So Much to Be Done

Women Settlers on the Mining and Ranching Frontier

SECOND EDITION

Edited by Ruth B. Moynihan,
Susan Armitage, and
Christiane Fischer Dichamp

University of Nebraska Press
Lincoln and London

Acknowledgments for the use of
copyrighted material appear on pp. ix–x.
Copyright © 1990, 1998 by
the University of Nebraska Press
All rights reserved
Manufactured in the United States
of America
⊗ The paper in this book meets the
minimum requirements
of American National Standard for
Information Sciences–
Permanence of Paper for Printed
Library Materials,
ANSI Z39.48–1984.

Library of Congress Cataloging-
in-Publication Data
So much to be done: women settlers
on the mining and ranching frontier /
edited by Ruth B. Moynihan,
Susan Armitage, and
Christiane Fischer Dichamp.—2nd ed.
p.   cm.—(Women in the West)
Includes bibliographical references.
ISBN 0-8032-8248-6 (pbk.: alk. paper)
1. Women pioneers—West (U.S.)—
Biography.   2. Women pioneers—
West (U.S.)—History—
19th century—Sources.
3. Frontier and pioneer life—West (U.S.)—
Sources.   4. West (U.S.)—Social life and
customs—Sources.
I. Moynihan, Ruth Barnes.
II. Armitage, Susan H.
(Susan Hodge), 1937–   .
III. Dichamp, Christiane Fischer, 1947–   .
IV. Series.   F596.S68   1999
920.72′0978—dc21
[B]
98-15057
CIP

Contents

Illustrations

Acknowledgments

This book represents something of a triumph for the technology of modern communications; it is a collaborative production by three historians on two continents, two of whom have never met. We came together through the good offices of Yale's Professor Howard Lamar, who introduced Christiane Fischer (now Mme Dichamp) of Paris, France, to Ruth Moynihan of Connecticut twenty years ago. Then Ruth introduced Sue Armitage of Washington State to Christiane, by mail, as the work proceeded. We all owe particular thanks to Howard Lamar for his personal encouragement as the research progressed and for making such an enjoyable editorial collaboration possible.

Many of the selections in this book were gathered by Christiane during summer research in America while she was teaching at the University of Nancy in France. She especially wants to acknowledge the help of Archibald Hanna and Joan Hoffman of the Beinecke Library at Yale, as well as the staffs of the Huntington Library and Bancroft Library in California and the Arizona Historical Society in Tucson.

Ruth and Sue added other selections, and they wish to thank Vicki Ruiz for her help in finding Hispanic material; the librarians at Yale's Sterling and Beinecke libraries, at the University of Connecticut's Homer Babbidge Library, and at the Washington State University library; and the photo archivists of the Western Historical Collections at the University of Colorado.

We are all grateful to Kathryn Newton of Buena Vista, New Mexico, for information she sent us about Carrie Williams and Lee Whipple-Haslam to include in our second edition. This edition also includes a substantially updated bibliography and several new selections.

We wish to thank the following libraries and copyright holders for permission to reprint the items specified:

The Arizona Historical Society, Tucson, for Sadie Martin's "Memoir,"

Mary Barnard Aguirre's "Autobiography," and the excerpt from Effie May Butler Wiltbank's reminiscences, manuscripts in their Library Collections.

Chalfant Press, Inc., of Bishop, California, for Sarah Winnemucca Hopkins, *Life among the Piutes: Their Wrongs and Claims,* originally published by G. P. Putnam (Boston, 1883) and reprinted by Chalfant Press, Inc.

Jesse Lilienthal of Hillsborough, California, for the selection from *Gambler's Wife: The Life of Malinda Jenkins* (Boston: Houghton Mifflin Co., 1933).

The Sharlot Hall Museum, Prescott, Arizona, for Angeline M. Brown's "Diary," from the Angie M. Brown Collection.

The Western Americana Collection in the Beinecke Rare Book and Manuscript Library at Yale University for manuscript letters by Louisa Cook, Jerusha Merrill, and Lucetta Rogers and manuscript diaries by Mrs. E. A. Van Court and Carrie Williams.

The Archives of the Sisters of Charity, Mount St. Joseph, Ohio, for selections from *At the End of the Santa Fe Trail*, by Sister Blandina Segale (Milwaukee: Bruce Publishing Co., 1948).

The University of Montana Press for an excerpt from *Frontier Woman* (1973), by Mary Ronan.

The Bancroft Library, University of California, Berkeley, for the excerpt from Apolinaria Lorenzano's *Memorias*, BANC MSS C-D 116.

Betty Moynihan, of Morrison, Colorado, for the excerpt from "Reminiscences of Mrs. Augusta Tabor," in her biography, *Augusta Tabor: A Pioneering Woman* (Boulder, Colo.: Cordillera Press, 1988).

Introduction

Nearly every western community in America celebrates its pioneers, the hardy souls who came "by covered wagon" before 1850 (or 1860, or 1870, depending on the region). Women are often singled out for special praise. Monuments to the pioneer woman are also frequent items of nineteenth-century public statuary, as are sentimental tributes to her devotion, goodness, and diligence. But the very lavishness of the praise has sometimes obscured the reality. The process of settlement and community building, in fact, has generally been described in terms of men's accomplishments, with little attention to the creative achievements of nineteenth-century western women.

The twenty-three narratives in this book, by women of diverse environment, status, and background, reveal women's involvement in every aspect of the frontier settlement process. They tell what women did and how they coped not only as individuals but also as members of complex networks—sometimes of other women, sometimes of family or status groups. Their part in making hard decisions, producing essential income, and developing new communities was as important as their flexibility, humor, and sense of adventure. This collection, augmented in the second edition by four new selections, represents the diversity of the female pioneer experience—and the distinctiveness of individual personalities—while also revealing themes common to all western frontier women.

Women have not been well served in traditional assumptions about the American frontier. Western mythology is replete with stereotypes about the active role of men and the symbolic function of women. The activities of gold miners, ranchers, and cowboys have entered the American imagination through every medium of communication, the frontier man usually embodying masculine bravery, physical strength, and independence. Contrasting images of women abound: the frail, genteel lady damaged by the harshness and isolation of the frontier, the prematurely careworn drudge of a helpmate, the briefly glamorous bad woman soon to meet a bad end—all usually dependent upon male enterprise and valor for their survival.[1]

Yet the distinctively new environment of the West actually required an adaptation to primitive physical conditions from which no one escaped. Neither wealth nor status nor sexual "delicacy" could command creature comforts that were not yet available. Newness bred familiarity and some egalitarianism among both men and women, and the need to "do for yourself" encouraged independent decision making and entrepreneurial experiments. Few women could be passive or dependent under such circumstances.

Despite similarities of status or shared hardships, however, women necessarily developed their own specific methods of coping and adapting. The historian David Potter pointed out a generation ago in 1964, "The character of any nation is the composite of the character of its men and of its women, and though these may be deeply similar in many ways, they are almost never entirely the same." And Annette Kolodny has more recently demonstrated from literary sources that women's personal and imaginative responses to the western environment differed from men's and significantly affected their own attitudes and behavior.[2]

It may be hard to recall a time when such gender differences were not apparent to most historians, but Potter's perception, as it turned out, was an early sign of the dramatic change in attitudes and research that was to produce the now-flourishing field of women's history. Analyzing history through women's eyes and women's source materials has opened up for American women what the historian Edmund Morgan called "a usable past." Such analysis provides new insights into all of American history.

Narratives by women settlers—diaries, letters, memoirs, autobiographies—are rich in evidence about personal attitudes and about day-to-day existence in the frontier West. They include details about living conditions, work and economic activities, personal and group relationships—details seldom found in the more formal, public source material by men. In fact, that is why so many scholars ignored women's narratives in the past. Public affairs and notable men were the preeminent topics of historical research. Literary scholars regarded most personal writings by women as "subliterary" and most of women's published novels and autobiographies as, at best, "local color." Now that has changed. A considerable body of feminist scholarship has been devoted to developing perspectives and methodologies appropriate to women's narratives,[3] and many social historians have revealed the crucial interrelationships between private and public experience in the making of history.

The issue of gender difference in western history was first articulated clearly in studies of that well-defined topic, the Overland Trail. Scholarly analysis of women's trail diaries by John Faragher and Lillian Schlissel altered our thinking about the overland journey itself and about western history as a whole. We now know indisputably that pioneering was not necessarily synonymous with adventure, and that real people, both female and male, faced westward with mixed emotions of anticipation and loss.[4]

But there is no single, simple interpretation that can encompass all of western women's subsequent experience of settlement. In fact, two major surveys of pioneer women reached opposite conclusions. Julie Roy Jeffrey, in *Frontier Women*, found strong continuities between western attitudes and Victorian domesticity: many pioneer women brought eastern sex-role standards west with them and refused to modify their principles even when they proved a hindrance. In contrast, Sandra Myres, in *Westering Women*, discovered a predominant spirit of adventure, nonconformity, and adaptation in the women she studied.[5]

The writings of the various women represented in this book justify both interpretations; indeed, the individual women often exhibit both tendencies. Differences of time, place, circumstance, and personality account for differences of emphasis, and the documents themselves require interpretive analysis based on differences in form and purpose. Letters and diaries, for example, usually reflect immediate reality in candid fashion, although a letter's tone—of courage or complaint—may depend upon its intended recipient, and a private diary may be more introspective than one meant to be shared. Furthermore, when such works are retrieved from archives without any other biographical information, there may be little known about the rest of the author's life; such is the case with several of these women. On the other hand, memoirs and autobiographies pose their own problems. Authors tend to embroider dull patches or embellish mundane facts; they may also remember selectively, adding a romantic glow or a courageous lilt to the prose. The perceptive reader must always do some snooping between the lines.

Available source materials are mostly by women of middle- and upper-class status. Because poor or uneducated women seldom wrote letters or diaries—and what letters they wrote were not likely to be saved—we catch only occasional glimpses of them on the fringes of someone else's description. Sister Segale offered her help to poor "Crazy Ann," who never returned, and Mrs. Lee Whipple-Haslam would "never forget" the "poor, undesigning, ignorant woman" named Williams or the "unique personality" of "Irish Kate," who fell into "ten feet of slum" with her arms full of laundry. But Whipple-Haslam and Louisa Cook had no sympathy for the "human microbes" and "fancy women" who led the "sporting life" they commented on. They would no doubt have spurned the rough-and-ready Malinda Jenkins, whose story survives only because she lived long enough to dictate it to a twentieth-century writer. Abigail Duniway, despite her concern for women's rights, asserted her own social equality with wealthy mine managers by denigrating "unthinking" miners' wives—as if squalid living conditions were their own fault.

Most white women also disdained the Spanish Americans who had long occupied California and the Old Southwest under Mexican rule. Mary Barnard Aguirre, however, was intrigued by their culture and impressed with their hospitality. Married to a well-to-do trader of Spanish descent, she could describe them with interest, unlike other settlers, who feared their "alien" religion and culture. The testimony of Hispanic women themselves, however, has been mostly lost or ignored. But manuscripts like that of Apolinaria Lorenzana (new to our second edition) enable us to rediscover their voices and document Hispanic women's distinctive contributions in early Western history. Deprived of property rights and status when the United States took over, Spanish Americans were soon submerged by the predominant Protestant American culture, and the extraordinary independence of Hispanic women, upon which many early American observers commented, disappeared.[6]

Most white women were as prejudiced and culture-bound as white men in their attitudes toward the American Indians. Sarah Winnemucca's education in California lasted only three weeks because white parents objected to having their daughters in school with an Indian girl. Yet other white women, like Mrs. Parish, the wife of an Indian agent, did teach and care for Winnemucca, and their mutual respect was strong. Mary Ronan, another agent's wife, was also sympathetic and concerned about justice for Indians, though her understanding of their situation was limited.

Looking to the future. This rural postmistress typifies the spirit of many pioneer women. The responsibility of her position made her the hub of a widespread community. Courtesy of the Stevens County Historical Society, Colville, Washington.

Lack of sympathy and cultural myopia were common attitudes. Sarah Butler York could not understand why the Sioux and Fox Indians she had seen in Kansas preferred their "ragged tepees" to the "good stone houses" built for them by the government. Mary Aguirre was apparently unconcerned when she saw "the first installment of Navajo Indians brought in on their way to the reservation just given them at Bosque Redondo (Ft. Stanton) . . . the first of 7000." Sister Segale, however, who also championed the rights of poor Mexicans, actually conspired with an Indian friend to thwart the murderous plans of two white men who were planning a mine disaster. "A good Indian is the best ally in an emergency," she said. Still, her response was exceptional. Most other women considered Indians a nuisance, if not a threat.

Women's insistence on clinging to Victorian sex roles is evident throughout the selections in this volume and well documented elsewhere; there is no doubt that nineteenth-century ideals of gentility—that a "true woman" should be passive, obedient, pious, and pure[7]—affected behavior among frontier women. This was especially true of those who wanted to prove to themselves and others that they were just as "civilized" as any easterner. In the West, as in the East, women of the "better sort" became definers of respectability, fettering one another with social restraints. There was woe to any woman who stepped far enough out of line to be classified as unworthy of deference, a lesson that prostitutes knew and "good women" forgot at their peril.

But evidence from women's narratives indicate that female respectability could also be a means of self-protection and attaining status in strange new environments; maintaining respectability may have been an active attempt to control one's circumstances rather than mere passive endurance. Even the most respectable pioneer women were far from helpless dependency. Many, like Mrs. J. W. Likins, Abigail Duniway, or Sister Blandina Segale, were adept at manipulating standards of deference in defense of their own personal achievement or unconventional behavior.

A frontier woman's ultimate power, though frequently combined with deprivation and drudgery, came, however, not from male deference but from her own productive responsibilities. Women's vital role in western settlement was marked by a fervid desire to tame the wilderness to suit domestic necessities, as well as an equally fervent desire to reap the profits, personal or social, that the frontier might yield to entrepreneurial talent. In short, most women were eager and willing to *work*.

Despite the replication of some eastern patterns, western pioneering was a testing experience for both women and men. Letters, diaries, and memoirs reveal women's bravery, physical strength, and independence equal to any man's, even as they also reveal the failures, weaknesses, and tragedies that beset both sexes during the complex settlement process. Women's writings describe the multiple tasks they undertook, the daily routines of frontier living, the interactive networks of relatives and friends that made both male and female survival possible. Ways in which women asserted themselves or circumvented patriarchal authority can be discovered in such sources, along with evidence of their entrepreneurial and creative ingenuity.

In some accounts, one is amazed at the mobility of westerners, who crossed great distances not once but over and over, often at the mere rumor of gold or an offer of hospitality from a relative. Women like Mrs. Nat Collins traveled from place to place or job to job with a facility born of generations of previous moving. Accidents and disease and unassisted childbirth were accepted hazards of frontier life. They could be unusually dangerous among miners and on isolated homesteads because of inadequate medical care, though sometimes "expert" care, like that which Sadie Martin's husband sent her to town to obtain, could be even less reliable.

Loneliness, often cited as an element of western life that bore hardest on women, may not have been any worse for the frontier woman than for nineteenth-century rural women elsewhere in the nation. Mrs. Van Court complained about it bitterly because she had left all her relatives back East. Annie Green's book reflected her bitterness about the ignorance of those who had planned such a utopian experiment and encouraged her husband and others to join. But Carrie Williams, Sadie Martin, and others had close domestic relationships with relatives and friends who moved west with them, and Sister Segale's religious community provided a support network all her life.

Contrary to nineteenth-century notions about feminine helplessness and passivity, pioneer women took decisive action to manage their own lives and maintain their hopes. The narratives in this book show that they were often the breadwinners and wage earners who provided crucial capital for male accomplishment. "A few weeks after my father's death," wrote Mrs. Nat Collins, "my brothers left for the mountains on a prospecting tour, leaving mother and I at home alone, and the task of earning sufficient amount to provide necessaries of life was indeed an arduous one. . . . every cent which we could accumulate, over and above enough to buy us flour, was given them." In other cases, women were the organizers of other people's labor and capital. Sister Segale's resourceful method of achieving the construction of a territorial girls' trade school in New Mexico is an example of institution building that was by no means unique.

Western women, like their eastern sisters in factories and on farms, knew how to put their energies to productive labor. And they were usually not at all shy about the importance of making money. "I resolved now to do something to aid my husband in a pecuniary way," said the genteel Mrs. Green as she prepared to turn her house into a school. Next she started a bakery, kept secret from her husband, who disapproved of working wives. "Never was there a better field for making money," wrote Jerusha Merrill of her San Francisco boardinghouse. That the money went to support the men in their families as well as themselves did not leave these women feeling valueless; instead they were proud of their endurance and their entrepreneurial contributions.

A striking factor in all of these accounts is that most of these women were in the West or were doing what they were doing of their own volition. They had *chosen* to go or to do that work. "Money could not hire me to go back there [to Wisconsin] to live!" exclaimed Carrie Williams from Nevada. Lucetta Rogers insisted that her desire to join her sick husband in California "was not the wish of the moment I have considered it for past months." Sadie Martin, who soon became fascinated with the "great beautiful desert" of Arizona, insisted on leaving Iowa to join her husband in the hot summer of 1888 after five months of separation. "He had tried to warn me," she said, "to wait one or two months longer, but I would not listen. . . . I had no one to blame but myself and was not going to complain." Even when they would have preferred not to, and hated the conditions, as did Annie Green in Greeley, Colorado, women accompanied husbands westward because they were determined not to be left behind. As Mary Jane Hayden put it, "I said, 'We were married to live together, . . . and I am willing to go with you to any part of *God's Foot Stool* where you think you can do the best, and under these circumstances you have no right to go where I cannot.'"

Although one might claim that such choices were not truly free, one must also remember that it was common practice for nineteenth-century men to leave their wives for months or even years at a time for the sake of their work: there were businessmen in city boarding houses whose families lived in the country or in small towns elsewhere, engineers on mining or railroad expeditions, politicians in distant legislatures. The marriages of Abraham and Mary Todd Lincoln and of Henry and Elizabeth Cady Stanton are only two of many examples of this practice.[8] Upper-class urban women took their children to country resorts or homesteads for the summer while men stayed at their hot city offices. The majority of gold rushers made their expeditions to the mines in just such single fashion, most of them planning to return quickly. Women who accompanied their husbands west knew there were culturally acceptable alternatives, but they chose instead to assert that their marriages were egalitarian units. They refused to be excluded or to be protected from hardships, and they were determined to help earn the money that might improve the whole family's lot in life.

In women's narratives, men often appear only on the periphery of the action. This is not simply because theirs is the public world, from which women are excluded; rather, it seems to be more because women see their own activities as primary and male endeavors as secondary, sometimes even downright foolish. Angie Mitchell Brown deliberately went to teach in "the most 'barbarous' country" she could because her fiance had broken a promise not to run for political office. Carrie Williams frequently refers to her husband's "tuting machine" and performing band with great disdain, even remarking, "I think he is wasting his life fast away blowing that everlasting cornet." As for his gold mining and public debating pursuits compared with her own activities in 1858, Carrie's priorities—and her disapproval of his—are clear:

> Wallace . . . went to work in the new diggings and as a matter of course got himself quite wet & muddy, forgot his dinner to boot, then came home about 4 oclock, brought a can of oysters, made some soup for the whole family, reserving no small share for himself. Notwithstanding supper was served . . . the afforesaid W adjourned to Temperance Hall, where after the ceremonies . . . he took part in a debate. Subject: "Whether under a republican form of government woman has a right to vote or not." Of course she has, but Wallace took the negative side of the question, and it is his private opinion publickly expressed to me that he came off victorious. Beat this day's work of his if you can.

Whenever illness struck, women seem to have borne the brunt of the responsibility. It was Mrs. Nat Collins who saved her husband's life, and Mrs. Green her stricken helpmate. Women suffered great loss in other disasters too, like the murder of Mrs. Lee Whipple-Haslam's father, or Angeline Brown's encounter with Apache Indians, or Mrs. Van Court's frequent moves due to floods, theft, and government dispossession. The latter said of her husband, "Many a man would have committed suicide," but "his family was all the world to him and he would not be downed." Sadie Martin remarked that her husband was not strong enough for the ranching life.

Martin, however, apparently loved the Arizona landscape. Whereas her husband called it a "God-forsaken country" when he attempted to dissuade her from joining him on his canal-building project, she frequently commented on the "hypnotic influence of the desert" and its beauty. Some women seem to have been at least as adventurous as men, and, like Mrs. J. W. Likins, as quick of speech and repartee. Clearly, Angie Brown thrived on danger and greeted every new experience with resourceful curiosity. Louise Palmer included graphic descriptions of ladies going on mountain excursions and picnics with young single men while dull, workaholic husbands spent their time at the mines or studying the stock market.

The documents in this book were selected for readability, authenticity, and representative significance. We looked for information about western life during the white settlement process, although descriptions of how women got there were often so relevant to their stories that they had to be retained. We were interested in showing the variety of environments and the differences in status that so profoundly affected individual experiences.

Focusing on California, Nevada, and the Northwest; the Rocky Mountain plateau; and the Southwest during the post–Civil War expansion of the last half of the nineteenth century, most of these narratives have to do with mining or ranching—often both. Others, like those of Jerusha Merrill and Mrs. Likins, show how women "mined'" other opportunities in the urban communities that developed in gold rush territory. We have added Apolinaria Lorenzana's memoir to our new second edition, describing the Spanish-American missions and ranchos of early California. Mary Barnard Aguirre's narrative also tells about southwestern Spanish-American culture, which was soon to be overwhelmed and lost; and Sarah Winnemucca's is an eloquent representative of American Indians uprooted and resettled in the name of advancing civilization. Mary Ronan corroborates the "misappropriation of Indian and Government property" that took place at the hands of most other agents, and describes an Indian girl captured and mistreated by white renegades.

About half of our selections come from little-known and rarely available printed sources; the rest are from manuscript collections. In editing manuscript material we have, where possible, retained the original spelling and sentence structure, but punctuation has been added for comprehension, where necessary. Ellipses indicate our omissions, except for two instances in Malinda Jenkins's account and in Sister Blandina Segale's, where they appeared in the original published sources.

The women represented in this book were all unique individuals with unique experiences. They speak for the many other voiceless frontier women of their times and places. Each of them writes with what one might call a sense of "normality"; the letters and memoirs show an expectation that others will find their narratives believable, and the diaries express a sense of immediacy and personal identity. Like the best of modern oral histories, these documents reveal human beings in action, responding to their environments and thinking about their lives. Through the voices of these diverse women we may gain some understanding of thousands of others. We may also learn a great deal about "what life on the frontier and in the American West was like in the second half of the nineteenth century."[9]

Notes

1. Beverly Stoeltje, "A Helpmate for Man Indeed: The Image of the Frontier Woman," *Journal of American Folklore* 88 (January–March 1975): pp. 25–41.

2. David Potter, "American Women and American Character," in *American Character and Culture: Some Twentieth Century Perspectives*, ed. John A. Hague (Deland, Fla.: Edward Everetts Press, 1964), p. 69; Annette Kolodny, *The Land Before Her* (Chapel Hill, N.C.: University of North Carolina Press, 1984).

3. See, e.g., Leonore Hoffman and Margo Culley, eds., *Women's Personal Narratives: Essays in Criticism and Pedagogy* (New York: Modern Language Association of America, 1985), and Susan Armitage, ed., "American Women's Narratives," *Women Studies: An Interdisciplinary Journal* 14, no. 1 (July 1987).

4. See John Faragher, *Women and Men on the Overland Trail* (New Haven, Conn.: Yale University Press, 1979), and Lillian Schlissel, *Women's Diaries of the Westward Journey* (New York: Schocken, 1982).

5. Julie Roy Jeffrey, *Frontier Women* (New York: Hill and Wang, 1979); Sandra Myres, *Westering Women and the Frontier Experience, 1800–1915* (Albuquerque: University of New Mexico Press, 1982).

6. Janet Lecompte, "The Independent Women of Hispanic New Mexico, 1821–1846," in *New Mexico Women: Intercultural Perspectives*, ed. Joan Jensen and Darlis Miller (Albuquerque: University of New Mexico Press, 1986), pp. 72–93.

7. The first to define this notion was Barbara Welter, in "The Cult of True Womanhood," *American Quarterly* (1966); reprinted in *Dimity Convictions: The American Woman in the Nineteenth Century* (Athens: Ohio University Press, 1976), pp. 21–41. See also Gerda Lerner, "The Lady and the Mill Girl: Changes in the Status of Women in the Age of Jackson, 1800–1840," *Midcontinent American Studies Journal* 10 (Spring 1969).

8. Carl Sandburg, *Abraham Lincoln: The Prairie Years and the War Years*, one-volume ed. (New York: Harcourt, Brace & World, 1954), pp. 94, 98–99, tells how Mary Todd Lincoln could not bear living in a Washington boardinghouse with her husband, then a congressman, and so returned to her parents' home in Kentucky while he served his term. Justin and Linda Turner, eds., *Letters of Mary Todd Lincoln* (New York: Knopf, 1972), refers to Lincoln's refusal of an appointment as secretary of the newly organized Oregon Territory in 1849; he declined because his wife would not go west to such a place. Elisabeth Griffith's biography of Elizabeth Cady Stanton, *In Her Own Right* (New York: Oxford University Press, 1984), describes the extensive separations that characterized her marriage.

9. Christiane Fischer, *"Let Them Speak for Themselves": Women in the American West, 1849–1900* (Hamden, Conn.: Shoe String Press, 1977), p. 12.

Part One

Part One

California, Nevada, and the Northwest, 1800–1883

Spanish-Americans, by way of Mexico, had been settling in California for two hundred years before it became part of the United States in 1848. At highly structured Mission communities and on great land-grant ranches, women like our first narrator, Apolinaria Lorenzana, actively participated in Hispanic culture, which would remain an important part of western life. Anglo conquest, however, brought both dispossession and cultural chaos.

California's legendary gold rush, which began in 1849, gathered people from all over the world into a brawling, dirty, disorganized scramble for riches. Traditional legends about mining-camp life generally reflect the male experience. But women also accumulated gold dust, in exchange for their pies and stews and laundry skills, when they were not actually panning for gold themselves.

Women became an ever larger proportion of the population as the turbulence of the early years gave way to more permanent and settled ways of life. Nevertheless, gold rush attitudes persisted. News of each new gold strike created the same kind of excitement as the first. Residents of even the most established mining towns, like Virginia City, were temporary sojourners, ready to move the moment they heard of a richer field elsewhere. Fundamental economic uncertainty underlies every one of the following documents. Even farmers like the Van Courts were caught up in the cycle of impermanence, financial instability, and constant mobility.

A man might find it difficult to make a living in California; the sensible man brought his wife with him because she could cook and wash and take in boarders—a far more lucrative source of income than his own precarious one. In many cases, taking advantage of a wife's skills was the best means of becoming a substantial citizen, a respected property holder. Single women and widows could use the same domestic skills to make a living without disapproval.

There was a distinctively urban character to California society, however transient the urban populace. This opened up numerous other economic possibilities, such as door-to-door salesmanship. "Respectable" ladies in need, like Mrs. Likins, could make money that way and also promote the spread of "culture." This type of work was less feasible on isolated agricultural frontiers, although women lecturers like Abigail Duniway and traveling actresses sometimes reached the most distant communities, and even small towns needed storekeepers.

By far the most striking aspect of mining towns in general was the social disorder and violence. Almost all women's narratives comment on it, though usually from a distance. Women knew about the violence and cruelty and occasionally witnessed shootings or beatings, but they remained insulated from personal danger by conforming to the social code; ladies did not frequent saloons and dance halls. We must not forget that women *were* there, but they were usually labeled prostitutes or "sporting" types, outside the pale of genteel female concern.

The "respectable" woman's first response to frontier violence was self-imposed isolation, which was much more benign than rural isolation, but a limitation of mobility and experience nonetheless. A second response was more constructive: women participated in cultural and religious activities, organizing and raising money for churches, theaters, musical performances, and aid to the poor. Louise Palmer claimed that women organized the entire social life of Virginia City, and Jerusha Merrill took great pride in San Francisco's "fine arts." The hub of Carrie Williams's social activity was her church, though she and her mother-in-law seem to have consciously established a domestic life marked by implicit criticism of male business and associational activities. Mrs. Duniway campaigned for suffrage.

The urban character of gold rush territory allowed women to act positively within traditional female roles, both as economic partners and as "civilizers." For example, women who took in boarders were economic producers, but however hard they worked or how much money they made, they remained safely and properly within the domestic sphere. As civilizers, women used the deference accorded "ladies" to protect themselves from social disorder and to promote the development of social and religious institutions. But they also expanded their horizons by sharing in the excitement of acquisition and decision making, and by their own efforts they helped to mold disorder into stability and community.

"All was done under my direction and care"

Spanish Americans, from Mexico, who called themselves "Californios," were the first newcomers to arrive in the West, the first to take the land from Native Americans, the first to establish the system of self-sufficient "ranchos" that became so typical of western life. They brought their own cultural assumptions and organizational methods, just as later Americans would bring theirs. Apolinaria Lorenzano's testimony here provides a rare glimpse into the daily lives of such Mexican-Americans in the years before the United States conquered them in 1848. Her recollections are among the 150 accounts by Californios that Hubert H. Bancroft and his assistants collected in the 1870s for use in Bancroft's multivolume *History of California* (1884–88). Lorenzano clearly enjoyed the opportunity to describe her work as a nurse, teacher, and assistant housekeeper at Mission San Diego. She shows us not only her own accomplishments but the efficient organization and operation of the California missions, a key component of the Spanish colonial system. This capable, literate woman also challenges comfortable Anglo stereotypes about ill-educated, passive Spanish señoritas interested only in romance. Lorenzano's curt sentence about her lost property—"It's a long story and I don't even want to discuss it"—reminds us that Californios were dispossessed not because they were indolent or incompetent but because the new Americans seized their land.

I Apolinaria Lorenzana, was born in Mexico, and while very young, barely seven years of age, was sent together with a considerable number of families and children of both sexes by the governor of Mexico (which then belonged to Spain) to this California. We left from the same city of Mexico for San Blas, and there we embarked on the frigate of the king, the *Concepción,* bound for Monterey which was the main port. Upon our arrival in Monterey [in September 1800], the governor distributed some of the children like dogs among the families; others were left here in Santa Barbara and in San Diego. I remained with my mother and various other women in Monterey. Those that were already women, Francisca and Pascuala, were married very soon, the first to Juan Hernández and the other to Joachín Juárez. . . . My mother also married, an artilleryman, and when the relief came for the artillerymen, it fell to my stepfather's lot to return to Mexico, and he took my mother with him. Thus I remained, separated from my mother, and I did not see her again. She died almost upon her arrival at San Blas, perhaps from the grief of having left me.

. . . Don Señor Carrillo, who was married to Doña Tomasa Lugo, transported me to San Diego with his family. I was ten or twelve years of age. There I passed many years with that family, and after obtaining permission for leaving, I passed to the house of Sergeant Mercado, who was married to Doña Josefa Sal, the daughter of Lieutenant Hermenegildo Sal, who died in Monterey. Don Señor Sal had another Daughter, Doña Rafaela, who was the first wife of Don Luis Antonio Argüello.

I had been only a short time in the home of Don Señor Sergeant when I became very sick, and the Padres took me to the mission. I remained there until I had sufficient strength. I returned to the house of Doña Chepita Sal in which I had lived before going to the mission. I remained a short time more in that house, and the Padres, favoring me, again took me to the mission to make me a nurse as for some time they had been building two hospitals. When they had finished the two hospitals (one for men and the other for women) and the sick people came to them, the missionary Padre Fr. José Sánchez came to the presidio to say the Mass and told me to get ready to return to the mission as he was going to make me the nurse of the hospital for women. . . .

During the time that I was at the presidio, the worth of computing never occurred to me. From the time that I was a very young girl, before coming from Mexico, they taught me to read and the doctrine. Even when I was a young woman in California, I learned alone to write, using for this the books that I saw, imitating the letters on whatever white paper I found discarded. Thus I succeeded in learning enough to make myself understood in writing when I needed something.

When I was in the house of Doña Tomasa Lugo, I had begun to teach some girls to read and the doctrine; afterwards, I did the same in the house of Doña Josefa Sal. This woman, after she was widowed, opened a school to teach girls to read, to pray, and to sew. As she had a vegetable garden that required much attention, I had the school almost exclusively in my charge. Too, there were some girls who had been entrusted to me in particular by their parents.

I taught the three daughters that Alférez Don Ignacio Martínez had then, María Antonia, Juana, and Encarnación; the mother was Doña Martina Arellanes. Too, I taught the niece of Doña Tomasa Lugo who was called Bernarda Ruiz, and she lives here yet in Santa Barbara. Many others learned their first letters and to sew with me.

In the mission I was very sick. Padre Sánchez took me there for charity which was much better as I was unable to work because of having my left hand paralyzed in such a way that it seemed dead. Thus it was about two years and eight months without any movement and about four months recuperating very slowly.

I maintained myself with the work of my hands, sewing, making shirts, silhouettes, embroideries, or as they asked me for them, embroidered sashes, waistcoats, and by order, ornaments for the soft leather boots of the soldiers and civilians. Those ornaments were of silk with embroidered points arranged with spangles, blossoms, and other things that were much work. The men used neckerchiefs with the points or the edges embroidered, imitating the officers. I did that.

The three years that I had my hand crippled I was not able to work, but in the hospital of the mission that was built to cure the sick, although Padre Sánchez told me that I should not do it, I, myself, without the authority to do it, was present so that the servants would perform well, but always, as I was able, I gave a hand and helped the sick. . . .

The single women slept in a department apart that was commonly called the nunnery. In that same house, there was a great patio wherein they spun the wool or untangled and spun the cotton as there was much cotton produced at the mission. One of the places that was afterwards given to me was the little valley of San Jorge which produced much cotton. Every week in the months from June to October an Indian came with a mule loaded down with a large basket full of cotton that almost dragged on the ground. All the tablecloths and napkins, towels, and the many other cloths that they had at the mission were woven there too, of cotton spun by the neophyte girls. All the wicks that the mission used were of cotton prepared in the same way. . . .

The single women were in the care of an older woman who was like a matron. This one watched over them a great deal. It was she who took them to bathe themselves, and she never lost sight of them. In the afternoon after dinner, she shut them up and took the key to the Padre.

The Indians got up very early. Immediately at dawn, they had the Mass . . . [then] left for their jobs after breakfast.

All the Indians that lived in the rancherias came to the well before dawn to have their breakfast of atole of toasted, well-ground barley of such perfection that it seemed to have passed through a sieve served to the Indians on trays. The pregnant women and new mothers among the Indians were employed in the task of toasting and preparing the pinole. The keeper of the keys afterwards stored it and distributed each day at the wells the necessary quantity. . . .

The jobs of the mission were the sowing of wheat and corn, tending them, etc. Others were engaged in cutting and bringing wool. There were carpenters, blacksmiths, cart makers, chair makers, and various other occupations. Others were in charge of the pack animals. Others were cowboys who were always under the direction of a mayordomo "of reason." There were always three mayordomos in San Diego, one for the sowing in El Cajón, another in Santa Isabel where better wheat, corn, etc., were grown as that place never lacked water; it rained or they drew from the springs in order to irrigate.

There was a housekeeper who cared for the clothes, and after I cured my hand, I began to give many services to the mission because when someone came to buy a fanega of wheat or corn or some other thing, I was the one who witnessed the delivery for the housekeeper. On Saturdays, a vacation was given to the soldiers of the escort (a corporal and four soldiers), and I had to be present at the distribution.

I taught the Indians to sew, and I had them constantly working at sewing for the church or the Padres. All was done under my direction and care. I cared for the linen of the church, doing it alone but for the washing for which there were Indian servants. Naturally, I assumed the care of the sick women in the hospital.

When the ships arrived at the port, those in charge advised the Padres, and these selected from the invoices the things that were needed for the mission and made their notes. Afterwards, when I had employment, I went on board with the servants to receive the goods. I always had permission to take from the ships the goods that appeared to me to be useful to the mission even when they were not on the list made up by the Padres. . . .

The mission of San Diego was poor and did not have an abundance of livestock as did the other missions. For this reason, every fifteen days they slaughtered livestock and, in time of peace, lambs. The meat of the cattle was given raw to the Indians, but that of the lambs was placed at the well, and they cooked it for the mid-day meal.

The Indian men had their cotton work shirts and loin cloths, the women their petticoats of coarse cloth and their cotton work shirts; a blanket was given to one and all each year. All of the woolen goods were made in the mission. The cowboys were given sombreros, breeches and boots, and saddles with lariats.

The Indians that did not carry out their duties or who were delinquent in some way were chastised by the alcaldes by order of the Padres. The punishments were to be locked up in the jail, with or without fetters, or in the cellar according to the magnitude of the offense. If the offense was of minor importance, they were given lashings which seldom exceeded twenty-five in number and, on many occasions, less. But if the offense was of importance, the delinquent was handed over to the corporal of the guard who proceeded according to his instructions. The corporal investigated well the circumstances of the case and the witnesses that were able to testify, and afterwards, with a view to all, presented the case to the comandante of the presidio. If the case was important enough for the prisoner to be indicted, a corporal and a soldier came on horseback and transported the culprit to the presidio where the indictment was made by the prosecutor named by the comandante.

I was in the service of the mission many years; and although after the mission was secularized, it did not have neophytes, even in the final years when the Indians were free, I continued on at the mission caring for the church and the Padre. The last one was Padre Vicente Pascual Oliva who remained until 1846. . . .

. . . Señor Marrón [administrator of mission San Luis Rey] asked Padre Oliva to come to celebrate the feast of San Luis (August 25). The Padre said, "yes," and we went, but Juan María Marrón was not even at the mission because Frémont and his people had thrown him out of it.

We knew nothing about this, and upon passing by Agua Hedionda, the rancho of Juan María Marrón, we saw that all the family was there. . . . Marrón saw us too, and sent a boy to tell us not to go to San Luis Rey but to his house. So we did. Juan María Marrón and his wife told us that Frémont had taken away the post of administrator from him as the Indians had presented themselves to him, asking for Marrón's removal as they did not want him there and for the Americans to manage them . . . . The Padre celebrated for two or three days the religious feast of the Patron Saint.

The festival concluded, I told the Padre that I wanted to go to San Juan Capistrano where the family of Forster was. I was very sad about the capturing of the country by the Americans, and for this reason, I did not want to return to San Diego.

Then the Padre told me, "Well, yes, you can go to San Juan. I will go there too. What would I do alone in San Diego?" We went first to Santa Margarita, and we remained there about eight days. I told the Padre that he should remain there, and I would go alone to San Juan Capistrano. I was obsessed with the thing about the Americans. I don't know what I imagined, perhaps through my going away the Americans would go away too. The Padre resolved to go also to San Juan.

Our main reason for going there was to procure seeds and other foods to take to San Diego which was very poor as it did not have anyone who sowed or did anything. . . .

[There were rumors of war and warnings to evacuate the missions for fear of Indian uprisings.] . . . Padre Oliva went to San Juan Capistrano with a man assigned to escort him who had been enjoined by [Mexican Commander] Varelas to care well for the Padre. I remained to put everything in order, and when this was done, I went to sleep at Santa Margarita, and on the following day, I went to San Juan Capistrano in a cart.

There we remained until the death of Padre Oliva on January 1, 1847. I was at San Juan when Commander Stockton and General Kearny passed by there with their forces on the way to Los Angeles. . . . Afterwards, I went to Los Angeles, and from there, I went to Santa Inés to inform Padre José Joachín Jimeno and all the relatives of Padre Oliva of the occurrences. . . . I lived in Los Angeles about a year and then retreated to San Juan where all of my things were. There I resided a long time. At that time, I still had my three ranchos, one that I had bought called Capistrano de Secua which was located half-way between my other two ranchos and which I sold to my compadre Juan López. The other two had been given to me years before by the governor. One of these was Santa Clara de Jamacha, located near the mission of San Diego, and the other, nearer yet, was called Buena Esperanza de los Coches. It was my custom when I obtained possession of some property to have it blessed and to give it the name of a saint because I always had great faith in the favor of the saints after first of all faith in God, Himself.

As I did not return to San Diego, I put the ranchos in the charge of a man, or better, he was appointed by Don Juan Forster.

When the American forces came by the Colorado River (I believe it was in 1850 or 51) Captain Magruder arrived with them. He asked Señor Forster who owned Jamacha Rancho. Forster told him that it was mine and that he was in charge of it. Magruder asked him if he might borrow it to put there the herds of the troop, and Señor Forster, acting with the trust I had placed in him, lent the ranch to him. I never saw my ranch again, nor did I know anything about it because Don Juan Forster went to a rancho of his own, and I did not see him again. When the Americans had won the war, Señor Magruder came to San Juan Capistrano where I was staying and spoke to me about the rancho. He asked if I wanted to lend it to him again. It is certain that I received nothing for the use of the rancho and that finally someone, perhaps Señor Magruder, took possession of my rancho. He, the second time that he wanted to borrow it, insisted that I should sell it, and I refused. It is a long story, and I don't want to talk about it. The other two ranchos were taken from me in some manner. Thus it is that after having worked so many years, of having possessed properties of which I did not dispose by sale or by any other means, I find myself in the greatest poverty, living by the favor of God, and them that give me a morsel to eat.

Appolinaria Lorenzana, *Memorias*, 1878, BANC MSS C-D 116, The Bancroft Library, Western History Archives, University of California, Berkeley, California.

"I am willing to go with you to any part of God's Foot Stool" 2

Most Overland Trail narratives tell little about the decision-making process that preceded the journey. Frequent expressions of reluctance or regret, however, combined with references to wifely obedience in accordance with nineteenth-century sex roles, have led historians to claim that the decision to go west was generally made by men, whereas wives merely passively acquiesced. But the reality of the power relationship between husband and wife was often more complex, and wives considerably more assertive, than has been recognized.

This excerpt, from a much longer memoir, describes a young wife's determined participation in her husband's decision in 1849 to join two male relatives rushing west for gold. The Haydens did indeed make the Overland Trail journey the next year. But they went to Oregon, not California, and found their prosperity in farming, not gold.

In 1849 there was great excitement about the discovery of gold in California and nearly everybody had what was called the *gold fever,* my husband with the rest, and I soon discovered by their evening chat as we sat about the fire, that he was making plans to go to California.

At that time I was in very feeble health, having an ailing infant six weeks old. I knew it was impossible for me to go with them. (My uncle, Mr. Sumner Barker of Maine, and Mr. Edward Copeland of Massachusetts, were to be partners with my husband.) I listened to their plans which they had gotten pretty well formulated, when I thought it was time for me to take some interest in affairs, and so put the question, "what do you propose to do with me?" "Send you to your mother until I return," was his answer, which did not meet with my approval, but I made no answer at that time.

I was very fond of my husband and was nearly broken-hearted at the thought of the separation. It was getting late in February and if they went to California they would have to start by the tenth of March, and it had to be finally settled. This is the way it was done.

I said, "We were married to live together," (he saying "Yes"), "and I am willing to go with you to any part of *God's Foot Stool* where you think you can do the best, and under these circumstances you have no right to go where I cannot, and if you do, you need never return for I shall look upon you as dead." He answered, "Well, if that is the way you feel about it I will not go." Mind you,—no word of this was said in anger, for we had never differed in our two years of married life, and so it was settled that *we* should go the next year to the California gold mines.

It was now December, 1849, two young men returning from California bringing each about a thousand dollars in gold, which was *wealth* in those days and which set the whole country agog. It was not so much the money they had as the glowing accounts of how easy it was to get the gold, one could pick it out of the rocks with a pocket knife. Is it any wonder we had a return of the fever. . . .

Mary Jane Hayden, *Pioneer Days* (San Jose, Calif.: Murgotten's, 1915).

"We are satisfied to dig our gold in San Francisco"

JERUSHA MERRILL

3

Jerusha Merrill, with her husband and three children, rushed to California from the small town of Newington, Connecticut, immediately after the news of gold discovery in late 1848. By March they were "in place" and prepared to profit at the great entry port of San Francisco as hundreds of thousands followed. In these letters to her brother and sister in Connecticut, Merrill views the social chaos of the early gold rush with a wondering, but veteran, eye. Noting the financial opportunities for women and describing her own twenty-room boardinghouse, she says, "Never was there a better field for making money than now presents itself in this place."

But Merrill suffered the death of her child in a measles epidemic, and sought to alleviate homesickness by maintaining connections with relatives in the East. She also sought stability in the growth of religious and cultural institutions in San Francisco, not just as amusements, but as a significant step away from social chaos. She provides practical advice about coming to California, notes the costs of produce and land, and is optimistic about her husband's farm sixty miles outside the city. Within two years she reports her pleasure in the city's "seven daily papers," "fine arts," and "the most splendid balls you ever heard of."

San Francisco March 1st 1849

Dear Brother and Sister

Yesterday your welcom letter came to hand   I was much gratified to hear you wer all well   you informed me you had previously written all particulars   we have received but one letter from you which was writen soon after ouncle Levi died   it would be very gratifying

to me to hear all particulars from home   you say you hear so many stories
it is diffeult to tell what is true   almost evry one tells a differant story.
many times it creates much excitement among us but I shall endeavour to
tell you what you may rely uppon   a very great excitement is existing
among us at this time   people are daily ariving from all parts by the hundreds   many land with not one penny to help themselves with   immagin
for one moment what their situation must be   board at eighteen dollars
per week   not one half can get accomodations at that rate or any other
rate   a room just large anough to turn around in rents for onely twenty
and thirty dolors per month   you may immagin me in a house with elevon rooms on the first floor,   nine on the second,   in the midst of sixty
boarders,   trantient ones not mentioned,   with hourly applications for
more   you can then have onely a faint idea of my situation   some times I
have sevon servants   at others but one or two   with my family it is quite
an item to be placed in this situation   our house is quite a resort for most
of the parties we having the largest room in town   my boarders consist
[of] American English French Polls Chillanas and some from no country
atall   yet a more orderly set could not be obtained in a place like this   I
have two from Windsor Conn that have been with me six months   our
terms for board are eighteen dollars per week including lodgeing   without fourteen   provisions are very high   for instance beef twenty five cts
per pound   ham one dollar   flour varies from ten to twenty   butter one
twenty five   chees one dollar   milk fifty cts per qt   potatoes eight dollars
per bushel   other vegitables not to be obtained   egg four dollars per doz,
at the mines one dollar a pease   all provisions in the same proportion   I
have been very much favoured by becomeing acquainted with the new
comers and secureing what ever we want at a redused price   never was
there a better field for making money than now presents itself in this place
at this time   yet many leave with less than they bring   if any one thinks to
get gold and keep his hands white he had better be off in the first boat   it
is not to be obtained without hard labour   any thing that is business will
sucksead   labour of all kinds being very high   carpenters from six to ten
dollars per day   Lumber is selling at four and five hundred dollars a thousand feet   we got ours in the nick of time and are now reaping our reward   property is daily rising   lots that wer sixteen dollars when we
arived have been sold at three four and even fifteen thousand according to
the location and still rising   we have had some hard rubs to contend with

we trust the worst is over   as to this place seeming like home to me it does
not   the uncultivated state of society and the many inconveniencies render
it extreemly unpleasant   in the summer we have cold unpleasent winds
from the north west but no rain   the first winter very pleasant   the winter
past very cold and insesant rain   our rainy season is now nearly over
now a word for the gold mines   many of our acquaintance have been at
the differant diggings   some have dug one hundred a day uppon an average   others less   some have retired with disgust   but let me tell you it is
a good deal like work to dig gold   those that have been hard labouring
men say they never worked as hard before   the trade with the Indians has
been great but is becoming dull   those located in business can do best at
home   many have already lost their lives some their health for months,
which has taken all they had in the world   they have what is called the
Sacramento fever, one of the most horrible diseases ever sent on to man
in the months of August and Sept this disease is contracted   those that
expose themselves the most and are the most irregular in their habits are
the greatest sufferers   not having places to repair to they suffer much for
the want of care   many months ensue before they recover   in many instances death is their lot   we are satisfied to dig our gold in San Francisco   a mans washing is no small item in this place it being onely from
five to eight dollars per doz just diped in to the water and rung out at
that   female labour is above evry thing else   many get one ounce a day,
servants obtain from fifty to one hundred and fifty per month   if you had
the produse of your farm in this place one year you would realise a small
fortune   I would like to see some corn onse more that is what is called
corn at home   also some of that good cider and apples   a few hickory
nuts would not come amis   farmes are becoming neglected for the mines
at what is Sutters fort they have what they call a citty of canvas houses.

2nd

I think if I laid my penn down onse yesterday while writing the above it
was somewhear near twenty   in the evening we had a ball which was well
reprisented by my sixty boarders   if you could step in about meal times
and hear the clatering you would think I would be crazy   at times I am
not far from it   we have writen to you several times by differant ways.
when a young man by the name of Griswould left I did not have timely
notes to write   he promised to call on you   I therefore thought he would
give you all particulars conserning us   when he [Griswould] left I had a

Women's work. Many women, like Mrs. Blankenship, found that their domestic skills—cooking, laundry, running boardinghouses—earned them good money in mining towns. Courtesy of the Western History Collections, University of Oklahoma Library.

lovely little boy that any mother would be happy to own but alas he has taken his flight to a better world to be transplanted in more congenial climes   he was too sweat a bud to bloom on earth   he was always happy   all faces afforded him pleasure   he was the pet of evry one that saw him   my friends have told me sinse his death they thought him an uncomon child   he had arived at a verry interesting age elevon months but them dear little armes will never entwine themselves around my neck again   he departed this life the sixth of january   I had antisipated much pleasure in bringing him to the United States   alas how vain are all things here below   in a moment when least expected they vanish from our view   I think in a former letter we informed you his name was John Selden   the measles have made great mortality among children   many mothers have been left childless   four have lain dead in one day   the north west winds I think will drive all pestilential diseases that so often sweap away such large numbers from our large cities   but the mines would be dreadful

6th

I am at preasent alone   the girls are at the sandwitch Islands [Hawaii] Frances was maried the 9th of january to a Mr Wood residing at the former place   his native place is Massachusets   I think him to be a very excelant man   he is soon to return to this place and open his business which is cabinet making   Jane has become quite a lady instead [of] the little girl when we left   Squire is tending store for his father and is quite a man of business   the long expected steamer has at last arived   it brought onely four hundred pasengers and news of three thousand more at Panama   the colara broke out just as they left   the enginear and all of the hands have left   therefore we cannot tell when she will leave   the second is soon expected in a few days   we are now supplied with a Baptist Methidist and Presbyterian minister at this place   it is thought an episcopal minister is on the next steamer   I think an episcopal church might easily be bilt in this place at this time   the ladies that arived in the steamer are not much pleased with this place   some will return the first opertunity   companies of gamblers are ariving and doing a smashing business   the sceans are beyond discription   they think nothing of taking a man up and sending him through a window and other outlandish things to[o] numerous to mention   drunkeness stalks it self abroad at all times in fact evry variety that can be immagined is presented in this place from the highest state of refinement to the lowest state of degridation   I sometimes almost immagin myself with my friends again enjoying the many privileges you are blessed with but on reflction find it but vexation and vanity for boundless waters and high mountains widely seperate us from each other   I would be much delighted to hear all particulars from my friends   I was sorry to hear Almira had been sick   not one word did you say about Charles   I suppose I must not say little C for by this time he is quite a man   how is that little neffew and many others to numerous to mention   as for advising you to come to this place I cannot   neither would I say stay away if you would like to come   I think if you wished to come you might make a fortune in a short time by manageing wrightly   those that come first are the best felows as a general thing   merchants must look well to their dollars   goods must come down   nothing is equal to houses at this time   a frame seven by eight is worth but four hundred and fifty dollars   if you had some of your good timber in this place it would bring any price you might demand   the publick mind is this way   many will make fortunes, many will not   provisions will bring the money for evry one must eat   I do not think of any thing more to interest you   as an opertunity presents of sending this tomorow I shall close by saying good by   we all join in

sending love to you and all other friends   Mr Merrill says tell him we shall
come back to see him as quick as we can

I remain your ever affectionate sister
J D Merrill

San francisco Oct 28th 1849

Dear Brother and Sister

I have been much gratified to hear from you by persons that have so
recently seen you   it is i can asure you pleasing to put my eyes uppon fa-
miliour faces again   all do not take the trouble to find me out   among
those that have are Bissel Lamb   Circum Brown and Hinsdale who re-
turnes home this steamer   his health has been verry bad   I think this climate would not aggree with him   I have not heard from Rodgers sinse he
left for the mines   I hope he is doing well but many are not   the number
of deaths is beyond all calculation   many have no friend to put them
under the turf   yet those that take care off themselves and are regular in
their habits enjoy good health   I warn all against the gaming house and
grog shop   we have rented our place   I am therefore more at liberty than
I have been at any time sinse we arived here   time would fail to tell the
wonderful changes that are constantly taking place in this far off country
and without doubt a wonderful revolution awaits it   the excited state of
things cannot long exist   that large fortunes are being made is true but in
the end many must suffer   many goods sent to this place will never be
accounted for   could you spend a week with us you would almost doubt
your eyes and ears   this place is not fit for any thing but business   no one
has time to spend a minet for any thing else   could I be with you a week I
could not begin to tell you of the wonders I daily hear and see   numbers
are constantly ariving   what they are going to do this winter I cannot
tell   It costes a fortune for a man to live here   therefore emty purses are
useless property   Lamb is stoping with us at preasent   much dissatisfac-
tion is felt among us at this time relative to the mail   three are now due to
the place   I received a letter from Mrs Robins by Brown   I begin to
think out of sight out of mind for no one has taken the trouble to write
before   if I can get the time I shall answer by this steamer   I have sent my
letters by private hands of late thinking it the best way   I trust you may be
able to see some one that has seen us   among the number that are leaving

all are willing to take letters   some promis to visit you but I fear forget
it   I hear of a great many from Hartford but see but few   uppon their
arival   they find things so differant than they expect their time is all taken
up   most of the companies have more or less trouble   evry thing is of
that nature that it is impossible to tell from day to day what is to
come   we have delighteful wether at this time   the pleasantest in the
year   we have an episcopal society and a little church most done   it is
called Trinety parish   the rev Mr Mines is rector   we have the rev Mr
Fitch Morehouse Burnham and Dr Vamear   you will see we are not wanting for s[p]iritual teachers   we also have Baptist Methodist Unitarian and
presbyterian   church servis has been held in our house   sinse I last wrote
you I have viseted a place called the Puebelow   the climate is much pleas-
enter than this place   the country more level   plenty of fruit and vegitables   people more social   yet I have no desire to make it my place of
residence   I can assure you if I wer quietly situated in the states you may
be sure that I would have no desire to viset this place again   as we are
about mooving it is impossible for me to say much   at this time we are all
together and enjoying good health   wish much to viset old friends   my
best love to yourself and family   also to enquiring friends

> Believe me sincearly yours
> Jerusha D Merrill

> San Francisco Jan 8th 1851

My Dear brother and sister

Having a good opertunity to send direct I will pen a few hasty lines   I
have previously writen several letters but have received no answers   I
think it is owing to some delay of the mails   we have just heard of the bad
management of some of the agents on the Isthmus and it is thought it will
not go right untill Americans manage the whole   I am at preasent a grass
widow   my husband has taken up a tract of land and commensed a
farm   it is about fifty or sixty miles from this place   he has two yoak of
cattle two mules an[d] a lot of chickings   eggs are six dol per doz   it is in
a valey well watered and wood[ed]   he has eight men   each one has a
lot   all are to join and assist one another   I have no[t] yet visited it   another man came over the mountains with over three hundred cows an[d]
has gone six miles beyond   he is going into the butter business   farming

is great in thi[s] country I can assure you   we have renovated our garden and have any quantity of plants to transplant   we have had the largest and best potatoes in our garden I ever saw   I would like to get some of your seed if it wer possible to get it   the seed you sent out the worms got in and distroyed most of it   I shall make out a list and send by Rogers which I wish you to put in a tin box and send by express   had I known he was going so soon I should have made a package but have but little time now   I have not been verry well of late   little Laura has been verry sick   we did not think she would live but is better now   she has four teeth   I would like you to see her and I would like to see your little ones   Mrs Wood has a little girl   we hear from her often   Mrs Whitney is with us yet   I have sent two papers to you and shall continue to do so you will be able to tell how things go in California   we have sevon daily papers printed in this place   we have many of the fine arts and it is impossible to keep pace wi[th] the improvements   all the days that are notised at home are here   for instance this day a large ball is given   we have some of the most splended balls you ever heard off   large dinner and various amusements to numerous to mention   I often think of the good apples and things that make the long winter evenings pass away so pleasently and would like an old fashion sleigh ride again   it is so sandy around us that we cannot have any rides to enjoy   the horse can onely walk   we are soon to have a plan[k] road from the town out to an old mision about three miles   most of our principle streets are already planked   the cholera has visited us   most of the cases wer those of intemperate habits   great rascality is caried on and some of the most daring roberies   they are so bold that they trip a man in the principle streets in the day time and take his bag of gold   9th I will pen a few more hasty lines   I this morn had radishes from our garden   Mr Merrill arived last night   I am going to town to meet Mr R   I shall send but a small trifle because I have not the time to look around   give my love to all and except a good share to yourselves

in haste   I remain your affectionate sister J D Merrill

Jerusha Merrill to Selden Deming, Newington, Connecticut, March 1 and October 28, 1849, and January 8, 1851, Western Americana Collection, Beinecke Rare Book and Manuscript Library, Yale University.

"I suppose you thought me foolish in wishing to go"

LUCETTA ROGERS

4

Lucetta Rogers arrived in California by ship in January 1853 to join her husband, who was sick with typhoid fever. He had left her behind in Connecticut when he went to seek gold, but by the time she got to California he had learned the hard realities of the gold rush. She reported, "He says he cannot advise any body to come   the better work here for 18 Dolars a month   untill they bring their wives and keep Boarders." As the Merrills came to realize, the Rogerses found that women's work was an essential economic asset on the mining frontier.

Although these letters are short and sporadic, they span almost thirty years, documenting the difficulties a working-class family experienced in achieving financial stability in California. Rogers wrote and sent the first letter just after her ship arrived in San Francisco. There were good times, like the sudden labor shortage caused by the Frazier River gold rush in 1858, and bad times, like the loss of both husband and son to death. Her concern for her new carpet during a fire is a poignant example of the way women cared about the domestic accoutrements that symbolized their re-establishment of "civilization" in the West.

January 15, 1853

I suppose you thought me foolish in wishing to go but it was not the wish of the moment   I have considered it for past months and to-day I wish I wer their   Rogers has written in every letter encouraging about my coming—it is true when I heard he was sick I was more anxious to go. . . . he says he cannot advise any body to come   the better work here for 18 Dolars a month   untill they bring their wives and keep Boarders. . . .

June 15, 1854

. . . Rogers has done very well considering his Sickness   I think at present the times is rather dull but the prospect is when the crops come in it will be brisker here again   he thinks he shall never return till he gets his pile. . . .

September 5, 1858

Our city has been all excitement about New diggins on Frazier River. Hundreds left good Buisness to start wher gold could be got faster than in the city and are now Sitting on the banks of Frazier River waiting for the river to fall   it must be very eazy work if not profitable waiting. many have returned to the city to seek if possible their Old buisness and are now Wiser if not Richer men   Rogers is draying and doing very well   wages was allmost any price here for a few days   house rents went down   Real estate was allmost given away and gowing to Frazier River was a House hole word   everybody seemed to be gowing but the excitement has subsided and we are again quiet at least untill the Steamboat Companyes can find another new Eldorado. . . .

March 10, 1877

. . . the house next to mine caught fire and I thought the fire man could put it out before it burned through to mine   the Chief engineer rang my dore bell to go through with his Ladders but I Objected untill he cleaned his feet for fear he would soil my Carpets, but in fifteen minutes after that my roof was broken in and a large hose was flooding my house so rapidly that foot prints were not visible on new carpets that had just been lain down   I never shall forget the agony I experienced for a few moments and then I went to work with a will to save what I could   it happnd on my Birthday and it was anything but a happy celebration. we wer not burnt out but Flooded out   I hardley now wich is the worst   I think I would prefer the sweeping fire as it seemes more purifying and the Enjines make every thing so dirty   we had some very good friends in the department or we would have lost by theft as well as by the fire   thieves are very thick at fires in this town. . . .

September 1882

. . . I too have been called to pass through the bitter trial again   my only son Walter died last May 18 after a long sickness   he was thrown from a carriage and had two ribs broken and it resulted in dropsy   his suffering for 15 month was fearful, but with it all he never gave up his courage   was wonderful the doctors thought. he left a wife 24, but no children. I am now all alone as you now   my Husdband has been dead three years.

Lucetta Rogers to her brother Eno (last name unknown), January 15, 1853, June 15, 1854, September 5, 1858, March 10, 1877, and September 3, 1882, Western Americana Collection, Beinecke Rare Book and Manuscript Library, Yale University.

In this memoir about her family's life in California between 1856 and 1864, Mrs. E. A. Van Court describes a series of profit-sharing farm and ranch ventures, each of which ended in failure through no fault of the Van Courts themselves. Animal diseases, floods, illnesses, theft, and even government dispossession to settle Mexican land-grant claims led the family to feel, plausibly, "hoodooed." Like Lucetta Rogers and her husband, the Van Courts found the golden promises of the West elusive.

Remembering the most difficult years of her married life, Van Court is particularly revealing about the psychological costs for many frontier women. She was overworked and was acutely lonely for the companionship and assistance of other women, especially during several childbirths. She had many fears—of bears and rattlesnakes, of Indians (after a frightening encounter), of family illnesses, and of economic failure—all of them justified.

But she realized that her eastern origins made her anxieties even worse. "Many women that I knew in early days . . . suffered more than I," she admits, "yet the most of them had been raised on the frontier . . . and they were used to hardships which the Eastern women knew nothing of. . . ." Van Court thought that she had often been close to total breakdown, as was her husband. She says of him, "Many a man would have committed suicide had they been in my husband's place, but . . . his family was all the world to him and he would not be downed." Yet, writing at a much later stage in her life cycle and family circumstances, she finds herself comfortable and contented, proud of her achievements and her survival.

E arly in August 1856, my husband became restless with City life and was determined to go out in the country and so went prospecting through Santa Clara Valley. Found a large ranch that took his fancy and leased one hundred and fifty acres for dairy purposes. The owner, a lawyer of some note in San Francisco, agreed to furnish us with one hundred cows, my husband to build a fence along the county road in front of the ranch, build a milk room, buy all necessary articles for the dairy, and share the profits with the owner. My husband went to work at daylight in the morning and kept at it till dark and kept his part of the contract to the letter; hired help to get the fences in order all around the ranch to be ready for the cows. As soon as the rainy season was on, one cow was furnished us and that was all we ever had. It soon became plain to us that we were to be cheated out of that lease. The owner had come across a man in poor health with money that took a fancy to the place, as it had a good house and it had a fine artesian well, and every thing in order, though he claimed that the cattle had gone up so high that he could not raise the money to buy them, which we knew was not so. We had no rent to pay, plenty of wood on that place and a nice lot of poultry and could make a living; and we were bound to stay till something was done for us.

October 25th my oldest son was born, my first child having died in infancy before I came to California. This house was on a state road, the nearest neighbor a half a mile away, not a house in sight, very large old oak trees all through the Valley which gave the appearance of living in the forrest. I never lived on a ranch before, having been born and raised in a country village eighteen miles East of the City of Albany in New York State, and to be as I almost felt, in a foreign land, seven thousand miles from home among strangers in the condition I was. One can imagine my feelings day and night. Before I left San Francisco plans were made for a lady friend to come down and care for me. We were to send a note by the stage driver, he to give it to the lady's son-in-law at Wells Fargo's office in the City and she would come to us by return stage. My boy was born at three o'clock in the morning. The nearest neighbors came to me, brought a Spanish mid-wife with her who could not speak a word of English. I could not speak Spanish, but my neighbor could, and so we managed to get along. It was a very cold morning, the heaviest frost ever known in that Valley and it being the first night in five years my neighbor had been out, she caught a very severe cold walking through the wet grass, and I did not see her again in six weeks. She went home at seven in the morning. The Spanish woman left at ten, and from that hour on Saturday morning till the next Wednesday at two o'clock, my husband and I were alone in that house, not a soul in sight only as the stage passed eight o'clock in the morning. As was planned, my husband give the note to the stage driver on Sunday morning. The first note was given to the son-in-law and he jumped on his horse, rode quickly out to his home and started the lady on the stage, her baggage being sent the next day. It had seemed the very best way for news to reach her as we were ten miles from the Post Office, no telephones, no telegraphing, no cars, a day's travel to the City by stage. Only for the bravery of my husband and that Baby Boy, I think I would have lost my reason. My husband wanted to saddle the horse and go to Mayfield, try and find some one to come and help. I would have been left alone for two hours at least perhaps five and I would not consent. He insisted. I said "Just as sure as you go, I will get up and go out to the road." So together we fought it out. He caring for me as best he could, I caring for the baby. On Wednesday afternoon the stage stopped and the lady got off. I fell back on my pillow in a faint and never have had any recollection of seeing her enter the house. I came to and cried and cried till I was hysterical. I had surely reached the limit of my courrage. I was in mortal fear of the Digger Indians and there were a plenty of them all through the Valley and treacherous people they are.

However, I was well cared for and in a couple of weeks was around the house and with the help of the kind lady was all right. She staid with me six weeks. Then one adversity after another followed us the nine long weary years in that Valley of St. Clara. We remained on that place until the next February when the owner of the Ranch became convinced that he could not get us off without some pay for all we had done, so had a talk with my husband and he said he would buy us a small hotel a half a mile down the road towards San Jose, give us the cow we had and six months rent. So we concluded to take the offer, and we left the ranch.

The family that had the hotel before us stayed with us two months. We raised a large lot of chickens and there being a large amount of teaming down from the redwoods through the Valley, to San Jose, brought a good deal of travel to the house for meals and nights lodging. We had a large barn for stabling horses; also, two of the stage drivers taking all meals with us.

My baby was only four months old when we took this place. I had no mother, sister or friend to even give me a thought and worked very hard from five o'clock in the morning till nine at night. From four to a dozen men stopping for meals any time of the day, had to make all my bread, pastry, no bakery for twelve miles; could not get help anywhere. I never had been alone on this place until after this family had left. They gave me a large Newfoundland dog, which I quickly made friends with, fed him well and he became very fond of me. After they had gone to Canada, I was very lonesome and suffered with fear day and night. It soon happened that groceries ran short which were very necessary to keep on hand. My husband said he would saddle the horse and go to Mountain View as fast as he could and get a supply. I said "Well, be sure and don't let the dog follow you." "I will look out for that," he said and so he started. I watched him out of sight. The dog did not follow him and I went about my work.

Soon after I heard a loud tramp in the bar room, went in to see what it was; there was an Indian with a long dirk knife sticking in a sheath outside of his pants, the handle and half of the blade in plain sight. He said to me, "Where is your hombre" meaning my husband. I instantly thought I must lie to save myself, and I told him, "He is behind the barn chopping wood". With that he knew I feared him and he began to jump up and down, swear at me in his own language and said, shaking his fist at me, "You give me whiskey." I told him I had no whiskey. He said, "You told me one damn big lie. Your hombre vamoose to Mountain View on the carriage; me savee." "We do not sell whiskey," I said. He called me a liar again. He was in a very savage mood. My baby was sitting on the floor in the parlor with pillows around him playing. I did not know what to do. I thought the dog had sneaked behind the trees and followed my husband and I nearly died right then. We did not sell liquor; my husband was greatly opposed to that, though the bar room was just as the family before us had left it, plenty of glasses and decanters on the shelves where I stood. I felt that I had to defend myself and the thought came to me that if he made an advance towards me, I could throw the decanters at him, but there was that dirk knife staring at me and I so very weak and trembly. The next thought was to come out from behind the counter, go to the baby and let the Indian have the house. I did so, I came out and when I got in the middle of the bar room, along the porch came the dog who had been asleep and heard the noise. He growled and came right up to my side. I was as brave then as if a dozen men had come to my rescue, only so weak I could hardly stand. I put my hand on the dogs head and petted him and I said to that Indian, "Now you vamoose, my dog eat you up." I knew the dog and I knew that the Indian would never have a chance to pull out that knife if I said "Seize him, Watch." And he evidently knew the dog, too, as he began to go out backwards swearing at me all the time, but made no attempt to pull out that knife.

I just staggered to the porch, sat down on the bench the dog by my side and I am sure for ten minutes I could not have gone into the parlor and picked up that baby. My husband after being gone two hours, thought I had a sick headache. I was in such a plight and that experience unnerved me for a long time; that the last time I was ever all alone on that place. We both worked very hard, raised a large lot of chickens which brought us a good income and after we had been there about five months, a disease came among them and in ten days we lost every one, two hundred and ten in number. The disease (I have forgotten the name) was from an accumulation of fat all through the body and as soon as the fat covered the heart they dropped dead. I assure you we were very discouraged.

I could not stand the hard work any longer and was breaking down, and as our six months free rent was nearly up, we made up our minds to leave. We knew not where. One afternoon a man drove up to the door for dinner and also wanted some tools of some kind to mend his harness which was broken, and he sat there on the porch about an hour talking to my husband and in the course of the conversation, he said he was looking for a good dairyman. He had sixty-five cows and milked all the time thirty of them. He made us a very good offer, so we picked up and left the place.

We soon got on our feet again, though I did not regain my strength and in six months I went down flat with nervous prostration. I could not sleep, I could not eat and all looked dark for me, and my husband also, as the Doctor told my husband that I was going into a decline. So help had to be gotten to do what I had been doing. I could not walk a dozen steps from the house. We were lucky enough to get the same lady from San Francisco who had attended me at the birth of my boy and she staid with us through the winter; took good care of me and I rallied again and late in the next fall when every cow on the ranch got sick sores all over their bags and their eyes, it was impossible to milk them any longer. This was caused from the alkali near the Bay. Many of the cows died and it was a great loss to the owner and there were no profits to share with us any longer, and we had to give up. There was nothing else for us to do.

It was late in the season, the rains coming and the only thing that offered was to go up to Mountain View, rent a house there while something else offered. My husband worked at his trade through the winter;

while there my little boy took sick with lung fever. No Doctor was nearer than San Jose, twelve miles away and they would not come. The wind was terrible; there was nothing to do but take good care of him with the remedies of our grandmothers' days and after two weeks, he recovered, and I thank God he lives today.

My husband took a small place the next spring and raised a patch of potatoes and the next fall bought a ranch of thirty acres, kept a cow, raised another fine lot of chickens and put in a crop of hay and barley; had good luck and made a payment on the ranch. My youngest son was born there, September 21, 1860.

After two years there we made the last payment in August and we were dispossessed by the United States Government. Our land was included in the nine leagues of land given to Castro, being the first ranch lying between New Mountain View and the Bay. This was one of the famous Mexican grants. We had the same as all others on the claim, a squatter's title, but it was not considered. We had no money to buy it over again at the price asked and so had to leave all improvements and go, leaving home and every thing behind; I with my two little boys, went to San Francisco with friends for a couple of weeks, while my husband went prospecting, still determined on a ranch, or country life which was far different in those days from what it is now, very, very different. To leave that place which we surely thought was our own with all the improvements, good fences, large fine chicken corral, chicken house, granary, a good house, a large fireplace that made home so cheerful, get nothing for it was heart rending to me, and it was with a very heavy heart I left. I turned my back on our home just six months before my last child was born. Many a man would have committed suicide had they been in my husband's place, but he was of better material than that. He was game through it all. His family was all the world to him and he would not be downed, so went prospecting through the San Mateo Mountains, Coast Range to within three miles of Pescadero, leased five hundred acres of land. The owner to put on one hundred cows for dairying, make butter and cheese, share the profits with him. My husband came to San Francisco after his family. He had moved our belongings while I was away. The early part of November, we went from Mayfield to the ranch in a buggy started early in the morning. We were well supplied with lunch for the day and milk for the baby; fourteen months old, and after passing the foot hills, we rested, staked the horse out for feed and ate our lunch. Then we started across the mountains to the ranch, which was a half mile to the Ocean. It was very dark when we reached the worst place, called Bear Gulch, where we got down at the bottom of the Gulch. The mud was so bad that the horse stopped and refused to go another step; it was so dark I could not see the horse's head. My husband urged the horse on, but he would give a start and stop. I often wonder how I lived through that night and kept my senses. Finally my husband give me the lines stepped over the dash board and along the shaft of the buggy and got hold of the horses head. He told me to urge the horse on as he pulled his head. With a prayer to Almighty God, I did so and the horse made three efforts and a plunge and pulled us out of that mud hole.

There were real live bears all through those mountains and the road was right through this Gulch. When we reached the top of that mountain, we could see the light in the house of the owner of the ranch we were to take. We reached that house at nine o'clock where we were kindly treated, stayed three days, then went to the other house we were to live in. We had a fine lot of chickens, one horse, buggy, twelve pigs and our household goods. In less than a month on Christmas morning, the great flood of '61 and '62 began. We were too far up the mountain for our house to be carried off, but in one month everything we had was gone, but the buggy and chickens and household goods. Our old family horse we found one morning dead at our kitchen door. The bears came down the ravine near the house and ate up our pigs. The chickens were safe in a good hen house. Cattle all around the mountains perished, what were left could not be milked, they were living skeletons. We managed to keep the cow, so as we had in the barn barley and some hay brought from our old home, when they moved our live stock. The rain was on for five weeks, just pouring torrents; the valleys were ankle deep with water and the mountain slides terrible; during that dark and awful month we got out of light and had none for three weeks, only three miles from stores in Pescadero, but it was impossible to cross that San Gregaria Creek. You can imagine what must have been the feeling of a mother with two little ones, liable to get sick in any of those dark and terrible nights. Coyotes coming down the mountains in droves, barking like hungry wolves, cattle bellowing and rubbing up against the house for shelter, the ocean roaring like mad.

Our next neighbor towards the ocean lost every thing they had but their

lives: big barn well-stored with hay and grain, their garden of winter vegetables, chickens, cow, horse, all went out into the ocean. The mother and
nine children, standing ankle deep in the water while the husband went on
his horse for help a half mile to the nearest neighbor, who was the owner
of all the land around that way. The mother told me afterwards, she never
expected to see one of those children when she saw the light go out of her
house and it washed into the ocean. They were rescued by the neighbor
and three hired men in the dark and during a heavy torrential rain.

My little boy, five years old, waded across that creek before the rains
began, trees two hundred feet high went down that stream like pipe stems,
every thing they struck had to go with them. Two miles up the mountain
from us towards the mountains, three young men lived in a cabin and were
shingle makers. A big land slide that came buried them and their bodies
were not dug out for a month.

In February, it began to clear up and the weather was fine. The owner
of all this land could not buy the cows as he expected and promised. He
was honest enough and very kind to us; all the stock he had, less than a
dozen perished, he could do nothing. He had to give up the 500 extra acres
he had yet unpaid for only a small homestead left. There was certainly
nothing left for us to do but get out of those mountains and go back to
Santa Clara Valley and try our luck, but it was impossible to leave then as
the roads were all broken up. So we worried along till the middle of May
when my last child was born. No nurse, the nearest Doctor twenty miles
away. When this child was born there was a lady with me through the
night. The morning she was four days old I got up at seven o'clock, began
to pack our belongings. The morning she was ten days old, we started out.
The fog so thick we could not see the mountains so very near us. Five of us
were seated in the buggy and rode sixty-five miles to the home of a friend
near Saratoga. On going over the ridge to Half Moon Bay, twelve miles we
had to get out of the buggy. My husband tied the wheels to keep it from
pitching down the banks. I carried the baby in one arm leading the boy
baby, twenty months old by the hand and the five years old boy trotting by
the side of his father who lead the horse. We all got into the buggy when
we came to hard ground and many a steep place we crossed before we got
to Half Moon Bay on the main road. We stopped at a farm house, the lady
of the house making me a cup of tea and urging us to stay with her a
couple of days. She thought it terrible for me to be travelling over the

rough roads with three little children, the youngest only ten days old. But the fog had all gone the day was warm and bright and I more than anxious to get out of the mountains and reach our destination. Which we did that night at dark.

The friends we stopped with let us have an empty house they had on the ranch close to the one they lived in and as soon as our household goods came in three days after, we settled there for the summer. My husband worked hard at harvesting. My baby took sick with marasmus, a disease that drys the body up with fever and was sick all summer, very sick, until we were induced to try homeopathy and she was cured in three weeks, weighed eight pounds when born and exactly the same at four months old.

In this place I was in perfect terror all the time for fear my little boys would be bitten by rattle snakes which were all through those hills. One small rattler was found on a log in the hen house, another one was found in the road near the house with nine rattles on and by watching the boys and caring for that very sick child, I had a hard time of it and very glad when the harvest was over and the summer ended.

In September we moved from there, took a ranch on shares, ploughed the ground and put in a crop of wheat and the dryest season known in that valley followed the winters flood and the hot sun burned everything all up and we did not raise a pound of wheat. On this place we had no water, had to go two miles to Campbell's Creek once a week; the men folks would take a large lumber wagon holding six barrells and go after the water. For my part, I was really and truly discouraged and the country was no place for us and a hoodoo was over us. My husband had let a fine chance go by him in San Francisco and if he was discouraged, would not own it. As our oldest boy was then seven years old and must go to school and so we decided to go back to San Francisco. After nine years of hard struggles and privations all we had to take with us was one cow giving a fine mess of milk. We thought with the three young children we could not leave the cow behind; we sold our chickens, one horse and buggy. My husband had been down to the City and secured a house for us on the corner of Laguna and Hayes Street near good friends and with the house was a large back yard, well fenced and in that we put the cow. We had all the milk we wanted and sold enough to pay our rent, $18.00 a month. We got started; my husband had a good position in a shoe house and all seemed bright when we had been there less than a month, I opened my back door to go out for water and that gate was open, the cow gone and from that day to this, we never hear of that cow. My husband spent three days down the road to hunt for the cow: no trace of her did we get. We wrote to our neighbors where we had left; no one had seen her. We surely thought that the ill luck would follow us wherever we went.

There was nothing left for us to do but face the music, go on, let come what would, do the best we could. So we stayed in the City until all our children were out of school, eighteen years. Then we came to Oakland March 4th, 1882. My husband worked in a mill. I began taking boarders which I made a success of (twenty-four in number), on Harrison Street between 14th and 19th, sold out April 15th, 1912 at the age of 80 years and four months, and I will say here that many women that I knew in early days crossing the plains in '49–50 and '52 suffered more than I, yet the most of them had been raised on the frontier when many states were un-settled and they were used to hardships which the Eastern women knew nothing of, the settling up of new countries and that made it harder to endure. It was here on Harrison Street that my husband died at the age of 72 surrounded by his family and in comfort. He passed away at one o'clock on the 25th day of October, 1888.

This is the true story of my pioneer life in California and I am more than 82 years and three months old, living a very comfortable, contented, peaceful life, happy with the love of my children and many good, kind and loving friends. I hope the reading of it by the young people of the State that are surrounded with every luxury and convenience denied their par-ents will realize how very blessed they are. I thank God for my life, my health and beautiful Oakland, where I hope to spend my last days. When-ever the call comes I will be able to say, "My work is done, I am content."

> Dated, March 26, 1914.
> Oakland, California
> 5690 Ocean View Drive, Rockridge District.

Mrs. E. A. Van Court, "Reminiscences," pp.5–15, Western Americana Collection, Beinecke Rare Book and Manuscript Library, Yale University.

This reminiscence of a girlhood in the evanescent California mining towns of Shaws Flat and Cherokee is a curious mixture of dramatic description and sentimentality. The twice-married Mrs. Lee Whipple-Haslam was born Lee Ann Summers in Missouri in 1849 and came to California during the gold rush with her family in 1852. When she was seven her father, Frank Summers, was murdered over a land dispute. Her mother then opened a boarding house and became so respected that the town, located near Sonora, was called Summersville, and only later became Tuolumne. One boarder, the William Connally in this narrative, later married Mrs. Summers. Years before writing about her mining town girlhood, Lee Ann was hired for a unique assignment with Wells, Fargo & Company by her stepfather's friend, Leland Stanford. She was to ride the frequently robbed stagecoach to Sonora in order to identify the robbers. That she did, including height, size, clothing, blood seeping through one man's glove, and cataract in another man's eye. Her testimony served to convict the bandits. The circumstances of her childhood apparently provided her with cool eyes and calm nerves in time of danger. But, writing this memoir almost seventy years after her father's death, she still longed for revenge and was acutely aware of class distinctions, hostile toward the Chinese, and in favor of lynchings.

S onora, Columbia and Jamestown were the most important towns in Tuolumne county in 1852–53. Sonora was the county seat, Columbia the most beautiful and Jamestown the most popular. Each one of these flourishing little cities had its landmark. Sonora's pride was Bald Mountain, Jamestown had Table Mountain and Pulpit Rock and a little later Columbia raised the cross of St. Ann's church. It defies time,—a memorial of early days. I hope to live long enough to see it restored to its original beauty and usefulness.

The mining camps that flourished adjacent to Sonora and Columbia were Browns Flat, Douglasville, Springfield, Tuttletown, Hardscrabble, Yankee Hill, Saw Mill Flat and Shaws Flat.

Those of Jamestown were Campo Seco, Yorktown, Poverty Hill (now Stent), Chile Gulch, Montezuma, Hardtack, and a few others I cannot recall. Algerine, Montezuma and Chinese Camp were the largest and most important of the smaller mining camps of early days. Most of all the smaller camps had a store, a blacksmith shop, a mail box, sometimes a restaurant, and always from one to three saloons. . . .

It has been truthfully said that where the carcass is laid there will the vultures gather. In the early part of '53 strict laws and the vigilantes sent an ever moving stream of human microbes from the cities—gun men, gamblers, blacklegs, and all the low class of the sporting element (men and women) to this county. They considered our hard-working miners lawful prey; and immediately introduced methods to reap the harvest. They used the method unsparingly, mercilessly and thoroughly, introducing all kinds of new gambling games. In the most unexpected places they started groggeries, where both men and women lived, sold whiskey, and gambled; sometimes with music and dancing. And, of course, these dens of vice were the centers [of] gravitation. And, as we all know, whiskey makes a confused and helpless fool out of a man. The honest, hard-working miner entered these dens of vice, to be robbed of his gold, his health, and often his life. A man's safety and life often depended on the swiftness of his draw,—and the calibre of the gun he wore. . . .

Man can often destroy in a few hours the work of nature that has been centuries in the building. It requires twenty-one years by nature, and the laws, for nature to mature a man. But in early days I have seen all that made life worth living to a young and handsome man, vibrant with life, destroyed in five minutes, by a man's fists. There was a family lived near us on Shaws Flat by the name of Smith. Mrs. Smith was a nice-looking and good woman. There came to the Flat a gambler, well-dressed and flashy, proud of his good looks and fine clothes. He tried to impose his company on Mrs. Smith. One day Mr. Smith met him and beat his face nearly off; he broke his nose, and knocked out several teeth, and told him to leave the Flat. He certainly left. Before Mr Smith came in contact with him he was known as "Pie Face," but after the Smith episode he was spoken of as "Scar Face" and was soon forgotten.

The early day miners seldom wore guns, and never used them unless necessary to protect life. But, believe me, no man stepped on another's coat-tail with impunity.

Every succeeding year brought thousands to California. And, as a natural consequence, the weak went to the wall, while the braggart often died with his boots on. Conditions changed for the people, and not for their betterment,—men wore guns and shot to kill.

Not only conditions of the Pioneers changed, but the face of nature was fain to confess the superior predatory capacity of the newcomers. Denuded hillsides, banks of gravel, tail-races, ditches, tailings, and stumps and boulders were in evidence, wherever gold could be found. . . .

. . . It is true the miners had to put the fear of the Lord, or His teachings, into the hearts of the Mexicans and Indians; and many a single-handed whipping occurred, as some miner would catch them stealing his clothing—often hung out to dry. The punishment was not ladled out with a silver spoon, but with a solid stick, and laid on whole-heartedly, without reservation and with enthusiasm.

That mob violence and drastic action was necessary, I will not deny; for in those days it seemed an utter futility to await the legal process and uncertainty of the law. Human life was not valued; it must demand a life for a life.

While the morning glory, black-eyed Susan, and a few other flowers beautified our log cabin on Shaws Flat and were admired by so many, one day there came to our door a woman I will never forget. Her name was Williams and she lived at Springfield. She came to the Loomis store and passed our cabin; she walked up close to the door. "For masseys sake, Miss Summers! The sight of your cabin just near give me the fan-tods! It looks like Old Missourey. Lawsey a me, Miss Summers, do you put on table kivers all the time? Say, ain't they the orneriest, sentimenterest ijuts you ever seed in Californy? I reckon I knows sense when I sees it. I get so mad when they laugh at me—their betters! The meanest, treacherest men are greasers; but I ain't skyeerd of nobody. Well my visit has hoped me up. I want to get home and get my shoes off, and have a smoke. Miss Summers, save me some morning-glory seed. Say, I am honing to get back to Missourey, and I'se agwine to when we make a stake. Fo' de Lord! think of wild turkeys, blackberries, strawberries, persimmons, and all we left!"

Poor, undesigning, ignorant woman! One of the units of a cosmopolitan population of Pioneers of early days.

Another unique personality on Shaws Flat was Irish Kate. She did laundry work. There were hundreds of ground sluice holes filled with slum, that were a menace to safety. Kate was walking one of the narrow trails, her arms full of neatly washed and ironed laundry. She made a misstep and went into ten feet of slum. It required half a dozen men with ropes to land her on terra firma.

It causes a longing, homesick feeling when I pass the spot where the little log cabin we lived in at Shaws Flat stood prominently, to be admired, as something unusual and beautiful. Its commonplace and homely walls were covered with morning-glory and other simple vines—from seed that we had brought from Missouri. We were thankful for the roof, even if we lived on a dirt floor. It was an humble and sweet home for us, both in theory and reality, because love radiated around and through, hither and thither, lighting up the dark and ugly corners with peace, contentment and happiness. Let turmoil, hate, and antagonism reign elsewhere, it never entered our door. Dear old Shaws Flat! Around you some of the fondest memories of a long life cling! For then I had youth and a dear mother and father.

In the Fall of 1854 my father moved from Shaws Flat to an unbroken wilderness, where feet of white men had seldom trod, and never those of a white woman. After working his claim on Shaws Flat to a near finish, he sold it, and filed a squatter's right to land now owned and occupied by the West Side Lumber Co., and where the town of Tuolumne is located, in the eastern part of Tuolumne county, ten miles from Sonora. It is now known as the "East Belt" of the Mother Lode. There were no roads; nothing but trails made by wild animals and wilder Indians. Our faithful old oxen, Tom and Jerry, were our main dependence for transit through the wilderness. It required two days to reach our new abode.

We had left what few conveniences Shaws Flat and Sonora could offer and the end of our pilgrimage seemed far worse to mother and me than the beginning.

We moved into a log house with a dirt floor and a big fireplace. We did not mind the storms of winter, for we were warm and dry. As time is the arbiter of all things, we in time lost the fear and dread of the unknown.

The advent of spring in 1855 opened up a vista of enchantment of bud and flower, and we loved it. Today I hold the ground sacred to the memories of the happiest days of my childhood. We had passed the winter in comfort and plenty. The woods were full of game. The cattle were fat. The world—or all we desired of it—was ours. As the summer advanced, we reveled and rejoiced, gathering wild grapes, gooseberries, elderberries, greens, and everything that gave variety to our larder.

Father fenced ground for a garden and planted seeds brought from Missouri.

I then became an important member of the family; and, I will say, a busy one; for it was up to me to keep the ground squirrels and rabbits out of the garden.

Later in the fall of 1855 the Scott brothers, half breed Cherokees, wandered into the mountains, near our place, prospecting. They found good prospects at Cherokee, as they afterward named the place, not much over a mile from our house.

They built themselves a comfortable log cabin as quietly as possible, located their claims, and, borrowing father's rifle, killed some deer and cured the meat. They hired father to move their long tom, cradle, rocker and tools, also some provisions for the winter and were soon ready for the winter snows. They knew they had good claims, and they wrote for their brother, Dick, to join them, locating a claim for him. They would not drink; were the soul of honor. They were gentlemen in the meaning that all the word implied. They wanted my father to join them, but he was clearing land for grain and hay.

Very early in the spring of 1856 the news of a rich gold discovery leaked out, and the country was soon overrun with prospectors. Cherokee soon became a lively, flourishing mining camp with two stores and two saloons. Of course the saloons were the center of gravity in all camps. Selling vile whiskey to vile men can have only one result. The men had already been inoculated with the virus of evil. They would drink and only taper off when tankage facilities failed. Whiskey created antagonisms, and their faces would remind one of a personified day of judgment, untempered by mercy. Then they were ready for anything—robbery or murder, but above all they loved to fight.

This is only a history of the vultures that preyed on the honest class of miners. Cherokee represented the subsequent camps on the East Belt during '56 and '57, during the placer craze.

The first murder that occurred was done by Wilse Walkingstaff in May, 1856, in a cabin on Turnback Creek, not far from Cherokee. Walkingstaff was a Cherokee Indian and a very dangerous man. The trouble was caused by jealousy over a woman—a young squaw. He became jealous of James Ham, almost a boy, that was new to conditions then prevailing. He had not been initiated into the gambling class. Walkingstaff met him alone and cut his bowels open so that they protruded to the ground by his dead body; and then fled in terror from the mob that he knew would hang him. Ham was buried under a beautiful live oak tree and laid first claim to what was afterward known as the Summersville (or Carters) cemetery.

In June, 1856, without warning of the awful shadow of death that was hovering over our peaceful home, my father was shot to death in French Bar, now known as La Grange. Oh, the awful sorrow and desolation of that bereft home! Another cold-blooded murder. My little brother (I forgot to state in proper sequence) was born April 2, 1855, and was too young to realize our loss.

The miners—God bless them—threw a cordon of protection around that humble but desolate home, and none of the rough element ever dared to intrude or molest the helpless and sorrowing inmates.

My dear mother had a problem to solve, alone and unaided. We must live, and in order to live, we must eat; and to pay the exorbitant prices for provisions seemed impossible. After mature and deliberate thought she opened a boarding house, my father having built a comfortable dwelling house the year before. It was not long until she had all the boarders she could possibly cook for.

Our new house was built very near and on the east bank of Turnback Creek. The creek was located and miners at work very near our house. They had cabins, of a sort, everywhere close to us. They were quiet, fun-loving men. They all wanted to board. Mother must have a cook, but the men all refused a China cook. As she could not get a white cook she told them it was a China cook or move boarding house, they consented. With the new help mother took on more boarders.

Everything was quiet, considering new men were coming in. One Sunday a fellow that had been bumming for several days went to Cherokee, filled up on "oh be joyful" and, coming down the creek to a cabin of three quiet miners he was offensive, with perfectly appalling results. He was ordered away in no gentle tone of voice. One of the rightful inmates of the cabin turned to fill his pipe, and received a bullet in his brain. The pardners grabbed the murderer and gave the alarm. In such times men act quickly and often without reason. Impulse is one thing and judgment another.

Inflamed by the injustice, and cruel murder of their comrade, two hundred miners, to a man, demanded the instant death of the murderer; the vulture in human form, whom they had housed and fed. There being no other rope available they removed the rope from a dry well at our house. Willing hands make quick work, and he was soon hanging between earth and sky. In the shadow of that tree, with its mute evidence of sin and mistaken ideals of life, one of the miners spoke words of warning. He said: "We are living in primitive surroundings; but there is strength in unity, and the strong hand of justice and retribution will not fail to exact a life for a life. Beware!" So ended the fateful year of 1856. That is, there were no more fatalities to record.

The fall and winter passed as quietly as could be expected. The boys taught me woodcraft; the compass, by reading rocks and trees. They taught me how to use firearms and I was an expert; and, old as I am, could take the head off of a gray squirrel in the tallest pine, in this day and generation.

By this time some families had moved onto the East Belt. Two or three had moved into Cherokee. Soulsbyville was still unpopulated, but contained the nucleus of a clean flourishing mining camp; for Ben Soulsby had discovered the Soulsby mine. This mine necessitated a different class of miners, men that understood hard rock drilling. Nearly all the quartz miners were Cornishmen, from the old country. . . .

The question of introducing Chinese labor into the placer mines was bringing a feeling of antagonism between miners and sentiment seemed to be about equally divided; so they decided to leave it to a miners' meeting and vote, and the place selected was Carter's store on Long Gulch. After a short and, as everyone thought, a friendly debate they proceeded to vote. Those in favor of the Chinese lost out by a large majority. Saying nothing, they all walked out of the store into the darkness of a starless night, leaving the door open. Like the crack of doom, pistol shots were the only warning the men in the store had of the horrid pandemonium of death that was to follow. Before the lights could be put out, Bob Clod was shot through the heart, William Connally was shot through both shoulders, Ben Edmondson was shot through the thigh. As soon as the room was in darkness men in the room made for the open, shooting in every direction. The murderers fled, leaving no trace. It was believed by every one that the brutal work was instigated and done by one John Page, aided by Bill Ake and Tom Rich. They left their claims and all their worldly goods, and an unpaid board bill, and were never heard of again.

The little store resembled a slaughter house; the window was completely shattered.

The question of coolie labor was effectively settled. Bob Clod was buried near the scene of strife. William Connally and Ben Edmondson recovered after long days of suffering, for medical treatment was uncertain in the early days.

Some time in the spring of 1858 news flew like wild fire that Jim Lyons had killed John Blakely and shot Bill Blakeley's arm off and was in jail. All the mountain folks knew Jim Lyons and liked him; no man ever left his house hungry; the latch string to his door always hung on the outside. The Blakely brothers, John, William and James, were Englishmen. They did a great injustice and a dishonest and low down thing to Lyons. He could not read, and having faith in human integrity, he unknowingly signed away his right and title to his land near Sullivan's creek, later known as the Hughes place, the Snyder and Frank Gilkey ranch.

I do not know the date of their location, but William and James Blakely discovered the Eureka mine. They did not have much money and mother trusted them for board for a while. But it was not long before they had money to burn. Soon the little town of Summersville (they named it in gratitude for mother's kindness after her) was a busy hive of industry and prosperity. The Blakely boys continued to board at our house until they sold the mine. . . .

In those days the miners did not exact an eye for an eye and a tooth for a tooth, but they demanded a life for a life. Consequently McCauley, with Jim Lyons and Bob Poore, received the death penalty and in the fall of 1858 they were all three taken from the county jail to "Dead Man's Gulch," near the Odd Fellows' cemetery, and all of them at the same time paid the debt of a life for a life. They were buried where they were executed. Vengeance could go no further with them than the portals of the grave. Wild flowers bloom over their unmarked graves, and birds sing their carols to hearts that are dead and ears that hear not. God is merciful.

Joaquin Murietta, the noted highwayman, always, like the "under dog," was painted blacker than he deserved. He was a peaceful, quiet miner, with his wife, living near Columbia, or Saw Mill Flat. He was mining some little distance from his cabin when it was entered by three white men. Brutes of the lowest type, after they had heaped every indignity on his wife, they robbed the cabin and set fire to it. Joaquin, seeing the smoke, hastened to his cabin, but too late to aid his wife or save the cabin or its contents. In an untutored, savage heart like his, what more natural or sweet than revenge? I have seen him and talked with him. He never was known to molest women and children. I had a souvenir that once belonged to Joaquin—a silver saddle horn.

During the fall of 1858 a miner on Turnback Creek sold his claim to a company of five Chinamen. They rented a cabin from mother, that she had taken in lieu of a board bill. After they had worked for some time, the miners all along the creek commenced to miss things. The thievery became a menace to the miners. Loss of mining tools and cleaned up sluices became of daily occurrence. A miner's meeting was called, and a still hunt for the stolen property instituted. The property was found under the floor of the Chinamen's cabin—picks, pans, shovels, sluice forks, rocker irons; they were found on a Saturday and left where found. The Chinks were at work on their claim. At night they returned as usual, not dreaming of the awful catastrophe awaiting them.

That night a miner's meeting was called for the whole district, and it was decided to whip them publicly. Five men were chosen to do the whipping; three others to guard the house through the night. The five were instructed to lay on good and plenty, but certainly not to overdo, and the whipping place selected is directly in front of where the Methodist church is now, in Tuolumne. At ten o'clock the Chinamen were taken by about forty miners (all wearing guns) to the place—I will not say of "execution"—and before a crowd of over two hundred people each Chinaman was stripped to his waist, and received on his quivering back twenty lashes. After they were whipped, they were given their shirts and told to go home, gather their things, and leave. They did not delay on the order of their going, either.

This proved a salutary lesson, for there were no more sluice boxes robbed. This was justice, or law, administered by the people and for the people.

I am a typical pioneer, and having lived so many years of my life, and seeing turbulence and evil of every description in early days and quick retribution of the people, single-handed or in mobs, I will say I have an unholy desire to see some of the brutish criminals of the present time man-handled as of old. Crime is ubiquitous; it bids fair to darken the canopy of our country—a shadow, a menace far worse than in '49. Evil companions and environment pit the character like the smallpox. There are many things today that lead to crime that the early days never thought of. Idleness in the growing generation of today is the mainspring or great factor of crime. . . .

At this time (1859) the important towns of Sonora, Columbia and Jamestown, with their prosperity depending on the rich placers, had begun to wane; many and various business houses closed. Quartz mining had reached a sure and paying basis, but on a safer, and saner foundation. Quartz miners would not support the sporting fraternity as had the placer miners. Times were changing. Families were making permanent homes, and wherever water could be procured gardens and small orchards were in evidence. Instead of dance halls, saloons and pool rooms, comfortable residences were built. The wild maniacal ways of mobs and unlawful hangings were things to be forgotten.

Mrs. Lee Whipple-Haslam, *Early Days in California* (Jamestown, Calif.: Mother Lode Magnet, 1925), pp. 12–21.

In 1871, Mrs. J. W. Likins (whose autobiography never reveals her first name) became a door-to-door sales agent for Bancroft's Bookstore, traveling throughout the towns of the San Francisco Bay area. A fire had just destroyed her family's home and belongings, and the illness of her husband and child made their situation desperate. Bookselling was too low paid for most men, but impoverished female agents could claim gentility as purveyors of culture to newly settled communities. Mrs. Likins peddled books like Mark Twain's *Innocents Abroad* and engravings of General Grant's family, taking her work and her respectability very seriously.

She had reason to be serious; she never knew when her gender might make her the subject of rude remarks about a woman's place or of improper jokes, usually about General Grant (he was reputed to have another, illegitimate, family). She was a most diligent salesperson but was always uncomfortable in the role. Invoking the rules of propriety, she appealed to the hospitality of women and the gentlemanly aspirations of men—abusive ones were accused of forgetting that they had mothers—to make her work possible. In her door-to-door canvasing, she showed a keen eye for class distinctions and urban conditions, and a quick tongue when she suspected mistreatment. She also had a sense of humor, which was useful in the midst of a California earthquake.

N ow begins the one great struggle of my life. I scarcely know where to turn or what to do. As I look around the room, I see nothing but want and poverty on every hand. Something must be done to get out of this place. Bidding my dear ones keep up courage, I start out. Never before did I know the meaning of the word poverty. Now I felt it in all its keenest pangs—everything looked dark and cloudy. I started for the Post-office. Not being able to pay car hire, I went on foot.

On my way I passed the book-store of H. H. Bancroft, then on the corner of Montgomery and Merchant streets. In the window I noticed a card, with the words "Agents Wanted" on it. Stepping into the store a gentleman advanced to meet me. I asked him "Do you employ lady agents?" "Yes," he replied, "allow me to take you to the Subscription Department." There I was shown to the gentleman in charge. I found him to be a frank kind-hearted gentleman.

Will I ever forget him, for it was he who cheered me with his pleasant words. After talking for a few moments, he showed me an engraving of Grant and his Family, in upright form; told me his terms, what to sell it for, and how much commission I would get. Knowing as I did that something must be done by me, we made a bargain; he giving me a book to take orders in, and two of the pictures, told me to go on Montgomery street. I left the store with more elastic steps than I had since my arrival in California. I started up the street, but did not have the courage to stop until I reached Mr. M., on Washington street; he bought the two and gave me the coin for them. How I thanked him; I think if he had refused, I should not have had courage enough to ask any one else. I hastened back to the store, paid Mr. S. for them, and had four more rolled up for me. It was now three hours since I had left home.

Taking them on my arm, order-book in my hand, I started up Montgomery street, calling on one and all, up stairs and down, in every room.

Some looked at me curiously, others with pity, and *some few* with contempt, while I endeavored, in my embarrassment, and in an awkward way, to show the picture.

I worked on faithfully until three o'clock in the afternoon, when I returned to my miserable room; but it contained those dear to me, where I found them very anxious about me. They soon cheered up, as I told them the events of the day.

Tuesday morning I again resumed my work; for five days I canvassed steadily, nothing of importance occurring.

In this time I made many dollars, which I put to good use, buying comforts for myself and family, and preparing my little girl for school again.

Eight o'clock every morning would find me in the street-car on my way to the business part of the city. I had one of the pictures mounted on canvass and rollers, that I used as a sample copy, taking orders, to be delivered in two or three weeks, and sometimes as far as two months.

It was now just before Grant's election, and great excitement concerning it prevailed. The Democrats arguing in favor of *their* candidate, and the Republicans in favor of *theirs*.

In almost *every* room, in front of every store or business house, and on every street corner, I would find gentlemen in groups, whispering or conversing in low tones; I suppose plotting and planning for the coming campaign; while others were loud and boisterous in expressing their opinions.

It was a great trial for me to know just how to approach them, for the one almost frightened me, and the others so grave and solemn, still I did not pass any of them; with a heavy heart I would step up, unroll the picture, saying, "Gentlemen, I have a fine engraving of General Grant and his family."

After they had looked at it, which they very seldom failed to do, I would present my order-book, take them in rotation, and insist upon one and all to subscribe, and was generally very successful. They would treat me kindly, and were very polite, with the exception of some few ruffians who seemed to have forgotten "their mother was a woman," would hurt my feelings, in many ways, with regards to Grant's life and character, on this coast, before the war; as though *I* was accountable for the way he had acted.

I will here relate a circumstance. I went into a lawyer's office on Montgomery street. It was richly furnished, with care and neatness. At a table were seated two young gentlemen; at a desk was seated a person whom I took to be a gentleman, from the looks of his back.

When I spoke to the young gentleman concerning the picture, he whirled around in the chair, and, oh, horrors, what a repulsive face. I *had never* seen any thing to equal it.

With a snarl, and the authority of a king, he said, "I don't want you to bother those boys, woman; what is it you want? I will attend to you." I politely showed him the picture. He looked up, with his blinky eyes, and crooked mouth, in which there was an attempt to grin. "I would buy the engraving if it had his squaw wife and Indian babies on it; we cannot trade madam," and he turned around to his desk.

I left the office, without daring to again ask the young gentlemen to buy; but as I passed them, and although they were busily writing, their faces showed they were deeply mortified.

When once alone in the hall, I sat down on the bottom stair that led to the third story of the building, and had a good cry.

Many passed me, looking at me wonderingly, but none addressed me. I dried my tears away, drew down my vail, and passed into the street. I had canvassed California street on both sides, from Front to Montgomery; on Montgomery, from California to Washington, and now made up my mind to try Front street, as Mr. S. had told me he *thought* I would be very successful there. I started in at California street, passed down the lower side to Washington.

The gentlemen whom I met were all pleasant and jolly. Democrats joking Republicans by saying, "Don't back out *now;* if the lady had a picture of Seymour *we* would buy it." Others would say, "Don't let him off, madam; he is as black as ever was." After many more jokes I passed up the other side.

Here I met a gentleman from the country, who was trading at one of the wholesale houses; he seemed very angry to think a woman should be selling pictures among so many men. He said I looked old enough to be married and have a family, and ought to be at home taking care of them.

I told him I knew I looked old, but he need not remind me of it; that I *had* a family and was trying to make an honest living for them, at the same time telling him I presumed he was a bachelor, who would not know how to appreciate a wife if he had one.

The proprietor laughed heartily, and said, "Madam, you guessed right." As I was wasting time I left him.

When I got to California street, my order-book showed fifty-three names I had taken on Front street. I next tried Davis street and took more orders than on any street of its size in the City. After this I took the rest of the business streets in rotation, canvassing them thoroughly, walking all day, and running the sewing-machine until late at night. I kept this up for six weeks, and was now canvassing on Third street, not succeeding very well.

An old man was standing in the door-way of his shop; I spoke to him, unrolled the picture and asked him to subscribe. He was a strong Democrat and was not long in letting me know it.

"You d—— women think you will rule the country. There is a clique of you who go prowling around, having secret meetings, lecturing all over the country on women's rights; *here you* are roaming around with that d—— picture of that loafer Grant. There was one of your *clique* in here the other day, lecturing on temperance. I told her in plain English to leave my shop; I would have no women's rights around me."

I replied, "Thank you for your hint; I am not in your shop, nor do not intend crossing your door-way, for fear I might become polluted, for you certainly are the most profane ruffian I ever met."

At this he became very angry, and I *think* he would have struck me, *had he* dared. I passed on and canvassed for several blocks; all the gentlemen were polite and kind, until I came to Mr. B——e's large grocery store. Inside were a large crowd of gentlemen talking politics, some of them seemed very much excited.

I stepped inside, unrolled the engraving and held it up for inspection, but did not say a word. One red-faced half drunken fellow stepped up and with many airs took hold of the engraving, examined it for a minute and said: "This picture is very imperfect." "In what respect," I asked. He replied, "It has not Grant's Indian babies." I told him it was better to be father of Indian babies than, like Seymour, not the father of any.

At this they laughed loudly. I looked at them for a second before I thought what I had said. I hurried away without asking any to subscribe. One of the gentlemen came out and called to me. I went back and four of them subscribed.

Next day I tried Kearny street, and took many orders, before I reached the City Hall; here I turned down Merchant street, until I came to the lowest story of the building, determined to take the officers in rotation. I found Mr. B—— behind the counter, who was very kind. After examining the engraving for some time he took my order-book, and signed his name. There were a great many of the street contractors in the office, among which he secured me some eight or ten names.

He returned to where I was standing, and showed me what he had done. I did not wish to take the money, as I could not deliver the pictures to them for two weeks. "Take it along," he said, "if you are mean enough to run away with so small a sum the country is well rid of you." Thanking them for their kindness I visited every room in the building. By the time I reached Washington street, I had twenty names on my order-book taken in the City Hall.

That evening, when I returned to the restaurant, I went to Mrs. T.'s room. . . . After telling her how well I was succeeding, I tried to persuade her to take Sacramento, and some of the upper counties, also telling her I had contracted with Bancrofts for the whole Pacific Coast for the upright picture of the Grant family, in connection with many others.

It was some days before she would give me any definite answer concerning it, though finally consented to try and canvass Sacramento; for she, like myself, was very tired of the restaurant, and was willing to do anything that was honorable and honest to get away from it.

She went in company with me to the store, where I introduced her to Mr. S.; at first, she was somewhat embarrassed, but his kind and easy manners soon reassured her.

I told him I did not wish the whole Coast. That Mrs. T. could have Sacramento, Marysville and Grass Valley. The bargain was closed.

I now selected out of the remaining territory what I desired, which were San Francisco, Santa Clara and San Joaquin counties.

It was two months since I first began to canvass, and I had several hundred names, also had the money for many small engravings. Bancrofts were looking daily for a new supply from New York. I had made up my mind to go to San José to canvass and take orders, during the Fair in that place, which was to commence in a few days.

The afternoon before the opening of the Fair found me in a railway car, bound for San José. I thought how lonely it would be there in not finding my friend, Mrs. F., as they had gone to San Diego.

Although I had passed over the road four times previous to this, I could see new beauties in almost everything. In fact, in the former times, I was so home-sick I scarcely noticed anything. But the prospects looked much brighter to me now.

As I sat and gazed from the car-window, I could but compare the autumn here with that in the East. There, at this season of the year, I have often wandered through the woods, looked with admiration at the leaves, with their many tints, listened to the soft, low murmuring of the wind, while in the distance I heard the notes of some merry bird, keeping time with the sad rustling of the leaves beneath my feet, while here before me lies the Coast Range, sunburnt and barren in its uneven appearance, looking as though some great convulsion of the earth had thrown it there. This scene is both grand and sad, while the thoughts of the other are sublime.

We pass on, and are soon at San Mateo. The town is not very striking in its appearance. But the country on either side, as far as the eye can look, seems fine and well cultivated. The next place that takes my attention is Belmont. Off to the right is a winding cañon skirted with heavy timber, making it look very beautiful to me.

As we pass through Redwood City, I was told it was the county seat of San Mateo county; it seemed to be quite a lively and flourishing little town.

There is Fair Oaks and Menlo Park, which are beautiful places for private residences.

At Santa Clara I did not get a view of the town, as it lies at some distance from the depot.

San Jose.

When I arrived at San José, I directed a hackman to take me to the Morgan House. The landlord recognized me at once, and seemed very glad to see me, but said he hadn't a vacant room in the house and recommended me to Mrs. M—— on Third street.

At Mrs. M—— I was shown to a nicely furnished room. When the bell rang for dinner I descended to the dining-room. At the table were several ladies and gentlemen; all strangers to me. The landlady inquired my name and introduced me to all.

The meal passed pleasantly. I found them to be polite and genteel in manners and appearances.

Next morning I went to the hall where the Fair was to be held, to try and secure some space where I might put a small table and a chair, but there wasn't any vacancy. The agent for the Florence Sewing Machine, who had a large space, kindly offered me room in one corner. Mrs. M—— the landlady, loaned me a table and a chair. After they were conveyed to the hall, I arranged my pictures on the table and took my seat behind them, feeling more like a culprit than anything else. ·

Although it was a short time since I had commenced to canvass, and knew it was an honorable and legitimate business, still it *seemed* to me very much like begging. As ladies and gentlemen would pass me, I would try in many ways to gain their attention, but I acted so awkward and out of place that I did not succeed very well.

Some would stop for a moment and admire the engraving; few ladies would insist upon their husbands buying, but I scarcely took any orders.

I soon found it was not the place for me; if I wish to sell anything I must get out among the crowd.

Standing close to the entrance, I tackled every one I would see, something after the fashion of a little news-boy.

"Ladies and gentlemen, here's a fine engraving of General Grant and family," insisting upon one and all, who stopped to look at it for a moment, to subscribe. In the afternoon as I was going around among the machinery, I overheard an old man, who had a patent wash-boiler, and I suppose feeling very important, say to one of the superintendents of the Fair, as he passed by him, "Why do you allow that woman around here with that picture, trying to get everyone's attention; why, a minute ago, while a gentleman was looking at the boiler; she had the impudence to ask him to patronize her."

He answered, "This is a free country, and as she don't seem to be doing any harm, she has as much right in here as any one else." At this the patent boiler man seemed to become a little embarrassed, but made no reply. In the evening I attended the Fair as a spectator, not as peddler.

I could not help but notice everything was arranged with good taste. I think there were the finest and largest apples, pears and grapes I ever saw. The canned fruit and jellies, in glass jars and tumblers, looked very inviting.

I stopped to examine the needle-work, wax-flowers, and paintings. The most interesting of all to me was the silk worms. I listened to the man in charge, while he explained their habits and customs, and could not help looking on them with curiosity, to think that mulberry leaves could be converted into material for our finest silk fabrics through the agency of these homely-looking worms.

The next day I went around to the Court House. The officers were all very kind and polite. I received several orders. During the day I visited many offices and stores; being very successful. Mrs. M., the landlady, told me in the evening she thought I would do well to go to the Fair that night and take my picture. I did so, and had quite good success, taking orders for several of "Lincoln and Family," "Washington and Family," also of the "Grant Family," saying they wished a group of the three great men of the United States. In the evening, I heard some one talking about a gentleman who had small photographs of different varieties, and a book written by himself. I inquired whether he was in the hall, and was told he had a small space at the far end of the building. I concluded to go and see him; when I came quite close to him the thought struck me to stand and watch *his* manner of doing *the* business.

He was standing, with his books and pictures lying on an oval table in front of him; they were arranged neatly, and showed well. I listened to his fast talk in recommending his goods; my thoughts were, "I'll have no chance while this gentleman's around."

I stepped up to his table; he turned politely and commenced urging me to buy. I told him I did not wish to purchase, as I was in the same occupation. I told him, upon inquiry, what subject I had. He said he had seen the engraving; it was very fine, and hoped I would be successful. I thanked him and wished him the same. I learned afterward his name was D——.

When I returned to my seat again, I found one of the ladies who had charge of the sewing-machines trying her best to sell one of the pictures. I helped her to close the bargain, and thanked her very much for the interest she had taken. It being late, I returned to the boarding-house, well pleased with my day's labor.

I continued my work there for several days longer, then returned to San Francisco; next day, after my arrival, I went down to Bancroft's. I showed Mr. S. my order-book, with which he seemed to be well pleased, saying, "You have done splendid." I thought so, too, as I had taken sixty orders during my absence. He told me the engravings of the Grant family had come, and I could commence delivering that day if I wished; counting out as many as I could conveniently carry, I left the store and went up Montgomery street. Using my order-book for a guide, I called on each one in succession who had subscribed; they all treated me kindly, taking their engraving, and some gave me orders for frames, on which I also made quite a good commission.

In this way, I worked very hard all day; as fast as one lot was delivered, would return to the store for a fresh supply. I now began to realize that taking orders for pictures, and delivering them were quite different things, the latter being very laborious.

I continued to work for several days, as I was in much need of the commission I was to get on them. At the same time, felt anxious to deliver as many as possible each day, so that my employers should have no cause of complaint.

I now began to think about looking up a house, so that we might go to house-keeping again. After some difficulty, I procured rooms on Fourth street, near Howard.

This morning I had concluded to go down into the City and buy some furniture, for the purpose of fitting up my rooms. I had just got my little girl ready for school, and about to put on *my* hat and shawl to start on my

Female enterprise. Millinery and dressmaking could be lucrative trades; Emma Gibbs and her satisfied customers celebrate her success. Courtesy of the Nevada Historical Society.

errand, when the *house commenced* rocking and shaking at an alarming rate; my little girl said, "Mamma, what is the matter?"

The cars never shook the house so before. The Polly was flying around in her cage, and seemed very much frightened. I did not realize myself what it was, until the second shock, then I exclaimed "Oh, this must be an earthquake, let us run into the street." We started, she gathering the cage in her hand containing the Polly. As we passed through the hall, I heard the whatnot fall in the ladies' parlor, breaking the vases and other things on it, and making quite a noise. Before we got clear of the house, an old wardrobe standing in the hall fell behind us with a great crash; then I thought *surely* the *house* was coming down on our heads, and expected every instant to be crushed to death.

But amid all the danger and confusion, as I passed through the hall by the landlady's room-door, I could not help noticing her, lying full length on the floor throwing her hands wildly about, exclaiming, "Oh Lord, save us, Oh Lord, save us," at the top of her voice.

When we reached the street, the sidewalk seemed to be still moving. We hurried down the platform toward the baggage-room in search of my husband, who had gone there but a few moments before. I found him standing in the door-way laughing. I said, "How can you laugh at anything so terrible as this?" He replied, he "could not help laughing to see those piles of lumber in front of the office dancing;" also said, "that as far as that was concerned, if the earthquake was going to sink the City, he did not see why we might not as well go down laughing as crying, as crying would not save us."

Many gentlemen came into the office laughing, talking and jesting about the earthquake, which seemed to me to be perfect mockery, for from my feelings then, I thought at every shock we should all be swallowed up.

I often smile now to myself when I think how ridiculous I must have appeared that morning, running down the platform with my hat in my hand, my shawl dragging, and almost crying; my little girl closely following, dragging after her the large cage with the Polly in it.

I stayed around the platform all day, and no one could persuade me to go into the house, until night drove me there. *Then* I lay down with all my clothes on, ready to run at any moment, and wished myself back in Ohio a thousand and one times.

It was two days before I could get up sufficient courage to venture up into the City to commence work again. I selected furniture for our rooms, and moved what few traps we had at the restaurant, and *once more* commenced house-keeping. Everything passed off pleasantly for two weeks, with plenty of work and liberal patronage.

I now concluded to go to Santa Clara and canvass that town, before delivering my pictures in San José. Eight o'clock in the evening found me seated in the ladies' parlor at the hotel, conversing with the landlord concerning the severe shock of earthquake we had two weeks previous.

He explained to me how the sliding iron doors of the hotel had come together, and he thought had shut them in at first, but as the convulsion of the earth continued, they opened again, and allowed the inmates to pass out into the street, which they were not long in doing. The shock was so severe, that they had apprehensions the house would fall before they could escape.

After conversing awhile on different subjects, he bade me good evening and went below. As I passed through the hall on the way to my room, noticed the ceiling was bare in some places where the plastering had fallen off; the walls were badly cracked. Taking a light from the stand, I went into my room almost fearing to lock the door, lest another shock might come, and I could not escape.

I thought, if the Lord spared me, I would not stay another night in a brick house. I had partially undressed when the house commenced shaking. Frightened all but to death, I scarcely knew what to do; but found myself in the door-way with the candle in my hand, thinking I must not go into the street in this condition. There came a second shock. I blew out the light, threw it on the floor, and rushed into the street, not caring how I appeared. It was full of people. Some of them looked at me curiously; but I drew my shawl close about me and stood my ground, nor could I be persuaded to return to my room. The clerk brought me my shoes and baggage, and took me where he knew I could obtain lodgings, to a lady's, a few doors away. She gladly offered me shelter, as her husband was away from home, and she was very lonely.

There were several light shocks after I had been there. Next morning, many joked me about my appearance the evening previous, especially Mr. W., who said he never would forget how comical and frightened I looked.

During the day I took several orders, sold a great many and received the coin for them. I had taken some eleven or twelve to Santa Clara with me. I made arrangements to stay with the lady until I should leave town, so I went back and spent the night.

After breakfast, I started for Mrs. W's., who lived a half or three-quarters of a mile from town. I found her and husband living on a fruit ranch. She did not recognize me at first.

I told her I had brought the picture she had subscribed for one evening, at the Fair in San José. She remembered it, took the Grant picture, and gave me an order for the engravings of Washington and Lincoln's families. She gave me some choice pears, grapes, and a *piece of pie,* insisting upon my eating them, as she said I looked very tired. Everything in and around the house, so far as I could see, showed a neat and tidy housewife. I promised to bring the engravings in a short time, also thanked her for her kindness, and returned to Santa Clara.

After lunch I started out along the Alameda, toward San José. I had sold all the engravings I had brought with me, so I made up my mind to call at every house and take orders, to be delivered in two weeks. The houses were very scattering, and I found it slow and tiresome work; but I enjoyed walking in the shade of those stately old trees that line either side of that favorite resort of San José and Santa Clara for driving. It reminded me of portions of Bourbon County, Kentucky. In that county is *one* of the dearest spots on earth to me, for it was my childhood home. I came to the place where they were about to establish the depot of the Santa Clara and San José street railroad. Here were several gentlemen collected. Among them was one without a coat, who did not seem to be working very hard, although the perspiration was streaming down his face. I did not wonder at it, he was so large and fleshy; he reminded me of the darkey song, "he's tree foot one way, six foot tudder, and weighs tree hundred pounds," and as for his coat, it was nowhere around.

However, I ventured up and addressed him, unrolled the engraving for his inspection; he looked up, politely bowed, viewed it for some time, occasionally wiping the perspiration from his face with his hand.

Turning his head to one side he laughed jovially, and said, "Old Grant is no favorite of mine; but if you will bring me a good engraving of his Indian family I will buy it. Will you?" I replied, "The demand for such an engraving seems so great I certainly shall order some for the accommodation of people of such refined taste."

Then the three hundred pounds looked at me sharply, as much as to say, "I don't sabé," but I kept a very grave look on my face, and said, "I shall most assuredly bring you a picture of the kind you desire, and shall expect you to take it off my hands."

I showed the engraving to a number of other gentlemen standing around, and insisted upon their buying it, but did not get a single order.

I bid them good day, and took up my line of march toward San José. It was now getting late, so I did not stop at any more houses, but hurried on, until I reached the Morgan House, on First street; here I partook of a light supper, went to my room very tired, having walked about six miles during the day.

Next morning I arose not much refreshed, partook a hasty breakfast, and visited the Express Office; found my package of engravings all right; had them sent up to the hotel, where I soon followed.

I found Bancroft's had also sent a number of small engravings on different subjects. Taking an armful of the Grant pictures, I started out to fill my orders in this place.

I worked very hard for several days, and with good success, selling a great many small ones, and taking orders for Grant, Lincoln, and Washington families. I had now canvassed the business part of the town thoroughly, and made up my mind to try what success I would have among the private families. Many ladies had been recommended to me, as being very liberal, and believed in patronizing their own sex; so I concluded to make one of them my first victim.

She lived several blocks from the business part of the town; while on my way I had plenty of time for reflecting, and wondered how I should be received, as this was my first effort to canvass among the ladies.

My somewhat long walk brought me in front of the residence of my intended first victim, who was the dashing widow of the lately deceased Mr.——, as I shall call her. I opened the gate and passed in through the neatly laid out and well-kept grounds.

I passed up to the front door, and timidly pulled the bell, and waited for the appearance of the servant, or I thought, maybe the lady herself might appear to admit me, and perhaps might invite me into her parlor, and might even go so far as ask me to stay for tea, as it was getting late in the afternoon.

After waiting sometime, with as much bashfulness as a young miss of sixteen awaiting her first beau, the door opened just sufficient for the dashing widow to see who the intruder was; instead of the cordial hand-shaking and hearty welcome I had expected, while awaiting her appearance the first words that greeted my ears were, "What is wanted, Madam?" at the same time holding a tight grip on the door, I suppose lest I might burst it open, rush past her and take the castle by storm. I had no such intentions, but politely told her I had a very fine engraving of General Grant and family; would like her to look at it, and perhaps could induce her to buy.

She said she had no use for such things and had no money to fool away for such purposes; still keeping her hold on the door, which was so nearly closed I did not get a full view of her august person. This liberal lady, I learned, was a leading member of one of the fashionable churches, and gave quite freely of her wealth, whenever an opportunity offered for it to be proclaimed publicly that the dashing widow had given hundreds for such, and such, a charitable purpose.

I had always been used to civil treatment from my own sex at least, and turned away with disgust *from this,* what the world calls a *liberal lady,* and must confess with scarcely sufficient courage left to call on another of the same liberal reputation.

When I reached Mrs. J—— I concluded to go in. She also was a descendant of the same family, but I found her very different, treating me kindly and politely, conducting me into the parlor, and inviting me to rest myself, while she examined the engravings. After looking them all over, she stepped into another room, and brought out an engraving of the Grant family, which her husband had purchased of me a few days previous.

We conversed awhile, then thanking her for her kindness I bid her good afternoon.

As I passed down the street, I saw a new and neat house, and inquired of a boy, who lived there; was told by him Mrs. C——, whose husband was a buyer of grain. I went up the steps and rang the bell; it was answered by Mrs. C——, in person; she is very nice looking, well dressed and a perfect lady in her manners, she cordially invited me in, and with her easy conversation made me feel quite at home. She examined the engravings and purchased two of the smaller ones. It was late and I returned to the hotel, concluding to take a new start next day.

In the morning I set out for Gen. N——'s residence; this I found at quite a distance, but did not mind it much for the morning was pleasant, and the air balmy.

When I reached the gate that led into his grounds, it was just nine o'clock. As I passed through the wide winding carriage-drive, thickly skirted on both sides with evergreens and ornamental trees, it looked dark and gloomy. I did not see his cottage until I was right upon it. The appearance of the dwelling outside is not in keeping with his grounds.

After rapping at several of the doors, I did not find any one at home. I looked around me; saw at a distance the gardener; in answer to my inquiry, he told me the General and family were away. I asked his permission to go over the grounds, which he readily granted, thanking him, I started down the wide foot-path, bordered with flowers, and small shrubs of the choicest variety; now and then a tree thickly entwined with creeping vines.

Sometimes I would see a narrow path leading off to the left, so thickly covered overhead with honeysuckle, making the entrance so low, I would have to stoop to see where it led. A few yards away was a neat small summer-house, dark and gloomy looking as though it might be a romantic lover's retreat. I wandered on, passed over a rustic foot-bridge that spanned a small stream, while overhead were large weeping willows, their branches dipping in the water beneath.

I stepped back upon the bridge, for the spot seemed delightful, although gloomy. To the left was a small grove of weeping willows, while around and about them were many rustic seats.

In front of them, on an elevation was a small artificial lake, supplied by a flowing well, the waste water forming the stream beneath my feet.

The wide path through which I had just come led to the hot-houses. I did not visit them, as my time was limited. Turning to the left, I passed around the lake, watched the numerous fishes playing in its waters, passed down the stone steps into the same dark drive I had first entered, out through the gate, and was once more on Santa Clara street.

I now went out to Tenth street, down Tenth until I came to Mrs. Dr. S——'s, whose husband raised fruit. I had met them one evening at the Fair, and promised to call at their residence. I inquired of a small boy, who pointed out the house. They have a beautiful place. At the edges of the sidewalk around the grounds was planted maples, which are now large and stately trees. I noticed the yard was tastefully laid out; there were many choice flowers and shrubs. I crossed the porch and rung the bell.

Mrs. S—— answered the bell, recognized me, invited me in, bought three different engravings, and sent for her married daughter, who lived next door, to come and examine them.

Mrs. F——, the daughter, purchased a few. They invited me to stay for lunch, which I gratefully accepted, as I wished to canvass that portion of the town in the afternoon. After lunch, thanking them for their hospitality, I started out, calling at every house in rotation. I was treated kindly and politely, and found the ladies very liberal.

It was almost dark when I reached the hotel. In the morning I went in the direction of the San José Institute. It was quite cold; by the time I reached Mrs. W—— I was chilled through. She invited me into a neat sitting-room where there was a bright fire.

Although she was a *widow* and a lady of considerable wealth, she *condescended* to treat *me*, a *canvasser*, with respect, and gave me her patronage, also a pair of warm gloves.

Calling at several houses, and being in the vicinity of Judge D——'s residence, I concluded to call and fulfill his order, given to me a few days previous, for a picture of General Grant and family.

His married daughter was sitting on the porch; she asked me to be seated while I told her my errand. She called her father, who came out, accompanied by his wife and youngest daughter. He took the engraving. I found him and his daughters polite, but I must say his wife was rather abrupt in her manners.

During the day I called on Mrs. C——, whose husband is a house-painter. A litle girl of six or seven years answered the bell, a timid and very delicate looking child. I stepped inside; Mrs. C—— came forward and offered me a chair. She took the roll of engravings and spread them out upon the table, telling her little girl to select two, as she would buy them for her.

All the while they were examining them, I could not keep my eyes from Mrs. C——; clad in a dark muslin dress, with a spotless linen collar, she looked more stylish than many others in the finest of fabrics. Though not strikingly handsome, still in every line of her features could be seen a true and noble woman.

She looked like one who, if you could once gain her friendship, would be firm and steadfast; one who had a mind and will all her own, not ready to change with the slightest breeze. If the rough winds of adversity should sweep over you, sunshiny friends turn away, she would stand by you, and do all in her power to shield you from its *second* blast.

I have tried her, and now know I was not deceived. But to my subject. The little miss selected two of the engravings; thanking her, I hurried away, as I wished to see Mr. P—— before the bank closed. I had a slight acquaintaince with him during the short time we resided in San José. He recognized me, and gave me an order for an engraving. I returned to the hotel, where I remained the balance of the day.

Gilroy.

Next morning I took passage in the stage for Gilroy. The railroad was not completed any farther than San José at that time.

There were several gentlemen in the stage; one of them bound for Hollister, where he had purchased a ranch. I was very much amused at his description of the fertile and rich soil in and about Hollister. "Why," said he, "anything in the world will grow there. Mr. H., that I purchased the ranch of, would always raise three large cabbage-heads from one stalk; also, said he raised a sweet potato, so large that the family of five made a good meal off of it, and *all* of them were very fond of sweet potatoes. He also raised a beet that was so large the first season he concluded to let it stand for two or three more; until it grew so far out of the ground the wind broke it off, and it measured four feet across." That must have been a *dead beat*.

Near the Eighteen Mile House I saw a large flock of sheep, tended by a herder. When I first caught sight of them they were some distance away, feeding on an open plain, beyond a strip of woods.

I inquired of *dead beat* what that was growing off to the left, pointing in that direction; he said he did not see anything growing; just then I saw them moving, and observed what they were; by this time all the rest of the passengers were looking at them. I acknowledged myself sold, and joined in their merry laughter.

We passed over several tracts of land covered with timber, among which were many live oaks, some of them very large and beautiful, with their wide-spreading branches covered with thick foliage, looking as though they might be a safe retreat for man or beast, and would protect them from a heavy fall of rain.

We crossed the creek, and followed it for some little distance. The country around Gilroy seemed low and flat, as though it might be easily undulated in the rainy season. When we entered the town, I was surprised to see so small a place; but there were many new buildings going up, among them the Williams House; everything appeared brisk and lively. At this time there was but one hotel in the place. The stage drove up to the door.

It was a long, rough building, with several live oaks in front, which made it look much more inviting than it would otherwise have done. I was shown into a room they called the parlor. It was very poorly furnished; but on the hearth a bright fire was blazing, which made the room have a cheerful appearance.

In a corner were seated two ladies. I was not long in discovering they were Southern people. The youngest was trying to get the village school; the elderly lady, her mother, was very communicative, and gave me her whole history in a short time.

I sat and listened to her, and thought she would make a splendid agent, for she was such a fast talker in her way. She tried to find out my business in Gilroy, but I did not give her any satisfaction. She would look at me sharply when I avoided her questions, and finally turned to her daughter, saying, "Sal, that poor critter is to be pitied, for she is *mighty* deaf, and not got much *larning*, no how."

She then crossed the room to the table, where I had laid my engravings, picked up the sample copy, took it close to the window, and put it to her eyes, as though she thought it was an opera glass, unrolled it, saying, "Humph! picture, hey?" came to where I was sitting, held it up before me, screamed in my ear, until it made me jump, "Peddling, I reckon." I looked at her in amazement, but made no reply.

She returned to the window, saying, "That's mighty queer how *she* peddles; Sal, what's that thare reading?" Sal took the engraving, looked at the name on the bottom, spelled it over two or three times, and finally drawled out, "Why, it's old Grant and family, the darned old thief." I thought to myself, you would make a splendid school-marm.

The old lady stormed and capered around the room in such a manner, that I thought it time to interfere, for I was afraid she would tear the sample copy to pieces. She, at first, refused to give it to me, saying she "would burn the darned thing up." I told her it was not mine, that I was taking orders for Bancroft and Company; also, told her I, too, was a Southern woman, in reduced circumstances, and had to work for a living. She replied, "No, you ain't, you're a darned Yank, an imposter. There ware a heap on you going round in the Southern States, before the war, 'tending to peddle, all the time stealing nigs." She came close to me again, shaking her head, "I know you ain't much, else you wouldn't played deaf."

I replied, "Madam, you are mistaken; I did not say I was deaf, nor act as though I was. I did not wish to answer your numerous questions, nor treat you impolitely, so I did not say anything."

At this, she stormed at me in such a rough and unladylike manner, I think it best not to repeat what she said. I had intended not to go to my room until bedtime, for the evening was cold, and the warm fire felt very comfortable; but I could not endure her abuse, so I gathered up my traps and started for my room, laughing at her as I went, which seemed to enrage her still more.

When I entered the room, I locked and bolted the door, for fear she might follow me. When I awakened next morning, I heard the rain, as I thought, dripping from the branches of the trees on the roof of the house. The thoughts of having to wade around in the mud during the day made me feel anything but comfortable. I arose and went to the window, and was much relieved to find it nothing more than a heavy fog.

After breakfast, I commenced to canvass, calling at every house. I found it to be a lively and bustling town, the citizens kind and very benevolent, giving me a liberal patronage. In the afternoon I called at the pastor's residence of the M. E. Church. There I met a lady from Marion County, Ohio, who was well acquainted with my father-in-law and family. She had been in California for many years, and lived on a ranch close to old Gilroy. We had a pleasant chat for some time. I promised to call and see her if I ever happened to be in that part of the country again. Bidding her good afternoon, I returned to the hotel.

In the evening I made inquiries concerning my *Southern friends,* and was told they had returned to their ranch, some fifteen miles from Gilroy. The accomplished young lady was not successful in getting the school.

Next morning, early, found me in the stage, on my way for San José. Upon arriving there I took the cars for Mayfield. It is a small village in Santa Clara county, on the line of the railroad.

As I went down the street, towards the hotel, many looked at me wonderingly, and then at the large, long roll of engravings I carried in my arms. I did not address any of them.

When I looked around me, I saw many neat dwellings, with well laid-out grounds, which looked cosy and home-like. When I reached the hotel, the landlady showed me into a neat, comfortable room. She seemed to be a jolly, kind-hearted woman, full of fun and quite witty. I told her I had come to canvass the place; she gave me all the information I desired.

Taking my bundle, I started out; called at the several places of business, and had tolerable good success. I called on *one* gentleman I pitied very much; he had to use crutches. He told me he was a cripple, from rheumatism. Still he seemed energetic, and full of business, carrying on a drug-store and keeping the Post-office, and was contented and happy. He said, when I came around again, he would take Mark Twain's "Innocents Abroad," if I would bring it to him, as he was a great reader. I called at the blacksmith shop, above his place. There was a man working there, an apprentice, I think, who was so low as to be abusive and vulgar, forgetting he ever had a mother.

He was a stout, raw-boned, thick-lipped, flat-nosed, tangle-haired, uncivilized creature, who depended mainly on his strength more than his brains to make his way through the world, and would just as lief strike a *woman* as a *man*. With the exception of this ruffian, I was treated with the greatest of respect by all of the citizens of Mayfield; and was more liberally patronized than I had expected from so small a place.

I returned to the hotel well satisfied with my afternoon's work. Next morning I took the first train for San Francisco. When I arrived there, I went directly to my home on Fourth street, where I remained for a week resting myself, as I was very tired and worn out. It was now late in the fall, and I was afraid the rainy season would set in, for I had to canvass Stockton, so I concluded to go at once. I called at Mr. Bancroft's and told Mr. S—— my intentions. He offered no objections, and showed me some new engravings they had; most of them were small and cheap; two of them were very pretty, entitled the "Sale of the Pet Lamb," and the "Burial of the Pet Bird."

I was not long in making a selection of those I thought would be most likely to sell; I told Mr. S—— he could do them up and send them to me by express. I went to the wharf and took the boat for Stockton. I had a severe headache, and laid down, so I did not see any of the country through which we passed. By the time we arrived there I felt much better. I took a "bus" and told the driver to take me to the best hotel in town. I was soon in front of the St. Charles, and was shown into the ladies' parlor, a large, well-furnished room, with a bright fire in the grate. After warming myself for a few moments, I went to my room, which was very pleasant.

Mrs. J. W. Likins, *Six Years' Experience as a Book Agent in California* (San Francisco: Women's Union and Job Printing Office, 1874), pp. 52—80.

"No persuits in common between us anymore"

CARRIE WILLIAMS

8

This uniquely detailed diary covers seven months in the day-to-day existence of a young married woman in a Sierra mining town. The diarist's exact descriptions of household tasks like ironing, washing, dressmaking, and treating childhood diseases, combined with the expression of her own feelings, make this manuscript unusually appealing and historically valuable. Its portrayal of intense domesticity exemplifies the immediacy of a diary narrative in comparison with more filtered reminiscences.

Carrie Williams led a family-centered life, caring for her young child in warm companionship with her mother-in-law, while their two husbands were constantly involved in the community—panning for gold at their flumes by day and "tuting" horns in a band most of the night. Williams was proud that her Wallace was a "temperance man," but she resented his absences and was not afraid to let him know it. Although her most frequent comments are about housekeeping, sewing, and childcare, we also learn that she favored woman suffrage (in 1858), read *Godey's Ladies' Magazine* and many books, and had strong opinions. Her religious convictions tended to be more social than theological, but she was a strong supporter of temperance. In fact, her father-in-law owned the town's Temperance Hall and rented it out for numerous social events besides temperance meetings.

Married on July 4, 1855, Carrie and Wallace Williams had experienced several disasters before this diary begins in November 1858. A fire had burned the whole town in 1856, and a flood had destroyed it in 1858, including the town water works owned and maintained by Carrie's father-in-law John Williams. Also, Wallace Williams had been involved in an accidental killing. Both men were working hard to recoup their losses during the time of this diary.

Located high in the California Sierras northeast of Sacramento, Nevada City was a gold-mining town founded by the Williamses in 1850 after they came west in 1849 from Wisconsin. They were followed by Carrie's family, headed by Thompson Humes. The Williamses lived together on a ranch in nearby Gold Flat and later shared a mansion in town, which John Williams built on the top of Prospect Hill. Among those mentioned in this diary, Adelia Humes was Carrie's youngest sister (who later came to live with her from December 1859 to February 1861); Mary (called Mollie) and George were adopted by Abigail and John Williams after their parents died on the overland trail; Amanda, Teresa, and Thompson were Carrie's sisters and brother; and "Toad.I.buss" was Carrie's pet name for little Wally. Carrie's mother or stepmother, Teresa Humes, came from Ireland and is mentioned only twice in this diary; Carrie obviously felt much closer to her mother-in-law.

Carrie ceased making daily entries not long after becoming aware of her second pregnancy. Later she had two more children, one of whom "never made much of himself"; the other was either retarded or mentally ill and finally had to be hospitalized. Wallace, her husband, who was renowned for his physical strength as well as for his abilities as a lawyer and leader, died after a long, painful illness in 1874 at the age of forty-one. Carrie herself died at forty-nine of a heart attack in 1883.

Novembcr 26th Friday   Wallace today bought this book for me to commence a journal. How faithful I will be to the trust time will show. Ever thoughtful for Carrie, he today made her a present of a gold pencil & pen. How thankful I ought to be for his kindness to me. Adelia returned from Marysville yesterday, 25th, Thanksgiving day. Her and Thomp were down in the evening. T had his flute along & Wallace with his violin, they made some pretty good music. My sewing today consisted in finishing a couple of night gowns for Walla and the hemming of a three breasted purple callico apron for your humble servt. A & M went to town today & bought each of them a pair of shoes, A's morrocco $1.75cts, M's congress gaiters $3.00. Yesterday W & [his] father bought $5200.00 worth of diggins! Dew tell, I want to know! Yew don't say so! I sent little Mary McDaniel a small pair of gloves today. Walla's granma finished Mary a black silk spencer today trimmed with green fringe. Now she is working on the skirt of a foullard silk for her. Work work work work till you die is her mottoe both in precept & example. Hers is a persevering nature through difficulties, as the raising of such a boy as George will show or prove. She will have her reward, if not in this world in the next, is one of the hopes she cherishes.

27th Saturday   The weather is very pleasant. What a contrast to Old Wisconsin's freezing this time of year. Money could not hire me to go back there to live! all though there was my childhood's home. I have not been very well today and therefore have not accomplished much in the house-keeping line. Wallace collected as usual, then went to work in the new dig-gings and as a matter of course got himself quite wet & muddy, forgot his dinner to boot, then came home about 4 oclock, brought a can of oysters, made some soup for the whole family, reserving no small share for himself. Notwithstanding supper was served this evening as usual, when the afore-said W adjourned to Temperance Hall, where after the ceremonies pertain-ing to that institution were over he took part in a debate. Subject: "Whether under a republican form of government woman has a right to vote or not." Of course she has, but Wallace took the negative side of the question, and it is his private opinion publickly expressed to me that he came off victorious. Beat this day's work of his if you can. Teresa moved today into the house that Jack built. Her & Tom went to town tonight and left their baby with me. They signed the deed of their home to strangers. T bought herself a love of a bonnet. Tis getting late, and I must to bed or the noon of night will find me not sleeping.

Sunday 28th   Wallace overcame his repugnance to such a bore as he styles going to church & went to hear Mr. McCollom hold forth at the brick church. I did not accompany him. His mother went in my place. His father worked all day on the old flume regardless of the day, as is his wont, and on reflection I do not know that I have spent the day any more worthily than he has. When Wallace came home him and I went riding over in the neighbor-hood of Wood's Ravine, I never having been in that direction before. Some of our Calafornian scenery is certainly very beautiful, especially here among the Sierras. So thought W and I as he stopped the buggy and we stood up and surveyed the surrounding prospect with the sun shining so pleasantly on the woodlands around. We came back just as the sun set. Walla was left with his grandma. Well I suppose I must draw this to a close and go wash that little responsibility for bed. What a kind friend he has in his granma. She has not read any today for care of him.

Monday 29th   Today has been bright and pleasant as spring. I was the first up this morning, but Walla required so much attention that I could not get breakfast before his grandma made her appearance as was my intention. I have not accomplished much today, only the mending of some aprons for Walla and the finishing of one for myself, sweeping, getting supper and the like. Walla's grandma put down a new oil cloth on the dining room floor. Wallace helped her a little, then went about his business in town. As usual his father went as soon as he eat breakfast to tending to his flume, and there he tarryed all day. Ws mother says she is afraid he will hurt himself, but I guess when the new fangle wears off he will be out of danger. Adelia was down today with Teresa['s] little girl, and Walla could not come near the little witch for fear of her scratching his eyes out. I am thinking if on some occasions 20 years from now she evinces the same disposition it will be well. Walla is a dear little fellow. O how dear he is to our hearts Wallace and I only know. Wallace just now came in to tell me that he was lieing on the lounge with Walla playing around when he called him to bring him a drink of water, which the little fellow accordingly done for the first time in his life. Sarah Fraser came home from school to stay all night with Mary.

30ieth Tuesday   Today has been cloudy and quite cool. I commenced ironing about 11 oclock and did not get done till 6. Wallace's mother stoned raisins and baked all day. Then in the evening after supper she killed 4 chickens, which I dressed. Mother did not get to bed till somewhere in the neighborhood of midnight. Wallace's father as usual tending to diggings. Mary & George came home from school with more trouble than they could contain themselves, and consequently their mother had to sit down and hear a recital of griefs and wrongs never before endured by anyone, they firmly believed, and in return she bestown some very good advice in which she vainly strove to convince them that they were wrong and the teacher right. Adely went to town today and [bought] herself a pair of kid gloves for which she paid $1.50. Wallace bought a large beutifully clasped Bible today which he made a present of to his mother, cost $10.50, also Frost's *Pictorial History of Washington* & 2 volumes titled *Ancient Egypt under the Pharaohs*.

December 1st Wednesday   Today has been clear and bright but quite cool. Nothing of any importance to write. The fact is I am not in a very good humor, for this reason, trifles light as air &c. Well, Miss Gibson was to have come to cut and make me a dress today, but alas for all human calculations no Miss Gibson appeared on the horizon this day. Walla's grandma mopped the dining room & kitchen, washed 4 aprons for Walla and ripped up Mary's flounced dress preparatory to remoddeling it. Wallace cleaned up the flume below the garden. His father parted off to the diggings in town before daylight. I today darned Walla's red merino dress that was moth eaten, a dress that his granma embroidered with red silk braid last winter. Mary did not attend school today, not having been very well.

2ond Thursday   Today has been the coldest day we have had this winter, wind very high. Plenty of exercise to keep fires agoing. Miss Gibson appeared not today. Walla's grandma mopped the kitchen and dining room today. I made the skirt of a plaid merino for Walla. Wallace panned out the cleaning up of the flume, and it was a matter of doubt whether he would freeze or not during the job. The proceeds amounted to $150 I believe. Mary did not go to school. Wallace came home this evening with another tuting machine and said that he had told the Union Brass Band Company that he would occasionly take a part with them, which piece of news I did not at all fancy, but I suppose I must try and not be too meddlesome or perchance I may forfeit his good oppinion, and that I would not have happen for worlds. W['s] father working [in] town digging as usual. Really, I am getting so cold in here that I must adjourn to the fire or some other more congenial clime than this cold little room, that is certain.

3d Friday   The weather today is considerably warmer than yesterday. No wind at all this evening. Walla's grandma mopped as usual today. His grandpa diggings again. I bought Walla 2 pink aprons 50cts and have cut them out. The fun of it is that they are not yet paid for. I do not think that I ever done such a thing before. Looks are against me, yet I am perfectly honest. I cut the waist of baby's dress out also. Adelia was down and brought me a song that Thompson had written down for me, the name Erin's Green Shore. I this evening took Walla and went up to see Teresa in her new house. She is quite unwell, has a violent cold. The little Adelia has also. Wallace came up after me just as I was starting. Walla's grandma cut him out 3 pair of stockings and made one pair while I was writing last night. I cannot write any more now, for the young gent in question bothers me so. Well so mote it be.

4th Saturday   Quite cold and snowing pretty much all day. How drear and dark tis out of doors. I pity those who have no good shelter this night. How ever mindful of the goodness and kindness of God I ought to be for the many comforts with which I am surrounded. I finished Walla's dress today and mopped my room and part of the hall. Walla's grandma mopped the dining room and kitch. Wallace and his father staid in town all day and are not yet back. Wallace gave me 50cts to buy a magazine. He brought me a beutiful little bottle of perfume last night called Kiss me if you dare, or the extract of Touch me nots. Now I must leave off writing and go tend to Walla, for he is sleepy and would be washed for bed.

5th Sunday   We were all up late this morning. Today has been quite pleasant notwithstanding the snow that fell last night to the depth of about a foot. No Sunday school going of the youngsters or church attendance of the elder ones. I have spent the time very pleasantly reading. This afternoon Wallace went to town and bought me *Godey's Magazine* and a *Waverly*. He also bought the *Life and Essays of Franklin*, which he made me a present of, I have several times in his hearing expressed a wish to possess that work. Walla's grandma is now reading from Godey to Wallace and Mary, and although tis past 9 oclock little Toad.I.buss is not asleep. His grandpa sits by the stove reading a *Union*, and I am here in my little room writing, as these pages will show.

Monday the 6th   On looking out this morning what a wintry landscape presented itself, sure enough, the limbs of the trees in every direction bowed down with snow that fell during last night. Today has been quite uncomfortable and cold. I have been washing a two weeks wash, 2 sheets, 4 shirts, 2 table cloths, 17 towels and other things too numerous to mention. Walla's grandma mopped the dining [room] today. Little W has not been very well. Wallaces father working all day in diggings. Wallace went to town and staid this evening to practice with the band. All the folks are in bed excepting him, his Muse and I, and I am thinking tis high time we were, for tis nearly 12, but no, I feel in a communicative mood, therefore will stay yet a while longer with you, O Journal. I bought 50cts worth of cotton edging for night caps of a pedlar, the one we have styled Bob Tail, but ah, tis late. How true the lines of Young that "we take no note of time. But by its loss."

Tuesday the 7th   Quite pleasant today. I rinsed and put out my washing and mopped the kitchen. Twas 8 oclock before any of us were up this morn. Wallace nor his father, neither of them came home this evening. They staid to the lodge. Dear little Walla is quite unwell to night, has considerable fever. I hope tis nothing serious. God grant that he may be better by morning. John L came down to borrow my last magazine, and I loaned him the two last numbers. Aunty wants to see the last fashions; that and young ones is her two hobbies. Well, tis all right. She is one of the different kinds it takes to make a world.

Wednesday the 8th   Walla's fever continued all night, though he rested pretty well after he went to sleep, which he did not do till about 11 oclock. Today has been pleasant although cloudy. Some of the more enterprising of the town folks have been improving the snow by sleighing it out to Gold Flat and back again. They have genuine sleigh bells too. Darling little Walla I think is some better this evening. We gave him some oil today, and he immediately vomited it up. He has not eaten anything since but meal gruel. His bowels keep running off just like he had taken medicine. I do not know what can be the cause, unless it is that he has taken cold. Wallaces father diggings. Wallace has been practicing pretty much all day, and he is now sitting with his music at the table on which I am writing, his violin in hand, keeping up such a racket I can scarcely write at all, as this page will testify. Walla's grandma finished Mary's flounced skirt today after a lingering siege of many days, and she rejoiced not a little. She cleaned the dining room and kitchen. Mary did not attend school. The young lady sewed on her yaller spencer, as she calls it, yesterday and today. Tis about 8 oclock, and Walla's poor grandma, as he sometimes calls her, has laid that little boy in question to sleep in his cradle, and I will just stop my writing and see if [I] can read a little while.

Thursday the 9th   Pleasant & warm today. Walla is better but very troublesome. I finished a pink apron for him and got supper this evening. Wallace has been in town practicing tonight. I now hear his horn on the way home. Walla['s] grandma mopped as usual. This afternoon she commenced on an allapacca sack for Mary. I have had the blues this evening and felt so miserable that really I can not write.

Friday the 10th   We were up early this morning, for Wallace's father has been summoned on the grand jury and has to be there in time. The first person that made their appearance at the house this morning was Miss Gibson. Therefore my time has been taken up with that old but worthy ancient maiden lady and my cashmere dress, which she cut out today. I made the skirt. Walla's grandma mopped, got dinner, supper, and tended to Walla all day long and let me sew. When she has her dress made I will do the same for her cheerfully. Raining all day, and quite hard now. In conclusion I cannot refrain from saying that I think Miss Gibby, as Walla calls her, is a real old gossip. I was quite amused today at some of the yarns she spun about the widow Sweeny. Walla, dear little fellow, has been quite unwell this evening and restless. Wallace went to town this afternoon and got me 2 ½ yds of florence silk to line the sleeves of mine and his mother's dresses, 50cts yd, also 3 do of slate paper muslin. Wallace is always kind to me, although I am cross sometimes.

Saturday the 11th   Raining all day. Miss Gibson and I worked steady on my dress. It is done and fits me beautiful. How glad I am that it is done and becomes me so well. Walla's grandma has had a hard time today taking care of him and cooking. He was very sick in the night and kept Wallace and I awake till about 2 oclock. We had to bathe his feet in water with mustard before he rested at all. He has required constant attention all day. We undertook to give him oil again but got but very little down him if any at all. I must now go and bathe his feet as before and fix his gruel, for we cannot allow him to eat much of anything else.

Sunday the 12th   Gloomy and cloudy, some snowing this evening. Walla rested very well last night. He has been very fretful and cross today. Miss G went home this morning after eating breakfast and promising to come again tomorrow. Lockwood came over this morning while the folks were eating breakfast. I had not sat down yet, and what does Wallace do but ask him to sit down in my place. Then I would not come in at all, but staid out and nearly froze myself. Then when they went down to the barn to practice on their old brass horns I made my appearance in the dining room, bawling, and Wallace's mother and Mary comforted me all they could & so after awhile I got better. Mary got breakfast this morning all by herself. Wallace sat up last night till half after one working on his mouth piece, and I was so vexed with him about it. Adelia was down today, but no one went to church or Sund[ay] school. Wallace's father worked all day on the diggings in town and came home this evening all wet. His mother chid him for so doing. It grieves her to think that he has so little regard for the sabbath. When I think about it I have a dissatisfied feeling at heart with myself, for I am conscious that I do not pay that respect to sacred things that I should, and I know that Wallace and I would both be better and happier if we would take such into consideration seriously and act accordingly.

Monday the 13th   Today has been warm and thawing the snow fast. I have had a pretty rough time of it this day. Miss G is making Mrs W a delain[e] dress, and she is making the skirt by way of helping. Walla was pretty good till about dinner, and since that time he has required constant attention. I mopped the dining room and kitchen before I got dinner, had soup, and some being left, I sent it to mother. Mary took care of Walla while I got supper. [We] had mackerel for supper, which Gibby made a great fuss over. Walla kept us awake a good part of the night by spells of crying that he would take about evry 15 minutes or half an hour. I got up with him at 11 oclock and bathed his feet in warm water, but it did not seem to do much good, for he slept but very little till after 2 oclock. Wallace sat working on his mouth piece till one. We gave Walla, or tryed to do so, 2 pills pulverized in peach juice, but he has not had an operation from them. Therefore I think we did not get much down him. Adelia went to town today and bought herself a new green satin bonnet, for which she paid $10, a present that Teresa had made her. Tis half after 9. Walla is not yet in bed. I have been tending him and reading a little in my *Rome*. My reading was the death of the good and honest Pertinax after a reign of 86 days. How contemptible was the conduct of the Praetorian guards towards him, and it did not stop there, but extended towards their country, in such a manner as to prompt them to offer her for sale to the highest bidder. Everlasting disgrace to their memory for these two acts, say I.

Tuesday the 14th   Gibby has not yet finished Mrs. W ['s] dress, and she helped her all day with but little interruption. I mopped the dining and kitchen and got dinner and supper, ironed Wallace a shirt and baby an apron, fried cabbage & bacon, made corn bread for dinner, fried potatoes for supper. Old man Stilt came dragging his weary length along again this morning after breakfast was over. I went and set him something to eat, which he done justice to without much solicitation, poor victim, outcast, of rum. How I pity thee, yes from my heart I do. Bob Tail was along today, and I, contrary to many resolutions, got in debt $2.50: a collar for Adelia 75cts, undersleeves 50cts for her, 18 yds linen edging 1.00, fine toothed comb 25cts. Dear little Walla rested very well last night. He seems to be considerably better today. Wallace did not come home last night till after 1. He said the band of brass horns went out serenading. I suppose all the bridgets in that neighborhood were beautifully tuted at, from his description. Wallace's father was tormented into taking $60 of Gibby's money this morning to buy scrip with. O, I am perfectly sick of the word, for there is nothing else to be heard the minute she gets sight of him till he goes away again. Wallace and him are at the lodge tonight. Now Walla's grandma and Gibby keeps up such a ripet with their tonges that I wont write any more for fear I might accidentaly get some of their converse into my document.

Wednesday the 15th   Miss Gibson went home about 1 oclock. I paid her 8 dollars. The facing on my dress was not straight. Therefore I ripped out the hem and she basted it over again, so I this afternoon hemed it down again and made the pocket. This forenoon she finished Mrs W ['s] dress. I got 2 ½ yds of dark calico for aprons for Walla, 50cts. Dinner I got today in quick order, yeast powder biscuits, which were very good indeed, Gibson said she did wish that she could have as good when the sewing circle met at her house; broiled steak and stewed potatoes, which Wallace praised. Walla's grandma tended him while I sewed this afternoon. Wallace's father did not get the scrip for Miss G, and she felt dreadful about it. I guess she almost thinks that this world is all a fleeting show for her delusion given. Without any doubt Toadibus is getting well fast. I have counted it up, and my cashmere dress, first and last, cost 20 dollars.

Thursday the 16th   How time flies. I have just come into my little room after supper. By the way we had a very pleasant tetatet, Wallace's mother, Mary & I, W nor his father neither of them being to supper. They have been working in the town diggings, his father till 7 oclock. This evening Wallace is practicing at the hall. His papa is now eating supper, just having come a little while ago. I commenced washing 15 minutes of 12 & finished hanging out my clothes about 6, did not have many things, 13 towels, 1 table cloth, sheet, 4 shts, 6 aprons for Walla & so forth. Wallace's mother cleaned the parlor after Gibson. She said she had a sweet time of it, and I can readily believe it when I think of the volumes of dust that rolled forth. Well dust we are and to dust we will invariably return, thought I as I stood out in the kitchen freezing on account of the doors having to be flared open to let it out. I have a desperately miserable cold and sore throat. Adelia was down this afternoon & I gave her a pair of my sleeve lasticks. Walla has been very good today. He keeps talking about Gibby, as he calls Miss Gibson. He can say a great many words but is not very proficient in sentence making as yet. He says get out, get up, take care, put it up, give me. I rubbed Wallace's mother's shoulder last night and the night before with Electric Oil. She is troubled very much with an affection of the shoulder and spine, and I am going to give this oil a thorough trial to see if it is all that is represented.

Friday 17th   Tis 10 oclock, and I am so tired. My throat is sore, and indeed I feel miserable, but I must write a little if I do. I put on my cashmere, my carochia collar and sleeves today and took the sleeve pattern of my dress up to aunty. The dress she seemed to think decidedly becoming. This evening after supper I starched 2 shirts, a bonnet, 2 collars and [a] pair of undersleeves and since have done quite an ironing. Wallace went to town to work all night on the diggings, putting in boxes. His father has not yet come home. I expect he too will stay.

Saturday 18th   Wallace came home about 6 this morning tired and cold enough. He and I forgot all about his taking anything to eat during the night, which placed him in an unplesant situation. One of the men that was working with him invited him up to his cabin. Therefore he helped him to eat up his provision. His father started over before breakfast. Wallace slept till noon. He is going to practice music after the Division is through with business. I have had a time of it cleaning Wallace's coat & pants this morn that he wore in the diggings yesterday. If he had the trial I did this morning a time or two I think he would be a little more careful of what he wears. I cleaned out my room and part of the hall. Walla['s] grandma cleaned dining & kitchen. She cut the top of her old geranium and dug up the pink rose that grew by the parlor door and set it out in one of the mounds. Part of it she put in a can. The gophers were undermining it. My geranium grows beautiful. It was a little slip last summer with only one shoot growing out of the side. I have it in a vase setting on the table, shading my book as I write. I have another slip that has just started a leaf or two.

Sunday 19   I went to hear Mr. Warren preach today. He is up from the Bay awhile, but I am afraid there was more harm done in my going than if I remained quietly at home and never expressed a wish to go anywhere. The reason is, Wallace so hates to take me or go himself. I wish it were otherwise, but I cannot help it. I felt unhappy and discontented all day. Wallace's mother took charge of Walla while we were gone. The little fellow seems not to be so well as usual tonight. Dear little toad, he waked up about 4 this morn and kept trying to climb up in bed so that Wallace had to slap him to keep him in the bed. He sobbed and grieved himself to sleep finally. Adelia went to Sunday school today and wore her sky blue merino and new bonnet for the first time.

Monday 20ieth   I washed 7 towels, 1 tablecloth and such like. Miss Gibson came about 7 this evening for the purpose of altering Mrs. W's slate merino. Wallace went with the band to serenade Mrs. Waite. I felt sad to see him go. He wanted me to kiss him before he went away, but I would not. Then he said that perhaps I would never have a chance to again. I have felt very miserable all the evening whenever I think of him. O how I wish he would give up going to town so much evenings on one pretext or another and stay with me and I would lay my head in his lap and read to him as I used to do. Those were happy evenings, but soon they passed away, and here I sit alone evening after evening with no companion but my own sad thoughts. Walla's grandma is now holding Walla, for he would not stay in bed where I put him before I commenced writing. She cleaned the dining and kitchen and cut out and made Mary a cape out of her cloak that she brought from the States.

Tuesday the 21st   Today has been dark, cloudy & raining part of the time. Wallace has been working hard the most of the day putting in false bottoms in the flume. He came home about 4 oclock, wet and muddy. He had not taken time to go to town to get anything to eat. He is now gone to the lodge. His father has been working in the diggings. I have not done much today, helped about dinner some, about supper a little, and ripped up my green plaid preparatory to washing and making [it] over again. The band went out serenading last night. Mrs. Waite shewed herself out on the balcony and made them a graceful acknowledgement, but the fun of the evening was they were standing on the bridge over Deer Creek playing just before starting home. Well out back at one end of the bridge is a house where there is liquor sold. Well the boss of the establishment, thinking himself serenaded, came out and in flattering terms thanked them for the honor and invited them very politely in to take something to drink, which invitation they declined, most of them being sons of temperance. I had a good laugh at Wallace about the termination of his serenade. Miss Gibson has been sewing on Mrs. Williams' dress all day, that is, all the time that she could spare from gossiping. Mr. Warren called today. I did not go in to see him. Adelia was down today. She said Thompson subscribed 6 months for the *Pacific* $3.00. I bought a quarter of yd of green merino to face the sleeves of my dress and a card of hooks & eyes 50cts of Simon, not paid.

Wednesday 22nd   The sun shone bright and warm all day. I washed and pressed out my plaid dress, and it looks very much like a new one. Wallace's mother commenced washing today. Miss Gibson went away this morning before breakfast. Wallace today threw a club at a turky and accidently broke its neck. I took the fowl and dressed it. Adelia went to town and bought me a yard and ½ of twill to line my plaid, 3 bits. She attended the training at the Methodist church of the children that are going to sing Christmas. The children of that Sunday school and Mr. Straton's day school are to have a Christmas tree, and Mr. S is to make a present to each of the scholars that attend his school. The youngsters anticipate a fine time. The children of the Presbyterian school are invited to attend and help sing. Adelia & Mary will not take a part!

Thursday 23rd   It began snowing about 1 oclock and kept steadily on till dark. Therefore we now have another deep snow to wade through. Tis a heavy, wet snow. Bobtail was here to day, and all I bought was a pair of mittens to put in Walla's stocking Christmas, they just fit the little toad, 25cts was the price; a braid for the skirt of my cashmere, 12½cts. Wallace is in town tonight practicing. He said the teacher would be with them tonight for the last time. Mr. Chittenden's school closed this evening. Mary is delighted that it is so. Mr. McColum takes his place next week, I believe. Before I go to bed I will have finished a dark calico apron for Walla. His grandma finished her washing about dark and has been taking care of him since. I fried onions for supper at the request of his grandpa. I was so affected that I cried all the time during the getting of supper. I cleaned the dining and kitchen.

Friday 24th   I have been pretty busy this day. I cleaned the dining room, kitchen, my room and part of the hall, made starch and starched 4 sh[ir]ts, ironed one. Walla's grandma is now busy baking cake for Christmas. Wallace brought home last night two primers for Walla. One is the history of Jack Horner and his Christmas pie, with which Walla is very much delighted. The other is a primer printed on linen with the alphabet in great large letters. Mr. Hamlin sent him a large glass ball. Mr. Chittenden was here today, and he allowed that my geranium was looking fine, and really I think he is sensible on that subject, for as I look up at it sitting so gracefully in its vase on the table I think so too. There is a grand ball at the National tonight, but none of the Williams from Gold Flat will be there. Well I will dry my pen and put up, as Walla would say. There is to be 6 chickens killed tonight, and I have volunteered to dress the fowls.

Saturday the 25th   Well Christmas has come round again, but I cannot say that I enjoyed it much. The traveling is so bad that tis hard to get around. Therefore we have had to stay within doors. I cleaned the dining room and kitchen this morning, then about 4 dressed up a little myself. Walla has been very fretful all day and [we] have seen but very little peace with the young-ster this day. Wallace and his father both condescended to be home to sup had a bread puding that was capital and plum cake not to be beat. You see, she baked 10 loaves of cake last night. Now about Sant Clauses pranks, I found a bundle of candy tied on the door knob of my room and on opening a drawer in the beaureau found one of my old ragged stockings containing a beautiful embroidered hand kerchief. That was the amount of Christmas gifts that fell to my share. George had his Christmas tree full, and little Walla's stocking was filled to overflowing. The little toad was very much de-lighted when he saw the varieties of candy that it contained. Strange to say, he did not know enough about candy to know that it was to eat, never hav-ing had any before.

Sunday the 26th   Cloudy, gloomy and lonesome today. George went to Sunday school. A & M did not go. Tom was down with his baby this morn-ing, and Mrs. Williams curled her hair in spite of all her fidgeting. Adelia was down, and she had a beautiful pair of ear rings, a Christmas gift. Lock-wood was here today practicing with Wallace. I went up to see mother the first time since Adelia came back. Thompson was shewing me some of his compositions on different subjects, and I was astonished at the fluency with which he writes, and his book of drawings (done spare times) is quite a treat. Mother, father, Adelia and Thompson all took dinner with Teresa Christmas.

Monday 27th   Washed today, had my new spread in, wash towels &c. Mary and George started to school this morning to Mr. McColum. Walla was very good till about 4, when he waked from his afternoons nap of about an hour's length, and he then was very fretful, so much so that his grandma quit her work and tended to him till she went to get supper. Wallace is at the hall tuting. His father worked in the diggings today. He went before break-fast. Walla's grandma cleaned the dining & kitchen and this afternoon fitted Mary['s] alapacca sack. The first of this month I got the last of my year's number of *Godey's Magazine*, and in the conclusion of Margaret's Home, a beautiful story from the pen of the gifted Alice B. Haven I have spent many a happy evening, following the trials of Margaret the good and patient to their final happy conclusion. May she be happy the rest of her life.

Tuesday 28th   Last night Wallace did not get home till 11. He brought me a pair of coarse calf skin shoes, 1.75cts, and his mother a pair of the same kind, $1.75cts. Raining and snowing all night. This bids fair to be a hard winter. Wallace came home about 15 minutes of 12 and said he wanted a clean shirt. I had none ironed. I was out hanging my white clothes on the line, not having done it last evening for fear of rain. I immediately went to work and ironed him a shirt, and his mother quit her mopping, broiled a steak and got up some dinner for her large son. The Odd Fellows were to attend the funeral of Mrs. Coleman, and Wallace wished to be in town again [at] 1 oclock. He brought Mary a pair of shoes the same as mine. George received a thorough whipping today from his mamma for not coming directly home from school. He stopped to play by the wayside and had to suffer the consequence of such conduct. I have been ironing since two oclock.

Wednesday 29th I have been sewing all day on a pink apron for Walla, but Walla was so fretful in the evening that I did not get it quite done. His grandma cleaned the dining and kitchen. Wallace was at work all day in the diggings. He came home about 6 oclock all wet and muddy, eat his supper and went back again and worked till [illegible] clock. He took something to eat with him this time. His father did not come back till he did. Mrs. Wentworth called on Mrs. Williams this afternoon. I did not go in to see the lady.

Thursday the 30ieth Finished the apron this morning and bought him two more dark ones, 3 yds 50cts, and cut them out. Have commenced one. Mary cleaned Wallace's muddy pants and coat, for which he gave her a dollar. I cleaned a pair of awful muddy ones too. Adelia went to town and got me a red & black braid for my bonnet, price $1.00. Wallace today took 700 dollars of Tom's money on interest, at 2 per cent. When Wallace came home this evening he brought Mary & I each a bottle of Lyons' Katharion for our hair, 75cts a peace. The thieves in our vicinity are beginning their winter's depredations again. Last night, so I am told, the houses of Judge Searls and Mr. Davis were visited by some of the light fingered gentlemen in question. For supper this evening Wallace's mother got up a "huge great" dish of chicken, dumpling, potatoes &c all in one. Wallace came near foundering. I did not have much of an appetite this evening. I have been troubled for a few days past with a kind of dispectic pain in my breast. I think it has been brought on by eating plum cake. Walla's grandma finished Mary a black sack today trimmed with plaid.

Friday 31st The last day of 1858. 6 hours more and it will be numbered among the years that were. Let us stop on the threshold of the new year and glance back through memory's halls. Some verses that I learned in an almanack long ago will fully express the thoughts that come crowding up, these:

1 Tis sad, tis sad, to number oer
  The faces glad and gay
  Which we have loved. Some smile no more
  Around us as they did of yore
  And some have turned away.

2 Tis sad, tis sad, to think upon
  The joyous days of old
  When evry year that wearys on
  Is numbered by some friendship gone,
  Some kindly heart grown cold.

3 Tis sad, tis sad, to come again
  With changed heart and brow
  To our youth's home where none remain
  Of those who made it blessed then,
  Who leave it lonely now.

Sentimentality aside now, for Wallace's mother is down to the chicken house doing whole sale slaughter in honor of this new year, and I must draw this document to a very unceremonious close for the purpose of dressing the unfortunate fowls that may fall into her unmerciful hands tonight, but before I do I must record the new leaf we have turned over with Walla today. We did not let him take his usual afternoon's nap, and the consequence was a certain little boy after being washed went promptly to sleep and was laid in his cradle without farther preliminaries, much to the delight of his grandma and mamma. Wallace bought him a rabbit on wheels and a box of blocks, $1.25 for the two. He also brought home a mamoth pear and divided it with us all. He is gone to practice tonight. Well, the 5 chickens have been dressed and a huge turkey, and I have read a sermon to Walla's grandma, one delivered by William H. Hill of Sacramento, [an] Episcopalian minister, the same that married Wallace and I. It was on the death of one of the firemen No. 1 Engine Co. Sac., the text: Watch, for ye know not the hour in which the son of man cometh. The language he uses in his discourse is persuasive and affectionate, evincing a depth of feeling and interest both for the dead and the hearer that leaves a good feeling instead of arousing contemptuous and rebellious ones.

January the 1st 1859 Saturday   I begin this year with the determination to read evry day not less than 3 chapters in my Bible and with the help of God to try and profit thereby. Today I cleaned the dining room, kitchen, also some little starching and ironing. Adelia came down in the afternoon, & her and Mary went to town. She took the velvet braid and went to Coen's, where she found a beautiful sheniel [chenille] braid for me. In the evening Teresa & Tom came down on his way to the Division. Thomp and Adelia eat supper with us. Then the girls after supper sent Thompson up after his flute, and they all three came into my room. A & M got their Carmina sacra. Thompson accompanied their singing with his flute, and so they had quite a singing school for about an hour. When Wallace, his father and Tom came home we had a down right candy pulling. Then after that was over Wallace got his fiddle and Thomp with his flute played for us and we danced till 15 minutes after 11. Thompson danced with me, the first time he ever tried to. We had considerable fun over the old fashioned french four that Wallace's father would persist in dancing, none of us having ever danced it. Well, the amount of it was there was a terrible dust kicked up. Then all hand took their candy & went home. Little Walla did act so cunning that I cannot refrain from speaking about it. When they commenced playing he kept his body going to and fro, till he would get tired. Then he would keep his hands going up and down, keeping perfect time with the music. It was quite amusing to see him perform. He looked just as serious all the time. He did not go to sleep till ½ after ten. I did not get to bed till one. So passed off New Year's day 1859 in this house, district of Gold Flat, County of Nevada.

Sunday 2nd   I got up this morning about 9 and tried to get ready for church, but did not succeed. Well, after breakfast, which I got, and burnt up the bread, the dancing room of the preceeding evening was so impure that although twas Sunday I could not refrain from mopping it out. Lockwood came over after ½ after ten to practice with Wallace. He staid to lunch. Teres and Tom came back from church, and Mrs. W & I persuaded Teresa to sit down and take a snack with us. Adelia and Mary went off to Sunday school, flaunting, in their blue merino dresses. Wallace staid with me this evening, and I read to him a very interesting Sunday school book, with which he was very much pleased. The title of the book is *Ten Mile Stones in the Life of Jesse Palmer*.

Monday 3d   I have felt quite unwell today, but I thought I would feel better if I wold turn in and work right hard. Therefore my Monday's washing is done, all but the rencing of the white clothes. They are now on boiling as I write. Wallace's mother has been quite miserable all day. She took ten drops of Electric Oil last night and this morn. It is her intention to take it regular, while I rub her shoulder, to see if it will relieve the rheumatic pains with which she is affected. Adelia & Mary went to town today. A got a braid for my green plaid. Neither W nor his father was to supper tonight. Walla's grandma washed and put him to sleep at 6 oclock this evening. Wallace wanted me to go to a slight of hand show in the theatre, but not fancying that kind of performance in the least I declined. He went, and he practices with the band also.

Tuesday 4th   Today has been bright and pleasant as a May day. Only think of it, in the depth of winter too. I rensed my clothes this morning & mopped the dining, kitchen and porch before 12. Walla's grandma took the entire charge of him while I was doing it, and the little toad went [to] sleep on the lounge, the first time he ever done such a thing. About two oclock I got redy and went up to see Teresa. I hauled Walla and also tipped the little chap over by Wentworth's Mill. He was very much afraid of "palling" after that, as he calls it. When his grandma fixed him to go he kissed her and said "By by Granma." He speaks a number of words quite plain. Wallace and his father went to town this morning and have not yet returned.

Wednesday 5th   What beautiful weather we have, almost as warm as summer, and quite as bright and plesant. I cut out 6 night caps today and made one after Mary's pattern. It runs up into a point, sugar loaf fashion, before it is buttoned down, and Wallace thinks it an odious fashion. Mrs. Wentworth came down this afternoon to invite Mrs. W to go up and take tea with her this evening, her and the squire. Well the sq came home about dark, all mud as usual, and M[rs.] W could not prevail on him to change a thing he had on. They went and said they spent a very pleasant evening. Wallace brought me an apple.

Thursday 6th   Lovely day this. My geranium looks superb, and the new shoot that my flower[ing] pea made two or three days ago looks fine also. Wallace and I, Mary and Adelia talks some this morning of attending a little dance in Temperance Hall Friday evening. Mary is as usual in a peck of trouble about what she will wear. I put a braid on my cashmere today and starched 4 shirts for Wallace, ironed 2 and the rest of my week's washing too.

Friday 7th   Pleasant as yesterday. Mrs. Williams expected Mr. & Mrs. Turner over to spend the day with her. She sent word she would be here at 11, but the children came home at noon and she had not yet made her appearance, so Mrs. W was all expectation yet. She had got Walla washed and his hair curled, herself all ready too, so as to receive them, but little W could not stay awake. I in the meantime was busy scrubbing. I mopped the dining, kitchen, hall and my room before she got here, which event happened about 1 oclock, she having taken the wrong trail over the hill. Mr. T did not come with her but came in the evening in time for supper. I staid in the parlor this afternoon, a great wonder for me. Mrs. Turner is a very amiable lady, I think. Wallace, Mary, Adelia and I went to the dance this evening before mentioned. We all had a good time generally, danced till 1 oclock.

Saturday 8th   Nice day, but I felt very much like someone that had been to a ball. Wallace is having trouble with the water works. He went to town this morning but came immediately back to turn on more water. The folks in town, he said, had no water at all, for some cause or other. The water works, I think, are a great trouble and so trying to the temper, Wallace says. Walla's grandma mopped the dining room today. Adelia wore her blue merino double skirt and Mary her maroon with velvet down the sides last night. Wallace brought me a pair of congress gaiters to dance in, black, $3.00. Adelia was down today. I gave her some oiled silk to put in hers and Teresa's bonnet[s].

Sunday 9th   Another lovely day. I was very good today, did not say one cross, ill natured word, and so I coaxed him to go to church with me, which he done without a single word of impatience, and the consequence was we have both been happier today than any Sunday before in a long time. Our intention was to go to hear Mr. McCollum, but we saw Lockwood standing at the church door, and he said there would be no service there this afternoon. The court house bell was ringing for Episcopal service, so [we] went there and listened to a very good sermon. The text was: be not afraid, only believe. Walla's grandma staid at home and took care of him. I wore my cashmere dress and white bonnet. Walla has come running in and reached up to the table, got a pin and commenced picking his teeth, so I'll have to stop and tend to him. Last night some one asked him what his name [is] and he said John, just as big as though he was 6 years old instead of a little tyke 22 months old. He sticks to it that his name is John. No one has ever trained him about it either.

Monday 10th Tuesday morning 11th   Really I was so tired last night, and it was so cold to go off in my room to write that I did not do it. Therefore the task this morning, and I am stealing time to do it too. My washing was done yesterday. Walla's grandma tried to commence the making of a winter bonnet for herself but did not get much done at it for running after him. Wallace worked hard all day making a reservoir up at the head of the spring that supplies us with water. He had an Irishman helping him, one that I think from Wallace's account ought to carry cloves with him and use the same freely. Wallace's father had his troubles yesterday too. To quote his own language, it was a blue Monday with him. In the evening Wallace talked of going to town to practice with the band, and then he talked of going to the theatre, but by dint of some coaxing from me and being tired as he was, he finally decided to stay at home, so he went and got his horn and rendered night hideous about here with the thing. Today I cleaned the dining, kitchen, and commenced making a pair of linen pillow cases. Walla's grandma worked hard today trying to make a pair of drawers, linen, edged with embroidery, for him. Wallace finished his reservoir about noon. When he came home I was busy mopping, and his mother turned in and got dinner for him. She made soup. Then about 2 clock his father came home, and she had to set dinner for him. He was going to Wentworth's for lumber to fix some boxes about the flume. He seemed very much care worn and troubled about those diggings. I hope the constant care he experiences on account of them will not have a bad effect. They work all night tonight. He was not to supper. W was. I was thinking some today of going up to call on Mrs. Wentworth tomorrow. I don't know whether my courage will hold out or not. Wallace and little Toad.I.buss are to accompany me.

    Wednesday 12 Thursday 13th   Half past 8 oclock. I sit down to record the ups and downs of the last two days. I did not write last night for this reason. I got interested in a story that I accidentaly came across, and I was bound to finish it, to the exclusion of Roman history, my writing, Bible reading &c. I read aloud to the family. The story was The Glorious Forth in Boston. During the reading we all laughed not a little at the misfortunes of Mr. & Mrs. Ben on that memorable day. Mrs. Furston called yesterday afternoon with her young son all dressed in an officer's uniform, cap and all. He did look so comical when I opened the door to let them in (for I did do it) that I was tempted to laugh. Wallace, Walla and I have made the long talked of call on Mrs. Wentworth. That lady received us very placidly and invited us into the dining room to sit down, there not being any fire in the parlor she said. She made a great parade over Walla and his curls, and he in return was as saucy to her as though it had been Mary or Geoge, as he call[s] them. He told her his name was John, and finally when we came away he went up to her and kissed her, said by by, and shook hands. Mrs. Furston came in while we were there. Tuesday I plaited a green satin ribbon into Adelia's bonnet braid, took out the black velvet in it. I today have been heron bone stiching on my linen pillow cases, done my week's ironing this evening. Wallace's father still in a great deal of trouble about the diggings, working hard all day, came home wet this evening. Wallace came home about 4 oclock all wet, had to change. He was completely out of patience with the flume. Him and his father were both to supper. Wallace is practicing tonight. Yesterday he got some new music from below. Two or three days ago he received a long drawn out letter from a man in Tuolome county wanting him to send him a description of the improvement on quartz mills that Wallace got a patent for last winter. He said he had saw something of it in the *Scientific American*.

Friday 14th   I mopped the dining room this morning, cleaned up my little Walla. He then went to sleep, and I made out to finish my linen pillow cases, all but the lace. That I do not intend to put on till I have used them some. Adelia came down with her bonnet, and I put in the braid, before mentioned, made of green and pink satin. The bonnet now becomes her very much. Walla's grandma baked pies and cakes this afternoon, and Walla troubled her not a little, running around teasing for a good sing. She made him a little turnover that is to be all his own. Bless his baby heart, when he beed so dear. Wallace's father went to the diggings this morning and has not yet returned. Tis ten now. Wallace had some trouble today with some person or persons that will persist in cutting wood off his land whether he will or not. Now I must go and rub Wallace's mother's back with Electric Oil. Then I must try and get to bed some time before midnight, for twas about that time before I did last night.

Saturday 15th Sunday 16th   Evening about 9 oclock. Yesterday I was very busy all day, mopped the dining room, hall, kitchen and my room, then cut out a night shirt for Wallace. Teresa and Tom were down in the evening, and her and I had so much running to do after little Kate and Walla that neither of us accomplished much but a little neighborhood gossip. Then twas so late when they went away that I did [not] write any, read some in the *Book of Life*, tended to a few little chores about and went to that receptacle for the weary and sleepy of earth, that matter of fact concern, a bed. Wallace practiced after Division. Wallace brought Walla a little whip with a whistle in the end, 25cts, and himself a small lamp for which he paid 2.50. This morning we were up later than usual, and the consequence was Mr. Lockwood, one of Wallace's fellows in the horn operation, catched us at breakfast. He sat down and took a cup of coffee. Walla[ce] and him then adjourned to the barn to tute (as little Walla styles playing the cornet). I went up to mother's this evening and staid till Wallace came after me, which he did about 7. I eat supper with them. Mother and I had such a good time talking over about the shadows and sunshine of the past, the trials that mother and you children, as she is wont to style her great grown up daughters and son, have borne unknown to any but ourselves. Wallace's mother this evening received a letter from her friend Mrs. Kelso in the States. Now I will just stop writing and go into the dining room and read awhile. Wallace is now down to the chicken pen making night hideous with that odious horn.

Monday 17th Tuesday 18th   My washing was done yesterday. During the day little Walla gave Wallace and I quite a fright. The little toad was missed, and I looked out of the back door and saw Mr. Wentworth looking very hard from the road down in the direction of the bridge. I turned my eyes in that direction, and there stood Walla on the extreme end of the bridge, where there is a plank, one end on the bridge and the other resting on the bank, which had partly caved away. His hat was thrown down at his feet. Wallace run down after him, when baby commenced climbing up the railing, to look down at the water. Wallace told him to come and get a pretty sing, when he let go and came running as fast as [his] little feet could carry him, so he was captured. Yesterday was the first day this winter that the ground was dry enough to let him out to play. Therefore his adventure. Wallace and his father both went to the theatre last night. Wallace played for the establishment, or rather the Union Brass Band of which he is a member are engaged to play this week (outside). They get free tickets and 50 dollars in money for the week's playing.

Tuesday   How busy I have been this day. Mopped dining, kitchen and part of [the] porch, starched 7 shirts for Wallace, ironed one, mended considerable on two of them before starching. Also cleaned, or tried to, a very dirty, muddy pair of pants, broiled steak for Wallace's dinner and boiled a mess of bacon and cabbage to end with. The reason why I did not write any in my diary last night was that I wrote a long letter to Amanda, which was sent off this morning. I forgot to mention in my writing last Sunday that

Saturday Walla got hold of a match and eat the sulphur end off. We felt some what uneasy and went immediately and gave him a good dose of sweet oil and in the course of 15 minutes after gave about a half pint of warm milk. Wallace to day received a letter from H. Merrow, also one from Old Man Fool, and O what hyeroglypicks.

Wednesday 19th Thursday 20   About 2 oclock in the afternoon that I am now writing. Walla is asleep, and I must improve the moments as they fly, for baby is very cross and will not let me do much of anything. Yesterday I felt very unwell, indeed the most part of the day. My head felt heavy and miserable, though along towards night I began to feel better, so that when Wallace's father came home and asked me to go to the theater why I went. Wallace had to be there in the evening to play with the band. That is the reason why I could not go with him. It was to see the celebrated Mrs. Wood that I wished to go, and she certainly is a very beautiful woman. The plays were both comedy, the first *Sketches in India*; I forget the name of the other. We were there early. The band had not been playing long when we got there. Walla's grandma took good care of him. Thursday. This morning Wallace whipped Walla for laying down and screaming when some books were taken away from him. I felt so bad about it that I cried too, but he deserved it, I suppose. I know though that Wallace will feel bad all day when he thinks about it. His grandma finished the waist for his linen drawers that she made. I feel very stupid and miserable all day today. I can hardly hold up my head it feels so oppressed somehow. I commenced supper 5 oclock so as Wallace could eat with us before he went to town. I went to bed at 9 oclock tonight.

Friday 21st   Today has been so pleasant that it has been hard for me to stay within doors, and particularly so for to keep Walla in. I commenced supper a few minutes past five, and so we had Wallace to eat with us again but not his father. The band went out on a playing excursion this afternoon, for tonight is Mrs. Wood's benefit. How I do wish Wallace did not belong to the concern. Him and his father have attended evry night this week. Adelia went to town today, and when she came back she teased me to let Walla go home with her, and so I did. Bless his sweet soul, he is always talking about some "poory chicky dead" whenever he sees a feather or dusting wing. I commenced making me a merino skirt today, sewed up the breadths and basted the hem, hemmed half a breadth. Now I must go and pick over a mess of beans to soak tonight.

Saturday 22nd Sunday 23rd   In the morning after sweeping and putting to rights, George being out hauling Walla in his little waggon, so I may write a little now without being disturbed. Wallace and Lockwood are down in the barn practicing on their machines infernal! Yesterday was a very busy day with me. I hemmed 2 ½ breadths on my merino skirt, cooked a capital kettle of beans! washed out my room, the dining and kitchen and then ironed till eleven oclock. Walla's grandma worked at her bonnet all day but did not get it quite done. She is some in the bonnet making line, and not a proffessional hand either. George took almost the entire charge of Walla yesterday. His grandma washed and put him to sleep after supper. Sunday Well I guess none of us will go to church this day, but I know what I will do. I'll go and clean Walla and myself and then perhaps he will go to sleep and then I can study or read just as I please in the afternoon. Wallace went to town and brought me two magazines, 75cts for the two, *Harpers* and *Graham's* that used to be but is now changed its name to the *Ladies Magazine*.

Monday 24th Tuesday 25th   About ½ after 12. I have just laid Walla in his cradle. The sun shines pleasantly, but there has been quite a high wind and cold today. Yesterday done my week's washing. Walla's grandma finished her bonnet, and I think she has made quite a bonnet. Wallace was summoned on the jury Saturday, but he did [not] understand and so did not attend. He was again summoned yesterday to appear this afternoon. He dressed and went to town for that purpose, but having some work to do on the flume, he came home for a saw and walked it from town here in 8 minutes! Almost locomotive speed! A man named Hanson and a Miss Mead were married last night at the brick church. He had his wedding advertised in the *Journal*, and the public were invited to attend. None of the Williams however made their appearances. Mary staid all night with Adelia. She says A is ½ an inch taller than her. Today I mopped the dining room, kitchen and porch thoroughly. Wallace's father eat supper home last night for a wonder, after the rest were done however.

Wednesday 26th Thursday 27   8 oclock, raining and snowing all day. Yesterday nice and pleasant. Teresa called on Mrs. McCutcheon yesterday afternoon. She has a feminine baby born last Tuesday 25th. Walla's grandma commenced to write a letter to Mrs. Kelso last night. She intends to finish it this evening, but she took little Walla to bathe his feet in mustard water, for he is quite unwell this evening. I think he felt feverish and bad about 4 oclock this morning when he first awaked. He has considerable fever tonight. I think this spell has been brought on by his running out on the damp ground the last day or two. I allowed him to stay out too late yesterday evening. I was so busy trying to finish a merino skirt I was making. This was wrong, and if heaven spares him this time I will try to be very careful in future as to how I let the little darling be exposed. I have just rocked him to sleep. Mary received a letter from Jany Kelogg this evening, and her mother one from Louisa in which she says Frank has another boy, born the last day of the last month in 1858. Wallace has worked all day in the diggings. He got off the jury for that purpose. He practiced last night and was to again tonight, but being tired and raining so he did not go. I ironed from 6 yesterday evening to 11 last night, about the time Wallace came home. All I have done today besides taking care of Walla has been to mend a pair of pants for Wallace and put feet in a pair of stockings for myself.

Friday Saturday Sunday morning 30ieth   Snow laying on ground, raining off and on all night, cloudy and chily this morning. I have not written any for two days. Friday footed another pair of stockings for myself and commenced the making of a pair of pillow cases. Walla was quite unwell and required so much attention. About 4 in the evening he went to sleep and slept about 3 quarters of an hour. In the morning we had given him two pills, but he vomited them up. He was out of his head till about 3 in the morning. We did not sleep any at all with him. He had a high fever all night and a bad cough. I was very much afraid he would have the croup, he was so hoarse with all. His grandma finished herself a black moire antique hood lined with ashes of roses satin. Saturday was a weary day to me, eqaly so to baby's grandma. He was very nervous and uneasy all day, and it required all the energy she could muster to keep him any way amused while I done the sweeping and scrubbing. About 9 oclock we bathed him to his hips in a tub of warm water. Then she took him out and put his feet in a pan of strong mustard water, and in spite of all his kicking and screaming she managed to keep him in about a quarter of one hour, which I think done him good, for although he coughed continually, he slept pretty well after he was put to bed, 10 oclock. Wallace staid after Division to practice, did not get home till eleven. Sunday none of us attended church. Wallace gone all day practicing! With the exception of a very little reading I have had to pay constant attention to Walla. He is so troublesome and nervous. He has a very bad cough. Indeed we are giving him Bull's Balsam for it. How tedious and tiresome

Mining-town girlhood. In spite of rough surroundings, children of both sexes delighted in the freedom of mining camps. Courtesy of the Western Historical Collections, University of Colorado, Boulder.

pass the hours, now days to me. Wallace's whole time and attention are directed here lately to practice music to play with the band. No persuits in common between us anymore, no more pleasant readings together, no more evenings spent talking and making plans as we used to. We go on day after day, without speaking a dozen of words to each other some days. I feel more and more evry day that this is not as it should be, but Wallace does not seem to think. What is going to become of our happiness at this rate? is a question I often ask myself. Wallace is just now coming in, and I will ask him.

Wednesday morning 2ond of February   Breakfast is about ready, and I have stole off in here two or three minutes to write a little. Monday I done up my week's washing. The rain poured down all that day without intermission. Walla's grandma took care of him, while she managed to rip up and remodel her traveling bonnet that was. About 4 I turned in and ironed Wallace a shirt, for he wanted to go to the theatre to play. Mrs. Wood has finished her engagement in Grass Valley and came to Nevada again, and so the band have another engagement, but alas for human calculations, the rain kept on and they did not perform, and Wallace had his clean shirt and walk in the rain by the light of his bull's eye for nothing, which he did not like, and when he got home he talked about building and going to live in town. Tuesday, that was yesterday, I felt quite unwell, and Wallace's mother complained very much of a sore throat, bad cough and so on, all occasioned by a violent cold that she has some how ketched. Walla was extremely troublesome all day. In the evening he came to me, and I took him up and as I supposed got him to sleep, but when I went to put the young gentleman in the cradle he made decidedly a fuss, so I had to take him up then. I was so aggravated that I slapped him a little, at which he screamed lustily. His grandma came running in, pitying him up, and wanted to take him from me, but I, being as stubborn as he was, would not give him up, so she give me a down right talking to about my cruelty, as she called it. Perhaps I was hasty in what I done. It will be a lesson to me in future, but I really felt so bad myself that I did not stop to consider about what I was doing. Bless his sweet heart, in a short time afterwards he put his hand up to his ear and kept saying hurts, hurts. He could not sleep but kept waking evry once in a while and crying. Then I begin to think that perhaps he had the ear ache, though he never had it before. So his grandma got some cotton and wet it with laudanum and put it in his ear. Then he went to sleep quietly and no more trouble about that, till when we went to put him to bed after washing his feet; then he would not be still, so his grandma slapped him several times, which finally quieted his nerves. Wallace and his father worked till 4 oclock this morning putting in boxes. Yesterday the band were out playing up recruits for the theatre.

Thursday 3rd Evening 7 oclock. Supper has been eaten and Walla (for a wonder) is asleep. Wallace came home about 4 and said he had not eaten anything today, so I turned in and got him some stewed potatoes, coffee and broiled steak, so his supper and dinner went together. He had been working hard at the flume. Tonight is Mrs. Wood's last night in Nevada, and I am not at all sorry. Yesterday Wallace's mother received a letter from a neice in the States, her brother Philander's girl. Mary got supper last night and breakfast this morning. I mopped up the dining room today and took Walla quite a ride in his waggon, the first time the little toad has been out any length of time for two weeks. Wallace brought him a huge apple this evening, with which he was very much elated. I just now hear the band commence to play. Tuesday Wallace gave me two dollars to pay for some hoop wire and 2 yds ½ of checked callico to make aprons for Walla. Mrs. W got some telegraph needles and gave me two paper. I finished a pair pillow cases today and marked each one with a W.

Friday 4th   was an extremely pleasant day, warm as any day in May. Fever is in Wisconsin. The honeysuckle is growing as nice as in summer, and my Baltimore Bell is starting out leaves, as is also the Persian Queen or cloth of gold. The grass in the yard looks so refreshing and green. I starched 5 shirts, 3 skirts and some other little things today. In the evening I cut out the lining of my green plaid dress, which I am going to make over again. Walla is fast regaining his former health and strength, and consequently he is getting less troublesome than he was.

Saturday 5th   Cloudy and threatening rain, sprinkling a little like April showers. I set my geranium out to ketch a little of the refreshing drops as they fell. I mopped my room, the dining room and kitchen. Adelia and Mary went to town today, and the burden of Mary's conversation this evening is Mr. Hamlin and his blushing face. I have a couple of shirts to iron yet tonight.

Sunday 6th Monday 7th   Evening, about ½ after 8. Walla's grandma has washed and got him to sleep, and my day's toil is done. I have been washing busy as I well could all day. This has been a showery, cloudy day, yesterday raining all day. None from here attended church or Sunday school. I felt very stupid and energeless all day yesterday. Wallace went to town in the afternoon to practice and did not get back till night. His father for the first Sunday since he bought those diggings staid to home, not however till he had been over in the morning before breakfast to see about things. Yesterday after Wallace came home I made him listen to me while I read the trials, loves and disappointments of Miss Shimmens, a fashionable milliner in her time. Wallace became somewhat interested in her in spite of himself. I feel very tired, very weary indeed tonight. Wallace brought me a can of strawberries this afternoon. He is in town playing tonight by way of practicing. His mother's health is very miserable and has been for the last two months. It seems to me unless she can get relief from the distressing weakness of which she complains that she will certainly go into a decline that will not easily be arrested. I can not see how she can be so patient with us all when she feels so bad, and we are all of us, big and little, impatient, hateful and aggravating a great part of the time.

Tuesday 8th   I crept out of bed this morning and dressed in the dark so as not to awaken Wallace or baby and got breakfast by ½ after 6. Mary, she took Walla up and dressed him this morning for the first time. This day set in by raining. Wallace did not get home till II last night. Walla's grandma set up last night and made him two pair of net drawers, while she fit the lining of my plaid dress. Today she was quite unwell all day too. Raining all day with but little intermission. Wallace and his father came home this evening wet to the skin. They had hard times with the flume. It was filled up, covered up, and evrything was the matter. I hurried and had supper soon after they got in. The rain just poured down this evening like the windows of heaven were open indeed. Wallace commenced a letter to Merrow this evening.

Wednesday 9th   I had my breakfast this morning just one hour later than yesterday. George took Walla up this morning and dressed him. My dress is progressing slowly. Walla's grandma fixed and peaced the back, put the form on so that it looks quite nice, if it is composed of five peices! Mary got supper this evening. Wallace is practicing tonight. Raining all this day too. I went not to bed till ½ after II last night.

Thursday 10th   Got breakfast. Sewing on my dress. As usual raining all day, also.

Friday 11th   Rained pretty much all day today. Finished my waist and sleeves this evening. George came home from school tonight quite sick with a violent diarohea he has somehow contracted. Wentworth's waggoner came down this morning to borrow our buggy to take a lady home, he said, and when he came back left the barn open so that Charlie got in and tramped things over to suit himself. So goes the world's gratitude for favors granted. Discouraging, say I, but I will not dwell on such a thought; tis unworthy. John L told George this morning that Mrs. Wentworth was very sick. Wallace practiced tonight some. Wallace brought me an orange. I also got breakfast this morn, had a little too much salaratus in my bread.

Saturday 12th   Got breakfast and then mopped the dining room, kitchen and porch, notwithstanding raining and snowing all day. My clothes that I washed Monday have had to lay all week in the tub and for what I see are likely to remain there a while longer. I baked bread, enough bread to do all tomorrow. Walla's grandma gave him a good scrubbing tonight all over, got him to sleep and then laid him in his cradle. I feel very tired indeed to night. Tis now about 9, and I think that I will just stop and go to bed.

Sunday 13th   Snowing and raining alternately all day. Wallace went over to town to practice, and then after that he worked several hours on the flume. His father was tending to the concern pretty much all day. He did not get home till seven and was quite wet. Wallace was also. He brought Walla a little pair of morrocco congress gaiters, $1.75, no. 6s, and me he brought 3 apples. I got breakfast this morning by 9. Adelia came down between showers and could not get back till near night. She eat dinner with Mary. They could not go to Sunday school.

Monday Valentine's day   I got breakfast this morning by 20 minutes past 7, did not get up till 20 minutes past 6. We were in bed last night by 8! Tis snowing some this morning. I had too much saleratus in my bread.

Tuesday 15th Wednesday 16th Thursday 17th   9 oclock in the evening. I have not written any since Monday morning, have been so busy trying to get my dress done and I could not possibly find time between that and my other duties. The dress is done this evening thanks to Wallace's mother's indefatigable encouragement and help too. Monday I put my last week's washing that had laid in the tub since the Monday before. The sun shone till the clothes had about half dried, when some snow began to fall, and I run out, gathered in and finished the drying by the stove. This week's washing, which I accomplished the same day, is still in [the] tub. I have regularly got breakfast evry morning, this and with the exception of one morning have had splendid bread evry day. This week has been stormy, especially today, snowing incessantly all day, decidedly the worst storm of the season. Wallace's mother is in a very weak state of health. I was really shocked this morning when she came into my room and told me how she was affected. She explained it by showing me a portion of her apparel the like of which I never saw before in a case of her kind. I must try and do all I can to lighten her care relative to household matters, for she has done a good part by me and mine, and now is one of the times I can show my gratitude for past kindnesses. I bought of Simon this week a pair of slate merino stockings, canton flannel for a night gown for Walla, 25cts, also paid him a dollar that I owed him. Then I got over 3 yards of green plaid ribbon for book marks, 75cts, not paid. I gave half of it to Adelia for her hair. I got 4 yds of marine for a hooped skirt, 1.00, of Henry. Mary has been unwell the last two days and did not attend school, for her mother would not permit her, and she does not submit very gracefully to staying at home, gives her mother a great deal of trouble by snarling and grumbling. Darling little Walla has been threatened with inflammation in the eyes the last two or three days, and [we] have put eye water in them now for two nights. He rebels like evry[thing] at the opperation. Wallace bought a book for me today titled *Life in California Illustrated*, $1.00. Wallace was a jury man on a trial today. The man whose side he was on won the trial and had to borrow the money of Wallace to pay the jury $20 or so.

Sunday the 20ieth   Today as usual has been passed at home alone. Wallace gone all day in town. Friday I thought I would do part of my Saturday's work so as to make it come easier Saturday, & I mopped my room and the hall and cleaned most of the paint in those appartments. In the evening Wallace brought me two yards of wattered green trimming for the sleeves of my dress, which I immediately put on. Then the dress was finished entirely. I then cleaned a very muddy pair of pants for Wallace. His mother still remains very poorly. I got supper as quick as I could. Wallace was not to supper. Saturday was a very busy day notwithstanding what I done Friday. I cleaned all the paint in the dining room but two windows, mopped the floor, the kitchen also. In the evening Wallace bought an immense pike fish, weight 14 lbs. He dressed it for me. It was 6 oclock before I got done scrubbing, and I had promised Wallace supper should be ready again that time, but I bustled about right smart and had supper not long after. Mr. Diehl visited the Division tonight. He is traveling lecturer in the cause of temperance. Wallace does not like him as he did poor Carter (who went down with the ill fated *Central America*). Wallace is slow to place confidence; therefore his real friendships are few. Carter, I think, was a sincere good man. He was an eloquent lecturer. His former experience in the downward path, as related by himself, gave more weight to his lectures, so that when one contrasted his former life with the present they could but listen with wrapt attention, and I think he occupies a place in Wallace's memory that time can not efface. Wallace's mother feels quite unwell this evening. She helped to get supper, and I expect the exertion over the fire was too much. I had splendid bread for breakfast and nice fried fish, good bread yesterday morning. A and M went to Sunday school today. Mr. D visited the school and exhorted the children to cultivate a love for the cold water principal.

Wallace brought Walla a huge apple this evening for which he paid 50cts, also a box of candles on his shoulder from town. We got a dollar's worth last night. I wonder how long they will last.

Monday 21st Tuesday and 22ond Wednesday 23d   7 in the evening. I got supper and it has been eaten. I have just come in and sat down to write a little with the pleasing thought in mind that I have done my duty the last three days to the best of my ability, with all cheerfulness too. Monday I commenced washing about 11 oclock after having got breakfast and done the sweeping. I went into Mrs. W['s] room and stole out 8 fine shirts and 2 under do. and 4 pair of drawers for Wallace's father and two sheets, 5 pillow cases, a gown and handkerchief. My washing and all together counted 40 odd pieces. I did not finish till dark yesterday, could not dry the white ones, because snowing set in this morning about ½ after 10 and has kept it up ever since. This day has been very cold indeed. Yesterday morning I starched Wallace 5 shts, and Wallace's mother ironed one for him. She has been working the last two days all the time she could get from tending Walla on a black velvet basque for Mary. A and M went over to the Methodist church and joined the cold water company organized by Brother Diehl. Today I mopped the dining and kitchen. My bread for breakfast this morning was unexceptionable. Wallace is not at home tonight. Mrs. Rider died yesterday morning.

Thursday 24th Friday 25 Saturday 26th Sunday 27th   ½ after 8 in the evening, the last but one of this stormy February. Thursday was a cold, stormy, disagreeable day. I did nothing out of the usual routine of my monotonous day's employments, finished the making of [a] shirt for Walla out of two old ones he had and cut him out a canton flannel night gown. Then I 5 oclock commenced baking corn bread and stewing some apples to make pies Saturday. Friday Tom came down and got his money Wallace had on interest. Wonderful to relate I got started at 11 (after my breakfast works and sweeping was done) up to see Teresa. I left Walla with his grandma. The roads were in such a condition he could not walk, and I did not feel able to carry him. Teresa was much pleased to see me. Her and I had a real old fashioned sociable time. She would in spite of my intreatys get dinner. She fried ham and eggs and stewed potatoes just for her and I. I got home after 5, after having had to borrow an umbrella to come through the rain. Saturday was a snowing, raining day, but I washed and ironed 3 handkerchiefs for Wallace, mopped the dining and kitchen and then in the evening made 7 apple and raisin pies. Walla's grandma took care of him and sewed at intervals on

Mary['s] basque. I was very much fatigued last night when I finished my work. When Wallace came home he brought Walla two apples. Adelia came down, and Mary went up with her. Sunday Snowing when I got up to get breakfast and has continued on with but very short intervals all day. Wallace has been at home all day, the first Sunday in a long time that he has not went to town. I have been reading some for him today in *Calafornia Life Illustrated*. We went over some of the trials and self denials of Rev. Taylor, a missionary sent to Cala in the spring of 49 around Cape Horn. For supper I had mackerel and stewed potatoes. Walla's grandma got him to sleep, and he is now in bed. Wallace is doing and explaining a sum to Mary in the dining room. George is in there abed and asleep. Wallace's father and mother are in the parlor, the one reading and the other on the sofa asleep. Out of doors is rain and snowing and evry thing cold and cheerless. Wallace's mother is still weak and miserable. Now I will just go in to the fire, warm myself and read awhile and then off to bed.

Monday 28th March Tuesday 1st   Yesterday I done my week's washing notwithstanding the snowing but dried calicoes in the house. This morning dawned upon us as serene and bright as the two last days of February have been tempestuous and cold. Verily I think part of the old saying has been verified the last month, for it certainly went out like a lion, and a roaring one at that. Today I put out the last Monday's wash and the one before that has lain in the barrel ever since. Mary nor George neither went to school the last two days. Mary has done quite a day's washing besides mopping the pantry and cleaning the shelves. I had good bread yesterday morning and extra good this morning, Wallace said. Wallace played for the theatre last night, that is [in] company with the band. Him nor his father neither were to supper. He plays again tonight. Potter has a company under his management occupying the theatre now.

Wednesday 20nd Thursday 3d   Cloudy and threatning rain today. Weather about the same yesterday. A and M went to town this afternoon. M bought a hooped skirt with which she is perfectly delighted. Wallace got Mary another pair of shoes today, morrocco, $2.25cts. Adelia bought for me 4 yds of marine for a hooped skirt that I intend making, 40cts a yd. Yesterday I finished another canton flannel night gown for Walla. Today I have sewed busily on an apron for the little chap. Wallace bought some nice raddishes of a vegetable, the first we have had this season. I cooked salmon for supper. Tis the first that has been along. O I have been so vexed this evening.

In my hurry to get supper, for Wallace was going to town, I burnt the toast, and the potatoes shared the same fate. I know not when I have been so bothered. Wallace staid after playing to the theater last night. He did not tonight though. Wallace brought George a pair of boots, no.3s, $3.00.

Friday 4th   Wallace's mother starched some of the clothes (shirts) that I washed for her. Mrs. Hait called today on her way to see Mrs. Wentworth. A & M were in town today. A received a letter from Amanda and Thompson one from Vanhook, who is rusticating to his no great delight (I am thinking) in the vicinity of Sweet Fraser river. Wages are $1.50 per day in that Eldorado for nervous adventurors. A says Amanda writes that she has a Chinaman hired for $1.00 a day.

Saturday 5th   I was up by ½ after 5, and Wallace's father got off to the diggings by 7. I mopped my room, the hall, dining room, kitchen and porch and in the evening baked 3 pies. O dear, how very tired I was when done, no one but those that have tried the experiment can know.

Sunday 6th   I was up earlier than is usual Sunday mornings in order to get ready for church, but alas! Wallace would not go, and then I cried about it. A and Mary went. They attended the Methodist church. In the afternoon Wallace carried Walla for me, and I went up to see mother. Thomps looks very bad and complains considerable. Dear little Walla got such a fall off of a chair up there. I neither read nor wrote any Sunday.

Monday 7th   I done mine and Wallace's mother's week's washing. Wallace played over in the hall practicing last night. Dr. Smith, no, not Smith but Collins was here canvassing for schollars to attend his seminarey in Stockton. His terms are $50 a term board and tuition.

Tuesday 8th   Today has been a cold, disagreeable day, and we are having quite a snow tonight. Wallace and his father have just returned from the Odd Fellows. Tom says that his baby was delirious all night last night. Adelia was down here yesterday with her, and I think that the ground was too damp for her to walk and that she has taken cold which causes fever. Wallace's mother has been ironing some of my washing this evening. I mopped the dining room and got dinner. She cut out my marine hooped skirt, and I have sewed on the gores this evening.

Wednesday 9th Thursday 10th Friday 11th   Sewing all the time I could get this week on my hooped skirt, and with no little assistence from W's mother it was finished this morning. She is now sewing on a blue merino cape, to be trimmed with bias plaid, for Walla. Wallace is in town practicing tonight, and he was Wednesday night. His mother has a violent head ache this evening. She bought for me today a nice dress cap for which she paid $2.50. I bought 2 hemstitched handkerchiefs, 50cts. Adelia this week hemmed 3 handkerchiefs for me and today took home 6 towels to whip or overcast fringed ends. I mopped my room and the hall. Wallace brought me a beautiful little box with a glass in the top. It was filled with delicious prunes. Mary and her mother and myself had a spirited discussion this evening on black hair. She always differs from anyone else on the subject of color.

Saturday 12th Sunday 13th Monday evening 14th Tuesday 15th   I have finished my week's washing and consequently am pretty tired tonight. Saturday was spent as usual mopping &c. Nelly Pooler was here in the afternoon. Mrs. Wentworth has a daughter that came last week. Sunday I was up early, got breakfast, and Wallace got up the buggy, and him and I went to church, the Methodist. The elder preached a sermon from somewhere in Mathew. His text: progress to perfection. He preached a very interesting sermon. Even Wallace, who is so hard to please in such matters, found himself interested. Adelia and Mary and Thompson were there. The day was beautiful indeed. In this evening I took Walla and went up to see Teresa. I took supper there. Wallace came up after me. Trece and I had a rather tiresome time than otherwise, because Kate and Walla disagrees so. Tuesday I mopped the dining and kitchen and commenced another dark apron for Walla. I felt quite unwell all day, had the head ache in the evening. Teresa came down and staid till he came from the lodge. I bought 5 yds of linen for which I paid $2.50. I gave half of it to mother and Adelia, also a hemstiched handkerchief to A, 25cts.

Wednesday 16th   About noon the pedlar Simon was here. I paid him 75cts that I owed him for ribbon and also purchased 4 yds of cambric for pillow cases and a strip of work [?] for pants $1.5 bits. Walla was 2 years old yesterday, and he can tell it as well as any of us. Also he can say when anyone asks him that his name is John Williams and that he is papa's baby boy. His grandma ironed 10 pieces for him alone last night. She has got him trained so that he can tell the names and explain the pictures in a pictorial history of the Indians of North America that we have. He does it quite intelligibly indeed for a little boy only 2 years old.

Thursday 17 Friday 18th Saturday 19th Sunday 20ieth   Somewhere in the neighborhood of 12 oclock. Let me see, I have some days to date back.

Wednesday afternoon Mrs. W and I started out calling. She went to Wentworth's and untie's and I to Mrs. McCutcheon's. Adelia spent the afternoon with Mary. They took care of Walla. The day was lovely. Thursday A and M went to town. I finished an apron for Walla and cut out 2 more. Friday gloomy and cold. Wallace went to town that evening though. Thursday Mrs. Stevens called in. She intends moving next week over in the vicinity of the Town [?]. She says she has been solicited to take charge of the district school there, and she has given her consent so to do. Yesterday Wallace went Lockwood's security for the sum of $500, payable in May. I do hope L will come promptly up to his engagement. I think Wallace has run considerable risk. Time will determine all this though. Yesterday my father completed his 54th year. He has ascended to the summit and is now slowly but surely descending. Where now alas! are many of these that knew him half a century ago. His mother lies in the grave yard of Monroe, Green County, Wisconsin, to which she was consigned in '51 or 2, I do not know exactly which. His youngest child, Adelia, was 17 the 14th of this month. The oldest died in 1832, a few weeks after I was born. She was a little over 2 years old. Today is a cold, snowing, disagreeable day. Wallace's brass horn, himself and co. have went a mile or so out of town for the purpose of practicing marches in anticipation of the coming celebration of the Odd Fellows that is to take place the 26th of next month. There is to be a procession and an oration, then a grand ball at the court house that night. I got up and got breakfast early this morning, thinking that I would go to church with A and M, but we have been disappointed by the wether. Well, I will content myself with a good day's reading and writing. In Roman history I have got as far as the reign of Diocletion, he who when he had reigned 21 years resigned the purple, a not very common thing for kings or emperors to do. Walla's grandma finished a nice linen apron for Walla last night. She worked the sleeves button hole stitch with scollops. Yesterday I scrubbed as usual and made corn bread and cooked apples for making pies. O dear, I am nearly froze here in this old kitchen to which I have retired to try and get away from the droning of George over his Sunday school lesson. Tis really dispairing to me to be compelled to hear him, but we are commanded to practice self denial, all in the hearing of George. When he has lesson[s] to learn (that do not run off) [I] have to endure the virtue, if not practice it.

Monday 21st Tuesday 22ond Wednesday 23d   3 in the afternoon. I have just laid Walla in his cradle for an afternoon's nap and am now at liberty to write a little, though I do not feel at all like doing so, but then I am loth to give up the habit. Today has been cloudy and gloomy, threatening rain. Monday I washed, raining very hard all day, washed all Mrs. W's things and mine. Tuesday morning the weather cleared off. I then put out my washing and mopped the kitchen and porch. Before I was done Miss Gibson came in to make a call. She has been very sick. Mrs. Williams was taken very unwell Monday night and still continues so weak she can hardly walk across the floor. This morning about 10 Adelia went to town, and when she came back Mary ran out to the fence, and A said she was going to Marysville this morning, but did not say how. Well I got my work all done and went up to mother's to see her before she started. Judge of my surprise when I found she was going to ride down in a buggy with Dempsey's partner, a man that I nor mother did not know. Indeed we neither of us had ever seen him before. I felt bad about [it], and the more I thought of it and the circumstances attending his coming the worse I felt. So bad did I feel that when I came home and considered the matter awhile I just put on my hood and went right back again and talked right seriously to mother on the subject, and she asked me to talk to Adelia, which I accordingly done, and she began to see in what a light she would place herself by so doing, and so when Mr. Pritchard came about 8 this morning she had made up her mind not to go. Then I think all hands that felt interested in Adelia felt considerably relieved.

Thursday 24 Friday 25th   Yesterday I finished Walla's last dark apron, which makes 6 that I have made him. Yesterday was a beautiful day indeed, and today is equally so. Mrs. Turner and Mrs. Pierre called in a few minutes yesterday afternoon on their return from Mrs. Wentworth's, whither they had been. I did not go in to see them. I bought 25cts worth of whale bone for Adelia's dress yesterday and today 7 yds of oiled calico and 9 do of french calico for the purpose of making me a double gown, price $4.00cts. I was up this morn and two mornings before this at 6 oclock. Wallace bought yesterday evening some young onions and radishes. The tops of both of them I cut off and made a capital dish of lettuce, so Wallace called it. Well there comes two pedlars, and I must go and see what they have got of course. Wallace brought Walla a nice little pair of rubbers, with which the little toad is very pleased. I got of a pedlar a pair of garters, 25cts and some hooping for my white bell skirt, $1.00 and 3 linen towels 75cts.

Saturday 26th Sunday evening 27th   I did not get up this morning till after 8. Today has been a cold, showery, dark day. Adelia and Mary got on their dress up bonnets and were starting for Sunday school when a little rain began falling, and so they had to put up with their yarn hoods or stay at home. I have lounged around all day in dishabille (not feeling very energetic). Yesterday was a bussy day. I got breakfast, done the sweeping and mopped my room and the hall, dining room, kitchen and porch, then commenced about ½ after 5 and made and baked 3 pies. I had damped 2 shirts and some other things to iron, but when I was at liberty to iron them Wallace's mother would insist on doing it, and she was not really able, but she would do it, in addition to letting down and otherwise fixing Mary's blue merino for her to wear Friday. I sent by Adelia and got 3 yds of canton flannel and 1 yd of twill for lining a dress. Yesterday my *Hesperian* came to hand, a third magazine style. There is two nice plates contained in it, one of birds peculiar to Cal. and the other a likeness of George Yount, one of our pioneers of 1831, who resides in Napa Valley. Annexed is a short description of trials and troubles experienced by him in those days of grizzly bears and savage Indians, which is quite interesting. Wallace brought home 3 new pitchers. He went to Grass Valley yesterday afternoon in company with the band to play for a theatre. He got back about 10.

Monday 28th Tuesday 29th Wednesday 30ieth Thursday 31st   The last day of March and like its predecessor is going out like that noted beast, the king of the forest or in plainer English lion. I washed Monday but did not put out the principal part of my washing till today, and that too at the risk of having it torn to pieces by the high wind. Monday Wallace had the tooth[ache]. Tuesday he suffered very much with it, so much that he went to Chapman and had a hole drilled through the root. That day I mopped the dining room and kitchen and laid off and commenced embroidering a shirt, that is, button hole stiching scollops on the yoke and sleeves. Wednesday Wallace's tooth was so painful that [he] took a sharp knife and pushed it into the gum, and it relieved him very much. Wednesday Wallace loaned Coggin $10 simply because he just came walking all the way from Sac. City flat broke and is a worthy young fellow. Wallace says he was sick there and otherwise unfortunate about getting his pay for work he had done. Very cold and snowing pretty much all day yesterday. I scolloped busily all day. In the evening Wallace's father came home and brought two letters, one from Philander to Mary and one from Erwin to Mrs. W. They contained the death of Jane Kellogg, who died the 15th day of March. We all felt very melancholy at hearing of her death. She died a faithful Christian. She lacked 2 months of being 14 years old. Wallace's mother has been fixing her slate merino all this week. Today our pianno was sold and taken away for $150. It cost $250.

Friday the first of Apr   I finished remoddeling a white bell hooped skirt that I had in the works, also took the hem out of the over skirt of my wedding dress that I think of fixing up for Adelia to wear the 26th to the Odd Fellows festival. Wallace's mother finished her slate merino today for a wonder. It has been in Mrs. Pooler's hands, who first made it over two years ago. Miss Gibson has made it over since, and now Mrs. W has finished [it] herself. I do not think she has worn it 3 times. Mary and A went to town today, M to get things for the ball and A some little errand for Teresa. M bought herself a pair of white kid garters, $3.00, and white kid gloves $1.25, ermine to top them with.

Saturday 2nd   I made starch and starched two shirts and a white vest for the ball, also 6 shirts for Wallace and two for his father, mopped the dining room and kitchen. George killed three chickens himself, the first time he had done any thing of the kind. I dressed them with his help. Mary got supper. Wallace's mother ironed two shirts for him and other ironing for me. She did not get to bed till after 2 oclock. Sarah Fraser was here today.

Sunday the 3d   I did not have breakfast till half after 9 this morning, could not get Wallace to go to church and so I did not go. I have never went without him, and I dislike to make a beginning. His mother could not get his father to go neither. Today is a beautiful bright day and nice walking. The girls went off to Sunday school in fine spirits with their blue merinos on.

Monday the 4th Tuesday 5th Wednesday 6th Thursday 7th Friday 8th Saturday 9th Sunday 10th   The first I have written since last Sunday. I have not made such a skip as this since I began my journal before. Today has been an April day indeed of sunshine and showers of rain and hail and snow turn about. Notwithstanding the forbidding appearance of the wether Adelia and George went between showers to Sunday school. Tis now 4 oclock. They have not yet returned. Twas my intention to have went to church this morning. I arranged so as not to bake bread this morning so as to have breakfast soon, but the elements combined against me. Monday I washed a large washing quite. Tuesday morning I put it out, though the day was cloudy and threatning rain. Adelia and I went to town a shopping, and while there there came up quite a shower of rain and hail. Before we came out though it stopped. I bought me a headdress of pink cheniel with satin beads $2.00, 3 yds of pink lute string with a satin edge for a sash for A $1.50

and 12 yds of valencines to trim double skirts of ball dress 1.50 and 3 balls of narrow rose colored ribbon for the same purpose. I got a bottle of Lyons Catharion 50cts, a bottle of Lubins double extract $1.00, 6 yds of thread lace 2.50, 4 yds of yellow flannel $2.00. Adelia bought herself a pair no 4 white slippers $1.75cts. I was very much fatigued when I got back. Wednesday Adelia came down, and Mrs. Williams cut and fit her dress for the 26th. It is fine swiss. I got 5 yds for the waist, sleeves and top skirt; the other two skirts are my wedding dress skirts. The 5 yds of swiss came to $3.12½. A staid all day. Miss Gibson came over in the afternoon in quest of sewing. She did not get a job though. Mrs. W gave her the promise of one as soon [as] our hurry of ball fixing is over. Mrs. W turned in Tuesday evening and pulled out the hem of my white dress and put it in again before she went to bed, besides mending a torn place in the dress. Wednesday was a beautiful bright day. Miss Gibson went out and hailed a teamster and got up beside him and so went home. A & M went to town after she started. I sent for hooks and eyes, 12½. Thursday a cold, cheerless day. Mary's dress was fit this afternoon, though Mrs. W has spent the most of two days on Adelia's. Today Mrs. Buckner and Mrs. Bostwick were here a little while. Mrs. Buckner was on her way to call on Mrs. Wentworth. She is the receiver of contributions here in Nevada for the Mount Vernon Association. Mrs. Williams contributed $2.00, Wallace $2.00 and his father $2.00. Mary made yest powder biscuit and some cake and tea all herself for the ladies. Friday I felt very bad in the fore noon. I suppose the reason was I did not sleep any at all the night before. Why I can not tell unless it was drinking tea too strong for supper. To day I commenced the upper skirt of Adelia's dress. Wallace's friend Coggin came over in the rain, and him and Wallace had a good time so considered by them tuting down to the barn. They did not wait for supper but went to town. The Templars were to have been organized this evening, but owing to the state of the wether they put it off till Saturday. I ironed my bordered wrapper this evening. Wallace quit smoking this evening, broke his pipe and throwed his paper of tobbacco into the fire. He commenced smoking when he had the tooth ache so bad some time ago. Saturday I mopped my room, the hall, dining room, kitchen and pantry, cleaned the mop boards in my room and part of the [omitted] and the doors from the dining room into the kitchen. Adelia went to town on an errand for Teresa and got caught in the rain coming home. We could not go to the hall this evening neither on account of rain, though the Templars met and the society was organized.

There was 5 or 6 ladies there and a number of gentlemen. We none of us got to bed till after 12. It now lacks a quarter to 6, and A and George have not yet come. I suppose they are having a tedious time with their Temperance society, for tis held evry Sunday after Sunday school.

Monday 11th Tuesday 12th Wednesday 13th Thursday 14th Friday 15th Saturday 16th Sunday evening after supper 17th   Another skip of a week. I had almost decided not to continue this old journal but on reflection have come to the conclusion not to give it up, so I must now try and keep my hand in, as I have last Friday evening assumed another obligation, that of uniting with the Good Templars, a society that has just been organized one week ago. The meetings are held every Friday evening in Temperance Hall. Adelia and I and Mary along with several others were initiated last Friday. I was up to mother's today and Thompson walked home with me, and so I got a chance to talk with him on the subject, and he promised me that I might take his name in next Friday to be proposed for a member. He also said he would use his influence to bring in one of his acquaintenances with him. Today has been a summer's day indeed. A good many of our peach trees are in full bloom and have been so for over a week. All the orchards in this vicinity look beautiful. Wallace went away to town this morning before I could get breakfast ready. Him and I had some trouble this morning; therefore his hurry to get away, though he said he had an engagement to play. He is not yet back. His mother and father went to church today. George harnessed the horse entire himself this morning. Monday I done mine and Wallace's mother's week's washing. The rest of the week has been spent, that is, Tuesday Wednesday Thursday and Friday, on Adelia['s] ball dress. Friday Mrs. W done up A's and M's long skirts, clapped them dry. They look as nice as the new. A's dress is all done but the gathering and arranging of the skirts, of which there is three, the two upper ones trimmed with 4 rows of narrow rose colored ribbon and valencines lace. The waists are low necked with puffed sleeves trimmed with a ruffle of the muslin and 4 rows of ribbon and lace the same as on the skirt. Mary's dress is finished, pressed and laid away. It also has 3 skirts, the two upper ones scolloped around, deep scollops, and trimming the same as Adelia's. Wallace's mother's health is improving very much within the last week or so. She done a lot of ironing for me last night, though since she came home from church she has suffered very much from a kind of nervous tooth ache. A, Thompson and Trece and Tom went to church this evening to hear Mr. Dryden preach a sermon on the Bible in common schools, a question that has been discussed over time and again in this state within the last month or so. Mr. Warren is now up from Sanfrancisco. He last Wednesday married Miss Colwell and Mr. Niles. The widow Sweeny was married week before last. Mr. Warren brought a prize for Mary, Adelia and George. M's is *Esop's Fables*, G's *Robinson Crusoes Adventures* and A's *The Life of Martha Washington*, the best prize given out.

Monday 18th Tuesday 19th Wednesday 20ieth Thursday 21st Friday 22ond Saturday 23d Sunday evening 6 oclock 24th   A skip of another week. How times flies. How bussy I have been the last week, Mrs. W and I both. All of our great hurry has been trying to get ready in time for the much talked of 26th. We put the finishing touch on A's dress last night. Mrs. W. worked hard all day yesterday trying to get mine done. I am going to wear a plain swiss double skirt, puff sleeves, the same that I wore at the children's ball last fall. It was made new for that occasion. Wallace has had a hurried time of it this week, practicing and writing music to play the 26th. His father bought himself some nice regalia to appear in at the ball, cost $20.00. Tis white silk fringed with silver fringe. Monday I washed and did not get my washing out till after 9 oclock. Tuesday auntie and Trece came down to see the girls' dresses. Mrs. W and Mary fit hers on, but I would not show Adelia's to auntie, and I understand that she is mad about it, but I don't care. A's two upper skirts are looped up with bows of satin ribbon, bows of the same on the sleeves. Thursday Mrs. W called on mother and auntie and Mrs. Wentworth. Wednesday I mopped the house from my room out to the porch. Mrs. Williams starched 8 shirts, 3 for Wallace. Thursday evening the girls went to town to get rose colored ribbon to finish their ball attire and came home with the news that Mr. Warren was to be here to dinner Friday, which peace of news put Mrs. W in a splutter, as we happened to be out of vegetables and the butcher would not be here till Saturday. Friday was indeed an unlucky day to me. Walla got hold of the inkstand and drank some ink. Then George took [him] out to play in the yard and got him mounted up on a wheelbarrow, when he tumbled off, striking his forehead on the corner of a box and hurting himself considerably. Friday was a cold cloudy day, but we all attended the Temple that evening. Thompson's name was proposed as a member. Friday Wallace's mother was taken quite unwell in the evening. Mr. Warren did not come. Saturday no scrubbing was done by me. Last week Mrs. W got breakfast two mornings, the first breakfast getting she has done since the 8th of February. Last Sunday evening Wallace came home with a new silver cornet for which he had paid $50.00. Saturday raining pretty much all day and today the same way. The prospect for the celebration looks rather dull. Wallace last night brought home a box containing some purchases he had made for himself; a broadcloth dress coat $30.00, a silk vest with a small crimson flower running over it $8, a pair of finest quality calf skin boots, two pr white merino socks, a black silk cravat & pair of cream colored kid gloves, white silk handkerchief thrown in by the merchant, a white merino undershirt—his bill all together was $49.00. I did not get to bed till 12 last night, ironed 3 shirts for Wallace after 9 in the evening. The girls went to Sunday school, under an umbrella however. I have just been writing one hour and a quarter.

Monday 25th Tuesday 26th Wednesday 27th Thursday 28th   ½ after 3 in the afternoon. I am all alone. Mrs. W has went up to see another Mrs. W that got sick going to town to see the marching of the Odd Fellows Tuesday. Mary and Adelia are in town, Mary to buy some articles of wearing apparel for the May party that is to come off next Tuesday. Walla is asleep. Monday I did not wash as usual but finished the arranging of mine and Adelia's dress for Tuesday evening.

Well the long talked of, looked for, prepared for Tuesday is passed and gone. Numbered are the anticipations, castles in the air, hopes and vanities of that day (and night) among the things that were! Wallace's mother went to see the marching and hear the oration delivered in the pavillion built for the occasion. Sargeant was the orator. His oration was a very good one; so they say who heard it. There was a large number of people present. The Union Brass Band acquitted themselves creditably, and they feel decidedly proud of the fact. Mary, Adelia and I saved ourselves for to dance that night. We dressed in the hall and then went up to the pavillion, A in company with a Mr. Parker that Wallace introduced to her. Mary went to supper with Mr. John Dickson. The supper was not so good as was expected.

April 29th   Adelia and Mary both wore their hair curled. Mrs. Williams done it up in papers the evening before. A looks decidedly well in curls. The Odd Fellows went parading through the room all night with their reagalia on, feeling quite important I thought. Wallace's emblems of office caught in the blouse of a ladies dress and she did not at all relish the joke. He then went and took it off. She was a Miss Downie from Rough & Ready and as it happened both deaf & dumb! Therefore she could not speak her displeasure, but she looked volumes! Friday 29th Thompson and 7 or 8 others were enrolled members of Union Lodge of Good Templars. His name is now where I have longed to see it. He has begun the race in the cause of temperance. God grant that he may never turn back or fail on the road. That very night he was proposed as candidate for worthy scribe, ballotted for and elected. He was 18 last Novem.

Saturday April 30ieth   A bright sunny day. Mrs. W mopped the dining room today, the first time she has done so for a long while. I mopped my room and the kitchen and porch. Adelia, Teresa and Tom went to the theatre tonight, the first time A ever was at one. The play was *The Stranger*. The star actor is a Mr. Anderson.

Sunday May Day, that is the first of May   Nothing out of the common transpired. O yes, I had almost forgotten. I attended church, Dryden's. I do not know the name of the minister that preached. I have heard him before at a camp meeting last summer. His sermon was quite edifying.

Monday 2nd   A done a huge great washing of two weeks standing, all of Mrs. W's clothes that I could besides my own. Raining all day, and tomorrow was to have been the May Day celebration. George was so eager to do something towards having it come off that he came near getting into a scrape. He had libberty to go and kill some chickens when the rain stopped, but he misunderstood or done so on purpose. Consequently he trots out and killed 4 of the old laying hens and comes triumphantly bearing them in after having chopped off their heads with an old dull knife.

Tuesday 3d   Rained some today. Mrs. W made a nice chicken stew. Wallace was here to dinner. I was up at 5 this morning. Mrs. [W] sat up last night till two oclock finishing Mary's May dress, thinking that in case she would need it it would be ready, but it was not used today. The May party was put off till Friday, and the chickens she cooked last night, two of them for the party. I finished my washing to-day but did not put it out.

May Wednesday 4 Thursday 5th   Passed off as usual; nothing of importance or out of the ordinary routine of every day life here transpiring. I was employed those two days embroydering a shirt for Walla, flannel; tis scollopped and the scollops worked with saddlers silk.

Friday May 6th   Day to be remembered in the lives of all the girls & boys that took part in the festivities of the May party that day. They crowned their May Day queen with truly royal ceremony. Miss Anna Irish was the distinguished of the day, the monarch of many loyal subjects. Miss Nina Churchman, last year's May queen, resigned the throne to her rival. Mary was the second maid of honor to her royal majesty, Miss Johanne Stone the first, & Miss Kate Overton the crowner. I was up by 5 that morning. Wallace's mother got his father coaxed up to go and take the buggy with her over to the party. I got breakfast, and she had George to kill two chickens, which she cooked besides baking 4 pans of cake and one of biscuit for the picnic. They were off by 10 oclock, the children by 8. Adelia took no part. Mrs. W had me label the box of provision she took:

> For the Union Brass Band!
> From the Ladies of Gold Flat

She says it was very gratefully received. Mary has hardly recovered from the effects of the sun shining on her uncovered face and neck yet. It blistered and peeled off. In the evening Thompson & Adelia called for us on their way to the Templars. T['s] first reading of minutes was this evening. He reads very well but will do better when the bashful wears off and he gets more accustomed to his new and strange position. I had committed the part I was to take in the evening's proceedings, but when the time arrived I was so scared that my voice would scarcely do its duty. Mrs. W mopped the dining room.

Saturday 7th of May Sunday 8th   None of us to church. The peaches are large as good sized peas. There is a dozen or so on a tree of my setting the spring of '56. It was in bloom last year, but the frost killed the peaches pretty much all over the state that year. The apple trees are in full bloom now. Indeed they have been for a week or more, some of them. We had a capital mess of green peas this evening, which little Walla enjoyed with the rest amazingly. It [was] pass Walla peas, Grandma, all the time during supper.

Monday the 9th of May   and with it came Miss Gibson. My washing I done as usual and Mrs. W's all I could get hold of. Miss G commenced a delaine (side striped) for Mrs. W, but she had the stripe put in front, wrapper style.

10th Tuesday morning   I put out my washing and commenced clearing out the winter's collection of chips and rubbish from behind the kitchen stove. Then I give the kitchen a thorough scrubbing, also the porch.

Wednesday 11th   sewing a dimity ruffle on to an article of ladies underclothes for myself.

12th Thursday   occupied in the same manner. I got breakfast readdy this morning by ½ after 6.

Friday 13th   Breakfast I had this morning about the same time. Gibson finished her job for Mrs. W today. She made her two dresses for 5 dollars, a delaine and double gown. She tried very hard to get to do some sewing for me, but I would not let her fit me a dress now for reasons best known to myself. Week before last I forgot to mention that Wallace gave me 20 dollars to a debt I owed a pedlar which I did and swapped my green wattered parasol with him for another, in style green with a flounce to it. The reason I done so was I had bought the other of the same man and it happened not to be very stout, so it broke about the first time I used it last summer, one of the ribs. He said he could get it mended. I gave him two dollars to boot. The one I now have is an 8 dollars one. I also got of him an 8 dollar green merino scarf. They are much worn now. I bought Wallace a small-pleted shirt 1.75.

Saturday 14th   Done no scrubbing. Mrs. W cleaned the dining room and made some pie plant pies. We had quite a shower that day. I made a pair of pillow case, all but the work, or trimming I would say. I made a bolster case last week also.

Sunday 15th   I unexpectedly attended church this morning. Adelia and Mary had made an agreement to go, but Mary got stubborn and would not eat anything at the breakfast table, so her mother said she should not go unless she did. A was waiting and rather than have her disappointed I jumped up from the table, ran into my room and got ready to go with her. By th time we were ready Mary had her cry out, her breakfast eat, and she was ready to go too, so we all walked to the Methodist church. Wallace and his father had taken the buggy over in a hurry. Wallace had a piece of mending to do on the lead pipe that had obliged to be done. That day was the first time I had ever went to church without Wallace since we have been married. It made his mother feel sad to see me starting off without him. When we came back in sight of the hall he was waiting with the buggy and little Walla for me, so I got in and we took a short ride around home. The minister's name I did not hear. He was a miner with a colored flannel shirt (an Englishman) who had unexpectedly been called upon about ½ an hour before the services began (to preach) in the absence of Mr. Dryden, who had sickness in his family and could not attend. He preached quite an interesting sermon for one in so short a notice, and he not a minister either. His text was: Be not afraid, tis your Master's good pleasure to give you the kingdom.

Monday 16th   My washing done, all I could steal of Mrs. W's also. I had for the house 16 or 17 dish and hand towels, for one week only too, got it all done and out about 10 oclock that night.

Tuesday 17th   I starched 6 shirts for Wallace and my sun bonnet, ironed one for W and set out two of my Maiden Blush roses that I made from cutting up the old bush in to slips that a gopher had gnawed off the roots of one year ago last winter. How very tired I was that night. Mrs. W called on Teresa in the afternoon, made a mistake of houses and got into the wrong one. Wallace and I had a good laugh at her when she was rehersing over her troubles. Wallace's father goes evry morning early to that flume in town, and there he stays till late evry evening. If he does not get his breakfast at ½ after 6 he is off with out it.

Wednesday 18   Mrs. W bought several things of a pedlar that was here. Among the articles for me were a large plaid muslin dress for a wrapper and shirting for 3 bolster cases and 8 pair of pillow cases which her and I tore out immediately. I last night commenced one of the bolster cases.

Thursday 20ieth   This morning about 20 minutes of 4 oclock there was a son born to Teresa, of which they are very proud. He came down and announced the news 7 oclock this morning. I went up about 9 and staid till noon. Wallace had a hard time of it wrapping the pipe with old rags somewhere up above where the water was wasting. Wallace's mother worked very hard today trying to help Mary do up some of her summer's washing and starching. Her health has improved so much since the warm weather set in.

Friday the 21st   I made a bolster case entire today. We all attended the Temple this evening. Thompson's first reading of minutes of his own composition took place this evening. He reads very well in the lodge room.

Saturday 22ond   Walla's grandma mopped the dining room and I scrubbed the kitchen. I went and raised the hall window and in so doing it slipped down again on my thimble finger and bruised it considerable so that I can not hope to [do] some of the many things I had laid out to do the coming week.

Sunday 22   I was very wicked all day both in thought and deed. I do believe that I was possessed of an evil spirit that day if such things are (which I think there is no doubt as to the theory). I finished the arranging of my book case that I had commenced Saturday evening, then ironed Wallace a shirt and Walla [a] pair of drawers, scrubbed out my room &c, had my finger tied up all the time too. In the afternoon Mrs. W went up to see Teresa, and I went in the evening, taking Walla with me. Wallace came after me about 9 oclock. We had quite a discussion before we left about the naming of their baby.

Monday the 23   I did not my washing today as usual on account of my hand but instead commenced to make a waist to my red calico skirt that [I] used to wear winter before last. Mrs. W cut and fit it. I sewed on the skirt, putting in side stripes or borders the same as I put on the sleeves.

Tuesday 24th John Lent was here to see us just up from San Francisco. Wallace has not been very [well] the last week or so. He looks very bad. I think he is wasting his life fast away blowing that everlasting cornet.

Wednesday 25th   Today I went up to see Teresa and Mother and on my way down stopped in to see Mrs. John L. She is very poorly and has been so ever since the celebration the 26th, when she got all of her children ready and then walked to town.

Thursday 26th   I washed a very large washing, two blankets and other washing. Wallace pounded the blankets for me. I did not however get done. Mrs. W and Mary went to town this morning, and they staid all day shopping and looking and examining the house Wallace's father bought of Tweed. They talk of going over to live there in town on account of the diggings having to be worked night and day and the walk from town here evry night being such a task at night after a hard day's work. Mrs. W bought herself and Mary and Walla a pr of shoes and Mary a fashionable dark leghorn hat with bugle lace trimming $5.00.

Friday 27   This morning I finished my washing and prepared to go to the temple this evening. I went and I was very tired indeed when I got back again. Wallace intended to go with the band to Grass Valley to play for Collins that has been performing for the last week in Nevada. The band has played here for him, but Wallace thought better of the subject, and I spared no pains to help him all I could so to do. Accordingly he did not go, but remained to attend to his office in the temple, which is that of Worthy Chief Templar. I am B. H. S.

Saturday 28   Mopped the hall, scoured out the kitchen and my room, then fixed up and went to see Teresa. Wallace came home to supper, and Mary and I went with him to the Sons of Temperance meeting. Mary and Nina were initiated members of the lodge. Adelia was to have been too, but Tresa was so unwell that she staid with her and let Tom go. She is to be made a member next Saturday. Wallace's mother sewed pretty much all day on the waist of my red calico dress.

Sunday 29th   I went up to see Tresa about 8 this morning, took Walla with me. Teresa took a bad turn Friday but is better now. Walla carried her a bunch of flowers himself, or boka, as he called it, the dear little fellow.

Monday 30ieth   Did not wash but Mary and her mother between them managed to get out quite a wash, the first [time] that her mother has tried to wash sheets or table cloths for 5 or 6 months.

Tuesday 31st   Wallace's father staid in town last night, slept in a bed of his own in the hall. Today Wallace's mother and I have sewed all day hard as we could on my two wrappers. She cut and fit the waists of both.

Wednesday 1st of June   How beautiful evry thing in nature looks.

Thursday 2nd   This morning John L came down before breakfast to announce the news that he had another addition to his family, a girl. I done my week's washing today, did not wash any for anyone but my self, Wallace and Walla. I washed my largest white spread. Wallace and George pounded it some for me. How tired a little exertion does make me, tis strange. John L came down and invited Mrs. W and I to go and see his new found treasure. She went up.

Friday 3d   Did not go to the temple, the first night I have been absent. I went this evening to call on Teresa, took Walla along. Kate & him quarreled so that I did not spend a very pleasant evening. Teresa is getting her strength fast.

Saturday 4th of June   This evening I attend Temperance Society at the hall. Adelia was initiated as a visitor. Wallace has been a member of this same Temperance association since the spring of '53. The society numbers but a few now. For the last two years it has been on the decline. Had it not been for a few determined spirits, Wallace and Father with a few others, the charter would ere this have been returned. I went with Adelia to Simon's to look at a Neapolitan bonnet that she wished to buy. She bought it, gave $8.00 for it. Tis trimmed with pea green ribbon with a white stripe.

Sunday 5th of June

March 6th 1861   A long long silence with regard to my journal, over two years since I have conversed any here in. Many changes have been experienced by our household, friends and acquaintenances since last I wrote, but thanks to our Heavenly Father our circle still remains unbroken. Many many blessings have been ours the last two years, the best and brightest of which has been the addition of little Frank to our home circle, a precious jewel he is too, a little sunbeam, little Paul, Walla's little bug, just one year and a half old. Adelia came to live with me the 1st of dec 1859. She staid till the 23d of last month (Feb) when she went to Marysville on a visit to Amanda. She commenced going to school to Miss Philips the 11th of July '59 and continued as long as she taught, which was a year. Amanda was here when she commenced, and curiously enough she was up on a visit when the school ended. The Sons of Temperance had a celebration the 23d of August last, grand procession and ball in the evening. They danced in the hall, the new edition just having been completed. Wallace's father and mother moved from the Flat into Mr. Hill's house the 1st of dec '59. Wallace and I, Adelia, Frank and Walla kept faithfully to the old homestead till the 11th of Novem '60, when the emigrating fever carried us to the brick house what is perched upon a hill. Well tis a nice house, can not say as much for the surroundings though. Walla's grandma received two loads of flowers today from the yard of an eccentric dweller on Piety Hill. The same came to hand by way of Expressman George. Little Rosy Williams went beyond the dark portals last May '60. Adelia and Mary sat up with her the night after she died. Wallace had Mary & Adelia likeness taken the 20ieth of last month, the shadows of friends when the substance shall have passed away. I think of many little items I should like to insert, but alas for tired finger and half after ten oclock, I cannot tonight. so ends the first lesson, as the ministers say.

Friday April 11th 1862 half after 8 oclock & all is well with us. Another leap over a year. How many events came to mind to be recorded. Since last I wrote here in I have been to San Francisco & Sacramento to the session of the Grand Lodge, where Wallace was elected to the responsible & honorable office of Grand Worthy C Templar for the state. I feel very proud of the preference shown for him. Twas in June. His term of office expires Sept next. Amanda was in San Francisco under the care of Doctor Toland. I & Mother went to Maryville last Novem to see Amanda again. We were telegraphed for by Adelia, who had been sent for a few days before, A having returned from the bay some months before. She is troubled with the liver complaint. We hardly thought she would live through the last attack she had, but thanks to a merciful Providence she is still spared to us. Teresa lost her baby 17 days old. He died the 2 week in Septem last. Herbert was his name. Sister Carter, wife of the Grand Lecturer of the name, was here last summer. I was requested by Brother Cutter to solicit donations for her benefit, which duty I performed to the best of my ability and to the amount of $103.00. Mrs. W & Mary went to Napa on a visit last Oct. Mary remained at school. I made all the preserves & peach pickles last fall myself & succeeded admirably, they all say. George was shot in the head by Conant Bryerly one year ago this month. They were playing duel. Doctor Hunt extracted the bullet. It was a hard struggle for master G to keep from kicking the bucket for 4 or 5 months. He also had that horrid disease diptheria, from the effects of which he has hardly recovered yet. God in his kindness has spared my darlings from the many complaints that have been among little children this winter & in so many cases have proved fatal. . . .

Walla & Franky

Commenced School with Mrs. Hibbard

Mond May the 9th 1864

A week or two before I commenced my journal Wallace bought me a pair of kid shoes 3.50.

Carrie Williams, diary, Gold Flat, Nevada County, California, 1858–64, Western American Collection, Beinecke Rare Book and Manuscript Library, Yale University.

"Odors not of Araby"   ABIGAIL SCOTT DUNIWAY

9

Abigail Scott Duniway of Oregon (1834–1915) was the most prominent early suffragist in the West. Her newspaper, *The New Northwest*, appeared weekly from 1871 to 1886, devoted to news about women, women's rights, and all aspects of western development. She herself traveled extensively for many months of the year, lecturing to all sorts of frontier audiences and selling subscriptions to her newspaper. Thus her "Editorial Correspondence," a column about her experiences that appeared every week in the paper, became a running commentary on the life and times of her "bailiwick," as she called it. Here is her description of an 1874 stagecoach trip to Nevada City and its hydraulic mining works (which Carrie Williams' husband and father-in-law had been so busily installing there fifteen years earlier). In 1880 she happens into a wedding in eastern Oregon, while in 1883 her visit to coal mines near Mt. Rainier in Washington Territory reveals more than she realized about working conditions—as well as her own and the manager's class prejudices. She also records Puyallup Valley hops production for the beer industry and environmental devastation incidental to development.

April 24, 1874

Dear Readers of the *New Northwest*:

*L*eaving Stockton on Monday the 12th inst., after having closed our lectures with a very large audience on Sunday evening in the Methodist church, we took the overland train at noonday, by the way of Colfax, for Nevada City, where we had an appointment for the evening. Our road lay through the lonely valley of the Sacramento, whose exquisite verdure of spring-time green was gorgeously variegated with every imaginable shade of floral beauty. Cattle stood to their knees in the muddy waters of lazy, sluggish sloughs, chewing the cud of sweet contentment, while jaded horses tugged away at the rolling sod, their drivers perched upon the spring seats of sulky plows, seemingly in need of nothing but umbrellas, fans and bottles of cologne to render the curse of eating bread in the sweat o their faces as imperative as the most devout of them fear that woman's curse of being ruled over by husbands will be in the new dispensation which is just upon her.

Arriving at Colfax, a little railway station, perched among the foothills of the bold Sierras, we learned to our disappointment that the staging to Nevada City could occupy us till far into the night, and prevent the possibility of our meeting our engagement for the evening. To make the best of circumstances was the only alternative, and we lugged our basket to the nearest hotel and took lodging for the night. . . .

Nine o'clock on Tuesday found us aboard the stage, with the usual crowd of passengers and baggage. We never saw a stage that wasn't capable of holding one or two additional passengers after it was already full. When about twenty feet from the hotel door, the horses plunged into a mud-hole, going down until, but for many similar observations, we should have expected to lose sight of their ears. But the horses came up and down went the coach, throwing the travelers into a heap upon the forward wheels and righting them again with the next lurch. . . . Miles of tedious repetition of the first moment's experience sufficed to reconcile us to our fate; besides, when you get your spinal column snugly telescoped, you become in a measure stage-hardened, and you learn to endure everything but the patient suffering of many pairs of rat-tailed, ewe-necked, ring-boned, knock-kneed horses, for whom we humbly hope there is a future life, where cruelty will be unknown forevermore. The lady passengers walked up some of the worst pulls and down some of the deepest gorges through pity for the patient animals and a laudable ambition to preserve their own bones unbroken.

In justice to the Colfax and Nevada stage company we make grateful mention that their horses are as well kept and kindly cared for as the nature of their occupation will permit. But the roads are lined with teams of the above description, drawing ponderous wagons which without a load would weigh a ton. These wagons cut up the roads with their broad, ladened wheels, making channels which the mountain torrents soon wear into gulches, and the traveling is fearful. . . .

Arriving at Nevada we were made welcome by our good friends, Mr. and Mrs. Crawford, in their elegant home, where all the implements of civilization are utilized in perfection. . . . The success of our meetings here was largely due to the efforts of Mrs. Emily Rolfe, a whole-souled, wide-awake, Temperance woman and earnest Woman Suffragist. . . .

While in Nevada we indulged in a visit to the hydraulic mining works.

Steady streams of water with over two hundred feet fall, are brought through large pipes, with six-inch nozzles, to bear upon the solid mountain sides with a force that disembowels the complaining earth, and sends it crashing to the plain below. Occasionally, blasting is resorted to, thereby aiding to loosen the solid mountain wall from its foundation, upon which the ceaseless waters play with such stupendous power as no army with strongest fortifications could long withstand. The flumes that gather up the debris of the elements extend for many miles through the gulches, and woe to the robber, who, when the waters are turned from their course to allow for the full "cleaning up" of the sluices, shall essay to "prospect" here for "tailings." His life would quickly pay the forfeit of his ill-advised cupidity. These mines yield an immense annual revenue, but are owned by wealthy companies and the laboring man's wages are but two and three dollars per day. . . .

In Grass Valley the Ladies' Temperance Union, assisted by our ever ready friends of the Methodist church, gave us three large and appreciative audiences, and much interest upon the woman's work in the movement has been awakened and will, we doubt not, go on till the great work is accomplished. . . .

From this place we are soon to retrace our way over the fearful stage road to Colfax, and from thence to San Francisco and Oakland, where we shall finish up our work and take the first May steamer for Oregon and HOME.

November 18, 1880

After mailing the editorial letter of last week from the Saltzman House, in the John Day Valley, we retired early to rest. After a dreamless sleep, we were ready to mount the Thursday morning buck-board, bound for the village of Mitchell, seventeen Cayouse miles away. Our route lay over and through alternate hills and valleys, creek beds and mountain gorges, and we experienced half a dozen varieties of climate in as many half miles, and saw more sidelong ridges than we would ever care to count. The valleys are low and level, and are capable of producing fruits and vegetables of both temperate and semi-tropical character. Everywhere, upon either hand, the great ragged bluffs rise up in bold array, casting black shadows into the gorges from one side, and reflecting back the sun's rays from the other, and so tempering the atmosphere that apples, peaches, tomatoes, pears, plums and cherries grow and ripen in profusion wherever they are cultivated. Irrigating ditches are noticeable here and there, the waters they supply being clear and pure, like melted snows. The basaltic rocks of The Dalles region have given place to concrete mountains, bluffs of sandstone, and banks of washed gravel cement. Sea shells abound on the highest peaks, and petrified trees, and even perfect leaves of stone, are found in many places, of a character to prove that inconceivable changes have occurred in these fastnesses at some remote period in the ages gone. Some of the great rocks are castellated, like those of the Wind River country, some of the billowy bluffs are variegated in color, and one great castle-like structure of sandstone slabs, with a huge dome at the summit, the driver told us, was called "senator Mitchell," in honor of the gentleman whose name it bears. A mile or two beyond this mammoth rock is the village of Mitchell . . . which consists of half a dozen new, unpainted frame houses, with the post office, hotel and store in one of them, and all cuddled cozily down upon the bosom of a friendly valley, around which great bluffs keep tireless and eternal vigil. . . .

Mr. I. N. Sargent, the leading man of the village, and proprietor of the aforesaid hotel, post office and store, welcomed us . . . and ushered us into the cheery presence of his amiable wife, who informed us that a wedding was in progress, and our help was needed to arrange the drapery of the bride. In a little while all was ready, and the groom-elect, an honest young rancheman from Baker county, led forth the bride, who was lovely to look upon in her floating veil and snowy orange blossoms, and Elder Rowe, who had halted by the way for the purpose, proceeded to pronounce Frank Hundsaker and Fanny Sargent husband and wife. The wedding was a private affair, only the parents of the high contracting parties and half a dozen invited guests besides ourself and the stage driver being present. But the occasion was all the more enjoyable because of its simplicity. In a little while we all sat down to a sumptuous feast, and the afternoon was spent in neighborly chit-chat and the friendly interchange of views upon many widely different topics.

Where the crowd came from that attended the lecture in the evening, was hard to conjecture; but it was promptly on hand, and a more respectful and attentive auditory we have never had. Ranche-men and ranche-women were there, the former roughly and warmly clad and fully equipped for the stock business, and the latter, for the most part, pale and anxious-visaged, and apparently in need of the ducking overcoats and fur-lined boots that made the men comfortable and kept them warm and jolly. When frontier men and women learn that women must clothe themselves as warmly as men do, there will be far less of ill health and mortality among pioneer farmers' wives than now. . . .

After the lecture, the "boys," as men of all ages are called on the road, to the number of a couple of dozen, began to tune themselves up around the freight wagons and camp-fires for the dulcet harmonies of a grand *charivari*. The newly-married couple took the hint, and, disguising themselves, departed in a hack for the house of a neighbor, several miles away. It was hardly nine o'clock before the fun began. And *such* fun! The "boys" threw stones at the house, and fired blank cartridges at the windows, and rang discordant bells, and drummed on dry goods boxes, and frightened a baby, and made good Mrs. Sargent nervous and angry—and all for nothing. The married couple had "vamosed the ranche." We thought the musicians had enjoyed about fun enough after half an hour, and the elder Mrs. Hundsaker accompanied us out to the teamsters' camp-fire, around which the serenaders had assembled for a few minutes' consultation; and when we graciously informed the amateurs that their victims had "skedaddled," it was our turn to enjoy the fun. Some of them held their guns awkwardly in their hands and gazed straight down their noses in silence, others toyed idly with the discordant bells and said nothing, and others asked questions incredulously. After being repeatedly assured that their game was gone, they felt that their music had been made in vain; but we begged them to believe it was all right. It was a grand serenade, we said, in honor of Mrs. Hundsaker and ourself in particular, and woman's rights in general. We were very thankful and complimentary, and bowed ourselves away at the close of the little speech accompanied by "Three cheers for the NEW NORTHWEST" and a grand "hurrah for Hardscrabble." The revelers then suspected the whereabouts of the bride and groom, and, after further consultation, departed for their place of entertainment. But the groom, anticipating such a visit, and determined to mislead them, had hidden his hack in a ravine over an adjoining hill, and, as they could not find it on the premises, they supposed he had gone in some other direction; and they returned, crestfallen but jolly, and consoled themselves by giving another outdoor concert in honor of their own discomfiture.

March 22, 1883

Monday noon, and off for Puyallup, the hop region, and Carbonado, the coal field of Pierce county.

The Northern Pacific Railroad Company has extended a branch line from Tacoma through the valley of the Puyallup and Carbon rivers, and our way runs through an immense tangled wildwood, where trees from six inches to half a dozen feet in diameter bestud the swampy soil, and great uprooted monarchs, from a dozen to twenty feet in circumference and as long as three Tacoma lots, lie prone upon the marshes, their matted roots kicked high in the air, and their slender tops long since denuded of the feathery foliage that was once their pride. Here and there are clearings upon the higher grounds, in which farm-houses nestle, surrounded by gardens and orchards, with hop-poles stretching away in different directions with little regard to regularity of outline, and lazy cattle basking peacefully along the roadsides in the sun. . . .

This valley, where the good people raise hops and preach temperance, is one of the richest localities in the Pacific Northwest. The hop yield is prodigious, the soil being a light, sandy loam, with a moist subsoil, particularly adapted to the growth of the beer-drinker's delight. There are some men in the valley who will not engage in hop culture, but their neighbors, who grow rich at the business, assure them that wheat, barley and even potatoes can be and regularly are distilled into worse intoxicants than can be made of hops—a convincing argument that makes new converts yearly; and so the occupation steadily increases, the last year's rise in the price of hops having added excessive impetus to the business lately.

Puyallup boasts a railway station, a school, a church, a public hall, three or four large and flourishing stores, a millinery store in charge of Mrs. Ross and her daughter, Mrs. Boatman (relatives of our co-worker), . . . a drug store, a post office, etc., etc., and last, but by no means least, a regularly ordained woman preacher, Rev. A. W. Jones, of the Baptist denomination, who is not only a minister, but an active Woman Suffragist, and of whom her intelligent husband is proud, and her parishioners ditto.

We had heard much of the Mt. Rainier coal mines, and were resolved to visit them. So, armed with a letter of introduction from Mrs. Barlow to her husband's partner at the Carbonado store, and accompanied by Mrs. Ross, who loaded a trunk with millinery, we entered a railway coach and proceeded on our way rejoicing. The beautiful weather was behaving its best, and the glorious day was aglow with sunshine. The clearings grew broader and more frequent for several miles, and the hop-poles more regular and conspicuous. Carbon River came tearing through the gorges and crossed our track often enough to have made profitable employment for bridge-builders while the road was being constructed. This river rises in the eternal snows of Mt. Rainier, and is fed by a glacier, which gives the water a milky look, and of course keeps it as cool almost as its parent fountain. The railway runs through a mountain gorge upon a serpentine track, so crooked and novel that nothing could abate our interest in it except a cinder from the engine, which, though not larger than a mote, so inflamed an inquisitive eye that we became as oblivious to scenery as the seasick swain whose first journey upon the ocean led him to anathematize the romantic author of "Life on the Ocean Wave."

The railway track ends abruptly at the foot of a tree-clad and almost perpendicular mountain, from which (we mean the track) another road diverges, forming a huge Y, up the stem of which an inclined grade goes crawling, so steep that the heavy loads of coal that regularly run down upon the rails could never be coaxed back by fire and steam and snorting locomotives. A few miles of laborious climbing upon this Y track brings us to the edge of an abrupt little table land, containing about four or five acres of stump-studded area, upon which are situated the store, post office, mills and dwellings belonging to the company, the store being under the management of Messrs. Barlow & Baker, and the mines and mills under the superintendency of J. W. Pinkerton, ESQ., whose handsome residence and its elegant furniture are peculiarly attractive in the wilderness, because of the strong contrast between it and the fifty-five tenement houses in which the families of the miners live, where children flourish like rabbits and women chatter like magpies, as happy as crows and as care-free as summer swallows. Mrs. Pinkerton, a lady of refinement and culture, who occupies the elegant home before mentioned, expresses herself delighted with the situation, so restful it is, and so different from the city life to which she has heretofore been accustomed.

About six years ago, a party of engineers, in surveying the township, discovered the outcropping of coal in these mountain fastnesses. A Mr. Henry built a crude wagon road leading to the new discovery, and afterward sold out his interest to a Mr. Chandler, of San Francisco. A corporation was then formed under the name of the Carbon Hill Coal Company, which was managed for two years under the superintendency of Mrs. Wingate, now of New Tacoma. The mines were again purchased eighteen months ago by Messrs. Crocker & Co., of the Bay City, for $750,000, since which time vast sums have been expended in their development. Twelve veins are now open, giving employment to 250 laborers, whose wages average from $3 to $4 per day. The unmarried miners live at the hotel or mess-house, and the married men in the tenements, which range like larger stumps among the blackened clearings. The houses and out-houses all look alike, and odors not of Araby fill the air with noisome stenches from the slops of many washings, frightfully suggestive of a forthcoming epidemic among the unthinking inhabitants, to a majority of whom sanitary measures are utter strangers. Yet there are notable exceptions among them—the young couple with whom Mrs. Ross and self find board for two days. . . .

Rev. G. H. Greer is here, engaged in teaching, and is doing his usual quota of good works among the people. He kindly presided over our one meeting in the place, which was not as well attended as we had expected, owing to a "wake" in the community, which, of course, found more congenial quarters in the one saloon, which, by the way, is soon to be converted by the efforts of Mrs. Pinkerton into a library and reading-room.

We'd like to take a ride down the almost perpendicular railway of the hoisting works and enter the tunnels to view the mines more closely, but Mr. Pinkerton objects because of recent disasters resulting from bad air, which requires the use of safety lamps; so we forego the experience, and content ourself with gazing long and curiously at the miners as they go and come, their clothing black with grime, and the extinguished lamps on their quaint caps suggesting the subterranean depths in which they delve, and from which they climb at stated hours for refreshment and rest. A miner's life, like a sailor's, has a peculiar charm, and the average employee never abandons his occupation. Yet here and there are sober, steady ones among them, who save their money, and in a few frugal years grow independent enough to retire to little farms and homes of their own.

Our time is up at Carbonado, and we leave Mrs. Ross, who has struck a land-office business among the untutored women for whom we have been engaged in trimming hats for two days, and we return to Puyallup, where an hour's rest in the hospitable home of Dr. and Mrs. Spining and their intelligent sons and daughters prepares us for the third evening's lecture in the town, which is given in the church in presence of a large gathering of deeply interested friends of equal rights, who accord our work the most profound attention. A goodly number of subscribers swell our former list, and we rest from our labors in unbroken sleep, to arise in the morning refreshed and invigorated.

From "Editorial Correspondence," *The New Northwest*, April 24, 1874; November 18, 1880; March 22, 1883.

Virginia City, Nevada, is the scene of this contemporary account, written to amuse the sophisticated readers of an eastern magazine. Palmer shows the freewheeling Virginia City society that developed out of early mining camps on the California border. Describing the social life of the small professional class in a mature mining town, Palmer depicts a gender-divided society in which the men have work and the women have amusements.

With irony and veiled sarcasm Palmer deplores the defeat of a women's rights law by the legislature, the ease and frequency of divorce, and women's interest in style and gossip. She describes ladies enjoying mountain excursions, fancy balls, and picnics with young single men, but says of their husbands, "The lords of creation are mere money-making machines." Unlike some other authors in this section, Palmer and her friends suffered no financial hardships, yet her brittle gaiety does not hide the basic insecurity of life in even the most prosperous mining towns. Gold fever exacted a high price from the land, from families, and from individuals.

*H*ow often must I declare that Nevada is not what it was when Ross Browne visited it, and wrote those atrocious, though I doubt not truthful, tales about its mines and mills, and above all its furious Washoe zephyrs?

These things were doubtless true then, but "*nous avons changé tout cela.*" Come to Virginia for a season and you shall see.

John is superintendent of the "Great Bamboozle" now, and is besides a member of the Legislature, so of course we move in the best society. I spent a week with him in Carson a little while ago—when they were attempting to pass a bill by which a wife might insure her husband's life without his knowledge or consent. The bill did not pass, though fair notes from fair ladies entreated the suffrages of the honorable senators. They were bribed also by the promise of a ball—a ball for the benefit of the church—but one of the senators remarked that those "sacred dances" had already impoverished two Legislatures, and so the sapient body refused to be thus beguiled.

But the "best society" gave us some excellent dinners, and placed their fastest teams at our disposal.

The roads were not good, but in Nevada horses are not expected to be particular about the state of the roads over which they travel, and so one day we drove over to Washoe Valley to see the palatial residence of a man who was created a millionaire in the early days—now six or seven long years ago—and who died in poverty some eight or nine months since. Poor fellow, he is buried behind the house which stands as his monument and that of the wild speculations and excitements amid which this young State was born.

In its present condition it is emblematical of the unsettled and un-finished state of the country—a speck of civilization and grandeur dropped upon illimitable waste of savagery. Behind it is the quarried mountain whence it sprang, and before it the beautiful lake, which lies like a silver horse-shoe dropped upon fields of snow. In summer time this valley is most lovely, surrounded as it is by the highest peaks of the Sierra Nevadas. Its meadows are of an emerald green; acres of wheat and barley sway in the gentle breeze, and yonder, where the long bridge spans the dark tule bed, bloom thousands of yellow water lilies.

I am not sorry the mills are mostly idle here; they should not with their clangor have invaded this peaceful spot. They have scared the fishes from the waters and the wild fowl from the sedges. Let them perish.

You see that great frowning mountain which lies at the back of the Ophir Company's deserted house and reduction works? See how a slice has been cleft from its side as if by a giant's weapon. Tradition says there was frightful havoc when that mile or two of land slid into the gorge be-low. There used to be an emigrant trail there, and of all the train that was passing at the hour of the slide, not one was afterwards seen.

If you would luxuriate in mountain grandeur go as I once did to the summit of that mountain. Ride through the cañon to the foot of the as-cent, and tell me if you ever before saw such beautiful cascades, such vivid tufts of green, and above all such lovely flowers as grow by the clear waters, or high in the clefts of the almost inaccessible wall upon your right and left. Leaving your horses at the saw-mill at the foot of the mountain, or perhaps at one of the woodchoppers' huts, you will proceed slowly, and with many a backward slide, to the two lakes which lie like gems half-way up the ascent.

Do not look back, but going around the mountain when far above the pines and chaparral, and upon the very summit of the bleak rocks, look around you that the full magnificence of the scene may burst at once upon the senses.

Hundreds of feet below you the white clouds of morning are floating, and through this misty veil is seen the sun-filled valley, bearing upon its bosom the horse-shoe lake—the dark fields of tule—the fairer meadows, and the fields of grain. Near the mountain sides rise the smoke of quartz mills, and more pleasantly placed that of white farmhouses. The little towns, too, are beautiful at this distance, and there is something truly grand in the sulphurous steam that arises in yon far-off valley to the left where lie the famous Steamboat Springs.

Now lift your eyelids higher. Ah, there is the Carson marked by a line of trees, meandering through yonder barren valley. There is the capital of the State. There Empire, made famous as the scene of Mark Twain's Hopkin's tragedy. There Dayton—and far, far away, Fort Churchill. The envious front of great Mount Davidson hides Virginia, but turn to the scene behind. Behold Lake Tahoe amid the peaks upon peaks that rise to the clear blue sky. Can there be peaceful vales beyond? Are not those wastes of rock and pines and snow illimitable? Standing there, it is impossible to think otherwise. But some mundane creature mentions lunch. The cloth is spread upon yon table-like rock. The first bottle of Champagne is spilled as an oblation to the genius of the scene, and *presto* the claims of hunger rival those of beauty.

But this excursion must be left for summer days. At present we had better return to Carson, and attend one of the Governor's quiet levees or Mrs. Y's ball.

Balls and levees are the same in most countries, though perhaps here you will see more ungloved men and bejewelled women than in any other place. You are surprised that Mrs. ———, who wore such magnificent diamonds last night, should live in so small and plain a house. But the fact is the house is their own. None but wealthy companies build grand houses here. Persons are not judged by the places they live in. Ladies may envy me for living in the stone mansion of the Great Bamboozle Company, but nevertheless they are not ashamed to receive me in their cloth and paper dwellings.

You would like to drive home by Empire and Dayton. Now as we drive across the flat you may see the Penitentiary, with the great granite quarry behind it, and the Warm Springs at its side. There is no better place than this for pleasure-seekers to obtain an excellent lunch. Willy-nilly the horses will stop, and we must too. Let me show you the great stone baths in which one may drown if he choose, or might do so whether he desired or no. To escape such a possibility I always sit upon the steps and simply bathe my feet. You may laugh if you please, but it is the safest thing for a poor lone woman to do.

There the approach to Empire is marked by the great brick house and dilapidated reduction works of the Mexican Company. I could not tell you how many fortunes lie buried in that pile of bricks, those crazy wooden buildings and the masses of machinery they cover. That is another monument of the speculative era. Passing through the village, having on one side a row of drinking saloons, and the inevitable hardware store and express office, and on the other the Carson, blocked with rafts of fire-wood, we come to an embodiment of the life and progress of the present—the fine mill of the Yellow Jacket Company with its busy surroundings. Long after its red walls have faded from sight we hear the dull thud of its stamps. Then comes the long drive across the flat, and over the chalk hill. The roads are execrable, but this mud of winter is far preferable to the dust of summer. Anon as we skirt the river more busy mills are seen, and the road is often blocked by the heavily-laden wagons that are bearing the wealth of the mountains to the powers of the river and the valley. A succession of these powers mark the entrance to Dayton. It is but a town of wooden buildings, enlivened by the red brick Court-house and the Judge's house, but it has gained its meed of fame; it has given fame to Lyon County, even to the State itself, for the ease—nay, eagerness—with which it grants divorces. It would appear as if there were some hidden law compelling ladies there to obtain divorces from their first husbands and to choose others. The society of Dayton expects its members to act upon this law. It is shocked by the man or woman who is so stupid and blind as to cling to his or her first love—formed in the immaturity of youth.

How charmed is Mrs. D to give her first husband, Mr. C, her hand in the dance, while Mr. D leads Mrs. C to the refreshment table and with attentive care procures for her the choicest ice. True, Mr. C may have been a little shocked a year ago, when he discovered that his wife's mode of paying her lawyer for obtaining her divorce was a promise to marry him. But the lawyer's sister was a very pretty girl, and so why should he contest the suit. And as all would live in the same town the children could run back and forth, and although at first it would be a little disagreeable to hear them call Mr. D papa as well as himself, that would manage itself in time.

And so the C and D families meet at church, and at the entertainments given by each other, or the public, as if no unpleasantness had ever occurred between them. Although churches do not flourish well in Dayton, who can deny a peculiar, if not Christian, forbearance among its people?

The drive from Dayton, through Silver City and Gold Hill, to Virginia, is very interesting. There is too much variety upon the road—even if it is not of the pleasantest character—for it ever to become tiresome. First we pass through a narrow cañon which seems at no long period back to have been riven out of the loose and crumbling mountains, and through which flows a turbid stream of slimes and tailings, from the mills that are huddled against its massive walls. There is a draught of air through this cañon, as if it had been blown through a funnel, and in winter time one is glad to emerge into the open country above, and from the hill-tops look down upon the busy life of the cañon. Presently one enters the great gorge in which Silver City is placed. Here a continual scene of activity meets the eye. The clangor of mills and of the forges, of foundries and work-shops, sounds on the ear, and above all the oaths of scores of teamsters, urging forward their straining mules.

Here as elsewhere there are a goodly number of saloons and drinking shops. One is, indeed, inclined to think that these compose the town, until a glance at the neighboring hills reveals small wooden houses, perched here and there upon apparently almost inaccessible peaks.

A mile or two devoted to mills and sluices brings us to Gold Hill. A deeper gorge, more houses, a series of mining works, more houses, more dumps of ore, more teams, more drivers, and more oaths. These make up the town, and driving across the divide, whence is obtained a magnificent view of the country we have passed over in our drive, and also a peep of the desert stretching towards Fort Churchill, we enter the city that lies on the slope of great Mount Davidson.

I must confess I liked Virginia better when the veins of the Comstock were less depleted. The yawning galleries of the Savage—the Chollar-Potosi—the Gould and Curry, the Ophir, and a host of other mines, warn us of land caves, and the tremor of some sudden settling seems to cry to us to flee from the wrath to come. Still, while there is an ounce of silver under its foundation, Virginia will not be forsaken.

John comes up from the lowest depths of the mine, where he daily runs the risk of suffocation by the extreme heat, besides other chances of death by the caving in of a gallery, or the slipping of the cage, and says this is the dreariest place in the world. He even says some harsher things, which I dare not repeat, and then he changes his clothes, and drives off to a mill in the cañon, or upon the river. I chance to meet him on C Street, in the course of the day, so busily engaged in conning the stock report, or talking "rock" with some eager millman, that he does not see me. However, that makes no difference, as I am going to a lunch party, and afterwards to call upon a friend, and do a little shopping.

It is curious that we all protest against lunch parties, yet continue to give and attend them. It is stupid to dress in one's newest silk, and handsomest corals to partake of chicken, creams, ices, and Champagne, with a dozen of one's own sex. Who can help being painfully conscious that each and every one of them have priced the silk at Rosener's, and the corals at Nye's, before they came to one's wearing. It is a trying thing for one's dress to be subjected to the test of its value, not of its adaptability, or becomingness.

However, there is a consolation for this last grief in knowing that Mrs. L's chicken is no more tender than it should be, and that her cream is not well frozen, and to learn besides that Mrs. R has quite decided to divorce her husband, because he lost a hundred thousand in his last speculation in K. Then, too, one learns the name of the next school-marm who is to be married, and that Mr. G has sent away that young lady whom we really would not consent to call upon, and has been introduced into society again by the charming Mrs. Y. All these entertaining articles of conversation, perhaps, account for the existence of lunch parties, and, besides, they help to exhibit the superiority of one's cook. Meanwhile John—still busied in discussing "stocks," or "rock," has lunched down town, and has refused one offer to "take a drink," and accepted a dozen. I pass him at the corner on my way home, and the youngest member of the group, of which he is the centre, leaves it and accompanies me home.

John is generally punctual at dinner; he knows that Bridget will scorn me and her forty or fifty dollar wage if he is not, and leave us in the lurch. Sometimes he annoys her by bringing a friend or two, and she threatens to leave, but, however, my humility generally conquers her ruffled dignity. I am very fortunate in this respect, for I have only had five different cooks within the last year.

After dinner John goes down town, just to see S for a moment, and settle about that little speculation they think of going into. I have heard of games of "poker" and such enormities in connection with these nightly business meetings, and I have a shrewd suspicion of billiards. But John tells me that though the rest of "the fellows" do indulge in those recreations, his hours, torn from his wife and children, are religiously devoted to business.

John seldom finds time to go to balls and parties, and it used to trouble me at first, especially as I had an unnatural craving for such things, caused by the many evenings John's business calls compelled me to remain alone. But presently I found that the unmarried men were not so closely employed as their encumbered brethren, and that it was their allotted duty to become the escorts of the ladies, while their lawful knights remained in billiard halls and club rooms to battle on their behalf with the fickle goddess fortune.

This proves an excellent arrangement where one's husband is old or disagreeable, or even where there are no such drawbacks, greatly lessens the chances of domestic feuds, by rendering impossible that familiarity which is said to breed contempt.

But does it not give rise to scandal? Certainly, but people must have something to talk about, and Mrs. V's open flirtation forms a pleasant variety to comments upon Mrs. L's dress, or her last failure at the Choral Society. You remember when Nelly Brookes became Mrs. Monkton, and went to Hillston to live, she found that her claim to respectability could only be established by her admission to the Choral Society. Seemingly, the same wise rule obtains here, for whether we can sing or not we try to do so on each Thursday night. Most of our attendant young gentlemen fidget through the singing, and only begin to enjoy themselves when dancing commences. In contrast to these parties, which the young men declare to be "neither fish nor flesh," we have club parties and public balls, interspersed with private card and dinner parties. And we are all very gay and fashionable—exhibiting our diamonds and laces to the eyes of rival mine and millmen's wives and daughters with as much eagerness as would a New York or Parisian belle.

Have I succeeded in convincing you that times have changed here, since Ross Browne wrote, or Mark Twain taxed his brain for horrible and fictitious locals? True, the hotels are nearly as bad as ever, and there are quite as many saloons. But a "man for breakfast" is not now to be had every day, and ladies of the *demi-monde* no longer expect to eat the dinners, and grace the parties of the *haut ton*.

We Virginians are a church-loving people, too, and although we do not endeavor to rival Carson in the number of our festivals (for there, it is said, if two strangers are seen to enter, a festival is improvised for their benefit), yet our churches wax rich and strong. Curiously enough, the religion of a family here appears in a great measure to be performed by proxy. Often the children by constant attendance at the well-organized Sunday-school do duty for both parents; but more frequently still the wife appears both in her own behalf and that of the husband, who is busy underground preparing his stock report, or driving through the cañon, crowded with quartz teams, towards his mill.

In fact, the entire religious and social life of Nevada is conducted by ladies. The lords of creation are mere money-making machines, with apparently no other human attributes than a hasty appreciation of a good dinner, the hope of a fortune, and of a home "at the bay," or in the dimly remembered East.

But this latter idea is absurd; no man who has ever breathed the air of excitement and speculation of Nevada can live and be content in the quiet of his Eastern birthplace. There is a charm in these rugged mountains which calls him back. It is not love of the glittering dross within them, but the bustle and activity which that dross awakens. There is a saying that one who has been in Nevada can never die until he returns to it.

We ladies say it is the charm of the cloudless skies that draws us back, after our annual visit to "the bay," and makes us gladly bear the discomforts or horrors of the journey across the rugged Sierras, to reach our homes over the catacombs beneath the streets of Virginia, or high upon the bleak sides of stern Mount Davidson.

But there are whispers now that there are fairer skies, and hills as rugged, and mines far richer, three hundred miles deeper in the heart of this great State. John has been there and says it's so. And there are dreadful warnings that this, the city we have built, is to be but of a day; that Virginia City and the region of the Comstock will yet be but a howling wilderness. But I, and the new railway company, know better than that; we are not going to sacrifice our household gods, or our certificates of stock, and rush to the wilds of White Pine. We complacently leave the outside barbarians to the snows of Treasure Hill, and declare that until the spring, at least, Virginia will not prove too civilized for us.

Louise Palmer, "How we live in Nevada," *Overland Monthly* (May 1869), pp. 457–62.

Part Two

The High Plains and Rocky Mountains, 1870–1890

As in California, the settlement of the Rocky Mountain frontier began with gold rushes in the 1860s and 1870s in Colorado, Montana, and Idaho. Mining remained an important industry in both areas, but in other respects the regional economies were very different. No other state or region had the luxurious abundance and diversity of California.

In the Rocky Mountains and high plains, aridity and high altitude created a much less temperate climate than in the Golden State. Whereas the hazards of pioneering in California were social and economic, those in the mountains were physical as well. Authors write of drought, tornadoes, winter blizzards, and dangerous travel through the mountains. Coming to terms with the land itself was a major aspect of the settlement experience.

Responses to that physical challenge varied among the women whose narratives appear in this section. Some rose to the challenge of harsh weather and primitive conditions, and some did not. In many ways, the failures are more interesting than the successes. Annie Green's dislike of the Union Colony in Colorado stemmed mostly from her belief that she was being forced to do things that were too hard for a woman to do. Sometimes this was a matter of physical strength, but often she simply found them inappropriate for *her* to do. Always there is her perception that the settlement itself was a mistake based on unrealistic male fantasies. She was at least partly right.

Dryland homesteading and ranching were distinctively new occupations in the high plains region. Homesteading was particularly arduous because of the marginal land; settlers expecting eastern farming conditions were unprepared for the aridity and harsh climate west of the ninety-eighth parallel. The Homestead Act of 1862, which had made such free land available, required continuous residence on the homestead claim, and this often condemned women and children to months of isolation while

Hunting. Finetta Lord's successful shot, photographed by her husband. Courtesy of the Montana Historical Society.

men worked elsewhere for needed cash. The "romance of pioneering" did not extend to the realities of tar paper shacks, no water, inadequate food, climatic extremes, and primitive transportation.

Ranching was more appropriate for the environment. As railroads and stockyards crept westward from Chicago, a market for meat in addition to hides developed in the expanding post-Civil War population. The first cattle ranchers could reap greater fortunes from the vast free grasslands than could gold miners.

Ranching bred its own life-style, along with that quintessential western hero, the cowboy. Herding cattle was a male enterprise, so much that it could spawn the dire warnings about cowboys that Sister Segale (whose memoir is included in the final section) found so humorous after she arrived in the West. It was difficult for women to find useful roles outside of the kitchen on a cattle ranch, unless they were, like Mrs. Nat Collins, the actual owners. Women did ride and shoot and help out with animals, within recognized limits established according to age and marital status, but they were more likely to be cooks and housekeepers even on the range. Or they might be wealthy hostesses and "financiers," like Mrs. Collins.

The challenge of the mountain environment also seems to have exaggerated the mobility so common to all frontier living. For Collins and Mary Ronan, frequent moves were common during their pioneer girlhoods and might account for their equanimity in the face of difficulties. Many women left destitute by disaster, desertion, divorce, or widowhood needed to make a living for themselves; this was the case with Collins before her marriage and the enterprising Malinda Jenkins. They searched for relatives across great distances or followed the advice of friends about job opportunities many miles away.

The shortage of female labor on isolated ranches or in rudimentary cities made housekeeping, nursing, and cooking lucrative sources of income, which could then be used to buy and sell property for further profits. If things didn't work out in one place, such working women were as free—or as constrained—as men were; they moved on to another place and job as quickly as possible. Fortunate ones might even discover old neighbors in the new places and find, as did Jenkins, that the "big world" was really small.

Another challenge of the Rocky Mountain region was from American Indians whose land was being invaded by white settlers and gold seekers. Mary Ronan's fair-minded reminiscence about life on the Flathead Indian reservation, along with Sarah Winnemucca's description of her tribe's forced winter march to be resettled on a reservation already occupied by a rival tribal group, offers a rare glimpse of the American Indian experience. Most whites paid no attention to the treaties that were supposed to guarantee Indian land rights. The "settlement" process experienced by whites was just the opposite for American Indians; they were *unsettled* by the destruction of their way of life and forcible removal from their traditional homes.

"$800,000 Worth of Gold Dust"

Augusta Pierce Tabor (1833–95) was born in Augusta, Maine, a third daughter among ten children. She married Horace Tabor, an ambitious stonecutter who worked for her father, and they moved to Kansas in 1857 with the support of the anti-slavery New England Emigrant Aid Company. Horace became a member of Kansas's first free-state legislature, a role that he would repeat when he later became a prominent Colorado politician. The following memoir, in which Augusta tells about their participation in the Colorado gold rush of 1859, was passed down to her great-grandson Philippe Laforgue of Versailles, France. For twenty years, Augusta continued to run boarding houses and tend post offices, carefully saving and investing and keeping financial records. She was helping her husband run a store in Leadville when local prospectors, with his support, hit the "fabulously rich" Little Pittsburg silver mine. The Tabors became millionaires overnight; their winnings continued in other mines for several more years.

Frugal, egalitarian Augusta did not like the lavish lifestyle that Horace now adopted. He opposed striking miners, she favored them. He took up drinking and gambling, she entertained old friends and servants in the mansion that he wanted to reserve for the elite. He turned their finances over to a hired bookkeeper and became a notorious womanizer. In 1878 Horace was elected lieutenant governor and in 1882 U. S. senator. He built an opera house in Denver, but he separated from Augusta and refused to escort his wife to the opening. Finally they divorced and Horace staged a flamboyant Washington wedding to the notorious "Baby Doe."

In her later years Augusta founded and supported the Pioneer Ladies' Aid Society, providing assistance to poor or despairing women who had been early territorial settlers and were now bereft. Horace died of appendicitis in 1899 without even money enough to pay for a funeral. Baby Doe froze to death in a mining shack in 1935.

*I*n February 1859, Mr. T. first heard of Pike's Peak through some one of Green Russell's party who was returning. He concluded to try his luck. He told me that I might go home, but I refused to go, and upon second thought he concluded that it would be best to take me, for if he took me to cook, he could get those two men that had been with us all the time to go and board with us, and their money would keep all four of us. Mr. T. worked at the Fort through March and April to get the money to outfit us for the trip.

The fifth day of May we yoked our cattle, our cows and a pair or two of year-old steers; gathered up our scanty means; bought a few months' supplies; baby and I climbed into the wagon; the two gents mounted the seat in front; Mr. T. took the whip and we left the town of Zeandale with the determination of returning in the fall, or when we had made money enough to pay for the 160 acres of land and buy a little herd of cattle.

What I endured on the plains only those that crossed in '59 know. There was no station until we got to within 80 miles of D. [Denver]—no road a good part of the way. I was weak and feeble, having nearly shaken myself to death with fever and ague in Kansas. . . . I had to cook for all our party and I did not find it a pleasure. Sometimes the wind would blow furiously and it is not very pleasant to cook over a camp fire in a wind storm when that fire is made of buffalo chips and every gust of wind would carry them over the barren prairie. By the time I would get them gathered together, another puff (and so on, lasting three or four days).

Every Sunday we rested, if rested it could be called. The men would go hunting, while I would cook, wash and iron, which kept me employed all day. My baby was teething and was sick all the way across, which, with my other work, made it hard for me.

We arrived in Denver somewhere between the 16th and 20th day of June, camped on the Platte River near where the West Side Bridge now stands. The cattle were footsore and we were obliged to stay until the 1st of July. Then we moved on up Clear Creek where the town of Golden now stands. Some one had come down from the Gregory Diggings from whom our men inquired the way to the Diggings.

Leaving me in the 7 x 9 tent to watch the cattle and keep them from straying, and with a baby to take care of, the three men took a supply of provisions upon their backs, a few blankets and telling me to be good to myself left on the Glorious Fourth. How sadly I felt, none but my God knew. Every morning and eve I had a round-up all to myself. There were no cowboys for me to shoot, cut and slash with then.

Three long, weary weeks I kept watch and ward. At the expiration of that time the men returned, and the 26th day of July we loaded up the wagon and started into the mountains. The road was a mere trail. At every few rods we were obliged to stop and widen the road so as to get the wagon through. Many hills we were obliged to take everything from the wagon and then help the oxen to get the wagon up, the men carrying the goods as best they could. In going down hill it was much easier, as it always is. We would often fasten a tree to the back of the wagon and drag it for a hold-back, or brake, down the hill. When night overtook us we were often in a place where we could not find a level place to spread our blankets. So we would drive stakes into the ground, roll a log against them, then lay with feet against the log and sleep, oh so sweetly, with Mother Earth for a bed and the blue sky for a roof.

We were nearly three weeks cutting our way down through Russell's Gulch, taking the first wagon through onto Pain's [sic] Bar, now known as Idaho [Idaho Springs]. We arrived there about the middle, or 20th of August. There was no woman there but many prospectors. The men cut trees or logs, laid them up four feet in height, mounted the tent on top for a roof, making me a comfortable 7 x 9 house.

Mr. T. went on to Spanish Bar and went prospecting. I opened an eating house; also made pies and bread to sell, and sold milk from the cows we had driven across the plains. I was very busy every moment from early morn until late at night, finding much more than busy hands could do.

With the 25th of September came the first snow, a few inches. An old Cal. miner came into camp and told Mr. T. that it would not do to keep a woman in the mountains in the winter. Said there would be fearful snow slides and we would be buried alive. Just think of it, you who have visited Idaho Springs. Snow slides from those foothills! Common sense ought to have told us better, but we had never seen a mountain, only as we passed through the Alleghanies en route West, and believing all an old miner would tell us, we pulled our tent and traveled toward Denver.

I had had what we called a profitable summer. I had made enough to pay for the farm and to keep us through the winter. Had found a trustworthy young man that would take the money and a dog that we had brought with us from home, one that I had raised back on the farm in Kansas. I did not feel able to feed the dog through the winter with the cheapest article of food that could be bought at 25 cents a pound and upward. So with many a sigh, I parted with my faithful "Petty."

Arriving at Denver, we took a room over Vasques' store. There was one window, a rough board floor, the roof reached to the floor—for which we paid $25 a month. The first house that I had been into for six months.

Mr. T. returned to his prospect hole and found it jumped. Might was right in those times. So he lost all his summer's time and had to sell the cow to raise money to get a new supply of groceries, as he wanted to go to a new camp that was much talked of.

The 14th day of February, 1860, we once more put our all into the wagon and I was lifted from a bed of sickness and laid upon the wagon and we left Denver, this time taking four men along. We drove out to a place about ten miles called Montana and camped. There were a few deserted huts, and we went into one for the night. No floor, no windows, nor door. I slept on the ground that night and awoke early, feeling better than when in Denver.

We were four days going down to where Manitou now stands. We camped near the Soda Springs and I mixed biscuits with some water. They were yellow and tasted so strongly of soda that we, with our outdoor appetites, did not relish them.

We lingered there one week, the men doing a little prospecting and some of them working upon the road up the Ute Pass. We started up into the mountains over the new road and for several days we made such slow progress that we could look back to the last night's camp smoke. The men worked hard to get the first wagon over the road. The weather was changeable, a few inches of snow falling nearly every night. I speak of this, for it made it wet and sloppy cooking over a camp fire, and my health was very poor that spring. We were two long, weary weeks getting up to the South Park. I shall never forget how beautiful the Park looked which I first beheld it. The sun was just setting, its beautiful rays reflected back, tinging the whole heavens with crimson and yellow clouds. It looked like a cultivated field with rivulets running through and herds of antelope; in the distance Weston Pass, and I beheld and wondered and exclaimed, "Who made this, O God!"

Then we drove down and camped on the bank of a stream now called Jefferson Creek. The men went up the stream, and I went to washing soiled clothes in the clear, running creek. We wandered around in the Park several days, trying to find the tracks of a party of miners that had come in over Kenosha Hill. We knew them when they left Denver. They had a packed jack [ass]. We could find no trace of them.

About the fourth day in the Park, we came to Salt Creek late at night. We tried the water and found that we could not let the cattle drink from the stream. Neither could we use it ourselves. So another night we retired hungry and thirsty. The wind blew furiously. . . . The night was cold. . . . A jack came to our tent door and stood in the hot embers of the campfire until he singed his ankles and the odor that was wafted into our tent was anything but refreshing. The men drew their carbines and watched for guerillas, and many were the conjectures as to whom he belonged. He stayed with us to the end of our trip and hours he carried babe and myself on his back.

We moved on next day toward water and camped on Trout Creek. The men shouldered their muskets and went in search of our Denver friends, one man going each way. The one that found the party was to fire off his gun. All day long I listened for the report and when night came I felt desolate indeed, alone with a babe, without a dog. How bitterly I lamented having sent my "Petty" away. The jack came into the tent and laid down. I was even glad of his company. I laid my head down upon him and cried with loneliness. The men had gone farther than they thought before turning, and it was midnight before they found camp and would not have found it at all but for the fire I kept burning. They did not find the trail, so we concluded to follow the stream downward. . . .

The river was rapid, with many large boulders, around which clung cakes of ice. We found what we thought was the best fording place and drove our oxen in. The water was icy cold. The cattle were thin, weak and tired and they halted in the middle of the river, and any amount of driving would not make them go. We shouted "Whoa, Ha" and "Gee, Ha" but to no avail. The men plunged into that cold stream, which was waist deep, tied ropes to their horns, went onto the shore opposite and tried to drag them along. They were numb with cold and would not heed. The men were obliged to unload the wagon, putting the goods upon the ice, not knowing but it might move downward any moment; unyoke the cattle, drag the wagon over and the oxen, too, return and carry the goods. The faithful little jack carried baby and me, although he could only keep his nose above water.

We were six hours in crossing the Arkansas River. We started a camp fire and dried ourselves and nursed the cattle all night long. We felt that we must save them, for our supply of food was getting low and we should have to eat them before long. Stopping about this place a week or more, one man would fish, one hunt and the other would take a pan and shovel and wash out dirt, always finding a few specks of gold to a pan of dirt. Our evenings were passed in playing cards and relating home news.

Our next move was to follow up the river. After many hard days over steep, rocky hills, we camped where Cache Creek empties into the Arkansas. Here we pitched our tent and went to work in earnest. Mr. T. and Maxcy whip-sawed some [boards], made two sluice boxes, sawed riffles from a log, made a ditch from the creek and commenced to work the bank away. Cleaning the boxes up every night, we found plenty of fine gold but more black sand and being new at mining, knew no way to separate the gold from the sand only with the slow process of lifting the iron sand with a small magnet. Every day I would work hard trying to separate the metals and when night came I would weigh my day's worth and find that I had only a few pennyweights of gold. Four weeks we tarried and worked this way. Our provision was gone. We were depending upon the aim of our guns for food. Our bill of fare for breakfast was broiled venison, fried mountain sheep. Dinner: venison roast, boiled mountain mutton. Supper: Fried venison, baked sheep.

We were getting discouraged when one morning we saw a man coming toward camp, riding a jack, being attracted by our camp. Our prayer was that he could speak English. He arrived and seemed surprised to see a woman in camp. He told us to move on up 20 miles or more across the river and turn up a gulch after passing a huge bald mountain: that he was with a party that had found gold in paying quantities; that it was coarse and easily separated from the black sand. At first we were doubtful, but he showed about an ounce in small nuggets. Said that he was going for supplies.

The next morning we left the camp. . . . We saw the bald mountain from the opposite side of the river, and plunged in. The river looked broad and shallow. When near the opposite bank, we came into a deep channel, our wagon bed raised above the wheels and floated down stream, myself and child in it. It was rapidly filling with water when the thought occurred to me to cling to the willows on the bank. I did so and held fast until the men who were coming on the shore rescued us. I knew nothing more until we were at the mouth of California Gulch.

We followed the stream up about six miles, passed the discoverers who were down on the stream at work while we were working our way through the thick timber.

This was the 8th day of May nearly three months since we left Denver. The first thing after we arrived was to kill the faithful old oxen that had brought us through and divide the beef with these miners that were there, they, too, being out of grub. Before night they had me a log cabin built. I think it was 12 x 18 feet—no door, nor window, no floor save the earth. I entered the place feeling queenly.

I at once commenced work, taking boarders, with nothing to eat but poor beef and dried apples. But this only lasted three days, for the man that had passed us en route for Denver met a pack train coming from New Mexico to Denver through the mountain pass. He persuaded them to go with him to the mountains with flour for which we paid $60 a sack, and it was one with sand.

We took our wagon bed to make some furniture, such as a table, sideboard, and the top to make three legged stools, to sit upon. But it mattered but little what we sat upon, for the only time that we sat down was when at our meals. There was work and good pay for it.

With the pack train that returned, word went that California Gulch had very rich diggings. Then came the rush of people. Before three months there were 10,000 people in the Gulch. A mail and express had been started— letters 75 cents each, express equally as high and they were kept at my cabin. Probably no other woman would be bothered with the crowd that it drew. I also had the only gold scales in the upper part of the Gulch, where we were centrally located, so I was called upon every evening to weigh gold dust for an hour or more.

When the men would clean up their sluice boxes for the day, they would go to town where Leadville now stands and gamble it all away, come home and try it again the next day. During the month from May to July, I weighed $80,000 worth of gold dust that was taken out of No. 20 above Discovery for Pat Wells and Jack Langon. Our claim was No. 21 above. I had the offer of No. 20 if I would board the owner for the summer when he was in the Gulch. He wanted to run an express from Denver.

When September came we had cleared $4000 from the diggings and my work. It seemed but little compared to what our neighbors had taken out. But it was so much more than we had ever had that we were satisfied.

From "Reminiscenses of Mrs. Augusta Tabor," in Betty Moynihan, *Augusta Tabor: A Pioneering Woman* (Boulder, Colo.: Johnson Books, 1988), pp. 118–125.

"I resolved to try and be cheerful"

MRS. A. M. GREEN

12

The Greens were members of an 1870 homesteading experiment, Colorado's Union Colony, sponsored by Horace Greeley and promoted through his *New York Tribune* articles. Encouraging westward migration as an opportunity for any ambitious young man of the East, neither Greeley nor many of those who took his advice had the kind of knowledge or practical skills to understand the land or the climate they were heading for. It was that eastern audience for which Mrs. Green wrote her book.

Annie Green had insisted on coming with her husband rather than let him go alone, but there were many times, she said, when she "wept and prayed to God for a change" in her "wretched life, winding up with a wish that . . . the founders of Union Colony" were " in the bottom of the sea." Consistently resourceful, despite her unhappiness, she tells with ironic humor about starting a bakery and trying to keep it secret from her idealistic husband, who disapproved of women working for money. She also opened a school, nursed her children and husband and friends through severe illnesses, had mountain fever herself, and endured several natural disasters. But she never accepted the primitive housing, harsh weather, and loneliness, conditions which she felt had been imposed upon her by the impractical choices of male reformers and their followers.

O f the founder of this place I have nothing to say except that I regret the sad manner in which he came to his death, for I really believe he was a very pure minded man, and one who sought the good of his fellow beings. After securing several lots in the new town, we pitched our tent, which was almost daily blown to the ground. To say that I was homesick, discouraged and lonely, is but a faint description of my feelings.

It was one of those terrible gloomy days that I sat in my lonely tent with my baby, Frank, in my arms, who was crying from the effects produced by the sands of the American desert, while beside my knee stood my little Sisy, (as we called her) trying to comfort her brother by saying: "Don't cry, F'ankie, we is all going back to grandpa's pitty soon, ain't we, mamma?" Not receiving an immediate answer from me, she raised her eyes to mine, from which gushed a fountain of burning tears. "Don't cry, mamma," said she; "sing to F'ank like you always does, and he will stop crying." I obeyed the child's request. . . .

As I closed my song the curtain raised and my husband entered, sank wearily on a three-legged stool and took up our little five-year-old, placed her upon his tired knee and then addressed me thus: "Well, dear, how do you get along to-day? I see the tent hasn't blown down." I attempted to answer in the negative, but failed, the meaning of which he comprehended in a moment. Notwithstanding any vain attempts to conceal my emotion, he pressed to his sad heart the little charge which he held in his arms, saying in a low voice: "Darling little one, you and your poor mamma have hard times, don't you? Then turning to me, he said: "Annie, I am very sorry for you. If I had compelled you to come to this country I could never forgive myself; as it is, I feel that you reflect on me." By this time I had regained my speech and endeavored with all my might, mind and strength to convince him to the contrary. Whether I succeeded or not I never knew, but I resolved there and then to cultivate a cheerful disposition, which I believe has prolonged my life, for, at the rate I was going into dispair at that time, I could not have retained my reason six month's longer, and doubtless the brittle thread of life would have been snapped long ere this. O how thankful I am that I still live to love, work and care for those whom to me are dearer than life itself! If I have one wish above another in this world, it is that I may live a long and useful life.

But I have wandered, and must return to that lonely little tent which was my first residence in Colorado. This we only occupied about a fortnight, when we procured a small cottage from a Minnesota gentleman, who had become sick of his bargain, and wished to return to his wife who had wisely remained in her happy home. Oh, how I reproached myself for not having done likewise! But I remembered the true saying that, "It is no use to mourn over spilled milk," and I tried to make the best of my mistake. Here we were truly strangers in a strange land. Mr. G. W. Beers, the only one who had accompanied us from our home, had tarried but a few days, then, bidding us an affectionate farewell, turned his back on Greeley and Union Colony in disgust.

I had made the acquaintance of a very dear lady, who, with her husband, had joined us at Meadville, Pa., which was their starting point for Colorado, and they, being members of the Union Colony, soon gained a prominent place in our hearts. We spoke to each other of our future prospects, mingled with hopes and fears. And now that our friend Mr. Beers had left us, I appreciated their friendship still the more. They, too, like ourselves, had purchased a small cottage with a vague prospect of one day being able to build a larger and more inviting one. But, alas! what short-sighted mortals we are, as this case will prove, for in less than five weeks from that time the dear Mrs. Lyon (as that was the name of my highly esteemed friend) was a lifeless corpse.

It was June 7th that we left the dreary little tent and took up our abode in the small cottage, of which I have heretofore spoken. I resolved now to do something to aid my husband in a pecuniary way. The first thing which presented itself to my mind was that of teaching school, and as there was no school house in the place, I determined to convert my house into one, providing I should succeed in getting a school, therefore I set myself to work. I canvassed the town successfully; the result of two days work gave me the position of teacher.

I remember vividly the first morning of my school. It reminded me of other days when I was engaged in the same pleasant occupation; but this was not to last. I had been teaching but two short weeks when the dear Mrs. Lyon, of whom I have spoken, was taken seriously ill with pneumonia. Her husband realizing that her case was helpless, requested me to give her my immediate and undivided attention, to which I consented; consequently I was obliged to give up my pleasant little school, which I did very reluctantly.

On the 3d of July, 1870, Mr. Lyon left us with the remains of his devoted and loving wife, for the home which she had so recently left with a spirit buoyant with hopes, now crushed forever. I will not attempt to describe the anguish of my heart on that memorable event, suffice to say, it was gloomy in the superlative degree. The next morning brought the first "Independence Day" ever celebrated in the far famed town of Greeley; yes, it was the glorious Fourth of July; most of the people repaired to Island

Park, a beautiful grove situated on the Cach la Poudre, and enjoyed a basket picnic together, after which speeches were made, poems read, sighs heaved, and no doubt many, many tears shed. In conclusion a beautiful song was sung by the Inman brothers of their own composing, entitled, "Greeley is My Home." I tried with all my soul to feel that it was my home, but vain were my attempts—no, no. I would ask myself the question, "How can I ever call this place my home?" At the close of that long ago Fourth of July, which seems to me a lifetime, though not quite eleven years since, I received a letter of inquiry from a friend of mine, in regard to Colorado; stating that if I considered it a number one country, to write and let her know, and if possible, she would join me in less than a month. Now I would have given almost everything I possessed to have had that friend with me, but I could not think of deceiving her in order to gratify my desire.

The 7th of July was Sabbath, and in those days I was usually found under the droppings of the sanctuary, for, though there was not a church in the town, we had regular services every Sabbath in the Union Colony Hall; but this morning I felt so depressed in spirits that I dispensed with going, and busied myself in writing to those for whom my heart panted continually. I had finished my third letter, closing up with a fervent prayer to Him whom I had been taught to believe would hear and answer the prayer of faith, for the preservation of my life, and also for those to whom I had been writing, until we should meet again (?) when the word *never, never,* sounded in my ear, and penetrated my aching heart with an arrow, the effect of which I feel to this day. At that moment my little girl approached me bearing in her hand the picture of her who loved me first and best on earth. I took it from the child, pressed it to my quivering lips, and cried: Oh, God, bereave me not of her! Until this time I had not ventured to open our album, but now that the ice was broken, I looked it through while tears gushed from my eyes. During this terrible emotion my husband returned from church, and again found me in tears and deep sorrow. This added pain to his already desponding heart. "Annie," said he, with a self-reproaching look, and in a pathetic tone which I shall never forget, "do you know you are killing me?" "I thought," he continued, "you had resolved to cultivate a more cheerful disposition; this will not do; it is cruel in the extreme for me to compel you to remain where you are so unhappy." My heart bounded for joy; and then, my pulse stood still to listen for the much longed for sentence,—we will go home; but, alas! it came in the singular number; "you must go home." "What!" I cried, "go without you, no, never;" and I repeat those words to-day; and ever shall, so long as circumstances control my husband's freedom. Again I resolved to try and be cheerful, but, my resolution and promise were but to be broken in less than twenty-four hours. On this occasion the physician was summoned and my disease pronounced mountain fever, from which I recovered, after an illness of six weeks. During all my affliction I had answered each letter from home without intimating that I was out of health, until the shortness of my communications excited their attention, and they demanded an explanation, which I was obliged to give.

It was now August, but oh! how different from any one which I had ever witnessed. Not a tree, plant nor shrub on which to rest my weary eye, to break the monotony of the sand beds and cactus of the Great American Desert. My attention was often called to the grandeur of the snow capped Rocky Mountains, towering toward the skies; and although I sometimes feigned an appreciation of their beauty in order to coincide with my other half, who displayed much anxiety to have me admire something in Colorado, I speak the truth when I say that the sun, moon, or stars never put on that brilliant appearance in my western home as they did in the land of my nativity.

About the first of September we were favored with a visit from that great man of renown, for whom we had the honor of naming our town; he announced before leaving the depot that he would address the people of Greeley at one o'clock p.m. The word was hastily dispatched through the village, and every Greeleyite was out to see and hear the old white hat, white hair and white coat philosopher. He discoursed largely on the art of irrigation, which was a subject of vast interest to us; he expressed a regret on seeing so many buildings in the town, and so few on the prairies: and closed by advising some of us to go without delay and erect cabins on our ranches. When he finished speaking there was a general rush to speak to, and shake hands with him; but on account of the throng I did not avail myself of the privilege, but was much pleased with his appearance, and his speech, which was the all absorbing topic for weeks. He tarried but a short time in the west, then returned to his home in New York; this was his last trip to Colorado.

September and October had passed away without the falling of a leaf, from a single tree, in our desolate little town, when the bright sun, of a November morning shown in through the window of a neat little cottage, which had just been finished, of which I confess, I felt proud. It afforded but three small rooms, yet it was a palace compared with the one which we had just left. "It is large enough" said I to my husband, "to take in boarders, and that is the best paying business in this town." With a look of surprise he exclaimed, "large enough,—nonsense, besides you are not able to do so if the house was twice as large." "But," I continued, "keeping boarders would help to pass the time away and you know I am so lonely." I was about to say "perhaps we can rent our house next winter, and go home until spring," but the answer came, I know not from whence, but it came in these words:

Oh! why, oh! why, should you repine
For blessings which will ne'er be thine?

I was at this moment aroused from my reverie by the shrill whistle, which announced the arrival of the Eastern train, and, as it was Saturday evening, I felt sure the mail contained one or more letters for me, as up to this time I had kept a regular correspondence with one of my sisters, with whom I had agreed to exchange communications weekly. I now forgot all around me except my husband, whom I urged with impatience to go for the mail, which he did in a very few moments and returned unusually soon, but, to my indescribable disappointment, had no letter for me. I readily understood the reason why, for I well knew that nothing short of sickness or death would prevent my sister from performing that which she had pledged her word to do. Oh, the awful suspense which I was subjected to during the next week! . . . Reader, have you ever experienced the untold misery of receiving a message draped in mourning? If you have, I need not solicit your sympathy, and if you have not I pray God you may never realize it as I have. Here let the curtain drop, the subject is too painful to dwell upon longer.

It was Sabbath night of this same month; all nature had sunk to rest; not a sound save that of the coyote, which howled in the distance, when lo! the terrible cry, *fire!* FIRE! rang out upon the stillness of the air. We had retired, perhaps an hour since, and the family, all except myself, were wrapped in the arms of Morpheus. I had allowed my mind to wander back to the happy days of the past until sleep forsook my moistened eyelids; but the cry of fire brought me instantly from my bed. I was followed by my frightened and bewildered husband, who rushed into the street half dressed. By this time I could discern the flames ascending from a hotel, only two doors from my cottage; every man and several ladies were soon on foot, and worked with energy until the flames were extinguished. The house, of which I speak, seems to have been dissatisfied with its location and disgusted with its surroundings, for, after four fruitless attempts to commit suicide, it succeeded in completing its design in 1879, and to-day a magnificent building is being erected on the ruins thereof. Ah, those were the days which tried the souls of the pioneers of Greeley.

It was during the spring of '71, the month I cannot give, neither is it necessary, the instance which I refer to is that of an attempt, which was made on Sunday by a party from Evans, (a sister village) to start a saloon, much against the wishes of the colonists who came here to found a temperance town. The building chosen for the purpose was an old cabin, built of sods, and thither an excited crowd gathered, after the morning services. Soon the building was discovered on fire, and the owner, which much difficulty, saved some of his stock in trade, and then concluded that it would not pay to make another effort, consequently the attempt was not repeated.

About the middle of March, in the same year, my husband, with several other men, engaged in prospecting for coal; the distance being about five miles from Greeley. I was compelled to live alone with my two little children. Oh, what a fearful undertaking it was for me, who had never passed a night without a protector, in the way of father, brother or husband! My husband knew how timid I was, and it caused him great sorrow to absent himself from home, a place more dear than any other on this earth, to a true and loving husband. But what could he do; we had then been living ten months out of pocket, and the prospects for the future were not at all flattering; hence it behooved us to sacrifice the happiness of which he had never before been deprived. Arrangements had been made with a young girl, aged thirteen, to stop with me at night, but, to my surprise and distress, I learned late in the evening of the first day after my husband's departure, that it was impossible for her to come. It was now dark and I was afraid to so much as look outside of the door. It was then that I realized, for the first time, that I occupied the responsible position of the head of a family. My heart beat with unusual rapidity, and my voice trembled as I begged the little ones, who had several times reminded me of my lonely situation by wishing papa would come, to be quiet, when, all of a sudden, I was brought to my feet by the sound of approaching footsteps, which halted at the door. Frantic with delight at the thought of my husband having returned so unexpectedly, my first impulse was that of flying to receive him, when thump, thump, came on my door in rapid succession. For a moment my tongue seemed palsied; but realizing that it would not better the matter to remain silent, I ventured to enquire who the intruder was, and also the nature of his business. Not receiving an immediate answer I repeated my demand. Horror of horrors! he wanted shelter for the night. I told him I was not prepared to entertain strangers, but if he would remain where he was a few moments, I would consult my husband, pretending that he (my husband) had just stepped into a neighbors. This he consented to do. I then took my two little charges and slipped out at my back door, flying in haste to the Greeley Hotel. I acquainted the proprietor of the affair, who soon went and informed the tramp that there was room for him at the hotel. After being assured that my unwelcome visitor was safely lodged, I returned home accompanied by one of the hotel girls, who remained with me through the night, but I did not indulge in sleep. I kept watch until the light of day dawned, when I dismissed my fears and sank into a sound repose, from which I did not awake until the sun was high in the heavens. I was then aroused by a rap at my door, which at first startled me, but after reflecting a moment I answered, then proceeded to arrange my toilet in haste and soon ascertained that my visitor was in search of bread. I directed him to the bakery, but he informed me that it was home made bread he was in search of. I told him I would bake bread for sale if I was sure I would have customers enough to make it pay. With this he appeared much delighted and assured me six to begin with. When I showed him one of my loaves he declared it was as large again as the baker's, besides he did not like their bread. After wishing my early visitor good morning, I proceeded to arrange matters as to engage in the capacity of a baker, and 'ere the sun sank behind the western horizon I had ten applicants for bread. When I finished the first sack of flour, I found that my profits amounted to four dollars, besides, I had gained the reputation of giving larger loaves than any other person engaged in the business in town. The only thing which I had to contend with was the anticipated disapproval of my husband in regard to my new enterprise, having heard him express himself in reference to my attempting to take boarders. I much feared the result would be a veto in this case. I therefore resolved to keep the secret from him as long as I could. The week passed by more rapidly than usual; every day brought new customers. I had baked the last of three sacks when Saturday came. This day was to bring my husband home, and O how glad I was, yet, how I feared that my secret would be divulged. I did not expect him until Saturday night and I knew he would only remain until Sabbath evening, or Monday morning, so I set myself to work to devise a plan to keep my customers away during his visit. I sent my two children to deliver the bread to each customer, requesting them not to come for more until Monday. When the last loaf was delivered and my little ones had returned home, I congratulated myself by saying: "The plan has worked like a charm."

"There comes papa! There comes papa!" cried the two children, "Let us run and meet him." With this they sprang out at the door and were soon encircled in their papa's arms, each doing his best to tell the most news and ask the most questions. After the usual "how do do's" and "how have you been?" were exchanged by my other half, and his better half, the little folks resumed: "O papa," said the younger. "Mind what mamma told you Frank," said his little sister endeavoring to put the child on his guard. "No I isn't going to tell papa not at all," said he. "Come children," said I, "you are monopolizing all of the time; mamma wants to talk." My husband, not being of suspicious disposition, took no notice of my embarrassment. Supper now being ready we all gathered around the table. I had not finished my first cup of tea, when a loud rap sounded at my front door. I instantly sprang up and hastened to receive my visitor. After bidding him good evening, I paused to learn his business. "I would like a couple of loaves of bread, ma'am, if you please," said he. "I have only bread enough, sir," said I, "to last me through the Sabbath;" and I turned to leave the stranger, but, he was not to be put off in this way. "Madam," said he, "perhaps I am not at the right place. Is this where Mrs. Green lives?" "It is," said I; "but there are more than one family of the Green's." "Is there, indeed, ma'am. Sure then I'm wrong, and I'll be after seeking them." I shut the door and returned to finish my supper. "Who was that and what did he want?" asked my husband. "O, a man hunting bread," said I, carelessly. "What brought him here hunting bread," said he, "does he not know where the bakery is? Strange," he continued, "that he should call at a private house?" I treated the affair with indifference and turned the subject to that of prospecting for coal. Everything went on in my favor until my little folks grew tired and sleepy and wished to go to bed. When the kiss good-night had been repeated, my little boy, wishing to assure me of his faithfulness, whispered in my ear loud enough to be heard across the room: "Mamma, I didn't tell papa, not at all." At this papa laughed heartily, for he well knew that he had a good joke on me. He did not ask the little fellow to divulge, as he feared it might teach him to break his promise, but he said to me: "'Murder will out,' won't it?" This compelled me to reveal the secret. When I had concluded he sighed, and then said: "Well if you think it best I have nothing to say." My heart sank within me and perhaps a tear glistened in my eye, but I brushed it away, saying: "You believe in 'Woman's Rights,' and I claim that it is my right and also my duty to aid you when I can, without interfering with my household affairs." He let me do the rest of the talking and I flattered myself that I convinced him. Sabbath I had several new applications for bread, but I informed them I would not keep my house open on God's day to sell them, therefore, they must get their supplies on Saturday to last until Monday.

Monday came, and my husband took his leave for the coalshaft. After relieving my lonely heart by indulging in a good cry, I bathed my head and eyes and then repaired to my daily task. While my bread was baking the thought occurred to me that I could use the fire for another purpose, at the same time, and, with coal at twelve dollars per ton, it was necessary to economize, and I determined to apply to the washer woman for ironing. This I did, and was quite successful. After resting awhile I, with my children, went out shopping, with the intention of returning in a few minutes, consequently, though carelessly, left my kitchen door unlocked; I, not being of a suspicious nature, apprehended no intrusion during my absence, and meeting with a friend of mine on the street accompanied her to her home. I had been there perhaps an hour and a half, when a knock was heard, and, in an instant, my name was called. This did not alarm me, for I supposed it was one of my bread customers; but I recognized the voice to be that of my next door neighbor, and, on seeing his face, I read at a glance that his mind was ill at ease. "Mrs. Green," said he, "You are wanted at home, and you must prepare yourself for a fearful sight." "My God!" I cried, "is my husband crushed? Oh, tell me quick in the name of mercy. Is he killed?" "No'm, my dear lady," said he, "it is nothing of that kind; but your house has been plundered." "Is that all?" I exclaimed with a frantic laugh.

"That is all," said he, "but when you see what has been done I guess you will think it quite enough." In this he was correct. When we reached the house, the first sight which met my eyes, was that of the doorstep covered with glass, and, on raising my eyes, I saw that every window pane from each window was gone. I went around to the back door and, oh, destruction! what a scene of desolation! The table had been turned upside down, smashing the bread and pies underneath it; my ironing accompanying them. By this time a crowd had gathered. One gentleman held in his hand one of my silver forks, which he had found across the street; another had several spools of silk, and cotton, and a third had a box of ribbons and lace collars, which he had found at the lower part of our garden. I pushed my way through the kitchen and entered the front room, when the sight left my eyes. Here I am again compelled to confess my carelessness, by acknowledging that I had left my trunks unlocked, and they had not escaped the fate of other articles; everything which they contained had been torn out, and lay on the floor. I had but one mirror in the house and that was smashed in pieces; my bedding was torn off of both bedsteads, and lay in the middle of the floor; my carpet, which was new, and had been put down a week previous, was covered by mud; my husband's watch, which he had left me, had been taken from under my pillow, and was lying on the floor, broken; our album, that had been filled previous to our leaving home in the east with precious pictures of our fathers, mothers, brothers and sisters, and many other dear ones, was found among the ruins, with every leaf torn out. Not having a book case I had converted one of our packing boxes into a stand, on which were piled about one hundred books; among others were two large volumes of the "American Conflict;" the cloth had been drawn from the stand and not one book remained to tell the fate of its companions, and to cap the climax, a gallon can of syrup had been strewn over almost every article in the room, including a black crepe bonnet and veil, for which I had paid thirteen dollars but two months before, also, a black silk dress; in short my entire wardrobe was literally ruined,—yet all this vanished into insignificance, when, on examining I found our most valuable books filled inside with adobe mortar, to such an extent as to render it impossible to remove by applying brush or cloth, therefore, I was obliged to use water. After washing and scraping those books, the reader may readily imagine that they were not very ornamental to a centre table. My neighbors all came in to condole with and assist me

Early days in the Greeley Colony. This community would have discouraged anyone. Courtesy of the Denver Public Library, Western History Department.

to restore order out of the most wonderful confusion I ever experienced. "But," says the anxious peruser, "don't make such a long story of it; tell us all about it; enemies, of course, and perfect fiends at that?" No indeed, they were too young to be either, as it was all done by three children, the eldest not being quite nine years of age. Now, this puzzles your brain, I know, and I cannot help you solve the problem. I have never been able to unravel the mystery myself; I only know that the parents of two of the children were intimate friends of ours; the other child's parents were comparatively strangers to me, but members of the colony. The children were detected while breaking the windows, and when asked what they were doing, replied: "O! having lots of fun." "But, what will Mrs. Green do when she finds this out?" said the man who addressed them. "Not anything," said the eldest. "We come here to play with her children every day, and she lets us do just as we please." I will say here as an apology for the children, that this is too true; I have always been too lenient and indulgent with other people's children, and it appears that those little folks took advantage of my kindness, for neither parents nor children owed me or one of my family a spark of ill will; nor did I ever change my behavior toward them from what it had been previous to my misfortune. "But," say you, "of course you recovered damages?" I answer, no; not to the amount of five dollars, notwithstanding several of the best men of Greeley estimated the damages at one hundred dollars; but, for lack of proof, that the child of the parents last referred to had been engaged in the mischief, the father of the same declined bearing his share of the damage, claiming that he did not believe his child had anything to do with the affair, except that she had received some articles from the boys who were engaged in the plunder; that she had only been a spectator, consequently, the conscientious father considered himself to be under no obligations to us, and said that whatever he might donate to make up for our loss, he should do only as an act of charity. When this reached my husband's ears, his indignation knew no bounds; whereupon he resolved to resent the cruel insult by giving vent to his exasperated feelings; he straightway repaired to the benevolent gentleman's office, and informed him that he was no object of charity, nor did he wish any of his contributions; he also gave him to understand that he had not the slightest doubt in his mind in regard to his child having been connected with the destruction of our property, and added: "Had I found her there, you would never have doubted it either, for," said he, "I would have switched her home, regardless of the result." The other two men being gentlemen of honor insisted on our accepting, at least two-thirds of the damages, but my husband's better judgment gave place to his sand, (as the old Colorado settlers say), and he utterly refused to receive anything in that direction. I will here say that the families of whom I have spoken as being special friends of ours, have ever remained the same, and, as regards my husband, in less than a week he had forgiven the one who robbed us of our just rights; but I cannot say as much of my spiteful nature, although you may stigmatize me as a resentful, unforgiving sinner, I never had one spark of love or respect for him, nor did I forgive him until I learned that he had fallen in that terrible massacre at White River. I suppress the names of each family, as the children are all living, though not residents of Greeley at present.

After a hard week's work, accompanied by many tears, I succeeded in replacing my soiled, indeed ruined household effects after a fashion, but I was so discouraged that I gave up my new employment and called it a grand fizzle.

About a week after this as I was hearing my children recite their lesson, I was interrupted by a call from a gentleman in search of a stopping place for himself, wife and little four-year-old, as he called their baby. I informed him of our inconvenience, to which he replied: "We can stand it if you can," adding, "we are not very hard to please, and my wife is tired of hotel life. If you will permit us to come we will do so at once." I paused but a moment and then said: "Well, sir, if you wish to risk it, all right." The gentleman assured me that I would be favorably impressed with his wife, and added: "Not wishing to flatter you, but I doubt not but that she will feel herself very much at home with you." Then wishing me a polite good morning, he departed, and in a short time returned with his wife and little daughter, Maggie, to take up their abode with me for the period of a month or six weeks. I found all in this lady that her husband had promised me. Her health improved so rapidly that at the expiration of six weeks she was able to resume her household work, notwithstanding she had been considered a confirmed invalid but two months previous to this time.

It was about the first of May, if my memory serves me correctly, that I made my first move to our ranch. Ah, me, then was when my trials commenced in earnest. I shall never, never forget that first long, lonely and fearful night on the plains of the "Great American Desert," eight miles west of Greeley. Oh, how often did I curse (mentally, of course), the founder of Union Colony, but as often asked God's forgiveness, for I felt that we were liable to be attacked by the red man 'ere another day should dawn. The moon arose in all her majesty and I fixed my swollen eyes upon her, for it appeared as though I beheld a beauty in its grandeur, such as I had never before. Do you wonder why? let me tell you. Because it shone in the direction where my heart was ever turning. Yes, it was away back east in that dear old home of mine.

I would like to give you a description of our shanty, and perhaps I may at another time, but I must pass. Saturday morning came and I proposed going to town to spend the Sabbath. This had truly been the longest and most dreary week of my life, and the first one without seeing and talking with those of my sex. Just think of it once; not one word from the late fashions; no chance to indulge in a little gossip, nor discuss the failings of my neighbors. My husband realizing my deplorable situation, thought it advisable that I return to Greeley for the summer, to which I did not object, feeling, however, much sorrow in regard to leaving him alone, but considering it best, I returned to the village, and for the first time during my pioneer life I felt at home, but this only lasted until Monday morning, when my husband gathered up his traps and left for his lonely little shanty on our ranch. After he had gone I would have given all my claim in Union Colony to have been with him, for I now felt my loneliness more intensely than ever before in my life, but I knew that I was doomed to wait, watch and wonder until Saturday night would come, which would be six tedious days and twelve long nights, as the nights were twice as long as the days. I had determined to accompany my husband to his humble abode when he would make his next trip, but he objected, on the grounds that things had not changed since I had tried it before, adding that it was not a fit place for women and children; this I had no disposition to contradict.

After his usual visit from Saturday night until Monday morning, I was again left with my two children to mourn the absence of one whose presence is ever indispensable in a loving and happy home. Thus passed the month of May. June came, but the beautiful prairie flowers, of which we had heard so much, failed to put in an appearance; there was scarcely a blade of green grass to be seen.

It was Monday morning again, a day which to me appeared to come oftener than any other in the week. I was busied packing up grub (as the old Colorado settlers call it) for my husband to take with him to the ranch. While doing so I had permitted him to go out in town for a few moments, as I had claimed his society from Saturday until this time.

"Hello, Annie," cried a voice, which I recognized in an instant. With a cry of joy I sprang forward and encircled in my arms the coat collar of as handsome a man as ever crossed the Mississippi, printing a kiss, not on his cheek or forehead, but smack on his mustache. I am not going to say whether he returned the favor or not, for he since that time has taken to himself a wife, and I do not like to cause coolness in a happy family. Perhaps my husband thought me imprudent, but I had not time to think of impropriety and have not interrogated him yet in regard to his opinion of the act. But it was a dear old friend of ours—not so much mine, however, as that of my husband's—and it was in view of this fact, I remember now, that I took the liberty of giving our friend so hearty a welcome in my husband's absence. But I had almost forgotten to state who this worthy and highly esteemed gentleman was, and as I hope many of his friends may read this book, I will now give his name in full—Mr. Samuel Thomas, Ex-

Sheriff of Franklin, Venango county, Pa. He was accompanied by Col. Lee of the same place. They remained but a few days in Greeley and then left for Puget Sound. Two weeks after this I was attacked with a relapse of mountain fever, and as it was almost out of the question to obtain domestic help, I was obliged to work until my strength gave way, and I sank beneath the withering blast of the acclimating fever. Medical aid appeared of no avail for many weeks. It was now irrigating season and our crops demanded attention hourly. I begged my husband to take me with him as he was obliged to be at his post day and night, for the cattle of the plains had begun to invade our premises. He at first objected, fearing that I would not be able to stand the journey; but I finally succeeded in convincing him that if left alone I would surely die; then after exerting all my energies I announced myself ready for the trip, and we started. Before we were three miles from town I despaired of ever reaching my destination, but I struggled with my fears alone, for I could plainly see that my husband understood my case better than I did myself. I looked at my helpless little ones and breathed a feeble prayer to God for their protection, for I really felt that my little deeds of kindness on this earth were about to end. When we reached our shanty I was too feeble to get to bed without assistance, but with this succeeded, and there remained during my stay on the ranch, which was about a fortnight, then our physician advised us to return to Greeley. This we did late Friday night, and early next morning our hearts were gladdened on account of the arrival of our dear old father accompanied by our cousin, Dr. Goodwin, who is now a citizen of Greeley. The excitement produced a wonderful effect upon my nervous system. For a while I was over-powered; my mental as well as physical strength failed and I wept incessant tears of joy; then I rallied and really imagined that my health was restored. During their stay, which was, I think, nine days, I was able to assist with the work, also engage in sports and jestings as of old. The society of my friends seemed to be medicine for both soul and body. I had but one trouble, viz: their departure, which I knew was inevitable, and as the time drew near, I felt my heart sink within my bosom. By the time they were ready to take the train, I was ready to take my bed in spite of all my efforts to bear the separation. When the last good-bye was exchanged, I took my seat by the north window to watch the fast flying train that was bearing our loved ones from our sight, and as it vanished my soul went up to God in prayer for their protection.

I then realized for the first time in my life what it was to have friends leave me, as it always had been mine to leave, and to be left, and I decided in favor of the former. It was on the second night after this painful event that I was awakened by the sound of distant thunder; I had always been very timid in storms east, but as I had always been told that it never rained in Colorado, and having lived here over a year without witnessing anything worthy of mention in that direction, I had concluded that there was no danger; consequently, let the thunder and lightning play all they had a mind to until I discovered with horror a terrible storm was rapidly approaching us; fortunately for me my husband was at home, but sleeping soundly; I awoke him and requested him to bring our little ones from the adjoining room as the storm had now begun to rage in its fury. He laughed, but complied with my request saying, "I hope you are not alarmed, when you know there are no hard storms in this country?" As he spoke, a vivid flash of lightning filled the room, and then came the most terrific peal of thunder that I had ever heard. This was repeated almost incessantly while the rain fell in torrents, until it turned to hail and then such a clatter, clatter, on our tarred paper roof, as I hope I shall never hear again. I was speechless, I could not so much as say, God be merciful to me, a poor deluded Union Colony victim. My little ones, who had been placed by my side, trembled like leaves and crept into my arms as if for safety. The storm continued for the space of an hour, at which time our roof was completely demolished; the water came through in bucketfuls until everything inside the house was saturated. Our neighbors shared our fate, as their shingles were of the same material; therefore we were obliged to remain in the Baptist faith until morning. When the storm had abated, my husband went out to examine the hail, which was several inches deep in the street.

When morning came the town presented a scene of desolation; every garden was supposed to be ruined and we had but little hope of our crops on the farm. We were obliged to obtain our breakfast at the restaurant and then proceeded to lift our soaked carpet which we stretched on the clothes line through the roofless house; then got a friend of ours to attend to drying our bedding, and we left the city for our country residence, expecting to find everything in ruin, but to our glorious surprise it had escaped the hail entirely, and had been much benefitted by a refreshing shower.

Here I am reminded of an incident that I have failed to mention, which occurred a few days previous to the visit of our friend Mr. Thomas. The wind had been blowing all the forenoon, so much so as to detain my husband from going out to the farm; but about noon there was a calm and he started on his journey. It was about three o-clock in the afternoon when the dust and gravel began to fly, rendering travel almost impossible, though I never witnessed so much force in the wind since I had been in this country. I was not nervous, however, for I had heard the old settlers say that they had never heard of a tornado or whirlwind in Colorado; thus I was comforting myself when I was startled by an approaching roaring, similar to that of the ears close by. In an instant darkness pervaded the room, my children screamed with alarm and rushed to my side; I caught them in my arms and then sank to the floor; this is the last I remember until I heard the alarm of fire. The little ones who had retained their senses better than myself, were now trying to arouse me to a sense of our danger. The darkness had disappeared, but the wind raged in its fury. I made my way to my north window, and was just in time to see a new house, belonging to Father Meeker, lifted from its foundation and hurled to the ground, dashing it in pieces. Also a house which stood near my own was lifted into the air and carried some distance, when it came in collision with another, stopping its speed by knocking in the side of the same. The air was literally filled with paper roofs, pieces of timber, clothes baskets, and men's hats; in short, every article which came in contact with that terrible wind. Then there came a lull and silence reigned, save that of the bustle of the people running to and fro seeking loved ones or hastening to assist the supposed wounded and dying. I was paralyzed and could only breath a prayer of thankfulness to my Protector, for I really thought it miraculous, the tornado having passed through my yard, lifting pieces of coal weighing several pounds. I clasped my hands and waited in a dreadful suspense to learn the fate of the inmates of those dwellings. In a short time dispatches from all parts of the town announced the glorious tidings, nobody killed, but a few slightly wounded.

Now let us return to our country residence, of which I was about to draw a picture, when it occurred to me that I had forgotten to give a description of that first and last tornado in Greeley, of which I have just finished giving a faint account. On entering our shanty everything appeared to put on an inviting appearance; our bed, twice the size of an ordinary one, afforded ample room for our entire family which numbered four; a rough plank answered as a table, and four three-legged stools completed our household furniture; everything was in its place, as there had been no woman nor children around to misplace them. A pair of irrigating boots were neatly placed on the table in close proximity with the dishes, accompanied by a pair of socks, which had been wet, but now as dry as a Colorado sand bed and as hard as a Texas herder's heart; the broom, dish cloth and face towel all occupied the same nail,—this showed economy as well as neatness;—table-cloth, which had formerly been flour sacks, had taken on the appearance of a mop cloth, (that is, a clean one, I mean, of course) and was neatly folded, lying on the foot of the bed, not on any army blanket, however, but on a pair of muddy overalls; but the mud was clean. I wish to have you understand that everything was in its proper place, as I have before stated, except the frying pan, which remained on the stove; but it was readily ascertained that it, too, had been provided for by the housekeeper, for near the head of the bed were marks of grease, (that is, good, clean grease) which had been accumulating ever since the batch business had been in session. On congratulating the housekeeper for his good taste, he assumed the dignity of a Chicago colored cook and said: "Yes, order is heaven's first law." I offered to assist in preparing the evening meal, but was kindly refused, giving as a reason that I had not learned the ways of the house yet; adding that I had better take a rest, to which I did not object. I placed myself in a position so as to watch the proceedings of my new cook. After making a rousing fire he proceeded straightway to the foot of the bed, picked up his table cloth and spread it partly on the table and partly on the floor. The dishes and part of the eatables were placed on and he was about to announce supper when it occurred to him that the tea-kettle had not been placed over the fire. He flew to the ditch for water and soon had the tea-kettle placed on the stove; then he thought of potatoes, which he washed in haste, putting them on to cook; he then seated himself with the "Greeley Tribune" to read an article on irrigation, written by the famous J. Max Clark, and he became so absorbed that everything else was forgotten until aroused by an unpleasant odor arising from the potato pot. Springing to his feet he seized the hot bail of the kettle, but released his hand instantly; thrusting his hand into his pocket he drew therefrom a snow white handkerchief as though to make it whole again, he replied "You bet;" then proceeded to lift up the supper, of which I partook, remarking that it was the best meal I had eaten for many weeks.

In the morning, breakfast over, I suggested that I would take charge of the housework, to which my predecessor did not object, providing that I kept everything in its proper place, as he remarked: "You are liable to play out at any time, which would compel me to resume my batching." I pledged my word to do all in my power to keep things in order, obtaining permission, however, to remove the frying pan from the head of the bed to a nail, behind the stove. Also that his boots be taken from the table to a less conspicuous place in the shanty. To this he consented; then, wishing me success, he went to irrigating his wheat and did not return until noon. Business had now commenced in earnest, our crops were as follows: five acres of wheat, two of potatoes and forty of oats. In the course of a week or so we had a refreshing shower which gave the farmers new courage as it had wet the ground thoroughly, giving them a chance to rest a few days.

By the first of August it was very perceptible that the Colorado soil was productive beyond our most sanguine expectations and we looked forward to a bountiful harvest. The like of the potatoes and tomatoes I had never seen. I began to build castles in the air. I could see our labors crowned with success in the not far future. I imagined my friends all flocking to Colorado, this would complete my happiness. I fancied my health improving, the color which had faded from my cheek appeared to be returning to its former hue; my husband's care-worn countenance was evidently fast disappearing and he joked and really laughed again as in the happy days of yore. But alas! I had forgotten the verse in that old Methodist hymn, which says:—

"The brightest object 'neath the sky
   Gives but a flickering light;
We should suspect some danger nigh
   When we possess delight."

But was reminded of it when we received our Greeley paper, as it stated that there were several cases of typhoid fever in that place; also recorded the death of two of our particular friends, one of whom had left four little helpless children to mourn and pine for that which earth could never given them back, and I shuddered as I thought of what might soon be the fate of my own little ones. It was at the close of a terribly sultry day in the latter part of August, that my husband returned from his work, with every symptom of the fever of which I have just spoken. He immediately sought his bed assuring me that he was only fatigued and that rest was the only medicine he stood in need of, adding, that by morning he would be all right. When supper was ready I endeavored to awake him, but in vain. After the lapse of an hour I resumed my efforts and succeeded, but could not persuade him to eat or drink. With the assistance of my children I removed his boots and bathed his feet. Then he retired for the night, reassuring me that he was only tired and would be all right by morning. To this, I replied, "I hope so," adding mentally "if not, God pity me." After locking my door securely and asking protection from the author of my being, I too retired to rest, but sleep had entirely forsaken me. My husband raved incessantly, at times he was irrigating, then expressing a wish for a shower; then his mind would wander back to our dear old home, where he imagined himself engaged in his former employment. "I will sell it low," he would say, "as I am bound to go out of the business." Here I interrupted him by saying, "What will you sell low?" "All the goods I have on hand," he answered, "for I am bound to go west." Then he aroused and apparently regained his mind. "O yes;" said he, "I am awake now; I've been dreaming; thought I was back home in the store and Carpenter, Kerr, Deacon Proper and Squire Richey, (referring to intimate friends in Wallaceville) were there." Father in heaven! I prayed, can I ever forgive the founder of Union Colony? At last the long dreary night wore away and morning dawned, but all was not right; although my husband got up, dressed himself and milked the cow, which had been neglected the night previous on account of his illness and my incapability of releasing him from the task. The cow was a splendid animal, for which we had paid sixty-five dollars; but she showed a decided repugnance to anything incased in crinolines, which were at that time indispensible articles to those of my sex. After breakfast, of which my husband slightly partook, he went to work on the farm; but, long before noon, returned with a flushed face and slow step. "You are all right, aren't you?" I said, speaking ironically, of course. "I am not going to have the doctor if I am not all right," he replied. "That will all be left for me to decide," said I; "once I am convinced you have the fever, I will send for a physician without delay, as you are aware, I will be boss in this case." To this he made no reply, but silently coiled himself upon the bed from which he was not able to arise without assistance for many days. In the meantime our little girl had come down with the same disease; this added greatly to my affliction. It was during one of those gloomy nights that I sat in my lonely cottage with my sick child in my arms, watching, as I feared, the life ebbing out from the one to me dearest on earth, that I wandered in memory back to the once happy family circle, which I had broken with my departure for this, my unhappy home; and a vision of the last night, that we, brothers and sisters, had joined in singing, came before me, with the heaven inspiring music I was quite familiar, but the words I could not call to memory, except these lines:

> "Let me go, why should I tarry?
> What has earth to bind me here?"

And after singing over and over these words, I composed the following verses, and sang them until worn out with fatigue and want of sleep I fell into a deep slumber, from which I did not awake until aroused by my husband, who had been awakened by the piteous cries of my sick child. It seems that the disease of father and child had reached its zenith, as from that hour they recovered rapidly. . . .

At the close of two weeks after my husband's attack we received the discouraging intelligence that half of Greeley were down with the same disease, notwithstanding the *Tribune* was extolling the healthy country to the heavens. And, although deaths were occurring daily in the colonial town, seldom was one recorded in that paper. At the expiration of three weeks my patients were pronounced convalescent. My little girl after the lapse of twenty-one days from the time she was taken ill was partially restored to her health, but so helpless that she could not walk across the room alone. A friend of ours in Greeley, having heard of our sickness, left his work to harvest what little wheat the cattle of the plains had left us. While engaged in shocking it a rain set in which lasted several days, at the close of which much of our wheat was gone. How is that for a country where it never rains? We had forty acres of the most promising oats I ever beheld, but it appeared impossible to save it. I remember one rainy morning in September that I arose from my bed and found about fifty head of cattle feeding on it. I softly slipped out so as not to disturb my husband, who was too feeble to attend to anything. With a vain hope of driving them I equipped myself for the task, taking with me the broom stick, which is termed the woman's weapon; but I gave out before I had got half way across the field, and sinking to the earth I wept and prayed to God for a change in my wretched life, winding up with a wish that Horace Greeley and N. C. Meeker, the founders of Union Colony, were in the bottom of the sea, and my family and I in the dear old Keystone State.

Mrs. A. M. Green, *Sixteen Days on the Great American Desert; or, the Trials and Triumphs of a Frontier Life* (Titusville, Pa.: Frank W. Truedell, Printer, 1887), pp. 8–31.

"To complain was never one of my traits of nature"

In this colorful reminiscence, a woman who became known as a "financier" and the Cattle Queen of Montana chronicles the hardships and adventures of her early life. Her attitude could not be a greater contrast to that of Annie Green, in the preceding selection. Amid crisis and danger, Collins simply carried on, her ultimate success apparently making it all worthwhile. She describes the first settlement of Denver, a six-month mining excursion in family wagons over the mountains to Taos, and her own work as a nurse in Helena and then as a cook in a Montana mining camp.

Some readers suspect that Collins's more dramatic adventures (including capture by hostile Indians) may have been embellished to please the tastes of eastern readers, who expected such thrilling stories of the Wild West. For example, to explain why she was not raped (as everyone assumed a captive would be), she claimed to have rubbed phosphorus from matches on her hands, which glowed in the dark and scared the superstitious attacker away.

This narrative is comparable to the many "self-made man" stories of the robber baron era. The author's uncomplaining attitude was undoubtedly genuine—perhaps one of the reasons why she survived and succeeded—but becoming an acknowledged "important person" in her society probably helped smooth the edges of her memories. The Collinses made the switch to cattle ranching on the high plains in the 1870s, just as new railroads and commercial slaughterhouses began to make it hugely profitable. They took advantage of the expanding post-Civil War market to accumulate a fortune and make Montana proud.

Soon after this we reached O'Fallon's Bluff, from which place we caught our first glimpse of Pike's Peak, and, although we were still distant nearly 100 miles from our journey's end, all felt that our weary traveling was nearing a close. At the end of six week's time from the start at the Platte River we reached Denver—or, rather, what is now Denver. At that time the only evidence of settlement was a small log cabin and one or two tents occupied by campers. Our first camping place was at a point midway between the foot-hills and the river, beneath the shade of a large, lone tree, and here it was that father decided to erect his first house. In company with him I left in a few days for the mountains to get the first load of house logs. The box was taken from the wagon, the ox team attached, a sack of provisions tied to the axle, and, seated on the "reach" of the wagon, we traveled fifteen miles before coming to a place where suitable timber was to be found. Our first logs were cut from timber on a high ridge, amid the most beautiful surroundings imaginable. The soil was of a redish clay nature, thickly covered with a lovely pine forest, through which little brown squirrels scampered from limb to limb and countless beautiful birds flitted from tree to tree. The odor from the pine, delightful in its intensity, operated upon the weary body and mind almost as an opiate, and, looking about upon the beautiful, vari-colored wild flowers, and surrounded thus on every side by primitive Nature, I felt almost that paradise had been reached and that henceforth all would be sunshine, happiness and repose.

For three days father was occupied in the work of chopping, trimming and loading, our nights being passed during this time in a little hut built of pine boughs. At last we were ready for the start home. Seven large logs comprised the load. All went well for a short distance but, in going down a steep incline, the wagon "reach" broke and the entire load, oxen, father and myself went rolling down the hill. Fortunately no serious damage was done, and, after much sweating, puffing and strong talking on father's part, the work of reloading was accomplished. Again was fate against us, for we had traveled but a mile or so further when the oxen suddenly cramped the wagon and over it went. Again the work of loading had to be done over. This was finally accomplished. About five miles from Denver it was necessary for us to cross the river. In attempting to do this we missed the fording place a short distance and were soon on our way down the stream. I was commanded by father to crawl out upon one of the oxen, and this I did, mounting "old Buck" after a fashion identical with that of a clothes pin on a clothes line. Father swam by the side of one of the oxen, holding onto the animal's tail and we finally reached the opposite shore several rods below the proper fording point, but fortunately at a place where the bank sloped back from the river, and soon had the team and load safe ashore. Thus was the first load of logs secured for our Denver mansion. This trip required eight days, and but seven logs were secured.

The work of hauling logs and building the house was more than father could accomplish alone, and, being without sufficient funds to allow of the hiring of help, there arose the necessity of earning money in some way. But mother came to the rescue by volunteering to take boarders. Our only table as yet was a large stump and our cook stove the camp fire, but even though food may not be served upon Damask table linen nor cooked upon a nickel-plated range, still it is a necessity at all times and places, and we found plenty who were satisfied to put up with the accommodations offered and pay therefor at the rate of $16 per week for meals alone. In this way funds were raised to pay for help in hauling the logs and building the house. By winter it was habitable.

When finished the house contained two rooms, the entire structure being about 18x24 feet in size. Lumber was worth $1.00 per foot, and, owing to this fact, but half of the size of one of the rooms was floored. Two windows, 8x10, costing $1.00 each, furnished light for the interior. Thus did we start in our new home and such was my initial experience in the far west.

The winter was indeed a long, dreary and discouraging one. During the early winter months mother was stricken with the mountain fever, and in order that she might be made as comfortable as possible, was removed to the cabin of a neighbor who had just completed a more comfortable and better house than father's. This left me to do the housework alone, and, as we still retained our boarders, the task was far from being an easy one. Our food was all cooked over a fireplace and at times it would seem that my face was fairly blistered from the heat and my eyes blinded by smoke. But to complain was never one of my traits of nature, neither was the expression "give up" ever included in my limited vocabulary, and I struggled on, hoping ever that better times and more comforts would soon fall to my lot. Our old home in the States was seldom heard from. Mail was carried only by horsemen, the postage on a letter being 25 cents, and seldom did we hear from those we had left behind. Our amusements and recreations were only such as we created for ourselves, and it is needless to say life under such circumstances was far from enjoyable. Still all battled manfully against discouragement and with the coming of spring all were ready to take up the battle anew and enter with zest into the struggle for wealth.

In the early spring there came to our house a very sick man who asserted that he was a stranger in a strange land, and entreated that he be allowed to remain in our midst until he was able to travel. Mother had by this time recovered from her sickness, and, prompted by the instincts of a true womanly heart, consented to shelter and care for him. In a few weeks he had recovered. During the time he had been our guest, he related glowing accounts of rich mines he had discovered in New Mexico, and soon succeeded in spreading throughout the entire settlement a species of "gold fever" of the most approved and irritating character, and by the latter part of April he had formed a company of from 150 to 200, who at once prepared to leave Denver and visit the gold fields of which he told. Shovels, picks, gold pans, provisions, etc., were procured and all made ready for the journey. On one of the last days of April or the first days of May—I do not recollect the exact date—the long wagon train wound slowly away and farewells were said to those remaining on the old camping ground. The first night out from Denver, camp was pitched on Cherry Creek, a stream so called from the fact of its banks being timbered exclusively with cherry trees. From Cherry Creek, southward bound, the caravan slowly passed on across a vast expanse of dry, sandy prairie, no water or shade being found until the stream known as Fountain Caboyeau was reached. Here good feed and water was encountered, but before reaching this place we were overtaken by one of those much dreaded hot wind storms which at times prevail in that section of country. To describe the suffering which people and stock undergo during one of these dreadful periods is beyond my power. Our hands and faces were burned and blistered, our lips swollen and parched to such an extent as to render eating almost a physical impossibility, and as we neared the banks of the river the stock became unmanageable, and, with their tongues protruding from their mouths, parched and swollen, broke from under control and regardless of wagons or packs plunged headlong through the brush down the bank into the river below. Considerable damage was done to wagons and contents, but three or four days proved sufficient time for repairs and we were soon again under way.

On the evening of our arrival at this point, after camp had been made I was sent to the river for the purpose of procuring a vessel of water. It was just dark, and as I passed along a narrow path to the brink of the stream, I was somewhat startled to see just before me the gleaming eyes of a wild animal. Pausing abruptly, and, keeping my eyes steadily fixed upon those of the animal in front, I called for the men at camp, at the same time standing perfectly motionless. Almost as I spoke the animal sprang at me and only by stooping quickly did I escape being caught by its paws. It passed on up the path and the foremost of the party from camp, who had heard my cry and started to my rescue, caught a glimpse of its flaring eyes as it neared him and by a well-directed shot killed the beast. It proved to be a mountain lion, and upon measurement was found to be over six feet in length from "tip to tip."

Another incident of our stay at this place worthy of mention was the stampeding of a large number of elk by the hot winds. The animals had been overtaken by one of these storms and, running before its blasts, plunged into a large thicket of cacti upon the banks of the river. They struggled fiercely to free themselves from the torturing situation into which they had blindly rushed, and the very earth trembled from their bellowing and frantic plunges. The plants at this place grew to a height of probably five or six feet, the main stalk being probably, on an average, some five inches in diameter, and the limbs or branches from 16 to 18 inches in length. The thorns were in the neighborhood of an inch in length, and a wound inflicted by one of these would cause the most intense pain.

After repairs had been made the journey was again resumed, an open prairie country being passed over, until the Arkansas River was reached. We stopped for repairs, and it was here I first saw a Mexican woman. From this point on to the range of mountains which we were obliged to cross in order to reach our destination the country was sandy, rocky and broken. The road was hard to travel and but slow progress was made. Arriving at the mountains, camp was located at the base and preparations made to cross the range. In the way of timber, balsam, fir, and pitch pine were abundant, while, in the way of vegetation, luxuriant grasses and numerous varieties of wild flowers covered the ground. The ascent of the mountain was a work of no small magnitude. Several teams were required to pull a single wagon, which, after being hauled to the top of the range would be left and another gone after.

One day while this work was going on I preceded the wagons and company, some considerable distance, reaching the summit of the mountains in advance of the main body. Well was I repaid for my labors, for a beautiful scene met my eyes. Upon the towering cliffs sported a herd of mountain sheep, skipping lightly from rock to rock in as confident and fearless a manner as if they were treading upon level ground instead of leaping through space across chasms of unlimited depth. These animals are creamy white, rather larger than ordinary tame sheep, and are provided by nature with enormous horns, gracefully curved in a single turn about the face. These horns develop to an enormous size and at times the animal bearing them is borne down by their weight, and lying down for rest, finds itself unable to arise. About my feet grew pretty wild flowers, among the pines were to be seen the beautiful white, red-eyed quail which frequent this locality. Here also were flocks of "fool hens," a bird resembling the ordinary prairie chicken, which will sit quietly upon the limb of a tree and allow the hunter to approach and knock them from their perch with a whip or stick. Huckleberries were present in profusion, growing luxuriantly within probably fifty feet of a huge snow bank.

Turning to retrace my steps to camp, the thought occurred to me that a "mess" of huckleberries would be relished by father and mother, so I started through a small grove of timber at my left, in search of a spot where the berries were plentiful, I suddenly came in close proximity to a large black bear. The animal was a curiosity to me, for, being as I was as yet, a "pilgrim" from the States, I was not aware of the nature of the beast. Acting upon the impulse of the moment, to drive the animal from the patch of berries, where it was quietly feeding, I picked a rock from the ground and hurled it. The aim was good and it landed fairly in his ribs. Immediately the bear assumed an upright position and proceeded at a rambling, although swift gait, in my direction. I stood my ground for an instant, but perceiving that he did not hesitate, and being by this time fully convinced that to retreat was now my only chance, I made haste to get from the spot as rapidly as possible. My pursuer still continued the chase and soon the fun was on in earnest. Fortunately I was able to scale a small tree before reached, but there I was obliged to stay. The afternoon had passed and the sun had sunk from view ere I heard my mother's voice calling in the distance, I answered, informing her of my situation and in a short time a party came to my rescue and succeeded in killing the animal. By this time half the train had reached the summit of the range, the remaining half still being at the foot of the mountain.

Much difficulty was experienced here in boiling water for cooking purposes, the air being so light that the liquid would evaporate before reaching a sufficiently high temperature to boil. Many of the members of the party were greatly affected by the lightness of the air and many of the horses bled profusely at the nose from the same cause.

The arduous task of reaching the top of the range having been accomplished without serious mishap, preparations were at once made for the descent to the plains of Pueblo. Ropes were brought forth and securely fastened to the rear of the wagon to be let down the grade, and by wrapping the rope about the body of a tree and loosening it slowly the wagon was allowed to move gradually down the side of the mountain until the end of the rope had been reached, when the wheels would be blocked, the rope wrapped about a tree lower down and the wagon again be allowed to descend. In this way the wagons were one by one taken to the foot of the mountain and finally the work of crossing the range was at an end.

The miner of whom I had spoken as being the organizer of the party and who was looked upon as the leader and guide of the train, now began to manifest signs of uneasiness, and this circumstance soon served to arouse the suspicions of several of the party that matters were not as he had represented them to be. Close watch was kept of his actions and no opportunity was afforded him to escape from the company.

After a rest of three days at the foot of the mountains, during which time search was made for the hidden treasure of which the men were told, it was decided to move on across the plains of Pueblo to the foot of another spur of the range. On the way across these plains Fort Pueblo was passed and a short stop made. Passing on about five miles, the company went into camp again, and prospecting was commenced in earnest.

At the end of a week's time the men were becoming greatly discouraged, and, after a lengthy council the miner who had induced them to undertake the journey was informed that unless he led them to the mines of which he had told within a reasonably short time, his life would pay the penalty of failure. With apparent sincerity he asserted that his inability to find the mines was owing to their having, after first discovery, been covered carefully to remove all possibility of their being found and taken possession of by others. He still expressed belief in his ability to find them provided he was allowed more time for search. His apparent sincerity and truthfulness coupled with the fact that at about this time Kit Carson, the celebrated western scout, visited camp and exhibited numerous nuggets of gold which he had received from the Indians in that vicinity, in a measure again restored confidence and hope in the breasts of the men and with renewed vigor the work of prospecting was again taken up. A few days of prospecting resulted in the finding of several specimens of quite rich quartz and for a time the company were in quite good spirits. But after a time they again became somewhat discouraged and it was decided to divide the camp, one party to remain where they were and the other party to move around the foot of the mountain to the opposite side, in order that more territory might be covered. This move was executed, and for a time I shall now wander from the subject of the mines and speak of sights, scenes and subjects foreign thereto. . . .

The preparatory work for the return to Denver was at once put in motion and in a week's time the train was ready to move upon the return journey. All were anxious to reach the old camping ground or settlement, and, urged on by this desire, more than ordinary haste was made. Recrossing the range at the point at which we first crossed, at the very summit, lying by the side of the trail or road was the body of a murdered Mexican. A halt was made, the body given decent burial, and again we proceeded onward.

While the southward trip had been far from a pleasant one, still the return was far more disagreeable, as it was now getting very late in the fall, the entire summer having been passed in the search for the mines, and the chilling winds, blasting frosts and dismal rains of the early winter season was in prevalence. It is needless, therefore, to assert that it was with a feeling of rejoicing and thankfulness that we found ourselves drawing close to our journey's end and finally, upon reaching the crest of a foothill, caught sight of the little city of Denver. To this pleasure was added the greater one to our immediate family of meeting, as we halted at the door of our little log cabin from which we had been absent so long, two additional members of our family—my brothers—who had, during our absence arrived from the States in company with a party of our former neighbors in Iowa. Happy indeed was that home-coming.

That dear old cabin, so humble and unpretentious, so rude and uncouth, still remains to me the dearest spot on earth, and for those dear friends of those trying days I shall always bear the most sincere and lasting love. These are recollections as pleasant as they are sacred and eternal.

There are words and faces and places that never lose their hold upon the heart. They may be words that we seldom hear amid the whirl and competition of life, faces that we may never see on earth again, places that we are seldom permitted to revisit; but they were once the scenes, the associates, the joy of our life; they had a controlling influence in training our aspirations and in shaping our future, and they can never be wholly forgotten. The flight of years cannot sully their innocence nor diminish their interest, and eternity will preserve them among the dearest reminiscences of earth. We may meet and love other faces, we may treasure other words, we may have other joys, we may mingle in other scenes and form other associations, but these old familiar faces and these dear old familiar scenes remain invested with a fadeless beauty, sacred in their exemption from oblivion and decay.

My brothers, who had arrived during our absence in Mexico, had, at once upon their arrival, set to work in finishing our log house. Lumber had been procured and the entire ground space was now covered with a good, substantial floor. The windows had been enlarged, the cracks well "chinked," and, taken all in all, the house was now so fitted up as to render it light, warm and comfortable.

The little town had grown to quite respectable proportions, being by this time a place of probably fifty or sixty cabins, and as lively a town for its size as ever stood upon the sod of Mother Earth, but still at that time opportunity for the making of money was lacking during the winter months, and by virtue of this fact, father and my brothers, soon after our return, decided to visit the mountains on a hunting expedition, hoping thereby to procure a sufficient amount of game to furnish us with meat during the winter.

When they returned, in the course of two or three weeks, they did so with father lying sick in the vehicle, suffering with a severe attack of lung fever. The disease soon resolved itself into quick consumption, and early the following spring he passed away. Then it was that I felt that all the world held near and dear to me had been taken away, but I had no time for nursing my grief, as every moment of the day now brought a duty to perform.

A few weeks after my father's death, my brothers left for the mountains on a prospecting tour, leaving mother and I at home alone, and the task of earning a sufficient amount to provide necessaries of life was indeed an arduous one. We still had a cow and our little home and by working almost day and night, sewing, and mending, we managed to struggle along. My brothers were unsuccessful in their search for gold and in order that they might be able to continue their work, every cent which we could accumulate, over and above enough to buy us flour, was given them.

During the early summer the younger of the two, while on a prospecting tour in the heart of the mountains, was overtaken by a band of hostile Indians and murdered. His body was brought to the door mangled and mutilated; as I stood there and gazed upon that dear face my cup of bitterness seemed full to overflowing, and Death would have been a welcome visitor. But it is not easy to die at will, and not until the appointed time does the Master call. We all have our destinies to work out and our allotted life to live, and coward indeed is he who seeks to die for want of courage to battle with life. Many years of work and hardship, many a discouraging event and many a trial and trouble were yet to fall to my lot, and as if the presentment of such were within my heart, I resolved to close my lips to complaining and strive to do well the work outlined by God for me to accomplish.

Denver was at this time, as I have already stated, a fair-sized, bustling, wide-awake western town, and were the truth told had the reputation—and well did it deserve the same—of being what in western parlance is termed "tough." Gambling and gaming, and the quarrels and fights always incident thereto provided constant excitement and "life." Desperate, lawless men thronged the street and scarcely a day passed but that the news would be whispered about from place to place that there was "another man for breakfast," which expression rightfully interpreted conveyed the intelligence that another human being had been shot down or knifed while in the midst of a quarrel over cards at the gaming table. Nor was the peaceably inclined person exempt from danger of being wounded by flying bullets from the gamblers' weapons.

I remember distinctly an incident which will serve to illustrate the prevailing state of affairs at this time. Walking along the main street of the town, I was about to pass one of the large tents in which gambling was being carried on when suddenly a quarrel arose within. In far less time than I employ in writing this brief sketch of the event, the sharp reports of the revolvers of the gamblers were ringing through the street in rapid succession. The fight was at its height in almost an instant, and, greatly startled, I turned to retrace my steps. As I did so a stray bullet pierced my dress and clothing and striking my right limb just above the knee, plowed a neat little furrow through the flesh at a depth of probably about an eighth of an inch below the surface, passing on through my clothing on the opposite side. The wound, as a matter of course, was but a slight one, and soon healed, but the sensation as I felt the leaden missile burn its way through my flesh was not of a very pleasant nature. Had I been six inches farther ahead I would have been badly wounded.

Murderers, desperadoes and gamblers were almost daily being shot down. Carl Woods, a gambler and murderer, was pursued, overtaken and shot down almost at my very feet as I was one day in the act of crossing Ferry street bridge. Among the poorer class great suffering existed and while women and children were almost starving for want of bread their husbands and fathers would be seated at the gaming table squandering their fortunes, all oblivious of their needs. Gold dust was the only form of money in use and with wasteful extravagance and apparent utter disregard of its worth would the precious article be lost or won, as the case might be, by the excited players. . . .

[Some years later] Bannack, at which I stopped on my return from caring for the injured miner on the trip to his home in St. Louis, was a place busy with pioneer life. The mines were paying well, the men who worked them were making enormous wages, and in consequence all was life and activity, but even though a more bustling and wide-awake town would have been hard to find, still as I reached the place and learned of my brother's absence a feeling of loneliness and homesickness was experienced such as I had never before known.

Although during my entire life I had been buffeted about by circumstances, hurried hither and thither by the decrees of Fate and pushed forward along unknown paths by uncontrollable events, still never before, with the exception of the time I was held captive by the Indians, had I been completely separated from the presence of a relative, and now that I found myself so situated, despondency settled upon me which was only shaken off by the greatest effort.

The first thing to do to bring about this result was of course, woman-

Western family. Dressed in their best, this Colorado mining family poses for the camera. Courtesy of the Western Historical Collections, University of Colorado, Boulder.

like, to indulge in a "good cry," following which I brushed away the tears from my red and swollen eyes and resolved to fight the battle life coura-geously, even if alone.

I was not without funds, neither was I without friends, and but a few days sufficed to see me comfortably situated in the home of an acquaint-ance in the capacity of housekeeper and nurse for a kind, respectable lady.

My knowledge of the care of the sick was at this time limited, but had I searched for years for an opportunity to familiarize myself with this par-ticular line of work I doubt very much whether I could possibly have found a place where I would have been able to learn as much in so short a time as here, for, without the slightest disrespect for the dear lady whom I cared for, I will say that she either in reality or imagination was afflicted with every disease known to the medical profession.

The pain from a corn on her little toe would scarcely be quieted before her body would be tortured with the more severe ailment of inflammatory rheumatism; a slight cold in the morning usually resulted—in her opin-ion—in a severe attack of pneumonia in the afternoon; typhoid fever and diphtheria were almost daily visitors; symptoms of peritonitis and whoop-ing cough usually gave evidence of their presence immediately following breakfast and supper respectively; as a dessert for dinner blood poisoning or smallpox was usually announced, while for an afternoon amusement a slight attack of consumption or softening of the brain would be indulged in.

Thus was I kept busy, engaged in the application of every known remedy and treatment for these various ailments, until at last as spring approached and I graduated from this nurse's training school with a case of obstetrics—it was an 8-pound boy; mother and child as well as could be expected—I found myself well fitted for the work of nursing, and soon after by the help of a friend and with the recommendation of the physician under whose direction I had, alone and unaided, so successfully conducted a general "hospital" during the winter months, secured a position as under nurse for the leading physician of Helena, to which city, with the coming of spring, I removed.

I was very fortunate in securing a home with a splendid family and also in the way of finding employment. Nurses were quite scarce and in consequence my services were much sought after and I received liberal compensation for my work, $25 per week being the amount I usually received for caring for the sick.

All went well with me in my new home and occupation for nearly a year; I had succeeded in saving a neat little sum of money "for a rainy day," when in February of the following year misfortune again overtook me and, as was the case with many others, my savings were taken from me and I was again left penniless and alone.

The event which brought about this condition occurred upon a cold, windy and blustering night in the month mentioned. By the bedside of a sick lady I was keeping watch, when, as the hour of three in the morning was about to be recorded by the hands of the little clock which was busily ticking upon a small stand by my side, through the small window on the opposite side of the room there suddenly flashed the ruddy glow of a distant flame.

Almost simultaneous therewith came the alarm of fire and as I peered through the glass into the storm I could see the hurrying of men, women and children as they made their way in the direction of the conflagration.

Soon the flames, fanned by the busy winds, gained headway and leaped high in the air, devouring with their fiery tongue every article, surmounting every obstacle, enveloping all within their path, and as the morning sun arose and shed light upon the scene nothing but complete and utter devastation lay in the path over which they had traversed.

Starting at the extreme upper end of the town, in a neighborhood thickly populated by Chinese and known as "Chinatown," the flames had burned a path the entire length of the city, destroying completely every dwelling, barn or other building along the line and paused in their work of destruction only when the farther limits of the town were reached.

So rapid was their progress, owing to the prevalence of the high winds, that nothing could be saved from the houses within the destroyed district, even though several persons lost their lives in an attempt to rescue their belongings.

Directly in the path of the conflagration was situated the house of the family with whom I made my home, and with them did I share the loss of every possession, excepting only the clothes worn at the time of the disaster.

My little savings—some few hundred dollars—together with every article of clothing, the carpet and furniture of my room and all else I claimed as my own, and for the possession of which I had forfeited many a night of sleep and labored many an hour, week and month, were irretrievably lost, and once again I stood penniless and alone, far from home and relatives.

As I stood that night pressing my face closely against the frosty pane and could see those fierce flames traveling on and on, never halting or swerving from their course, I knew full well that in all probability the home I had learned to love so well would be destroyed, and with it my hard-earned savings; into that sick room, stealthily crept the Angel of Death, leaving me with the emaciated form of the dead woman as a companion.

Was it a wonder that amid such surroundings and under such circumstances I should feel that my cup of bitterness was filled to overflowing?

Such were my feelings, I am free to admit, and though in after years I stood by the side of many a dying person and witnessed the flight of spirit from the body, still never has the presence of Death seemed so close nor life so little worth living as it did then.

Now that my home in Helena was destroyed, the summons of a friend to her bedside at Silver City, a mining camp some twelve miles distant, was accepted, and soon after the fire I changed my abode to that place.

During the early spring months I made my home with this friend, but in May a new life opened for me.

Barnyard chores. They were frequently performed by women and children—and had to be done in all kinds of weather. Courtesy of the Denver Public Library, Western History Department.

In the mining districts, during the time of which I write, it was the custom of the miners to work in their properties during the summer months only, suspending operations as cold and stormy weather approached and resuming again as early in the spring as the weather would warrant.

Most of these men were either unmarried or had left their wives and families in the eastern States, and consequently a practice prevailed of employing a cook for the camp, all paying a proportionate amount toward defraying the expense.

The miners at Canyon Creek had learned of my misfortune in losing my possessions at Helena, and, prompted by kindness and a desire to aid—as well as by a craving for good cooking, I firmly believe—placed the situation before me for acceptance, and, prompted by kindness and a desire to see these hardworking men as comfortable as possible—also craving for the $75 per month—I promptly accepted the offer, and with the coming of the month of May assumed the duties of cook of the Canyon Creek miners—the camp at which I so officiated being composed of eighteen men.

Here I remained during the summer and winter until just before Christmas, when I again returned to Helena for a couple of weeks, at the end of which time I became the wife of Mr. Nat Collins, whom I had been acquainted with for a period of about two years.

Mr. Collins was the owner of a mine at Silver City, near the place I had been employed as cook, and immediately following our marriage, which occurred on New Year's Eve, 1874, we returned to his home at the mines.

Arriving at our new home, we at once commenced housekeeping by the purchase of a large supply of provisions, and Mr. Collins, among other things, bought a small cow.

While this latter fact may not appear to the reader at first glance as an important event, still, if they but knew my feelings of pride as that little, scrawney, homely and apparently almost worthless animal was led through the deep snow and presented to me as I stood in the doorway of that little low log cabin, they would no doubt excuse the mention of the fact. Her purchase price was $75, and the hay upon which she was fed that winter cost from $20 to $30 per ton.

As the weather moderated with the coming of Spring, work in Mr. Collins' mine was inaugurated, and during the summer we prospered and were happy. The mine we owned—I say "we" for the reason that I consider it timely to now lay claim to a share of my husband's property—was of the kind known as a placer mine, and worked in the main by the "hydraulic process."

As he was at work one day during the summer of which I speak, he was visited by a neighbor miner, and as Mr. Collins worked, his visitor sat busily chatting, near the head of the "diggings," when a small, smooth and rather peculiarly-shaped boulder attracted their attention as it lay amid the dirt and rocks where it had fallen.

Commenting upon its appearance and great weight, Mr. Collins decided to investigate its nature, and, succeeding after a few blows with a heavy sledge in breaking it into pieces, was surprised and elated to find plainly visible to the naked eye large particles of pure gold and silver.

The outward appearance of the rock would indicate to the experienced eye of a practical miner that the boulder had broken from a "lead" some distance from where it was found, and traveled and rolled, perhaps a few feet at a time, down the mountain side to the point where it was finally noticed.

But where that "lead" was located, how it might be found and its extent after being found, were questions which remained to be solved.

With the breaking of the boulder and the consequent discovery of its richness as a mineral-bearing rock, Mr. Collins' visitor declared his determination to find the main body of quartz of which this was a disengaged portion.

He soon entered upon the work of prospecting, and, going far up the mountain side, began his work. For two long years that determined man labored with pick and shovel, slowly tunneling his way into the mountain, the loosened dirt and rock being conveyed to the mouth of the tunnel by means of a wheelbarrow.

Alone, and without a word of cheer, in the face of discouragements and despite the existing uncertainty as to whether his labor was being directed in the right direction, this courageous miner toiled slowly on, ever hopeful and always fully determined never to give up until he had at last found the hidden treasure.

As time wore on his funds became almost exhausted, and even the necessities of flour and meat were with the utmost difficulty procured.

But at last there came the reward so justly earned, and at the expiration of these many months of untiring labor the then almost penniless, but stout-hearted miner, and now the wealthiest and best known banker of the city of Helena, Montana, in the depths of that slowly excavated tunnel, struck with his well-worn pick the rich gold-bearing "lead" of the world-famous Drum Lummon mine.

This mine the discoverer in a few years sold for the sum of one million six hundred thousand dollars.

During the summer following our marriage all went well with us in our mountain home, and the season's work was a profitable one. That year, I remember, winter came upon us quite early, and by the middle of November the ground was thickly covered with a blanket of snow. The great number of the miners in the vicinity had suspended operations in their mines and abandoned their work until the following spring, so we were practically alone in the gulch.

Quite early on the morning of the 19th day of November—the date I shall never forget—Mr. Collins was at work with an unruly colt which he had a few days before purchased, endeavoring to "break" the animal to the halter and harness.

With a long rope the colt was tied to a tree near the cabin, and, finding itself securely held by the rope, was franticly struggling to break the fastenings which held it. Finally, with a series of quick and desperate plunges, the animal circled about the tree, and Mr. Collins, in endeavoring to get from its path, slipped and fell. His right leg became entangled in the rope, and when at last disengaged it was found that the limb was badly bruised and terribly shattered.

As best I could, I half carried and half dragged him to the cabin, and after repeated efforts succeeded in placing him upon the bed. With bandages torn from the bed-clothes I bound his injured limb and in every way possible sought to alleviate his pain and suffering for the time-being, intending to leave him alone for a few hours while I went for medical assistance.

As I was about to start, he asked for a drink of water, and, taking the pail, I started for the spring which supplied the cabin and which was located some twenty or thirty rods down the steep bank, near the bottom of the gulch.

The path leading to the spring was, in the summer even, a steep and difficult one to traverse, but now that snow had fallen, ice had formed upon its surface from top to bottom, and only with the utmost difficulty could it be traveled.

As I neared the spring I lost my footing and went sliding and rolling to the very edge of the water. Hastily scrambling to my feet, I started to step forward to fill the pail which I still held in my hand, but the first step was my last, for as I threw my weight upon my left foot I sank to the ground sick and faint with pain, for in falling my left ankle had been shattered and splintered.

As I regained consciousness I crept to the spring and, partially filling the pail with water, turned and started on the painful journey to the cabin.

Creeping on my hands and knees up that steep, slippery path, suffering untold agony from the pain in my broken ankle, I finally reached the door and at last managed, after many trials, to get upon the bed.

By this time both Mr. Collins' broken leg and my shattered ankle had swollen to an enormous size, and we were both almost frantic and dilirious from pain. Unable to move, even so much as to procure food or replenish the fire with fuel, we thus lay for two long, weary and tiresome days and nights, at the end of which time there came at the door of our cabin a gentle rapping.

Bidding the visitor enter, the door opened, and from the cold and storm without crept in a half famished, half frozen Chinaman, known throughout the camp as "Old John." Seeing us lying upon the bed, perceiving the lack of warmth within the cabin, and observing at a glance that all was not well with us, his first words were, "Missy sickee. John sorry muchee. Me helpee you," and at once he set about starting a fire, after which he brought us food and administered to our wants as best he could and then hurried away for other help.

In a few hours' time our cabin was half filled with sympathizing miner friends, and with the coming of a physician who had been summoned from Helena, we were relieved from our suffering to as great an extent as lay within the power of human hands.

A few days later witnessed our departure for the hospital at Helena, both of us being conveyed to that place upon a bed and attended by our kind-hearted miner neighbors. This was, as I have previously said, in the month of November, but our return journey was not accomplished until a greater part of the month of May had come and gone, and when we again reached our little cabin the buckskin sack in which was contained our little store of gold dust, was lighter by just $1,500.

But "it never rains but it pours" was to prove true in this case, as in nearly all others, and ere we had fairly finished our first meal after our arrival home, a terrific downpour of water carried upon its crest the large reservoir owned by Mr. Collins, which was situated some distance up the gulch and employed to hold a supply of water with which to operate his mine, and with it went nearly a mile of sluice boxes. The property was worth, at a conservative estimate, fully $800 to $1,000.

These events, following so closely upon one another as they did, as a natural consequence, greatly discouraged and disheartened us, and we at once decided to discontinue the business of mining and engage in that of cattle raising. A purchaser for our mine was found in a company of Chinamen, and in the August following the property was sold.

By November our cattle had been bought, and in that month we took up our residence on a rented ranch in the Prickly Pear Valley, about eight miles from our former home, with a "bunch" of cattle numbering 180 head.

The winter was an unusually severe one. Snow and storm, high winds and blinding blasts were the order of the day, and with the coming of spring the prairies were seen thickly dotted with the dead bodies of famished and frozen animals.

Our loss that year was very heavy indeed, but still we were hopeful for the future, and during the following summer labored diligently in an effort to prepare for the coming season of cold and snow, but again the storms were frequent and severe, and many a head of stock was lost from our little "bunch."

The following spring Mr. Collins decided to search for a more favored locality, and, having heard much in favor of the Teton Valley, visited this locality and returned very favorably impressed with the outlook.

Gathering our cattle for the start, we were about to undertake the journey to our new home, when Mr. Collins was taken very suddenly ill and had to be taken to the hospital at Helena for medical treatment; but after his recovery we proceeded on our travels, and on the 3rd day of August we arrived at Old Agency, Choteau County, now Choteau, Teton County, locating at a point about midway of the beautiful Teton Valley and distant some one-half to three-fourths of a mile from the present sight of the village of Choteau.

Of my life since that date much might be written were details indulged in, but this I shall not attempt, but, on the contrary, shall only refer to a few of the events which are the most closely connected with the history of Teton Valley and the town of Choteau, concluding with a short account of my first shipment of cattle and the events which led to the possession by me of the title of "Cattle Queen of Montana."

Mrs. Nat Collins, *The Cattle Queen of Montana* (Spokane, Wash.: Dyer Printing Col, n.d.), pp. 12–25, 42–47, 217–31.

"They go by the name of fancy women"

LOUISA COOK

14

This letter reveals the disdain of a proper lady for the gambling in mining towns and for the "fancy women" who flocked to such towns all over the West. It is interesting that Cook seems to have objected, perhaps with unconscious envy, to the way the women were together "in a drove," rode ponies astride, like men, and wore "mens clothes." Though the gulf between women of the "better sort" and such "soiled doves" was seldom breached, this letter is one of many sources that enable us to fill out the frontier story by recognizing their numbers and some details of their lives.

Louisa (pronounced Lo-EYE-sa) Cook had come to the west with her young daughter on the Oregon Trail in 1862. Her letters were written back to her mother and sisters in Ohio. She supported herself as a teacher at Fort Walla Walla and in Idaho mining communities before she was married in late 1864. She died one year later.

Boise, Idaho October 4, 1863

• • • *I* attended the Sabbath School in Centerville today about the only thing there that is like Sunday. The school meets in the dining room in one of the hotels right across the street from a bowling alley where you may hear the balls rolling from morning till night. The streets are crowded with people laughing, singing, swearing, running foot races, betting, etc. But there is nothing like getting used to it; in Bannock the only preaching there is, is by a street preacher who goes into a saloon and commences his sermon at one end of the room while at the other end gambling and playing is being carried on with the greatest fervor. . . . I have but two or three Lady acquaintances in this country. *Ladies* are not plenty. There are a great many in all the mining towns who wear the form of woman, but o so fallen and vile, a living, burning shame to the sex they have so disgraced. As soon as the miners began to flock to this country these women began to come out of Portland,   The Dalles,   Walla Walla, and other places, sometimes a dozen in a drove, astride an Indian pony dressed in mens clothes, rude boisterous and more obscene than the male bipeds who accompany them. Once here they dress very richly and in gay colors and go by the name of fancy women. . . .

Louisa Cook, letter from Boise, Idaho, October 4, 1863, Western Americana Collection, Beinecke Rare Book and Manuscript Library, Yale University.

The life story of Malinda Jenkins, written by an interviewer, seems to be colored mainly by the passage of a lifetime and the triumphant ego of the teller. This selection introduces readers to the down-to-earth discourse of a woman who obviously made no pretense of being a lady. One may even wonder if there is some unspoken truth between the lines, for Jenkins successfully managed an extraordinary number of boardinghouses, starting with the one described in this excerpt. Her behavior alerts one to important class differences in female attitudes toward opportunity in the West. Undertakings, both economic and sexual, that were inappropriate for ladies apparently posed no problems for a frank and straightforward woman like Malinda Jenkins.

Jenkins was married three times, the third time for forty-three years to a semiprofessional gambler. She was constantly moving, sometimes separately from her husband, pursuing opportunities all over the West, from Arkansas to Oregon, from southern California to the Klondike. She was unusually frank about sexual matters and may indeed have "knowed more about how things was than the girls around"; however, the availability of her sister's medical books (she was a midwife) shows that interest in and information about birth control were more widespread than one might think. Her experience illustrates the fact that leaving a bad marriage in the nineteenth century also meant losing one's children, but that marrying a rich second husband might help get them back.

Malinda Jenkins seems to have been even more of a gambler than her husband. When she told her life story at the age of eighty-three, having finally become a millionaire breeding racehorses, she said, "Do you know what I'd do if I was to get broke up? I'd go into business tomorrow. Yes sir, . . . and I'd make good like I always done."

I didn't want no more children. I had my home, my work and every-thing that a woman raised like me could wish for. Two children was enough.

There wasn't no quarrel with Willie, no words. I was his good wife in every respect—but I wasn't going to have no more babies. And when I said that it meant something because I was posted. The many times I lived with my sister Betty, the doctor, I was poking my nose in medical books. I knowed more about how things was than the girls around me.

Then we went to visit Mary Lindren, my niece, over Saturday night. I didn't carry no paraphernalia because Willie promised to behave hisself. He didn't, and that's where our troubles commenced.

When I found out I was having another baby I wasn't only unhappy, I had an awful bad feeling towards Willie, too. I had one thought all the time, I wanted to run for it, get clear away from everybody, to live among strangers. . . . It ain't to be wondered at the way my second boy turned out. How can I blame him, though he's been a tramp and a wanderer all his life? He's lived everything I wished for and thought and wanted for myself while I was carrying him.

Sudden like I lost my father. Alfred come and told me papa was very sick. 'Will he get well?' I asked him. 'No,' he said, 'and if you want to see him you will have to come now.'

I was expecting in six weeks. This was February. They fixed a feather bed in the sleigh and put me in the middle of it. It was twenty-five miles in a bad storm. We got there four o'clock in the afternoon, and the next morning papa passed away. He'd been asking for me, saying 'Sinney' over and over. Betty took me in to him but he didn't know me. How sad I was! Part of my world was gone forever.

When a man died and the estate was settled, the widow was supposed to get one-third of everything. My stepmother said she didn't want her share when papa died. 'I don't need it. I never earned it and all I'll take is a child's share. There's six of you, and with me there's seven. I want a seventh like the rest.

'I'll tell you what I'd like,' she said, 'jes' all of you chip in and buy me Susan's feather bed.' Sister Susan had finished one from her own geese. There was forty pounds of feathers in it and we paid Susan fifty cents a pound. We give my stepmother that and she was happier with it than all the other things.

She had five or six children of her own. They was all married. Her oldest, Jim Staton, went to Iowa in the early days and done good. Later he turned minister. The others was living in Iowa, too. My stepmother hadn't seen them hardly at all so she went there after papa died. We heard from her but never seen her again. ·

It was nigh on four years after I had May that my second boy come. I named him William—not after my husband, but after my youngest brother that died. Will was as pretty and fat a little thing as I ever looked at but he didn't fill my heart like May done.

Carrying the child and working so hard, from that moment my health begun to fail. Will was born the eleventh day of March. In the fall and winter before, I spun and wove four blankets. And made up all the clothes, the jeans and flannels for the whole family, knitted all the stockings and everything.

I had been cutting rags for two or three years. I must have been a glutton for punishment. I set at the loom—just four weeks before my time—and wove a rag carpet. With the breastpiece of the loom rubbing against me, and a grease cloth tied around my stomach to keep it from hurting, I finished the carpet and tacked it down. Sunday I cleaned house and got ready. Monday, after dinner, I had an eleven pound baby. . . .

We had been away from Boone County two dry years; two years of terrible crops. As lean as they was in the Wabash Valley we fared better than our Boone County tenant. He hadn't nothing to show for his toil and owed us two years' rent. He done the only thing the poor man could. 'Page,' he said to Willie, 'move in now 'stead of next March and take the crop for what it's worth. It's the only way I can pay you at all.'

It felt good to be back home and I thought maybe everything was going to go all right—even though we didn't have a dollar, only from what we gathered up and sold on the Burroughs place.

In March, following that fall, I fell sick with pneumonia. We'd been doing middling good, what I called blundering through. I know how I caught it—going out milking the cow in the cold. I didn't take care of myself—never had no time, the way Willie dawdled and loafed and left things undone.

The doctor's name was Tinkler, watching over me through this spell. I had five blisters that et into my flesh until there was sores like holes. We didn't have no cabbage like he ordered, but Annie Shepard, my sister-in-law, bless her, had it growing and she come and showed them how to manage it, drawing the corruption out with wilted, green cabbage leaves.

I couldn't stand a man that would let me suffer while he toasted his feet in front of the fire. I suffered terrible. I'd be crying, and asking Willie to put on some fresh cabbage. 'I will,' he'd say, 'jes' so soon as I finish my pipe.' Put-offs like that.

The God I believe in today is the power that's in us to do good. But them days I believed like the rest of them. I prayed to God to please to let me get out of that bed. I lay there crazy with worry. I seen how it was. I thought: Everything that he's ever had in life was give him. He ain't the sort to go to the bottom and climb up. It's up to yourself, or the Lord help you and your little ones!

I kept thinking what Willie should have done and hadn't. I had the time to study it out. I made up my mind it was sink or swim, and saddled to Willie we'd all sink. Leave him! Staying there meant hardship and want for the rest of my life. I was praying for the chance to find something else for my children. I promised God I would, if only I'd get well.

I cured up awful slow. On Ollie's birthday, the twenty-fifth of May—I couldn't much more than drag myself around the house—I made the children as nice a birthday party as I was able. I knowed it was the last meal of vittles I'd be fixing them.

Mind you, I never had been away from them a day. I washed their little feet and cleaned them up like always, before I put them to bed and kissed them goodnight. Next morning I said as how I was going to see their Aunt Mary down in Texas. Then I was coming back to fetch them. . . .

Ollie was standing, leaning up against the mantel piece. May asked him, 'What are you doin', are you cryin'?' She was about five years old, she couldn't understand.

'Well, don't YOU feel bad,' he said; 'don't you know that mama's a-leavin' us and a-goin' away? Ain't I got plenty to make me feel bad?' Ollie was nine.

'She'll come back after us,' May said, 'she told me so, and Aunt Sally's a-goin' to care for us meantime.'

I couldn't stand Willie's laziness another day. I wanted to get away from him bad enough to do anything. . . . I hoped and expected to gather up the children later on. I didn't know how, but I'd find a way.

Willie broke up the whole household after I left. He sent May with Aunt Sally, over to his sister, Annie Shepard; the two boys went with him to that hellcat Demarias that hated me. But he kept his promise by letting Annie have May, and if there ever was a good woman it was Annie.

Soon Annie picked up and moved off. It seemed like the family all moved to different places. Annie's husband was dead in the Civil War and she was drawing a pension. She went to Kansas and took May with her. Well now, Willie—that was one good thing about him—he didn't want the children scattered about, so he packed up with the two boys and went along.

When I started for Texas I was down and out, with nothing but a ticket and seventy-five dollars left from my inheritance. The train went to Fort Worth. My sister Mary lived out of Stephenville, over in Erath County. The rest of the way from Fort Worth, about sixty miles, I was fixing to make by wagon.

But at Fort Worth I was too sick and weak to go further. I found a cheap boarding house and got me a room and rested. I decided to stay there until I felt better.

Sister Mary was a money-maker. Her and Wesley Cunningham, her husband, went out to Texas and got a section of homestead land off the government. Later they bought another hundred and sixty acres close up. They had five children. Johnnie was their baby; I'm coming to him.

I wrote to Mary and give her my address at Fort Worth. I asked her to come for me in about a month, that I wasn't ready to stand the trip.

Then I seen that they didn't want me there at the boarding house. Mrs. Swenson that was running it, she come in one day and told me. 'Excuse me, for askin',' she said, 'but what's the matter with you anyhow? I know you're decent by your way of actin', but you ain't left your room, and all of us a-hearin' you cryin' your eyes out?'

I looked her in the face. 'Are you a mother?' She said she was. 'So am I, but through circumstances that I don't feel like mentioning, I left a little girl behind that I never was away from a night in my life. I was obliged to leave her; I'm a-tryin' to gain my health to keep from leavin' her always.'

I said that I was very satisfied at her house and that I would try to bear up. When she heard my story, she got real friendly. 'It's all right, now that I know how it is. I don't blame you at all. Forget what I said, and if the others don't like it they can move out.'

I thanked her, and I done my best. When I cried it was under the covers. But I seen that I had to make a fight, or what would I ever amount to? I asked Mrs. Swenson if she didn't have something for me to do. I went around with her and helped dust the rooms and fix the beds. I picked up, being with her.

No letter come from Mary. They got their mail at Stephenville; I'd wrote to her there from Indiana and never had no trouble reaching her. It made me wonder, maybe she didn't want me now. And that was a god-send, the best thing that ever happened; it begun to rouse up something in me that I had to fight this battle alone. So I just opened up and told Mrs. Swenson that I didn't have much money and had to go to work. I dunno; all I can remember I didn't have enough to keep on paying board, and later to hire somebody to drive me to Stephenville.

She wanted to know what I could do. 'Anything under the shinin' sun,' I said.

'There's an awful nice place here for a house girl. Mrs. Leonard, that I went to school with, she's the banker's wife—she wants a cook.'

Leonard & Adams was a private bank in Fort Worth. We went over to Mrs. Leonard's on the corner; the Adams place was right opposite. They was beautiful homes, both of them. Mrs. Leonard took me over the downstairs and showed me everything. They was swell. They was banker's wives; they was high-toned just the same, a class of people I hadn't never mixed with.

Mrs. Leonard told me I didn't have to do nothing but cook. I knew I could do it. 'We have a table waiter, all you need do is get it ready,' she said.

As I remember it, she paid me four dollars a week. She had a young darky named Adora to look after her two-year old baby. Adora come in and talked to me and that was all the company I had while I was there.

The first night I give them quail pie, and Adora said how Mr. Leonard told the missus, 'She's a good cook!'

Two weeks after I'd been there the coachman said that him and a friend of his was going over to Stephenville. Right then I told him, 'I want to go—not charity; I'll pay my way.' I heard from Mary, too. They was busy planting corn and hadn't been down to the post office for the mail. In her letter Mary set the time when she would come for me but that was still three weeks off.

We got to Stephenville, eleven miles away from Mary's ranch. I told them where I wanted to go, as near as I could. Both of these men was wide awake. The one that owned the rig said he'd ride me out but he'd have to rustle around to find my sister's place. He was going to see a man by the name of Jeff Cox. I never thought nothing about that, but the way it turned out it was the same Jeff Cox I was born and raised with, and him living neighbor to my sister in Texas!

After I got done hugging and kissing, all I said was: 'This looks like a family gatherin'. I thought it was a big world when I come out in it, but now it seems to me like an awful small one, seein' you people all neighbors.'

I begun to write Willie and tell him about everything. I thought I was through with him, but I forgot my animosity when I seen them homesteads. With the help of my brother-in-law I pictured it all out, and I done my best to wake Willie up. I wrote how I could borrow the money from Wesley to bring the children. Oh, he wrote me that he would come, but he didn't. I stayed there at Mary's all summer and the next winter waiting.

Come April, Mary decided she wanted to take her boy, Johnnie, to a place she heard of called Thorp Spring, about forty miles from Fort Worth. Mary had a fine span of mules and a brand new wagon, a covered wagon, of course. Johnnie had scrofula in the eyes. He was ten years old and I don't think he'd ever been able to look up at all, for the light. It did help him so that he could see the birds fly, and it liked to tickle him to pieces. It was the spring water done it. Johnnie got over that eye trouble and made a fine man.

We wasn't able to get into the hotel or any of the boarding houses at Thorp Spring—people come from all over in the summer for the water— but somebody that had jurisdiction over it told us about the schoolhouse that was empty in vacation time. We got permission to stay there; we bought cots and a stove and went to housekeeping.

At Thorp Spring I met Johnnie Ellis that had the grocery store. He wanted to call on me but I wouldn't let him. He didn't know that I was married—everybody called me Miss Jenny, or Miss Page. It wasn't none of his business and I didn't tell him. I said I hadn't no place to entertain in, living in a schoolhouse.

I was feeling that I was a wife and didn't want no company. But Johnnie kept on. You're dang right! He said, 'Why can't I come down Sunday afternoons? Your sister's there; you ain't alone?' . . . Well, I let him come. I thought it wasn't no harm, so I said all right.

Johnnie was a fine fellow and good looking. He was sure attentive and nice, it looked like every thought of his was to do something for me. He come Sunday afternoons; he got coming nights, too. One day, setting out in the shade under a big oak by the schoolhouse, I thought that I ought to tell him how it was with me, a married woman with three children—and I did. I told him all about it.

And one thing more, too. 'Even if I was a widow tomorrow,' I said, 'I never would marry again. One husband is plenty.' I felt it, and I thought it was the truth.

'Still, even at that,' he said, 'let's go right on and be friends. I'm awful sorry—I think a great deal of you, but I'm glad that you told me.'

One day a man turned up from Ladoga, Indiana. Jonah Small; he'd worked for Willie and lived with us for many months. Back in Indiana I helped him take care of his two little girls when his wife was sick and dying. We got to be very good friends, and in that way he knew that I had a sister down in Texas. So when he come down to Stephenville the first thing he done was to hunt up Mary. Wesley Cunningham told him that we was at Thorp Spring and here he was to see me.

With news, too! Jonah Small asked me, 'When did you hear last from Willie?'

I told him not for a few months, that the one I'd been hearing from regular was my sister-in-law Annie. 'I know about the children,' I said, 'they're fine. I'm fixin' so's I can go after them or send for them this fall.'

Jonah give me a look. 'Don't you know,' he said, 'that Willie's divorced you?'

'Why, my God no!' Not that I was so in love with Willie but I never counted on nothing like that.

Jonah Small told me why Willie wanted to be free. He got going with a woman that wouldn't stand for him being a married man. He didn't marry her though.

I didn't tell Johnnie Ellis for nearly a month. I let him keep calling on me and I begun liking him. I wasn't in love, I just liked him. One night I up and told him. I didn't intend to be mealy-mouthed about it, I put it to him plain: 'I ain't married no more,' I said, 'I'm divorced.'

'All right, what about you and me pairin' off?' It come so fast the breath went out of me. Johnnie sure had a mind of his own and a quick one.

'How do you know that I care for you enough?'

'Well,' he said, 'if you don't, I calculate there's time to get that way. I'll make you care for me!'

I did, I got to caring for him plenty.

Just then Mary, in place of going back to her home as we was aiming to do, decided she'd drive the forty miles to Fort Worth. 'Linnie,' she said, 'do you know what I've a mind to do? Load up'—and she could drive them mules like a man—'and head for Fort Worth. I'm a-goin' to buy me some property maybe.' We was reading how it was growing there and she had the real estate bug.

So the next time Johnnie come, that nailed the thing. 'Let's be married first,' he said.

'No,' I told him, 'I want to go with my sister, but after I get there we can talk about it some more.'

Johnnie aimed to sell out and move to Fort Worth; he liked the idea of a bigger place. But he seen he couldn't rush me. Besides he knew he didn't come first, as much as I liked him. He told me, 'Jes' as soon as we're married, or before if you want it, I'll give you money to go after your kids.' We pulled out in about three days, us two women and Mary's boy Johnnie. We had eggs, bacon and ham, and we camped just like men.

Mary bought a big, fifteen-room boarding and lodging house at Fort Worth. But she only bought the house, the land that it stood on was leased. There's where she made a mistake, because when they went to work on the Fort Worth end of the railroad, building a branch through to Weatherford on the way to El Paso, land jumped sky-high.

We was there and settled, but I wanted to do something to forget myself. I was grieving for the babies, but I done my bawling in my room. Mary had turned the upstairs into furnished rooms and rented them out. But she didn't like to cook. She was very fleshy, weighed nigh onto two hundred pounds. I was the skinny one.

'Listen here, Mary,' I told her, 'I want to make a little money. I studied out a scheme to do it. If you'll let me have your dining room and kitchen, I'll take in day boarders and I'll board you and the boy free.'

'Sure I will,' she agreed.

I knew I could make some money at it. There was a compress, a cotton

Homesteaders. Photographed by Evelyn Cameron, an Englishwoman who fell in love with Montana and produced many memorable images of its early years. Courtesy of the Montana Historical Society.

gin, over across the block from us. I went there and got six day boarders, at five dollars and a half each week. I bought dishes, tablecloths, towels and such things as I needed. And them men went crazy over my baking-biscuits—they was used to sour dough all their lives and they thought my biscuits was wonderful.

But Mary took another one of her notions. Wesley wrote her about all the work at home—it was branding time, they was gathering in the cattle—so she thought she was needed there. And good Lord, she sold out the rooming house right over my head.

I had to make up my mind quick. After buying and paying for them dishes and things I didn't want to give in. I had seven dollars and a half to my name but I wasn't going to ask Mary for nothing. Maybe she would have loaned me a hundred or two hundred dollars—I'm sure she would at that—but I was too proud to ask it. The boys all come to me in a bunch.

They felt so bad when I said I'd have to break up. They wanted to know why I didn't open up a vacant house, standing over there by the cotton gin.

The day before Mary left I went over to look at the empty place they told me about. It was a double house and a Mr. Bronson owned it. He lived right across the street from it. I asked him if he would rent me half.

Yes, he said he would.

'Listen, I'm fixin' to open a day boarding-house and I ain't got but seven dollars and a half. I can't pay you nothin' in advance.' I think the rent was twenty dollars or twenty-five a month. 'But I have a brand new Wheeler & Wilson sewing machine I'll put up till you get paid.'

I couldn't have said nothing he would have liked better. They hadn't none and his girls wanted to do some sewing.

Next I had to have a stove. Mary took hers back. I was starting out alone, without nothing except the sewing machine, a feather bed, and my dishes, towels and tablecloths. I went to the hardware store and told the man what I wanted. I had a long talk with him. I wanted a second-hand stove, see. He had one but, no sir, he wouldn't let me have it. 'You want a good stove,' he said, 'I'll sell you a new one, the best I got in the store.'

Wasn't that the funniest thing? It sure was. I asked him why he wanted to take a chance on a ninety-dollar stove.

'Because you'll make good and pay me for it.'

Then he piled that stove with enough stuff to start housekeeping with! 'You'll need 'em all,' he said, 'to feed that hungry bunch, and a stove ain't no good without cookin' utensils.'

This was a Saturday. 'I'll come in and pay you something on it Monday,' I said, 'and after that as fast as I can.'

I hadn't touched my seven and a half!

I went off to buy some lumber, enough for tables and benches for the men. And I needed some boards for legs; I got them for nothing by paying for one piece, twenty foot long and one foot wide. I bought ten cents worth of nails; and I borrowed a hatchet and a saw from Mr. Bronson. Also he give me a plank for a bench, to set along the outside of the house to put the basins on for the men to wash up.

When I opened my place for dinner Monday noon, after buying the meat and vegetables, I still had two dollars and a half left. The six men I had over to Mary's come, and four more they brought with them. They all paid me for a week in advance.

Next day there was ten more and I had twenty to feed; of course I had to have help. I sent for Emma McLaughlin, a widow woman that was glad to get the work. I done the cooking, and didn't they punish them baking-powder biscuits!

When Saturday night come I had to put on another ten foot of table and benches, and there was money enough to pay for my stove and my house rent.

As hard as I was working, every other day I went to the post office for Johnnie Ellis' letters. Me and Johnnie had arranged our plans; he could sell out his business any time for cash but until I wrote him to come he wouldn't do nothing. The last time I was with him he told me, 'I want to be honest with you, and you be honest with me the same way. If you find anybody you like better, you jes' write and say so; I'll take it standin' up!'

After a little while Johnnie's letters stopped coming. Well, he proposed the arrangements and it was him left off. I wasn't going to let it break my heart. . . . Besides, I was seeing Jonah Small. He drifted in to town and got him a job. I went out with Jonah Saturday nights; I hadn't no time for gallivanting week days.

Then I took down sick—just when my business was so wonderful. I went to aching all over, every joint in me; I was just reeling. Emma made me take some pills. 'You'll be back on the job in the morning,' she said. I took four of them; two would have been enough but I took four. In the morning I wasn't no better, so I took three more.

I just collapsed; the pills done it. Emma got me into bed and sent for Dr. Bell. He looked at me, felt my pulse and shook his head. He didn't say nothing to me—I couldn't have answered him back if he had. Emma asked him what he thought about them seven pills I swallowed. 'Seven bullets through her head wouldn't have been no worse!' And the thought come to me: I ain't got one of them encouragin' doctors, that's sure!

I lay there forty-four days with typhoid fever, and Emma setting with me and watching over me. Thank God I had money enough to see me through.

Jonah Small was around asking how I was getting along and trying to help out every way he could. And after a few months we was engaged to be married and I had his ring on. I was mighty happy. He knowed Willie and the babies; he was the only one around there that did. He was good and kind, promising how we was going back for the children. He meant all he promised. It was that more than love; I was grateful to him for his understanding ways.

As soon as I was strong enough I opened in the same place but I had to change my business. The compress was closed. I had a big sign hung up, DRESSMAKING, and I got lots of sewing—enough to keep going. Then I moved just across the street and opened up a millinery business, along with my dressmaking. I had all I could do. The hat part was hard work, specially the bleaching with sulphur.

How is it that so many things comes up in one person's life? It was probably six months after me and Jonah was engaged—I just don't know how long it was—when I went over to the post-office, and my land, if there wasn't a letter from Johnnie Ellis! He wanted to know what had happened, why I hadn't answered his letters. Asked me to tell him didn't I care no more.

Well, the way things had turned out, that's so, I didn't care no more. Not hearing from Johnnie I'd kind of forgot him and I'd stopped going to the post-office regular. . . . But here was something else. I was sure now, somehow it come to me, that Jonah Small had been stealing my letters. He knew about Johnnie for I'd told him everything. . . .

When Jonah come to see me in the evening I asked him, 'Where's my letters?'

'What letters. . . . I don't know what you mean.'

'I mean this; I want them letters from Johnnie Ellis that you stole out of the post-office. I got one here saying as how he was writin' right along!'

Jonah was dumfounded. He thought there wouldn't be no more letters, after Johnnie got disgusted and quit writing for a while.

I told him, 'Do you know I could send you to the penitentiary? The only thing you have to do is tell me why you done it.'

Yes, he owned up; what else could he do? 'I done it because I wanted you to marry me. I knew the kind of woman you was ever since I lived at your house. I made up my mind to court you, and marry you, and help you take care of the children, for the good way you treated me and my little girls. I seen that Ellis stood betwixt us and that's why I done it.'

There was a little ravine close by where we was setting. I throwed Jonah's ring down there in the bushes. 'Now you jes' follow it!' I said. 'I never want to see your face again.'

I run up my business to the best millinery store in Fort Worth. I had three salesladies working for me: big Alice, and little Alice about four foot high, and Emma McLaughlin. I done most of the making of the hats myself—except the frames; I bought them of course. I done the covers and the trimming.

If I wanted to buy anything I could go to Bennett's store and several others. There was times when I was short of cash but they give me credit; I never got turned down by no one, not even by Turk, the tall Jew with the little black mustache, that wouldn't give nobody credit.

Right then I took the typhoid again—in the glory of all my success. For the second time. The doctors couldn't understand it, only a little more than a year after the first time. I was just as bad but I was laid up ten days less. Dr. Bell brought in his partner, Dr. Fields, that become my good friend.

And another partner, Dr. Birch—he come in too. I told them, 'You look worried. Three doctors means something! Jes' cut out thinkin' I'm a goner cause I ain't!' I firmly believed I'd get well when I said it.

Emma McLaughlin was nursing me. Little Alice run the business and done it good. I went back to work as soon as I could. During that time I got in the habit of reading medical books that Dr. Fields give me. He said as I was calculated to make a good midwife. I didn't take that serious, but I went on studying for many years, knowing one kind of study was as good as another for a body's brain.

Willie Page begun writing me to come to Kansas. He had his divorce, but now that he got it he didn't want it. I actually packed a box with my sewing machine and my saddle that was my mother's, and some other things I had, and shipped them to Annie in southern Kansas where Willie had the children. That's how close I come to going back to him.

I was making good in Fort Worth and I thought that I could start my children off right in Kansas, even if my husband hadn't. Dr. Fields was the cause of me not going there. I got one of my bilious fever attacks and I told Dr. Fields I'd have to give up and go home if I kept on that way. I was ashamed to tell him I had weakened and was going back to Willie Page.

'Well now,' he said drawly and quiet like, 'I don't think we're beat yet.'
He started to joke. 'What am I goin' to do without you?'

'I ain't foolin' about this,' I went on, 'I sent my feather bed and a lot of
things to Kansas.'

He boiled up—'What's that you say? Are you tryin' to make me think
you're jes' an ordinary quitter? You ain't goin' back to that no-account and
spoil your life!'

I told him I didn't figure Willie would ever amount to nothing; I wasn't
fooling myself.

He answered me: 'Jenny'—that's the name they used to call me by,
down in Texas—'why can't you do for your own children and take them
away from him?'

More than once I had told Dr. Fields I couldn't force Willie. No court
would let me have my children, thinking I wasn't worthy after leaving
them. I said something like that now.

'Let me ask you,' he said, 'are you goin' back for your children, or is
there something else?' I told him true—'There ain't nothing else, it's only
that. I'd give up everything to get them.'

'You ain't crazy about lovin' a man if you was to go to marryin' him?'
I didn't know what he meant.

'I know a man that's got plenty of money,' said Dr. Fields, 'and I believe
he'd marry you twenty-four hours after he talked to you. Marry him and
you'll have the money to go back and fight for your children! Get 'em here
in Texas and you won't have no more trouble.'

I was willing to do anything Dr. Fields told me, I had so much confidence in him.

He knew that my sister Mary was coming back to Fort Worth with her
two daughters and little Johnnie. Dr. Fields had been doctoring the boy.
He said, 'I'll stop in to say howdy when they get here. I'll have a gentleman
with me and I'll introduce him. Then you can do the rest.' But he wouldn't
tell me nothing about him, who he was or what he looked like.

Mary moved into town and one day, sure enough, along comes the doctor in his buggy. 'I jes' dropped in to see how the family is gettin' along
and I brought a friend of mine with me.' He turned around and said,
'Come in, Mr. Chase, I want to introduce you to my friends here.' Dr.
Fields introduced him all around. I knowed it was the man and I felt
mighty peculiar.

First off I noticed his brown eyes, and his rosy cheeks and fair complexion. He had white whiskers, cut round and covering his necktie about two or three inches under the chin. His hair was brown, nearly gray and parted in the middle—on the sides it was curly. He was a handsome man, close on to fifty years old; medium size, perhaps a little too short.

'I feel like we're goin' to be good friends and I am awfully pleased to meet you, Mr. Chase.' Them was my words.

They stayed half an hour—it was about eleven thirty in the forenoon. Dr. Fields got up to leave. 'I'm a-goin' to eat dinner with the family and Mr. Chase is comin' with me,' he said.

Mary walked out of the kitchen with a fresh baked cake and wanted them all to have a piece. The doctor said as he was going straight to his dinner he wouldn't have none. Mr. Chase seemed to see that Mary was embarrassed. 'Doctor,' he said, 'I don't have no home to eat at; I will be pleased to get a piece of that home-baked cake.'

He was the grandest man in that respect; he was a gentleman. He was just being polite. But inside it made me smile, wondering if the old darling wasn't hinting already!

About two evenings after Mr. Chase stopped in to call. He brought us nuts and candy, and he had his pockets full for the boy Johnnie. He said as he was out walking and got feeling lonesome. He smiled and it went to my heart. We just set around and talked. He asked me if I cared for driving.

'Yes,' I told him, 'I am very fond of it, and I love best to drive after sundown.'

Fort Worth was beautiful to drive through at dusk. It was level and there wasn't no trees, and the horizon seemed so far off, with nothing in sight but maybe a slice of moon. In the day the wind was hot and heavy but at night there was a balmy zephyr breeze blowing. Them summer nights was the finest I ever seen anywhere. I have always been a great one for setting out in the evening. Texas nights is beautiful.

Dr. Fields come along after a bit. 'How do you like my friend?'

'I like him wonderful, ain't he a gentleman!'

'Never was a greater one,' he said. 'He's your'n if you want him, the way I size it up. But don't take him for his money and give him the go-by. No, you ain't that sort of woman.'

Some people is inclined, it's their way, to take all they can get. But I like the give side better than the take. 'No, I ain't,' I said, 'when I bargain, I pay. Even if I knew he wouldn't be good to me I'd risk it to get the children. And I'll do my best to make him happy.'

Mr. Chase come around for me one afternoon about four o'clock. 'There's a lot of country I want to show you,' he said. 'We'll head down Weatherford way and drive home by moonlight.'

We didn't do much talking; we was still strange. Every little while I sighed. I was in heaven. I was sure I was going to get my May back. Then I'd quail. Maybe he'd think I was a flip of a girl and wouldn't like me. Did he know about my being married? Most everybody called me Miss Page. I found out later that Dr. Fields hadn't said nothing.

I told Mr. Chase how I enjoyed the ride so much.

'If you have enjoyed it as much as that you won't mind comin' out again.'

'That sure will be grand!' I replied.

I made it strong! And I made it easier for him by saying again how I liked driving in the dusk best—seeing as how he was a business man.

But I done a mean thing to him about three weeks after that, on a Sunday afternoon. Another one of my beaux drove up in a brand new rig and I couldn't resist the temptation of taking a ride. I said to Mr. Chase, 'Stay here and keep house till I get back, I won't be gone long.'

We drove out about three miles; then this fellow thought as he'd get smart and try to hug me. I told him to keep his hands to hisself but he didn't. I reached out for a rein and give it a tug that brought the wagon around sharp. And I jumped out.

I started to walk home, him driving alongside and begging me to get in. It was taking me so long to walk them miles. And I was thinking about Mr. Chase setting there. So I climbed back.

'But don't you start pawin' me!'

'No,' he said, 'I have learnt my lesson.'

When I got home and peered in Mr. Chase looked terrible. Oh, he was scorching mad! He'd been playing with Trixie, the little dog he give me the week before.

'I'll be goin' now,' was all he said. He raised up with Trixie under his arm and started out.

I grabbed Trixie—'No you don't,' I cried, 'you can't have her!'

'Goldingit!' he said, 'you think more of that whelp than you do me!' That made us both laugh. It broke the ice.

'Come on,' I begged, taking his hand and leading him over to the sofa; 'you can hear all about it, then maybe you won't be so mad with me.' And I told him what happened. And a lot more. All about my being married, and about the children. . . . My voice was cracking and I had to stop to keep the tears back.

Mr. Chase set still as a mouse. After a bit he said, 'I have been married, too. I have been married twice. My first wife, Arvilla Bunn, was an orphan. We was boarding the same place. She hadn't a living soul on earth that meant a thing to her. I lost her when the baby come—and the baby.'

He told me everything. 'I grieved a long time over losin' her,' he said. 'You see this ring on my finger; it ain't got no set, it's very unsightly. There was a diamond in it. But I wouldn't let no one touch it when the points needed fixin' because Arvilla wished it on.'

He told me then about his second wife. He lost her in three years. There was two step-children, Milton and Katy, and he was supporting them, he said, though they did not live with him.

Bless his old soul, he was looking at me so serious. Then he said, 'I'm glad this has come up and we could talk it over. I'm a-goin' to make a proposition to you, too. I ain't askin' you to love me. I think it's impossible for a young woman like you to love a man as old as me. . . .'

I told him, 'I ain't no sucklin'. There ain't such a difference between us. Don't say that word again—hearts never grow old!'

'Ain't them sweet words!' he said. And then, 'I'm a-goin' to ask you to let me kiss you on the cheek.'

'Let's change that to the mouth! Cheek-kissin' don't mean nothin',' I told him.

After a time he said, 'I have a little property, I ain't never used a dollar from the estate of my first wife. There's a five hundred acre ranch in Tyler County rented out that pays me two hundred dollars a year. It's for you as a weddin' present.'

We understood each other before we ever tied up. We was married eight weeks from the day we met—by the Justice of the Peace at Wax-ahachie. In his parlour; the man's two daughters was the witnesses.

The first night Mr. Chase slept like a baby. I laid there and thought: So I am Mrs. Chase. Well, the honor of bein' a rich man's wife ain't goin' to bother me none!

We went next day to Fort Worth, to Mr. Chase's rooms where he lived above his office. He had a small private office up there. 'I'm a-goin' to rent a house,' he told me. 'We may be movin' along some day; I don't want to buy if it's all the same to you.' He had been out looking at some houses and he took me to see the one he liked best. It was on 'Quality Hill' where all the upstarts lived; that's what I called them. A nice six-room house, very high up and well-built, although it wasn't the finest house; there was others finer.

Mr. Chase moved all his stuff over and told me to buy what I pleased. I loved nice window curtains and I did get fine ones—and everything else in keeping.

'It's up to you when you want to go after your children.'

'I'll be goin' next week,' I said.

Malinda Jenkins, *Gambler's Wife: The Life of Malinda Jenkins* (Boston and New York: Houghton Mifflin, 1933), pp. 59–60, 78–97.

Mary Sheehan was a child of the frontier, following her father from one western mining town to the next. She married Peter Ronan, a Helena newspaperman, when she was nineteen. Four years later he was appointed as the government's agent at the Flathead Indian reservation in western Montana, where they lived for the next sixteen years. Although most Indian agents were notoriously corrupt and uncaring, the Ronans were different, and their relations with the Indians were close and cordial. Mary Ronan's account thus serves as a valuable contrast to those demonstrating the negative attitudes of some other women toward Indians. The contrast even includes a poignant description of an Indian girl who was captured and raped by white men. Her Indian father, Captain George, appealed to the Ronans for help as he searched for his daughter to save her and bring her home.

Constant hospitality was characteristic of frontier life and was a particularly important duty for a government official's wife. Ronan also provides details of domesticity, delighting, for example, in having a tub that could actually be drained through a rubber tube. She frequently mentions the warmth of close relationships with other women. This selection from her autobiography, which was written in collaboration with her daughter, describes her life on the reservation and the circumstances of the Nez Perce War of 1877.

"At the head of the Jocko Valley, on a small tributary of the Jocko River and distant about two miles from that stream, is situated the Flathead Indian Agency. One mile to the rear of the Agency buildings a chain of lofty mountains rises abruptly from the valley, forming no foothills and towering grandly. . . . The valley is about

five miles in breadth and twelve miles in length. Along the river and tribu-
taries is excellent farming land, cultivated by Flathead Indians and half-
breeds. Following down the Jocko to its confluence with the Pend d'Oreille
River the valley closes, and for a few miles the Jocko rushes through a narrow gorge, but before joining its waters to the Pend d'Oreille River and at
the junction of those two streams the valley again opens into a rich and
fertile plain where a large number of Indian farms are located. Good log
houses and well-fenced farms, with waving fields of grain everywhere give
evidence of husbandry and thrift.

"Leaving the Jocko to the left and passing through a narrow canyon
and over a low divide of hills the road leads to St. Ignatius Mission, some
seventeen miles from the Agency, where the Indian boarding and manual
labor school [founded in 1864] is established. This Mission is one of
the largest institutions of the kind in the U.S. and is presided over by a
number of Jesuit priests, lay brothers and Sisters of Charity. A large convent, church, schoolhouse and dwellings are surrounded by a picturesque
Indian village of some seventy snug log houses, where principally Pend
D'Oreille Indians dwell and cultivate the rich soil. The Mission Valley is a
broad and extensive plain, well watered from streams which flow from the
lofty and broken ranges of mountains that rise on both sides. From the
Mission to Flathead Lake, a distance of thirty miles, and around its borders there are farming lands enough for thousands of settlers. The Indian
name for the lake is *Skalt-Koon-See*, which means Wide, or Big, Sheet of
Water." . . .

I have quoted at length because the words reveal a situation for the
Indians quite different from the present one. I bear witness to the fact that
at that time many of them did have snug log houses, well-fenced farms,
waving fields of grain and grazing herds of horses and cattle, and there was
evidence of husbandry and thrift and of the advance of the Indians in the
ways of civilization.

The confederated tribes of the Flatheads, the Salish, Pend d'Oreilles and
the Kootenais at once bestowed upon my husband the title *Scale-ee-hue-
eal-i-me-kum,* White Chief. That he was indeed—he became their advisor,
mediator, patriarch, champion. So concerned was he in their affairs—in
counseling them, in seeking to solve their problems, in getting justice for
them and redress for their many and grievous wrongs—and so successful
was he in the administration of his office that he spent the remaining six-

teen years of his life among them on reappointments through Republican and Democratic administrations.

Once, in council with the confederated tribes, General John Gibbon, who looked upon the solution of the Indian question as dependent upon the transfer of the red man to the guardianship of the Army, suddenly put the question to the Flathead Chief Arlee, "Do you like your Agent?" Arlee replied, "As Agent of the Government we respect him; as a friend and adviser and neighbor we love him; and I trust I may never live to see the appointment of his successor." With a few notable exceptions, that, for instance, of Major John Owen, always the understanding friend of the Indians, the history of the affairs of the Flathead Reservation under the various agents had been one of everlasting trouble, or misappropriation of Indian and Government property and of constant court proceedings. . . .

True enough, just as my husband thought, I was delighted with the beauty of the place. There I spent twenty years, the most interesting and difficult of my life. Something stirring, exciting, dangerous was always pending, threatening, happening.

The old Agency was isolated from civilization, but the situation was lovely, and fishermen and huntsmen found the streams and country all about such a paradise for their sports that after the first summer as long as I lived on the Reservation I was never again alone in my home with my own family. As there was no hotel nearer than Missoula, a half-day's journey by wagon or horseback, and as my husband was lavish in his hospitality all comers were our house guests for as long as they chose to stay. Keeping my household organized, attending to the needs of growing children, the insistent demands of a baby—during most of those years there was a child under three years of age—counseling my husband when, in our mutual concerns, we felt that two heads were better than one, all combined to keep me in the midst of enthusiastic activity and burning with a sense of quickened and multiplied consciousness. My difficult[y] came upon me in having to play the gracious hostess almost continually to members of Indian commissions, Senatorial commissions on appropriation for the Reservation Transcontinental Surveys and Railroad commissions, Special Agents of the Government, Generals of the Army and other officers, a Papal Ablegate, archbishop, bishops and priests, an English and an Irish earl, a French count and other sportsmen from abroad and the East and

West, scientists, millionaires, journalists in search of a story, celebrities, friends, relatives, Indians—chiefs, tribesmen, squaws with their papooses.

No retinue of servants was in the background to prepare and serve food and to dispense other necessities and comforts for this multitudinous and very human pageant of guests. My help usually was a Chinese cook, an Indian laundress, and a young girl to act as nursemaid for the children and to help with the sewing—for I made all my clothes and the children's. I am glad to remember that I never felt overworked or abused or longed for my little children to grow up. Always something especially appealing about the worn little shoes scattered about in the evening made me resolve that the next day I would try to be more patient and sweeter. . . .

Mr. Ronan . . . came to Helena in "the nice spring wagon," and conveyed Mrs. Lambert, the children and me the hundred fifty miles to the Reservation "in a very comfortable manner,"—according to the ideas of that time.

Mrs. Lambert with her little daughter Grace, who was just Mary's age, and I with my baby Gerald, not yet three months old, sat on the back seat. Mary, not yet two years old, and Vincent, just past three, sat beside their father on the journey. . . .

Mrs. Lambert and I were young, happy and forward-looking. We did not find the care of children on the trip irksome. The weather was sunny, so sunny that my wrist, exposed between the sleeve and glove as I held the baby, was all but blistered. The country was beautiful beyond description. The spicy fragrance of June blossoms, especially of wild roses which hedged the road, and syringas, which almost embowered it, delighted us into forgetfulness of burned wrists, arms aching from holding the baby, hours and hours of jolting over rocky roads that followed river bottoms or clung along mountain slopes, of toiling up long, long grades or scraping down with brakes set, of pitching down steep banks into deep fords. Between Deer Lodge and Missoula, a distance of eighty miles, the Missoula River [Clark Fork River] had to be forded about twenty times.

On the evening of the third day we arrived in Missoula and went to the hotel on West Front Street, kept by Mr. and Mrs. William Kennedy. These old friends were expecting us and greet us warmly. Missoula was a little village in 1877, most of the log houses clustered in the vicinity of the bridge where the Missoula mills, the property of F. L. Worden, stood. On Front

Street the village extended a block or so east and west and north on Higgins Avenue. Early the next morning we started on the last twenty-eight miles of our journey. At the mouth of the Coriacan Defile (O'Keefe Canyon) we stopped at the log ranch house of Baron O'Keefe, for through all the years since Alder Gulch days I had kept up my friendship with Mrs. O'Keefe, nee Hannah Lester, by letters, and since my marriage Mrs. O'Keefe and her two little girls had visited in Helena. In spite of urgent invitations we did not stay long enough to get down from the wagon, for we were anxious to reach our new home.

The weariest, most wildly beautiful stretch of our way lay through the narrow Coriacan Defile. Besides following the windings of the canyon, the road twisted and turned around great boulders. The road bed was as rocky as a river bottom, in fact it lay along what must have been an old creek bed. We traveled next for four or five hours through the dense, majestic Evaro woods, slaughtered years ago, down Evaro Hill to the ford of Finlay Creek, then a roaring torrent—for none of the water had been diverted for irrigation. Just beyond the ford we emerged from a grand grove of yellow pines and I saw for the first time the fruitful valley of the Jocko, lovely and lush in June growth, the grass and flowers spread knee-deep across the prairies. Here was a great blue patch of lupine, there a rippling splotch of pink clarkia. A band of wild horses, grazing in this luxuriance, raised their heads, startled, whinnied and broke into a gallop. Pitched against backgrounds of occasional clumps of trees were smoke-stained tepees. Best of all, in the distance, at the end of the road that looped in long curves almost across the valley from west to east, was visible a little settlement, the Agency, our home, a cluster of houses showing white in the late afternoon sunshine.

Directly to the east and to the south of the Agency buildings, not two miles away, rose, without approaches, so abruptly that they seemed to lean forward, great, wooded pyramids of mountains, their dark blue intensified by deep shadows. To the northeast in a gap in the mountains was a magnificent view of one of the jagged snow-capped peaks of the Mission Range and a glimpse of a waterfall on its craggy side, barely distinguishable from the snow. To the north were rolling brown hills; back of us to the west were wooded hills and mountains. So beautiful the valley was that it seemed to me I had entered a place like the Garden of Paradise.

At the Agency stockade Harry Lambert waited to welcome us. We went into the house and found a delicious dinner ready to be served by the cook, whom Mr. Ronan had hired, a clean, efficient white woman. We were tired but not too tired to be gay during our house-warming dinner.

When Mr. Ronan had had sufficient time to make improvements, the Agency settlement, built in a hollow square covering in all about an acre of ground, consisted of our residence in the center on the south side of the square; on the west a building including the Agent's office, a storehouse for the Government clerk, a granary, a long narrow building with living quarters for the Indian interpreter and the Agency employees (miller, sawyer, carpenter, stableman and others); on the north a barn, a carpenter's shop and a blacksmith's; on the east a grist and saw mill; in the southwest corner, a house for the residence, office and drugstore of the Agency doctor. In the yard back of the Agent's residence were various small buildings—an icehouse, milkhouse, smokehouse, chicken house, washhouse and others. All the residences were weather-boarded and enclosed within low picket fences. The yards were planted with gardens and shade trees. All of the buildings were painted white or were whitewashed except the sawmill which was red like the roof of the big barn. A picket fence six feet high enclosed the whole Agency square; at the middle of each side was a gate wide enough for a wagon to drive through. At night these gates were closed, to keep out wandering stock. A fence-enclosed vegetable garden, a pasture with a zigzag fence, cattle sheds, houses for the sawyer and blacksmith were outside the stockade to the north and the west.

In time Mr. Ronan set out an orchard, planting several varieties of apple trees, wild plum trees, currant, gooseberry, raspberry and blackberry bushes and strawberry plants. In the midst of the orchard he built a cottage for the gardener, behind it a big root cellar, and still farther back was a pond for water storage in summertime and ice cutting in winter. He devised a system of waterworks—a cold stream was run through the milkhouse, cold water was piped into the kitchen sink, a bathroom with a tin tub was improvised in a small room off the kitchen. Hot water had to be carried in pails from the large tank attached to the kitchen stove and emptied into the tub, cold water in pails from the sink. But the water could be drained out through a rubber tube into a narrow irrigating ditch, a truly great convenience.

After a number of years a sufficient appropriation was allowed by the

Government for additions to several of the residences. On account of the numerous official guests that it was necessary to entertain the two-story addition to the Agent's house was somewhat pretentious for the times, consisting of a large parlor and several bedrooms. The house came to have during most of the years we lived in it eleven rooms besides a fair-sized storeroom, pantry, bathroom and three hallways. The largest of these hallways, the children named "The Hall of Death," because in it were many mounted trophies of the chase—a black bear, a mountain goat, elk, moose, deer and caribou heads. . . .

. . . Often in the late afternoon Mr. Ronan would walk, ride horseback or drive to the Jocko and return in perhaps an hour with twenty or thirty trout hanging from the crotch of a willow branch in plenty of time to have them cooked for supper. All about the Agency stockade were quantities of prairie chickens and pheasants. We would shoot the birds from the wagon. The children loved to be lifted down to run to get the birds. In season for each we went on gay expeditions to gather huckleberries, chokecherries, wild plums, Oregon grapes and elderberries. These I preserved or made into jelly or jam in great quantities and put away in gallon earthen jars.

We had need to use every resource. We were provided with shelter, heat, light, some staple supplies such as flour and sugar, and we were privileged to utilize for our own household products from the Government demonstration farm, garden and orchard. My husband's salary was $125.00 a month, payable in quarterly installments; oftener than not, however, until the railroad came through the payments were delayed a month or two or three. The currency to pay the salaries of all the Government employees on the Reservation and allotments to the Indians was expressed to Missoula, where my husband had to go to receive it and then to drive back with a pouch containing thousands of dollars over that lonely, twenty-five-mile stretch of hill country, mountain, forest and canyon to the Agency. The trips were always made secretly. Sometimes Mr. Ronan took with him a trusted guard, but oftenest he made the trip alone, armed. He was never accosted by robbers, but I was never a moment at ease until his errand was accomplished.

In those happy-go-lucky days before a household budget was heard of we would have regarded it as a breach of hospitality to submit to the Department of the Interior an expense account for the ubiquitous inspectors, special agents and other officials on Government business who stayed at our house and sat with us at table for days, weeks and sometimes months at a time. It never occurred to either of us to do so. I suppose we were simple, unsophisticated and unbusinesslike. We were products of our times. Every stranger was welcomed like a worthy, bidden guest. Our latchstring always hung out.

In our early days at the Agency we kept hearing stories of trouble which had been rife for some time among the non-treaty Nez Percé led by Chief Joseph and the white settlers in the Wallowa Valley in Idaho, backed by the U.S. soldiers under the command of General O. O. Howard. Except for an uneasy feeling when I listened to these rumors, the first weeks at the Agency passed like a happy dream. Soon, however, storm clouds gathered, the terrible red clouds of war. Every day brought us new rumors of the trouble between the whites and the Indians. Some Nez Percé lived on the Reservation. Arlee himself, the war chief of the Salish (including the Flat-heads), was the son of a Nez Percé mother.

One morning, a few weeks after our arrival at the agency when I was sitting on the porch drying my hair, which was heavy and wavy and hung below my knees, Arlee stalked up the steps followed by one or two of his men and the interpreter, Baptiste Marengo. He enquired for Mr. Ronan. I arose, shook my hair back from my face and started into the house to find him. I heard a moccasined tread behind me and felt my hair gathered by a hand at the nape of my neck. I was terror-stricken. There flashed into my mind childish fears I had had when trekking across the plains and the awful tales of scalpings related by emigrants by campfires at night. Fortunately, I did not have time to cry out or to show my fear in any way, for quickly I felt a second hand below the first, and so hand below hand the length of my hair. While the measuring was in progress Baptiste spoke, saying that the Indians liked long hair, that Arlee had never seen any so long as mine and that he wanted to tell the tribe how many hands long it was. . . .

One day a runner came with definite information that Chief Joseph and his band, flushed with victory over the United States soldiers in Idaho, were on the warpath and were headed toward Montana on their way to Canada. Mr. Ronan was away from home on business. Ovando Hoyt, the miller, really a better carpenter and painter, was doing some renovating around our house. He was a Spiritualist. Whenever I passed him, going about my household affairs, he would stop his work and, embellishing his revelations with much waving of arms and gesticulation with a paint brush, relate to me the visions that had been vouchsafed him of the Nez Percé sweeping in carnage across the Reservation and over the entire state of Montana. Without my husband to reassure me, this, to say the least, was very distressing.

Excitement possessed us all. The very air was charged with fear when a runner brought us the news from Missoula that on July 20 the Nez Percé had appeared in the Bitter Root Valley, forty miles from the Reservation, and that on July 23 they had actually appeared in war array outside Captain Rawn's encampment in Lolo Pass. *The Missoulian* issued an extra edition on July 25 which carried the headline, HELP! HELP! WHITE BIRD DEFIANT! COME RUNNING! *The New Northwest* of Deer Lodge, dated July 28, 1877, came to us several days late, carrying a story of the presence of Chief Joseph, White Bird and Looking-Glass in Lolo Canyon, with three hundred and thirty warriors; of Captain Rawn, the Seventh Infantry and a volunteer force being entrenched in the Canyon; of the call for more troops; of the coming of the Deer Lodge volunteers; and of Governor Pott's arrival in Missoula, twelve miles from Lolo Canyon, to ascertain the true situation. Mr. Ronan was in the midst of the stir, riding back and forth between the Agency and Missoula to keep informed, and here and there about the Reservation to check on the whereabouts and activities of the Indians under his charge, especially of Eagle-of-the-Light and his following.

Our baby Gerald suddenly became very ill. No doctor was at that time assigned to the Agency. There was no one to send to Missoula for a doctor, so Mr. Ronan himself went with a team of fast horses. While he was gone a runner brought the news that the Nez Percé were headed through Missoula and across the Reservation into Canada over the Kootenai trail; that all the women and children in Missoula had been gathered in the Courthouse, with guards picketed; and that already the Indians had launched their attack on Missoula. I have no words to express the intensity of my feelings. I scanned keenly every Indian who chanced into the Agency square, trying to pierce into their stolidity and to detect a look or an action that betokened friendliness or enmity. When, in the morning, I found the baby was much better and could be left with Mrs. Lambert, I went about among the Agency employees to discover what news or hope they could give me that my husband was safe and that the march of the Nez Percé was not in our direction. My terror was increased, for I found that the men had all stopped their work and were putting their firearms in readiness for use.

By noon Mr. Ronan returned with reassuring news. He said that there were no Nez Percé in Missoula and that there was no fighting. The women and children had been gathered in the Courthouse under guard merely as a precaution. He was assured, he said, of the friendly attitude of Chief Arlee, "the renegade Nez Percé," as Charlot, Chief of the Bitter Root Flatheads, called him. Furthermore, Mr. Ronan declared that among the two hundred volunteers entrenched with Captain Rawn were many Flathead Indians.

For all he said, that night I saw him, when he thought I was asleep, slipping guns, ammunition and even a hatchet into the wardrobe in our bedroom. That night we only pretended to be asleep. Our ears were alert for sounds of hoofbeats and warwhoops. At last morning came and runners from Missoula to say that still there was no sign of the Nez Percé there.

That morning old Michelle, Chief of the Pend d'Oreilles, and a band of his warriors pitched their tepees just outside the Agency square. He and a group of his headmen came ceremoniously into Mr. Ronan's office. Through an interpreter, Michelle announced to the White Chief (Mr. Ronan) that he and his people would stand with Arlee and with the whites against the Nez Percé. He had sent a message, he said, to Joseph that should he try to cross the Reservation it would mean the annihilation of his band. If the wife of the White Chief was frightened, he would picket a guard of his warriors around the house until all danger had passed.

I was summoned to the council. The Indians sat about the office, some in chairs, some squatted upon the floor, solemnly passing around the circle a tomahawk with a bowl and pipe stem, each one drawing and puffing in that slow, enigmatic way that I came to know as typical of the Indians. I stood beside my husband, scarcely concealing my trembling. The interpreter repeated Michelle's message to me. The Pend d'Oreille Chief's rugged old countenance and kindly attitude commanded belief and respect. My self-possession returned. After a brief consultation with my husband I asked the interpreter to thank Michelle and his men and to say that I would not require a guard. The encampment of Pend d'Oreilles so near the Agency and their Chief's pledge of friendship were assurance to me of the safety of my children and myself. . . .

After several days we heard . . . that early in the morning of July

28 Joseph had broken camp and with his entire following of warriors, squaws, papooses, equipment and stock belonging to his band of non-treaty Nez Percé, had skirted Captain Rawn's entrenchment and had pushed forward along the wooded slopes of the Bitter Root Mountains. For more than a week couriers kept bringing us news of the leisurely march of the Nez Percé through the Bitter Root Valley. "In view of all the circumstances, it was the boldest, most fearless, audacious and confident tactical movement we have ever known. Then we had the news of the terrible carnage of the Big Hole, beginning at daybreak on August 9. Little by little the news reached us of Joseph's retreat through Yellowstone Park, across the Missouri, and north across the state of Montana toward Canada, of the encounters with General Miles and General Howard in the Bear Paw Mountains, of the escape of Chief White Bird and forty bold warriors across the British miles on October 8 to save the remnants of his tribe—"eighty-seven warriors, of whom forty were wounded, one hundred and eighty-four squaws and forty-seven children." He was reported to have stated, "I said in my heart that rather than have war I would give up my country. I would give up everything rather than have the blood of the white men upon the hands of my people."

My husband, as a result of his conferences with the Jesuits, who knew the Indian so well and also because of the acquaintanceship and investigation among the Indians that he had been able to make even during the first two months in office, believed in the sincerity of Chief Joseph and regretted the course that was being pursued against him. Hostility had been forced upon Joseph. Many whites began to believe that he was indeed a man with grievance, a man to be respected and admired. We followed with interest all that befell Joseph, his removal with his people to Fort Leavenworth, and later to Baxter Springs, Kansas, where many of the Indians sickened and died. Through all of the years of Mr. Ronan's services among the Indians echoes of this tragedy kept coming to him. And more than that, he listened frequently to poignant appeals from Nez Percé friends of Joseph's on the Reservation, to do all in his power to bring an end to that tragic exile. "Take me back to my old home," the broken warrior chief kept pleading, "Where I can see the tall mountains and can count the stones at the bottom of the mountain streams." Because my husband believed that the plea of Chief Joseph and his friends was based on just claims he did exert his utmost in behalf of the dispossessed Nez Percé. . . .

Mr. Ronan recommended to the Commissioner of Indian Affairs that Joseph and his band be sent to the Flathead Reservation. His recommendation was not acted upon in every detail, but at last, in 1885, the broken Chief Joseph and the sick and impoverished survivors of his audacious tribe were sent to spend their last days on the Colville Reservation in northern Washington, near, at least, to their old home and where they could "see the tall mountains and count the stones at the bottom of the mountain streams."

After the excitement following the surrender of Chief Joseph had subsided, except for minor troubles with police discipline and the necessity of expelling some whites from the Reservation, peace reigned on our little domain and the year rolled happily around to July, 1878. . . .

One day in mid-July . . . two strange Indians, heavily armed, dismounted at our gate, tied their horses to the white picket fence and stalked into the sitting-room. I was alone in the house with my three little children and the nursemaid, Minnie Sullivan. Minnie at once recognized the warriors as Nez Percé. One of them, who walked with a limp, a grim, bruised, battered-looking man with a soiled and bloody bandana around his forehead, asked in English for Major Ronan. While Minnie hastened away to find him, the Nez Percé told me that they had come from a camp on the Jocko Lakes. I was terrified. In my mind this confirmed the rumor that White Bird's hostiles had indeed come over the Jocko Trail and would soon surround the Agency.

In a few moments Mr. Ronan entered the room. The Indians greeted him and then sat in silence for some time before the spokesman took three letters from his beaded pouch and gave them to Mr. Ronan. When my husband finished reading, Captain George (for that was the spokesman's name) told his story. He had joined the retreat of the Nez Percé from Idaho the previous summer. A young warrior from Joseph's band had carried off his sixteen-year-old daughter from his home at the crossing of the Camai in Idaho. She was with the Indians in all of their battles, including the Battle of the Big Hole, where fifty Indian women and children were among those killed. She was among the fugitives in the retreat across Montana. Her abductor was one of the band that escaped with White Bird and he took her with him to the camp of Sitting Bull. Captain George had traveled on horseback in search of his daughter more than two thousand miles before arriving at the Agency that morning of July 14, 1878.

One of the letters Captain George brought related part of his pathetic story:

> The bearer, "Captain George" (so-called) is a Nez Perce who came through with General Howard to get his daughter, who was in the hostile camp. He was very useful as an interpreter at the surrender of Chief Joseph and his band of warriors, and after the Nez Perce camp was secured. I sent him to Sitting Bull's camp for his daughter, and with a message to White Bird and the band who escaped. He secured his daughter, got as far as Carroll, or near there, where he was foully dealt with by miserable white men—was shot in several places, as his unhealed wounds will show, and his young girl used worse. I presume he was left for dead, but succeeded in reaching the Crow camp. His daughter was taken, I understand, to Benton, where she remained at last accounts.
>
> For his good services, and to repair, as far as possible, the wrong done, I send him with two government ponies to you, and one other Nez Perce, hoping that he may recover his child. Should he do so, please send him back to his home, or make such disposition of them as you deem best. The ponies I would like sent back, as they belong to my regiment.
>
> If the white men who committed the crime are caught I would suggest that you report to department headquarters, as the department commander ordered the affair investigated. I am, sir, very respectfully your obedient servant,
>
> Nelson A. Miles
> Colonel Fifth Infantry
> Brevet Major General
> United States Army
> Commanding

The second letter was from Major James T. Brisbin, the commanding officer at Fort Ellis, Montana. It was dated July 5 and read:

> To Whom It May Concern:
>
> The bearer of this, "Captain George," a Nez Perce Indian, arrived here, and goes to Benton to find his daughter who was stolen from him by some white men. Citizens along the road between here and

Benton are forbidden to harm Captain George and his companions, and should give him every assistance in their power to recovery of his child, as he has been badly treated by the whites.

The third letter, from an officer at Fort Benton, commanded safe passage for Captain George from there to Flathead Indian Agency and enlisted the assistance of the Agent in searching for the Nez Percé girl and restoration to her father.

Mr. Ronan found quarters for Captain George and his companion. He directed them to remain on the Agency grounds while he made investigations among the Indians. He knew that it was dangerous for them to travel through Missoula County, as they might be taken for members of the hostile Nez Percé band which only the week before had passed through the country leaving death along their trail. In a few days some Salish Indians reported to the Agency office that early in the spring a young squaw answering to the description of the daughter of Captain George had been rescued by members of their band from her white captors near Fort Benton. They had brought her with them over the Indian trail through Cadotte Pass to the Reservation and had sent her, under Indian escort, over the Lolo Pass to her home at Camai.

Mr. Ronan sent our runners to gather more information about the girl and he himself started to Lolo to meet a camp of Indians who were reported coming over the trail from Idaho. On the way he met one of the Bitter Root Flatheads, John Hill (*Tah-hetcht,* which in Indian means Hand Shot Off). He said that eight days previously he had camped at the lodge of Captain George at the crossing of the Camai, that the girl was at home with her mother, to whom she had been brought by a band of Salish braves who took her from the white men at Benton. When Mr. Ronan returned with this news Captain George's impassivity gave way to emotion. He was wild with delight. He said that *Tah-hetcht* was his friend, he would not lie to him, he knew that it was true that his daughter had been restored to him. With a trusted guard Mr. Ronan sent Captain George to Fort Missoula and from there Major Chipman sent the devoted Indian father home under military escort.

This incident and the continued and growing friendliness of the Indians, including Eagle-of-the-Light and his band, during all these turbulent times, sealed our trust in my husband's charges. That trust was never betrayed, not even in small matters. Indeed, as the years passed we came never to shut a window or door of our house except against the weather and no door or window was ever locked. Indians might stalk into the house at any time of the day—they never came with sinister intent or stole anything or did any harm; they either stated their business to some member of the family or told what their "hearts" wanted. Though their hearts wanted many things they accepted denials with stoicism, squatting down idly in silence until the spirit moved them to depart. If I requested them to go, they did so quietly and without offense. Of course, I always endeavored to put such requests tactfully and to accompany them with little gifts—a bit of sugar, a piece of bread or an apple.

Mary Ronan, *Frontier Woman* (Missoula: University of Montana, 1973), pp. 86–110.

Born in 1844 in what would become Nevada, Sarah Winnemucca was a daughter of the Piute Indians' chief and granddaughter of chief Winnemucca, who guided the explorer John Charles Frémont across the Sierra Nevada to California. She learned both Spanish and English at her grandfather's insistence and became a leader of her tribe during the turmoil that accompanied white settlement. Highly respected, she was also employed as an interpreter by army leaders and government agents.

Sarah Winnemucca wrote the book from which this selection is taken after she traveled to Washington, D.C., in 1880, and again from 1881 to 1882 with her white husband, to protest governmental injustices to her people. She lectured in San Francisco and many eastern cities, where her descriptions of Indian suffering and of cruelty and corruption among the government's Indian Bureau agents made her perhaps the most famous Indian woman in nineteenth-century America. Some white reformers took up her cause, but the government did nothing to improve the conditions of the Piutes.

Here she tells about the forced resettlement of the Piutes, who in 1878 were driven from their Nevada homeland to the Yakima Indian reservation in eastern Washington because the Bannock War (in which they had not been involved) had aroused the fears of the white settlers. The Piutes were ill prepared for the December journey over the high plateau and mountains of eastern Oregon and Washington, and the exhausting trip was followed by exploitation and starvation in a new and hostile environment. Sarah herself died in 1891 of tuberculosis.

O ne day the commanding officer sent for me. Oh, how my heart did jump! I said to Mattie, "There is bad news." Truly I had not felt like this since the night Egan was killed by the Umatillas. I got ready and went down to the office, trembling as if something fearful was waiting for me. I walked into the office. Then the officer said to me,—

"Sarah, I have some news to tell you and I want you to keep it still until we are sure if it will be true."

I then promised I would keep it still if it was not too awful bad news.

He said, "It is pretty bad." He looked at me and said, "Sarah, you look as if you were ready to die. It is nothing about you; it is about your people. Sarah, an order is issued that your people are to be taken to Yakima Reservation, across the Columbia River."

I said, "All of my people?"

"No, not your father's, but all that are here." I asked, "What for?" He said he did not know.

I said, "Major, my people have not done anything, and why should they be sent away from their own country? If there are any to be sent away, let it be Oytes and his men, numbering about twenty-five men in all, and the few Bannocks that are with them. Oh, Major! if you knew what I have promised my people, you would leave nothing undone but what you would try not to have them sent away. Oh, Major! my people will never believe me again."

"Well, Sarah, I will do all I can. I will write to the President and see what he thinks about it. I will tell him all you have said about your people."

I was crying. He told me to keep up a good heart, and he would do all he could for me.

I went home and told Mattie all, and she said, "Well, sister, we cannot help it if the white people won't keep their word. We can't help it. We have to work for them and if they get our people not to love us, by telling what is not true to them, what can we do? It is they, not us."

I said, "Our people won't think so because they will never know that it was they who told the lie. Oh! I know all our people will say we are working against them and are getting money for all this."

In the evening Mattie and I took a walk down to their camp. There they were so happy; singing here, singing there and everywhere. I thought to myself, "My poor, poor people, you will be happy to-day; to-morrow or next week your happiness will be turned to weeping." Oh, how sad I was for them! I could not sleep at night, for the sad thing that had come.

At last one evening I was sent for by the commanding officer. Oh! how can I tell it? My poor heart stood still. I said to Mattie, "Mattie, I wish this was my last day in this cruel world."

I came to myself and I said, "No, Mattie, I don't mean the world. I mean the cruel,—yes, the cruel, wicked, white people, who are going to drive us to some foreign country, away from our own. Mattie, I feel so badly I don't think I can walk down there." Mattie said, "I will go with you."

We then went down, and Major Cochrane met us at the door and said, "Sarah, are you sick? You look so badly."

I said, "No."

He then replied, "Sarah, I am heartily sorry for you, but we cannot help it. We are ordered to take your people to Yakima Reservation."

It was just a little before Christmas. My people were only given one week to get ready in.

I said, "What! In this cold winter and in all this snow, and my people have so many little children? Why, they will all die. Oh, what can the President be thinking about? Oh, tell me, what is he? Is he man or beast? Yes, he must be a beast; if he has no feeling for my people, surely he ought to have some for the soldiers."

"I have never seen a president in my life and I want to know whether he is made of wood or rock, for I cannot for once think that he can be a human being. No human being would do such a thing as that,—send people across a fearful mountain in midwinter."

I was told not to say anything till three days before starting. Every night I imagined I could see the thing called President. He had long ears, he had big eyes and long legs, and a head like a bull-frog or something like that. I could not think of anything that could be so inhuman as to do such a thing,—send people across mountains with snow so deep.

Mattie and I got all the furs we could; we had fur caps, fur gloves, and fur overshoes.

At last the time arrived. The commanding-officer told me to tell Leggins to come to him. I did so. He came, and Major Cochrane told me to tell him that he wanted him to tell which of the Bannock men were the worst, or which was the leader in the war. Leggins told him, and counted out twelve men to him. After this talk, Major Cochrane asked me to go and tell these men to come up to the office. They were Oytes, Bannock Joe, Captain Bearskin, Paddy Cap, Boss, Big John, Eagle Eye, Charley, D. E. Johnson, Beads, and Oytes' son-in-law, called Surger. An officer was sent with me. I called out the men by their names. They all came out to me. I said to Oytes,—

"Your soldier-father wants you all to go up to see him."

We went up, and Oytes asked me many things.

We had to go right by the guard-house. Just as we got near it, the soldier on guard came out and headed us off and took the men and put them into the guard-house. After they were put in there the soldiers told me to tell them they must not try to get away, or they would be shot.

"We put you in here for safe-keeping," they said. "The citizens are coming over here from Canyon City to arrest you all, and we don't want them to take you; that is why we put you in here."

Ten soldiers were sent down to guard the whole encampment,—not Leggins' band, only Oytes' and the Bannocks. I was then ordered to tell them to get ready to go to Yakima Reservation.

Oh, how sad they were! Women cried and blamed their husbands for going with the Bannocks; but Leggins and his band were told they were not going with the prisoners of war, and that he was not going at all.

Then Leggins moved down the creek about two miles. At night some would get out and go off. Brother Lee and Leggins were sent out to bring them back again. One afternoon Mattie and I were sent out to get five women who got away during the night, and an officer was sent with us. We were riding very fast, and my sister Mattie's horse jumped on one side and threw her off and hurt her. The blood ran out of her mouth, and I thought she would die right off; but, poor dear, she went on, for an ambulance was at our command. She had great suffering during our journey.

Oh, for shame! You who are educated by a Christian government in the art of war; the practice of whose profession makes you natural enemies of the savages, so called by you. Yes, you, who call yourselves the great civilization; you who have knelt upon Plymouth Rock, covenanting with God to make this land the home of the free and the brave. Ah, then you rise from your bended knees and seizing the welcoming hands of those who are the owners of this land, which you are not, your carbines rise upon the bleak shore, and your so-called civilization sweeps inland from the ocean wave; but, oh, my God! leaving its pathway marked by crimson lines of blood, and strewed by the bones of two races, the inheritor and the invader; and I am crying out to you for justice,—yes, pleading for the far-off plains of the West, for the dusky mourner, whose tears of love are pleading for her husband, or for their children, who are sent far away from them. Your Christian minister will hold my people against their will; not because he loves them,—no, far from it,—but because it puts money in his pockets.

Now we are ready to start for Yakima. Fifty wagons were brought, and citizens were to take us there. Some of the wagons cost the government from ten dollars to fifteen dollars per day. We got to Canyon City, and while we camped there Captain Winters got a telegram from Washington, telling him he must take Leggins' band too. So we had to wait for them to overtake us. While we were waiting, our dear good father and mother, Mr. Charles W. Parrish, came with his wife and children to see us. My people threw their arms round him and his wife, crying, "Oh, our father and mother, if you had staid with us we would not suffer this."

Poor Mrs. Parrish could not stop her tears at seeing the people who once loved her, the children whom she had taught,—yes, the savage children who once called her their white-lily mother, the children who used to bring her wild flowers, with happy faces, now ragged, no clothes whatever. They all cried out to him and his wife, saying, "Oh, good father and mother, talk for us! Don't let them take us away; take us back to our home!" He told them he could do nothing for them. They asked him where his brother, Sam Parrish, was. He told them he was a long way off; and then they bade us good-by, and that was the last they saw of him.

While we were waiting for Leggins, it snowed all the time. In two days the rest of my people overtook us. It was so very cold some of them had to be left on the road; but they came in later. That night an old man was left in the road in a wagon. The next morning they went back to get the wagon, and found the old man frozen to death. The citizen who owned the wagon did not bring him to the camp; but threw him out of his wagon and left him! I thought it was the most fearful thing I ever saw in my life.

Early the next morning, the captain sent me to tell Leggins that he wanted him to help the soldiers guard the prisoners and see that none of them got away. He said the Big Father in Washington wanted him to do this, and then he and his people could come back in the spring. I went to tell Leggins; but he would not speak to me, neither would my brother Lee. I told him all and went away. When I got back, the captain asked me what he said. I told him he would not speak to me.

"Did you tell him what I told you to?"

"I did."

"Go and tell the prisoners to be ready to march in half an hour."

We travelled all day. It snowed all day long. We camped, and that night a woman became a mother; and during the night the baby died, and

Piute mother and children. A Northern Piute family, near Bishop, California. Courtesy of the Nevada Historical Society.

was put under the snow. The next morning the mother was put into the wagon. She was almost dead when we went into camp. That night she too was gone, and left on the roadside, her poor body not even covered with the snow.

In five days three more children were frozen to death, and another woman became a mother. Her child lived three days, but the mother lived. We then crossed Columbia River.

All the time my poor dear little Mattie was dying little by little.

At last we arrived in Yakima on the last day of the month. Father Wilbur and the chief of the Yakima Indians came to meet us. We came into camp about thirty miles from where the agency buildings are, and staid at this place for ten days. Another one of my people died here, but oh, thanks be to the Good Father in the Spirit-land, he was buried as if he were a man. At the end of the ten days we were turned over to Father Wilbur and his civilized Indians, as he called them. Well, as I was saying, we were turned over to him as if we were so many horses or cattle. After he received us he had some of his civilized Indians come with their wagons to take us up to Fort Simcoe. They did not come because they loved us, or because they were Christians. No; they were just like all civilized people; they came to take us up there because they were to be paid for it. They had a kind of shed made to put us in. You know what kind of shed you make for your stock in winter time. It was of that kind. Oh, how we did suffer with cold. There was no wood, and the snow was waist-deep, and many died off just as cattle or horses do after travelling so long in the cold.

All my people were dressed well in soldiers' clothes. Almost all the men had beautiful blue overcoats; they looked like a company of soldiers, but we had not been with these civilized people long before they had won all my people's clothes from them. Some would give them one buckskin for an overcoat and pants, and some of them got little ponies for their clothes, but the ponies would disappear, and could not be found in the country afterwards. Leggins had a great many good horses, which were lost in the same way. My people would go and tell the agent, Wilbur, about the way his people were treating them, and the loss of their horses; but he would tell them their horses were all right on the reservation somewhere, only we could not find them. My people would ask him to tell his people to tell us if they saw our horses, so that we might go and get them. He told his Christian and civilized Indians, but none of them came to tell us where our horses were. The civilized Indians would tell my people not to go far away, for the white people would kill them; but my cousin, Frank Winnemucca, and his sister's son, who was named after our good agent, Samuel Parrish, were out hunting their horses. They were gone eight days. They travelled along the Yakima River, and saw an island between Yakima City and the reservation. They swam across to it, and there they found their horses, and two of the Christian Yakima Indians watching them. They brought them back. After that it was worse than ever. All our best horses were gone, which we never did find. My Meride was found three months afterwards. They were using my horse as a pack-horse. It was so lean the back was sore. I took it to Mrs. Wilbur to show her what the Yakima Indians were doing to our horses. I asked her if I could turn the horse into their lot. She told me I could, but the horse was gone again, and I have never seen it since.

We had another talk with Father Wilbur about our horses, but he kindly told us he did not wish to be troubled by us about our horses. Then my people said,—

"We have lost all our clothes and our horses, and our father says he does not want to be troubled by us." My people said everything that was bad about these people.

Now came the working time. My people were set to work clearing land; both men and women went to work, and boys too. They cleared sixty acres of land for wheat. They had it all cleared in about ten days. Father Wilbur hired six civilized Indians to plough it for them; these Indians got three dollars a day for their work, because they were civilized and Christian.

It was now about the last of April. I was told to tell my people that he had sent for clothes for them, and it was already at the Dalles. He was going to send seventeen wagons down, and have them brought right off. I told my people what he said, and I assure you they were very glad indeed, for they were almost naked. No money,—no, nothing. Now our clothing came; everything you could wish or think of came for my poor, dear people—blankets of all kinds, shawls, woollen goods, calicoes, and everything beautiful.

Issuing day came. It was in May. Poor Mattie was so sick, I had to go by myself to issue to my people. Oh, such a heart-sickening issue! There were twenty-eight little shawls given out, and dress-goods that you white people would sift flour through, from two to three yards to each woman. The largest issue was to a woman who had six children. It was six yards, and I was told to say to her she must make clothes for the children out of what was left after she had made her own! At this my people all laughed. Some of the men who worked hardest got blankets, some got nothing at all; a few of the hats were issued, and the good minister, Father Wilbur, told me to say he would issue again later in the fall, that is, blankets. After the issue was over, my people talked and said,—

"Another Reinhard!—don't you see he is the same? He looks up into the sky and says something, just like Reinhard." They said, "All white people like that are bad." Every night some of them would come and take blankets off from sleeping men and women until all were gone. All this was told to the agent, but he would not help my poor people, and Father Wilbur's civilized Indians would say most shameful things about my people. They would tell him that they were knocking their doors in, and killing their horses for food, and stealing clothes. At one time they said my people killed a little child. Their Indian minister, whose name was George Waters, told me one of my women had been seen killing the child. He said the child's head was cut to pieces. I said to brother Lee,—

"We will go and see the child."

I asked the white doctor to go with us to see it. I told him what had been said. They had him all wrapped up, and said they did not want anybody to see him. George was there. I said,—

"We must see him. You said our people had killed him, and that his head is cut in pieces." So the doctor took off all the blankets that were wound round him. There was no sign of anything on him. He had fallen into the river and had been drowned.

On May 29, my poor little sister Mattie died. Oh, how she did suffer before she died! And I was left all alone. During this time, all the goods that were brought for us were sold to whoever had money. All the civilized Indians bought the best of everything.

Father Wilbur said to my people the very same thing that Reinhard did. He told them he would pay them one dollar a day. My people worked the same, and they were paid in clothes, and little money was paid to them. They were told not to go anywhere else to buy but to this store. At this, my people asked him why he told them that the clothes were theirs. At this Mrs. Wilbur said they had to sell them in order to hold their position. This is the way all the agents issue clothing to the people. Every Indian on that reservation had to pay for everything.

For all the wagons they ever got they were to pay one hundred and twenty-five dollars, if it took ten years to pay it. I know this is true, because the agent told me to tell my brother Lee so, and he told Leggins the same if he wanted wagons, and that they could pay him little by little until they had paid it all.

We had the finest wheat that ever was raised on the reservation, for my people pulled out all the cockle and smut. The civilized Indians were so lazy they would not clean their field, and their wheat was so bad that after it was made into bread it was as black as dirt. I am sorry to say that Father Wilbur kept our wheat for his white friends, and gave us the bad wheat, and the bad wheat was ground just as you would grind it for your hogs. The bad flour made us all sick. My poor people died off very fast. At first Father Wilbur and his Christian Indians told us we could bury our dead in their graveyard; but they soon got tired of us, and said we could not bury them there any more.

Doctor Kuykendall could not cure any of my people, or he did not try. When I would go to him for medicine for them, he would say, "Well, Sarah, I will give you a little sugar and rice, or a little tea for him or her"; he would say laughing, "give them something good to eat before they die." This is the way the agent treated us, and then they dare to say that they are doing all they can for my people. I say, my dear friends, the minister who is called agent, says there will be or there is a time coming when every one is going to give an account of all he does in this life. I am a little afraid the agent will have to give an account of himself, and say, "I have filled my pockets with that worthless thing called money. I am not worthy to go to heaven." That is, if that book you civilized people call the Holy Bible is true. In that, it says he who steals and tells lies will go to hell. Well, I am afraid this book is true, as your agents say; and I am sure they will never see heaven, for I am sure there is hardly an agent but what steals a little, and they all know that if there is a God above us, they can't deny it before Him who is called God. This was in July, 1879.

We were now going to have a camp-meeting, and some visitors were coming from the East. Bishop Haven and his son and daughter were coming. The agent told me to be sure and keep my people away, as they were very poorly dressed. I did not do as I was told. My poor people were almost as naked as they were born into the world; for the seventeen wagons of supplies were not issued to them.

When the time came, I came with all my people, and camped near the agent's house, and during the meeting I made them all come and sit down on the benches that Father Wilbur made for his civilized and Christian Indians. I wanted all to see how well we were treated by Christian people.

Day after day my people were begging me to go east and talk for them. I told them I had no money to go with just then; but I would as soon as I got some, for I had a little money coming to me from the military government.

The military authority is the only authority that ever paid me well for my interpreting. Their pay to interpreters is from sixty-five dollars to seventy-five dollars, and the lowest is sixty dollars per month. For this pay one could live. All the agents pay to interpreters is from thirty dollars to forty dollars. One has to live out of this money, and there is nothing left.

I always had to pay sixty dollars a month for my board (or fifteen dollars a week) when I was working for an agent. When I was working for the government they gave me my rations, the same as they did to the soldiers. My last appointment was given me at Washington in 1879. It was to be very small pay. I wrote to the Secretary of the Interior (Mr. Schurz), telling him I could not pay my board with that; but he never answered my letter, and so it stands that way to this day, and I never got a cent of it. But their pet, Reinhard, without an Indian on the reservation, could be paid three or four years. I have worked all the time among my people, and never been paid for my work. At last my military money came. I told Father Wilbur I wanted to go back to see my people. At first he said I could not go; he stood a minute, and then said,—

"Well, Sarah, I can't keep you if you want to go. Who is to talk for your people?"

I said, "Brother Lee can talk well enough."

Then he said, "You can go after the camp-meeting is over."

Sarah Winnemucca Hopkins, *Life Among the Piutes: Their Wrongs and Claims* (New York: G. P. Putnam's Sons, 1883), pp. 203–15.

Part Three

The Southwestern Desert, 1863–1900

On the great desert frontier of the Old Southwest, heat, aridity, and hostile Indians only exaggerated the challenges settlers had faced in the Rocky Mountains. The last segment of the territory that became New Mexico and Arizona was acquired from Mexico in 1854. Although Anglos rapidly assumed political and economic dominance, the area retained its thriving Hispanic traditions for many years. Mary Barnard Aguirre's accounts of a bullfight and of elaborate christening and wedding ceremonies during the 1860s indicate her fascination with "the newness of every thing." But the strangeness of culture and climate deterred many settlers, and the incoming population remained much more sparse than elsewhere.

Though one might expect that only the most hardy women would attempt desert life, our narratives reveal just as much diversity as elsewhere. Despite wealth and status, Mary Aguirre could not avoid the physical stress of blinding snowstorms or the desert "Jornada del Muerto," for example, but she obviously enjoyed the security of her husband's social position and the elaborate luxury of an embroidered satin cloak, fancy balls, and frequent horseback riding. She even requested to stay when her husband returned to the States for a winter.

Sarah York, on the other hand, was seriously ill and "seeking health" when she went west. She felt that she had found the "land of promise" in New Mexico, even though she had to live in a house with a dirt floor and roof and eventually lost her husband to an Indian ambush. Like many other frontier women, she had to manage the ranch when her husband was away—and after his death.

The Apache Indians of the Southwest were hostile toward Anglo and Hispanic settlers and unpredictable in their interactions with them. Attacks on travelers and isolated ranches occurred frequently, and women felt justifiable fear. Some settlers, like Sister Segale, perceived that Indians were being mistreated too. Because she taught their children, she had learned enough about their customs to be able to speak in their terms, winning their respect despite her fear.

Many women learned a similar kind of diplomacy. Indians everywhere admired courage in an adversary and were usually respectful toward "spunky" women. Even fearful women could be moved to act forcefully in defense of their work and their meager domestic possessions, as did Angie Brown to protect her trunkful of precious photos. The dangers of the desert environment were real. Three women describe Indian attacks, two fatal; others describe deaths due to inadequate medical care. Some women perceived themselves to be in a strange place full of dangerous animals and equally dangerous human beings, both Indian and white.

Although isolation on far-scattered ranches was a frequent experience, it was balanced by elaborate codes of hospitality. There was much work for a woman in making visitors welcome, but women themselves reveled in the variety of visitors, who often stayed for days or weeks at a time.

The ranching household was usually quite extensive. Along with visitors, there were hired hands and sometimes their wives, servants, relatives, and often a tutor for the children or a boarding schoolteacher for several far-flung ranches. Sarah York savored the fame of her distinguished guests, and Angie Brown, a teacher, faced the rigors of the frontier in a household that was certainly never lonely. If isolation did limit opportunities, some women just moved to town during winter months for the sake of their children's education. Such independent living caused no loss of approval from the community; motherhood actually legitimized many forms of freedom.

For all the dangers and the harshness of the land, women also loved its beauty. In fact, Sadie Martin's memoir contains one of this book's most heartfelt appreciations of the western landscape. Many commented on the spectacular mountains or the nature of the plants and animals. They did complain about snakes and lions and skunks, yet they often learned to meet the enemy head on. Sadie Martin, for instance, claimed that she eventually became "quite expert at killing" rattlers; and Angie Brown made friends with a Gila monster.

The western frontier took its toll on women as well as men. But they responded with imagination, pleasure, courage, humor, and pride. There was, after all, "so much to be done."

"Set and rest and rock a spell"

EFFIE MAY BUTLER WILTBANK

18

Sarah Ann Prince was a Mormon, married in 1876 in Utah to Jacob Butler. They moved with other Mormons to Holbrook, Arizona in 1873. Her granddaughter later described many aspects of daily living among early Arizona settlers, but Sarah's simple "receet" for doing the family wash seems to epitomize the practical skill, determination, and common sense required of so many frontier women.

1. bild fire in back yard to hey kettle of rain water.
2. set tubs so smoke won't blow in eyes if wind is peart.
3. shave 1 hole cake lie sope in bilin water.
4. sort things. make 3 piles. 1 pile white, 1 pile cullord, 1 pile werk briches and rags.
5. stur flour in cold water to smooth then thin down with bilin water.
6. rub dirty spots on board. scrub hard. then bile. rub cullord but don't bile just rench and starch.
7. take white things out of kettle with broom stick handel then rench, blew and starch
8. spred tee towels on grass
9. hang old rags on fence
10. pore rench water in flower bed
11. scrub porch with hot sopy water
12. turn tubs upside down
13. go put on a cleen dress—smooth hair with side combs, brew cup of tee—set and rest and rock a spell and count blessins.

Reminiscences, Effie May Butler Wiltbank Biographical File, MSS W 755e, Arizona Historical Society, Tucson, Arizona.

"It was all a wonder to me"

MARY BARNARD AGUIRRE

19

Mary Barnard, born in St. Louis in 1844 (the same year as Sarah Winnemucca), spent her privileged childhood on a prosperous plantation near Baltimore. When her father opened a "large store" in the trading hub that became Kansas City, Missouri, he moved his wife and seven children west, along with their slaves, servants, and "no end of baggage," including a piano. Educated at private ladies' academies in Independence and back in Baltimore, Mary made Confederate flags and endured Yankee "persecution" when the Civil War broke out. At eighteen she married another prosperous trader, an aristocratic Mexican. In 1863, with a new baby, the Aguirres were part of a large mule-drawn freight caravan traveling over the long-established Santa Fe Trail to New Mexico.

This excerpt from the autobiography Aguirre later wrote for her family provides a rare glimpse into the flourishing Spanish-American society that was about to be overwhelmed by a flood of incoming Americans with scant respect for other cultures. Mary, however, enjoyed the novelty and ceremony as well as the beauty of the country. Like so many other frontier women, she apparently considered it quite normal to be constantly moving long distances from one place to another. When her husband was killed by Apache Indians in 1869, Aguirre was left a widow at age twenty-five with two small children.

*I*n September '63 we made preparations for another trip—this time it was to be to unknown lands "across the plains" & by the 19th all was ready & we started from Westport in ambulances—quite a party of us. There was my father & oldest sister, my husband, myself, Pedro (then not quite three months old) & a nursegirl 13 years old, named Angeline. In another ambulance was L. B. Elkins then a young man of 21—just begin-

ning the world (with no money in his pockets but plenty of brains in his
head from which to coin money to fill his pockets)   With a sunny temper
& no end of grit & a loving kind heart & with him came a member of the
Gov Goodwin party. That party had gone on with another train bound for
Arizona where Goodwin was to establish a Federal government. In another small wagon were two young men Messrs Wells & Giles. In another
a family by the name of Kitchen—mother & three little children & a cook.
The provision wagon was driven by Dory Jones a young friend of ours,
about 19 years old & we had an old german named Enders to cook for us.
The wagon train consisted of ten wagons—each one drawn by ten fine
mules & loaded with 10,000 lbs of freight for which they paid 15 & 20 cts
per lb. Merchandize for Santa Fe. We rode in ambulances which were
comfortable carriages—costing $500 a piece—& built so they could be
turned into beds at night just as a "sleeper" seat is arrainged now a days.
They had boxes under the back seat for clothes—pockets in the sides in the
doors which opened as back doors do. In these pockets were brushes,
combs & looking glass. Under the front seat was another box & there were
two seats faceing each other inside so that six people could be comfortably
seated. We had tents & camp chairs, a mess chest furnished as completely
as a ladys china closet & the top arrainged so it would spread out & make a
nice table. We had canned goods galore & all sorts of comforts that money
could buy or loving kindness suggest—so we started on that long journey
with every prospect of it being a happy one—so far as the temperal comforts of this life were concerned. I was like a child with no more knowledge of the responsibilities of life or the care of a baby & only glad to leave
that cruel war & the horrors behind me.

Our road lay thro' Kansas which was then in a fearful state of exaspera-
tion against the Bushwackers on account of Quantril having just burnt
Lawrence & murdered a great many people in revenge for something the
Jayhawkers had done to his people. So we could literally feel the *blood* in
the air & were thrown into a terrible state of excitement by the arrival one
night of a company of soldiers when we were 100 miles on our way from
Westport . . . sent ostensibly as an *escort* to keep the Bushwackers from
getting our mules. . . . And those soldiers & the Lieut Commanding went
on with us for weeks. My husband having to give them rations for which
he never received a cent. We journeyed on for weeks & weeks—Went thro'
Council Grove Fort Larned & many other points where there are towns

now on the A. T. & Santa Fe but then was a wilderness—Nothing to be seen but grass for miles & miles one long unending road—Not a shrub even & never a tree but an occasional one near a water hole. We made 30 miles a day when we done a good days driving. The tall grass was turning grey with the cold that came upon us gradually. The very monotony of it became pleasant at last. There seemed nothing more to expect—nothing to look forward to & nothing to do. I got so I could sew & read & make myself as comfortable as if I was in a house. Pedro grew & thrived apace & was the pet & delight of the camp. Angeline studied Spanish & made fun for us all with her mistakes & so we journeyed on & on 'till we neared Ft Larned where news was waiting us of my sisters death which caused my father & sister to return & I went on alone. About that time we began to meet herds of buffalo & had quantaties of meat. The tongues were something delicious—after these were smoked & we had plenty of them for my husband was a great buffalo hunter & kept us well supplied. I never can forget the first one I ever saw. It had just been killed & we rode to where it was off of the road. I had a curiosity to measure the hair on the neck which I did with my arm & it covered it from my finger tips to the shoulder. When we neared the crossing of the Arkansas river there commenced talk of difficulties—as that river is so very uncertain—'till I was quite anxious for it to be over, having that aforementioned horror of swift muddy streams. By the time we reached the crossing—the old Cimmaron crossing it was) the weather was quite cold & we had had several dust & wind storms. There was quite a formal camp made on the bank of the river. The wagons were lightened of their loads, the beds raised up & then twenty mules were hitched to each wagon & they were started with men driving & two men on horse back on each side of the teams. When they started they were never let stop a moment for if they did the treacherous quicksands caught the wheels & the feet of the mules & held them. So a good teamster never let his team stop a moment. When about half of the train was over the ambulances were rushed over because the sand was steadied somewhat. But the horror of it—that awful muddy water—It took two days to cross all the train & there was quite a jubalee when all were on the other side & the men sang & had a glass of whiskey all around & the whole camp was gleeful & they sat up around the fires telling yarns later that night. The teamsters sang a sort of chanting, long drawnout song. The first drive after the crossing had to be made a short distance & then they

Teresita Suaso. This sketch of a Hispanic woman, done in 1853 by Alexander Barclay, portrays a way of life soon to disappear. Courtesy of The Bancroft Library.

made camp & brought the mules back to the water because there was a 45 mile journey ahead without water. The afternoon after that first short drive there came up a terrible wind storm. The wagons were circled which means they were in the circle they always made by driving up one after the other & stopping just a little behind & to one side—half of the train on one side & half on the other—& the ambulances in the centre. Well, this had been done when the storm came up & the wind blew with such force that it nearly upset the ambulance in which I was with Pedro & the nurse, the redoubtable Angeline. Just as the wind was doing its worst & the men were holding the ambulance Pedro took the colic. The louder he cried the worse frightened Angeline got 'till finally she howled outright & commenced to say her prayers & declare that the baby would die—almost in the same breath—which I suppose was more than human nature could stand, and I too, commenced to cry—so that when the storm passed & the door was opened there we were in the depths of woe, the three of us. [. . . They rode all night through a blinding snow storm.] But we finally arrived at the house which to me seemed like a palace so tired & cold was I. And it was the first house I had been into since I left Westport two months before. The owner, Mr Raber, was kindness itself & tho' the breakfast was corn bread, fat bacon & black coffee—three things I detested in my normal condition—they seemed like nectar to me & the way I ate & drank astonished my husband & the rest of the party. We stopped there two days—& then went on to Krenigs (La Junta N M) ranch where there was an old fort & stayed all night. The next day we arrived in Las Vegas & I was "across the plains" & into a semblance of civilization once more. There we stayed a week in very comfortable quarters. The weather was like summer, so warm was the air. We rode to the Hot Springs which were 6 miles away & away up in the mountains. There was only one house there then & that was a one & one little room in which was a wooden bath tub. But the Springs were a curiosity to me & the sight of burros loaded with clothes coming & going to & from Las Vegas

All the washing for the town was done at the springs & the women sat all around the large spring rubbing out the clothes on stones. From Las Vegas we went on to Santa Fe taking two days to go 70 miles & travelling thro' those lovely mountains all so new—strange to me whose eyes had grown used to those unending plains. We stopped at a place called Kosloskeys for the night & for supper & breakfast had fine trout caught in the mountain stream near there. Just beyond that ranch is the old Pecos church & there we stopped to see the ruins then in a very good state of preservation. The rafters still held up part of the roof & were beautifully carved at each end. We could trace the outline of the town for a long distance. We arrived in Santa Fe the last of Nov. where we met the rest of the Arizona party & there I met Mr. McCormick. We stayed there a week & then went on down the Rio Grande river in company with Gov Goodwins party   Quite a number of dances were given to the Gov's party & they had quite a lovely time. While in Santa Fe I saw the first installment of Navajo Indians brought in on their way to the reservation just given them at Bosque Redondo (Ft. Stanton). They were the first of 7000 who were afterwards put on that reservation. At Albuquerque we stopped two weeks where the whole party were right royally treated by the natives. One ball was especially elegant. It was given at Paralta not far from Albuquerque—20 miles about & we had to travel right on the banks of the river in some such narrow places that my hair fairly stood on end. From Albuquerque my husband sent the gov's party across the country to Prescott with his train. They passed over what is now the line of the A. & P. road—encountering awful snow storms in one of which nearly all the mules were lost—one night—70 mules in one night & each one worth a hundred dollars. Mr Elkins was intending to go on to Prescott but was persuaded by myself & husband to go on to Las Cruces with us. Dory Jones went also with us. We went down the Rio Grande in the ambulance crossing the river several times to my dismay, finally crossing at Paraje the last time. This was the starting place across the dreaded Jornada del Muerto—Journey of death—We stopped at Ft Craig, near which the town of San Marchial now is. The Jornada is a desert of 90 miles without water & is the abomination of desolation, for even the earth looks like ashes. As the Indians were bad it was not quite safe for us to go alone so we waited for the stage & the paymaster, Maj Davis, also   so we all joined company & crossed the Jornada together. We went into Ft. McRea which is on the river & there rested the first night. The next day we went on & arrived late that night near Dona Ana (six miles from Las Cruces) a small town on the Rio Grande. The next morning we arrived at our long journeys end, Las Cruces, just a week before Christmas having been over three months on the road. On Christmas day we had a family dinner & one of the eatables was an immense watermelon as fresh & crisp as if it had just been cut. It had been gathered late & hung to the rafters of a store room along with many others of its kind & bunches of grapes—also—which tho' not quite fresh were not quite dry & were very nice. They raised quantaties of grapes in the Mesilla valley from which the celebrated El Paso wine was made. These grapes were so sweet & kept very nicely 'till late in the winter packed in chapped straw. That first winter was delightful to us all. The weather was so warm & the constant sunshine so lovely that we States-people enjoyed it to the fullest extent—staying out of doors the most of the time. We rode on horseback & in the ambulance all over the country. I found some old friends in La Mesilla,   Col Jones family & Judge Hackney who were kindness itself to me. On New Years day (1864) my husband & myself were invited to be "Padrinos"—(godparents) for the New Years high Mass, which we attended sitting in chairs in front of the altar with highly decorated wax candles in our hands. These were lit & my whole attention was devoted to keeping that candle straight—for I was so interested with the newness of every thing that I'd forget the candle for a moment & it would bob over to the imminent danger of my hat. This was a special attention we were shown because my husband was much beloved in the town.

Next came Pedros christening which was a grand affair. He being the first grandson in the family an especial celebration was made. For three days before there was a baker & two assistants in the house. They baked no end of cakes & confectionary, roasted fowls & pigs & were highly entertaining to me, on account of the way they made & baked things. Everything was baked in one of those bee hive shaped adobe ovens, that opened into the kitchen. It was heated red hot & then all the coals scraped out & things put in on flat pieces of tin & shallow pans. The number of eggs that were used was a marvel & in fact it was all a wonder to me. There were two hundred guests. People from far & near were invited, some coming from El Paso—60 miles away. All the officers from the Cal column, then stationed there, were on hand. First of all Pedro was taken in State to La Mesilla to be christened. In the afternoon his grandfather & mother standing for him. Then came the supper & afterwards the dance. Pedro was set at the head of the table & crowed & laughed in a wonderful way for a six months old baby. His health was drunk in champaign by all standing, he being held up by his proud father & then the supper commenced. The dance was kept up till the "wee wee hours" & every one enjoyed & long remembered Pedros christening.

The plowing was a great curiosity to me. The plows were two poles crossed so one made a point to the ground which was covered with steel. The oxen were hitched by the horns & as many as twelve plows followed each other in one furrow. This was done to deepen it sufficiently I suppose. The carts were made of wood entirely, not a piece of iron in them. The wheels, immense round pieces of wood with holes in them, & the way they creached & complained as they moved along was comical. I was constantly reminded of the Bible descriptions of the olden times.

There was something new to see all the time. The annual feasts came on in due time. Each town has its patron saint whose day was celebrated by high mass & then a week of games & bull fights & dancing in the open air by the populace. There were three towns near together—Dona Ana, Las Cruces & La Mesilla & their feasts came in Jan, Feb & March & we attended all of them. At the Mesilla feast which was in March there were much more elaborate preparations made. I was again invited to be the "Madrina" (My husband had gone back to the States then leaving me at my own request to spend the Winter)—and again I had to sit in front of the altar with a candle in my hand. I was attended by Steve Elkins, Miltie Jones, Jola, my sister in law & Mrs. Jones, & was dressed in a way that would be astonishing now adays, for part of my attire was an elaborate satin cloak, made in the City of Mexico & embroidered a half a yard wide on three capes, reaching to my feet. I had to go also to the vespers & the evening was cool. It was brown satin & the embroidery white. So you can fancy my astonishing appearence as we sailed up that church, climbing over the kneeling crowds—for there were no seats & all sat on the floor— till we reached the chairs set for us before the altar. Some one remarked that I must be the Virgin Mary.

The next afternoon we all attended a bull fight. The ring was in the church plaza, built of logs tied together with raw hide. Above one side were the private boxes "Palcos" they were called—which were made of boards loosely put together & covered with canvas. These were reached by ladders of the rudest description & the widest apart rungs one could imagine. It was terrible climbing for short folks like me. When we ladies started up that ladder (me in that wonderful cloak) two men held blankets over us as we went up. When we arrived at the top the boards of the floor were so wide apart that we came near stepping thro'. But we all enjoyed the bull fight immensely tho' there were no bulls killed & no blood shed. After we

got settled in Las Cruces Steve E. commenced the study of law & was admitted to the bar soon after. His first case was intensely interesting to us all
& was something about a division of goats & the next was an assault &
battery case & the next a divorce case for which he got a twenty dollar gold
piece & a government pistol. & then he went onto success & was sent to
the Legislature at Santa Fe. Dory staid with us for quite awhile—but finally went to Tucson, Arizona, & afterwards to Colorado where he now
lives in Pueblo, well to do & respected by all. Angeline was married after
a few years to some one in Ft. Union—& lives there yet. I lived in Las
Cruces seven months & then went to Las Vegas to be with my husband
who had what was then called the Interior freight contract from the government to supply all the military posts of the territory with provisions &
freight. The shipping point was Ft Union—& Las Vegas was the nearest
point. There I lived very happily—going occasionally to Santa Fe during
the winter of '64. One trip we made about the middle of Dec expecting to
stay a week & be home for Christmas. But a big snow storm came on &
blockaded the mountain roads so that we could not leave so spent Xmas in
Santa Fe. It was very gay & I was going constantly—visiting & receiving
visits. The military were very gay & the Gov. (Arnys) family tho' quiet
people were very pleasant—so the time passed pleasantly. One Sunday
Steve E & I went to high mass at the old cathedral.   I was dressed in my
best (but not in the aforementioned cloak) & was dismayed when we
found there were no seats in the church & we had to either sit on the dirt
floor or stand up all thro' the mass. Finally we concluded to sit down &
with many inward qualms on my part about my nice silk dress, down we
sat on that dirt floor, Steve doubling his feet under him. But this soon
grew irksome & we grew more & more uncomfortable. We were too well
bred to leave the church, so varied the position by kneeling up once in
awhile 'till church was over. By that time we could scarcely stand & felt as
if we had had a spell of rheumatizm of long standing. When we left Santa
Fe the roads were splendid, the snow being packed down solid & we enjoyed the lovely scenery. I went to a marriage in Las Vegas that was typical
of those times in the middle class, I also attended one of the upper ten. The
first one we went to the church & saw the ceremony, then went in a sort of
procession with the bride, groom, attendents & a dozen men, with fiddles
& guns. The men played & the guns were fired off at intervals all the way
to the grooms house, where a fine breakfast was prepared. At night there

was a dance, the musicians singing verses complimentary to the dancers, as they played, making up the words as they went along & bringing them in to suit in a wonderful way, the bride changed her dress three times in both cases, the only difference being in the value of the dresses & jewelry & that the upper ten did not go in procession from the church.

I remained in Las Vegas till Feb '65 when I returned to Las Cruces in a buggy, stopping at different points on the Rio Grande as my husbands business demanded. Crossed that dreadful Jornada del Muerto again. I had crossed it in the stage when I went to Las Vegas. Went in a stage to Santa Fe—300 miles—taking my sister Lola with me & Pedro just a year old. So this was the third time I crossed the Jornada. We travelled with the state & did not touch at Ft McRea but stopped for water at Point of Rock where the U.S. Government had tanks for water which were filled from the river. The water brought 30 miles in wagons made as tanks. We arrived in Las Cruces the early part of March & on May 12th my second boy, Epifanio, was born & there I remained till March of the next year when we again made preparations for a return trip across the plains, going as we had come with wagons but not by the same route from Las Cruces.

Mary Barnard Aguirre, "Autobiography," Aguirre Collection, Arizona Historical Society Library, pp. 7–17 of typed copy.

"A stopping place for travelers"

In this short, naive reminiscence, Sarah Butler York provides a graphic description of her three-month trip over the mountains from Colorado to join her husband in the Gila Valley of Arizona in 1877. She and her young children traveled in a large ox train manned by Mexican drivers, for whom she had little understanding and less sympathy. Later the family moved to a ranch, where their open hospitality meant that Sarah was, at least informally, constantly providing for extra boarders, just like so many other women in this book. Visitors, however, were also a welcome link to the outside world, and illustrious ones a source of local prestige. After her husband was ambushed and killed by Apache Indians, York continued to manage the ranch with the help of her five young children.

I have been asked to give you some sketches of my pioneer life, and if you will excuse a simple story told in a simple way, I will try to give you a few of the experiences which came to us: first on the long journey from Missouri to New Mexico; second, on the trip from New Mexico to Arizona, and others during our life on the cattle ranch on the Gila River, twenty miles south of Clifton, Arizona.

In the spring of 1873, a party of sixteen persons, four women, seven men and five children, started from the central part of Missouri to find homes in the far west; all were hoping to better their fortunes, and a few, including myself, were seeking health; some kind neighbors advised my husband to put a spade in the wagon thinking it might be needed, but I was anxious to make the trial.

Our train consisted of covered wagons, drawn by oxen and a herd of cattle, driven by the younger men who were on horses. Our long, tedious journey required four months. You will realize that our progress was slow because all our possessions such as food, clothing, bedding, cooking utensils and tents were packed in the wagons, besides the women and children. Nine miles a day was the average distance we covered. Travelers now going over the same route at an average of fifty miles an hour will, no doubt, think of us with pity—but though slow we were sure. We were fortunate in regard to the weather as there was not much rain. On stormy nights the men did the cooking while the women and children remained in the wagons or tents, but we were usually so cramped from sitting all day we were glad to get out for exercise, if possible. After we reached the plains, wood for cooking was our greatest problem and it was some time before the women would consent to use a fire made of buffalo chips. Afterwards we made a joke of it, and would laugh to see some of the fastidious young men come into camp with a sack of chips on their shoulders; the old chips that had laid there for years through all kinds of weather certainly made a wonderful fire. By that time another party of four men, driving a larger bunch of cattle, had joined us and we welcomed the addition, believing there was more safety in numbers. We could hear the prairie chickens most every morning and passed large herds of buffaloes at different times and saw many antelopes. Our men killed several antelopes and two buffaloes on the way and the fresh meat was very acceptable; however, I would not care for a diet of buffalo meat. One day they had wounded a large buffalo and chased it until it was very tired. Our camp happened to be in the way, so he came right through. The women and children took refuge in the wagons, much disturbed over the uninvited guest. The work that has been done to preserve the buffaloes reminds me of what I saw when we touched at one point in Western Kansas. The Union Pacific Railroad, sportsmen on board the trains had shot the buffaloes down until they lay by the hundreds, and were left to decay without even removing the skins. It was pitiful to see an act of such vandalism.

When we came through the Sioux and Fox Indian Reservations in Western Kansas one of the men missed his dog. After we were camped he went back to look for it, but was unsuccessful, but when he became angry and drew his revolver the Indians took him into a tepee where the dog was tied; no doubt they were preparing to have a feast of dog meat.

The government had built good stone houses of two rooms for these Indians, but they would not use them and were living in ragged tepees nearby. They had used the floors and the window and door casings for fires.

We saw many Indians, but no hostiles, although we had been warned before starting not to cross the Arkansas River. I was fortunate in being the first to see the mountains, which to me was a glorious sight, as it was just at sunrise. None of the party had seen a mountain and all were very much excited with our first view of the Rockies in Colorado; we rejoiced, too, that we were nearing the promised land, and a land of promise it indeed proved to most of us. Some felt they were too far from civilization and returned to the old home, but the families remained and prospered. It was a rough life, living in log cabins with dirt roofs, forty miles from a post office or supplies. An ox team was our only means of travel and yet we were gloriously full of life and health. We had lived at this beautiful place at the foot of the Rocky mountains three years when we learned that we were on the old Maxwell Grant and could get no title to the land. We had read of the possibilities of the Gila Valley, pronounced with a hard G, of course, so my husband decided to come still farther west and left us in the spring of 1877. In October of the same year he made arrangements with a Mr. Chandler, who owned and operated a large ox train, to bring us a distance of five or six hundred miles; so with my two little daughters of eleven and six years and a baby girl fourteen months, we boarded an ox train, which consisted of sixteen immense wagons, each drawn by ten or twelve yoke of oxen. The one provided for us was a good sized spring wagon with bows and canvas cover, trailed behind the last wagon. In this we carried our clothes and bedding; the bed was rolled up in the back of the wagon during the day; at night we spread it in the bottom and made a fairly comfortable bed. The man who owned the train promised to make the trip in six weeks, but on account of having poor oxen and encountering stormy weather, we were almost three months on the way. Some nights the oxen would wander so far they could not be found in time to move on next day and we would be compelled to remain in camp much against our will, for when we were moving, even if it were ever so little, we felt we were drawing nearer the end of our journey. The drivers were all Mexicans. After camp was made at night and the teams were turned loose a large fire was built for the men, and a smaller was made near our wagon. The provisions and cooking utensils were brought to my wagon as, unless it was very cold or snowing, I did my own cooking. In case of stormy weather food was brought to us. If there was snow the men would scrape it off, cut pine boughs and build a wind break, then we would wrap up and sit out by the fire. They were good to the children and would want to hold them. This would have been a rest for me, as I had to hold my baby all day to keep her from falling out of the wagon, but they were so filthy and infested with vermin I didn't dare allow them to help me, and as it was we did not entirely escape. We learned a few Mexican words, the alphabet and how to count. Mr. Chandler said we were not to ask the meaning of their songs as we could enjoy them better not to know. Since we were so long on the road our provisions gave out and we had to use the same food provided for the Mexicans; beans, flour, coffee, bacon and dried fruit. One night we camped near a white family who was going in the opposite direction; the man had killed a bear and gave us some of the meat, which we enjoyed. These were the only white people I saw after leaving Albuquerque and we passed through no towns except little Mexican plazas.

Mr. Chandler had told us what route we would take and the towns we would pass through so I could get mail, but after he started he changed his route twice and I had not a line from anyone for almost three months. My people back in the old home, thinking we were at the mercy of half savages, as they judged the Mexicans to be, were very anxious, and my husband was anxious, too, although he had confidence in the man's promise to bring us through safely. Fortunately, we were perfectly well all the time. If any of us had been seriously ill nothing could have been done. One Mexican did die one night in the wagon next to ours. We heard him moaning and calling on God to help; it was bitterly cold and no one went to him. The next morning they seemed very much surprised to find him dead. We had to stay over one day so they could carry the body to a little plaza and lay it in consecrated ground. I thought it would have been more Christian to have taken care of him while he was alive.

The train moved so slowly we would take turns walking in good weather and could easily keep up with the wagons. The children gathered quantities of pinon nuts and in the evening the men helped to roast them. We passed many hours cracking and eating them as we moved along.

The first word I had from my husband was a note sent by some teamsters. This message reached me fifty miles out of Silver City. Two days afterwards he met us with a light wagon and a team of large mules. That was a joyful meeting and we gladly said goodbye to the plodding old oxen. It seemed that we were flying as we bowled along the last twenty-five miles to Silver City, where we arrived at six o'clock in the evening to find our little adobe house all ready for us, even the wood was laid ready for a fire in

Branding cattle. This quintessentially male occupation involved some women: the Becker sisters brand cattle on their ranch in the San Luis Valley in 1884. Courtesy of the Colorado Historical Society.

the Mexican fireplace, built in one corner of the room. How good it was to feel a floor under our feet and to have a comfortable bed on which to rest! My husband was very proud to think I would undertake such a journey to be with him, but I told him to make the most of it for, knowing what it meant, I would never do it again, alone.

I have made other journeys equally as tiresome and dangerous, when one was afraid of Indians behind every tree or rock. If we were traveling by night we imagined every soap weed was an enemy running, but he was with us and told us never to look for an Indian, because he would always hear the shot first.

Silver City, where we arrived the last of December, 1877, was quite a small place then. It is the county seat of Grant County, New Mexico, and at that time the silver mines were in active operation. There were also many large and small cattle ranches and sheep herds scattered over the country and a number of small farms or ranches, as we call them in this western country. These were located in the valleys around and all were drawing their supplies from Silver City, which trading made the town a very flourishing and prosperous place. It is beautifully situated and has a fine climate. We remained in this place, where my husband was engineer in the smelter, for over two years, then he took a herd of cattle on shares from Harvey Whitehill, sheriff of the county, and moved them out on the Gila river only a few miles from the Arizona line. After the cattle were located he returned for the family and we again embarked in a wagon, but this time it was drawn by horses. We were only two days making the trip over the Continental Divide, through the Burro mountains by way of Knight's Ranch. There we saw the burned remains of a wagon, household goods and wearing apparel scattered about where the Indians had massacred a family a short time before. We passed over a long dry mesa to a crossing on the Gila and drove down the valley past a few scattered ranches to the cattle ranch where we were to live for a year in a Jacel house, made by setting posts close together in the ground and daubing them with mud. It had a dirt roof and floor. While we lived at this place I taught school in one of the rooms, having an enrollment of nine children, including my two. With the proceeds of this venture I bought my first sewing machine. After a year we moved fourteen miles down the river into Arizona and settled on government land, which is now called York Flat. There were a few shacks on the place, and my husband soon had built a large adobe house with shingle roof, windows and floors which were a real luxury. Here we felt at home once more. Our house was a stopping place for travelers going from the railroad at Lordsburg to Clifton and the Longfellow Mines, which were owned and controlled by the Lesinskys. We entertained a number of interesting people; men who would be welcome guests in any society and more than welcome to us. They were very cordial and friendly and made an effort to give us the news of the outside world. Some of those I like to remember were Colonel Lee and Governor Sheldon, of Santa Fe; H. W. Lawton, Gen. John A. Logan, the Churches, who were the first owners of the mines at Morenci; many army officers, and Archibald Clavering Gunter, a story writer, who wrote profusely. One of his most interesting stories is "Miss Nobody of Nowhere," a rather exciting story of Indian troubles in the neighborhood of the ranch. The Indians were hostile and made a raid somewhere through the country twice a year, in the spring and fall when the grass and water was plentiful for their ponies. One time all the settlers got together about twenty miles up the river, making the trip at night because the Indians never attack at night or during a storm. We stayed at that ranch a week; sometimes the men would fill gunny sacks with sand and pack the windows half way and we would stay at the ranch. At other times everyone forted at Duncan and on this occasion the cowboys followed the Indians several days and pressed them so closely a squaw dropped her papoose which was strapped in the basket. The baby was so filthy the women had trouble getting it clean. A family named Adams took the child, a boy, and as he grew he developed the Indian traits. He was very cruel with other children and often struck at them with a hammer or rock. At one time he slashed a little boy with a knife, but was caught before the boy was badly hurt. The Indians traveled fast, only stopping long enough to run off the horses or kill a beef or human being they found. I do not remember them ever attacking a house, for the Apache Indians are great cowards and never fight in the open. A rattlesnake is a more honest enemy, because he, at least, warns one before striking. At one time five hundred Indians passed the ranch and, as it was round-up time, they killed a good many cattle and one man in sight of the house and two others a few miles above. Another time we heard the shot that killed a young man who had been at the ranch an hour before, playing croquet. There are many other incidents I could mention, but will not at this time.

If the men were late coming in from their rides after the cattle I was very uneasy and could not rest. My husband would scoldingly say that he always trailed a cow until he found her, and that I must get used to his being away. I often told him the day might come when he would wish I would become uneasy and send men to hunt him. This proved true, for if I had known it was Indians instead of rustlers who had stolen our horses three years later I would have sent men to his relief and he would not have been ambushed and killed.

After my husband's death I was compelled to remain at the ranch, as all we had was there. With the five children, the oldest sixteen and the youngest eight months, I went through many rough and dangerous experiences. The children's education was a serious problem. I tried taking them to California, but things went wrong at the ranch and I was sent for. I brought with me a young lady teacher, who stayed with us two years and took entire charge of the children; then we had another teacher for the same length of time. Altogether we had four and this arrangement proved much more satisfactory than sending them away from home.

Many things crowd into my mind, but I shall bring my story to a close by saying to you dear young people, who are starting out in life and are feeling, sometimes, that you are having many hardships to contend with in these rough mining camps, that if you just stop and think how much better you are situated than we of the earlier days were, you will have very much to be appreciative and thankful for.

Sarah Butler York, "Experiences of a Pioneer Arizona Woman," *Arizona Historical Review* 1, no. 2 (July 1928): pp. 69–75.

Female members of Catholic religious orders played a more important role in the settlement and development of the West than most histories acknowledge. This twenty-one year letter-journal kept by Sister Blandina Segale of the Cincinnati Sisters of Charity was intended mainly for her own sister, but Segale undoubtedly knew it would also be read by many members of her order. Thus, she tended to emphasize courage and action more than fear or failure, but her methods of coping certainly produced enough adventure and achievement to justify her independent-spirited faith.

Sister Blandina was born in Italy in 1850 and came to Cincinnati, Ohio, with her family in 1854. Although she had prayed to be sent west ever since she had joined the order at age sixteen in 1866, her summons to go in November 1872 was sudden and unexpected. For the next twelve days this twenty-two year old, sheltered nun traveled alone to the raw frontier mining town of Trinidad, in southwestern Colorado, where she lived for four years. From there she went on to establish missions in Santa Fe and Albuquerque, New Mexico.

Included here are descriptions of facing down a lynch mob to ensure a fair trial for an accused killer, preventing a mine disaster by means of astute judgment and friendship with local Indians, earning the respect of Billy the Kid and his gang, and even forestalling an Apache attack by her fearless intercession. A brief vignette of "Crazy Ann" portrays another sort of frontier woman, who was not so fortunate. Segale's unique methods of achieving the construction of a territorial trade school for girls in Santa Fe exemplify her community-building skills.

Trinidad, Dec. 10, 1872.

My dearest dear:—Here I am safe in Trinidad, Colorado Territory, instead of in the island of Cuba where we first thought I was to go. No wonder this small pebble (Trinidad, Colo.) is not on our maps. "Angels guide your footsteps." This sentence has stayed with me from the time I left the Archbishop's residence in Cincinnati, and is with me still.

I ordered the stage for the morning of the 9th. Mrs. Mullen was very attentive. She had new clean hay put in the stage to keep my feet warm, and after I got in she wrapped a large comfort around me, remarking that "traveling on the plains and in winter was not a pleasant prospect." The driver must have had strict injunctions from Otero and Sellar—they own the stage line. For the first time I had indefinable fears. The cowboys were constantly in my mind. I expected there would be a number traveling with me on the plains. "Snow-bound and cowboys" came in thought to annoy me.

At noon the driver came to the stage door and said: "We take dinner here." I thanked him and said: "I do not wish any dinner."

"But lady, we will not have another stopping place to eat until six o'clock this evening."

I thanked him again, "but I do not wish any dinner." The jolting of the stage and my thoughts had taken all appetite away. Though I could see nothing from the stage (every flap was fastened), it seemed that the driver aimed to drive over every stone and make the wheels go into every rut. It was nothing but a jerk up and down all the way—in a stage that had no springs and traveling at the rate of twelve miles an hour!

At six o'clock we arrived at the station for supper. At every station the mules were changed. The driver came to ask me to supper. I thanked him, but said: "I do not wish any supper."

"There will not be another chance for a meal until twelve o'clock to-night, and you have not tasted anything to-day, so come now and take it if only a cup of black coffee."

"No, thank you, I have no desire for anything."

The poor man was quite distressed. He could not think I was trying to save traveling expenses, because the price of stage traveling included meals. Here is the mental attitude I was in: if the driver could surmise the vague fear that is preying on me he would know I have no appetite.

He went in to supper and presently returned. "Lady, if you do not want to eat—come in and let me have my supper. The woman who runs this station will not give me a drink of muddy water unless I fetch you in to supper—I told her how you are dressed and she goes off wild and says:

'Bring her in or you will get nothing to eat to-night, nor any other time you come.'"

I went into an adobe, log-raftered, mud-floored, mud-plastered hut. The sight of the red checkered table cloth and black coffee only added to my repugnance for food. The person who kept the station was an Irish woman of the good old stamp. I made an effort to sip some coffee, but not a drop would pass my lips. The cowboys were in my mind. I tried to ascertain if there were any in the vicinity, the answers I received were indefinite.

At midnight: "Now, lady, you will have a good meal."

"No, thank you, I desire nothing."

"What will Otero and Sellar say to me when they find out you did not take a meal during this journey? They gave me more orders about you than I ever got since I'm staging, and that's ten years."

"Say I wished for nothing. I will write the firm my thanks."

Oh, the lonely, fearful feeling! The night was dark. No passengers to allay my turbulent thoughts. Footsteps drew near the stage. My heart was thumping. The driver opened the stage door and said:

"You will have a traveling companion for some miles."

In the open door, by the light of the lantern, I saw a tall, lanky, hoosier-like man, wearing a broad brimmed hat. On one arm he had a buffalo robe. While I sat riveted, he got in—asked me if I would take part of his "kiver," and before my fright permitted me to speak, he placed part of the buffalo robe over the comfort that enwrapped me, and sat beside me on the rear seat. The driver closed the door and we were in utter darkness. By descriptions I had read I knew he was a cowboy! With crushing vividness—"No virtuous woman is safe near a cowboy" came to me. I made an act of contrition—concentrated my thoughts on the presence of God—thought of the Archbishop's blessing, "Angels guard your steps," and moved to such position as would put my heart in range with his revolver. I expected he would speak—I answer—he fire. The agony endured cannot be written. The silence and suspense unimaginable. Suddenly from the darkness I heard:

"Madam!"

"Sir!"

"What kind of a lady be you?"

"A Sister of Charity."

"Whose sister?"

"Everyone's Sister, a person who gives her life to do good to others."

"Quaker like, I reckon?"

"No, not quite."

By this time I learned from his tone of voice that I had nothing to fear. He asked me a number of questions, all prompted by a conversation he had had with the driver before he came into the stage. In my turn I asked him why he became a cowboy. He said he had read of cowboys and ran away from home to become one.

"Is your mother still living?"

"Yes, I allow she is—leastwise she was when I left home six years ago."

"Have you written to her?"

"No, madam, and I allow that's beastly."

"It is certainly unkind to one whom you can always trust and who, I am sure, loves you as much now as she did when you were a little fellow."

His voice got husky. "What do you say I otter do?"

"Write; do so as soon as you get off this stage. Tell her you will soon make her a visit, and see to it that you keep your word."

"I will, so help me God! I was mighty feared to speak to you when I got in, because the mule driver said you was more particular than any lady he ever seen. I allow I am powerful glad I spoke to you."

To think that this lubberly, good-natured cowboy had made me undergo such mortal anguish. He got off on the outskirts of Trinidad where the driver stopped to point out to me dugouts at the side of the foothills.

"This, lady, is Trinidad." . . .

Dec. 14, 1872.

I am sure, dearest Sister Justina, you will be interested in my viewpoint of things as I find them here. To-day I went to look at my schoolroom to be; 40 ft. long; 14 ft. wide; 8 ft. high; two small windows, low-sized door, no transom; solid adobe walls on two sides, log rafters as black as ebony. Of necessity ventilation said "Goodbye" when the house was completed.

But I must add all these adobe houses were built with a view to protect the inhabitants in case of a sudden attack from the warring Indians. That does not mean that every house has these dimensions. The head of each family built to suit his taste in the matter of length, breadth, and height— but material to date is unchangeable: sunburnt mud (shaped, of course)

4x9x18 inches; the foundation the same as walls, mud roof over rafters—mud floors. There are some seventy-five of these houses on "Mexican Hill." That will be my first objective point; the second will be the jail.

The Purgatoire River—corrupted into Picatwar, but the natives kept its correct name, Purgatorio—is below the *acequia,* (artificial canal) which is the boundary line to land and house given by Don Felipe Baca, one of the leading citizens here, to the Sisters for a school. The land on which the Academy is built (now in course of erection) was donated by a Mr. Heone, who lives a few miles outside of Trinidad.

This gentleman and Dr. Beshoar, our physician, have pews in the church—if you can call eight planks nailed together, pews. The Sisters use the choir loft. The church is an adobe structure—with a pretense of a gable roof and a double pretense of having been shingled; mud floor, mud walls, wooden candlesticks. Previous to the Sisters coming, bottles were used for candlesticks. The only restful spot about the church are the grounds to the entrance of it.

The graveyard is in the rear of the church with a street between graveyard and convent. There is a long stretch of an adobe wall from convent (academy) to public school, the only one here and taught by the Sisters. I am told there is an Academy (called "Rice") maintained by the Methodists.

We have twelve resident young ladies at the Academy, occupying the part that is built; very few in the select school. The Sisters are: Sister Marcella, in charge and music teacher; Sister Martha, Housekeeper; Sister Eulalia, Factotum; Sister Fidelis, Select School; Sister Blandina, Public School Teacher; Sister Eulalia, Assistant.

Here is the Trinidad of today: Commercial Street, a few scattered houses the length of two blocks. Main Street, a few scattered stores occupying one side of the street about the same length as Commercial Street. Convent Street, we use to the end of the Public School grounds, where there are a few small adobe huts. So far, Mr. Baca has the only house that looks like a residence. Then there is the Mexican settlement on the hill. I am informed that very few prisoners ever come to trial. They manage to burrow out from jail before the Circuit Court convenes. The Circuit Court comes from Denver.

Here, if you have a largeness of vision, you find the opportunity to exercise it; if a cramped one, the immense expanse of the plains, the solid

Rockies, the purity of the atmosphere, the faultlessness of the canopy above, will stretch the mind toward the Good. Maybe, dearest, it may please you to know my own attitude at the present writing. *Vede mio cuore.* (Look at my heart). I wish I had many hands and feet, and a world full of hearts to place at the service of the Eternal. So much one sees to be done, and so few to do it. I have adopted this plan: Do whatever presents itself, and never omit anything because of hardship or repugnance. . . .

Jan. 6, 1874. . . .

To-day, while acting as moderator on the playgrounds, a woman came staggering on her way to me. She asked: "Do you know me, Sister?"

"I do not remember having met you before."

She stammered: "I'm Crazy Ann."

I looked at her kindly. She continued: "Why can't I be like you?"

"You are the only one that can answer the question," I replied.

Meanwhile, she seemed to be regaining her equilibrium and she resumed: "Sister, I was a good girl. My father compelled me to marry a man I did not love. I married him and sailed the same day for America. This happened in Ireland. I landed in New York. Now I am here, an outcast."

"Poor, poor Ann! Why not start life over again?" Ignoring what I said, she straightened herself and soliloquized: "I'm coming to church Sunday."

Encouragingly I said: "Do, Ann, but wear something on your head and drink only water Sunday morning." Sunday came, and so did Ann come to church. She made sure to look up to the choir loft to let me see she had kept her word. Only once have I seen the unfortunate woman since our first meeting. At the second encounter, she was surrounded by a crowd of men enjoying whatever she was saying to them. Suddenly she saw me. She made a rush through the crowd and disappeared. Her audience turned to discover what had caused her sudden departure and saw only two Sisters of Charity wending their way to the post-office. . . .

June 30, 1874.

Dear Sister Justina:—

It is nearly one year since I wrote anything in the Journal I'm keeping for you. The reason is simply that the things I could write are so ghastly that they had better be left untold. Keep in mind that the only three aims I can read in the minds of those who, at present, live in Trinidad, and its surroundings are:

1. Health for invalids.
2. Strenuous efforts in money making.
3. Jesuits and Sisters of Charity trying to stem undesirable conditions.

For the last named, their effort is like attempting to stop an avalanche.

Fearing you may consider me ambiguous, I will narrate one instance I would prefer not to write. One of the most thoughtful members of our Young Men's Vigilant Club came cautiously to see me and related the following:

"Sister, you know Mr.——— and Mr.———?" I bowed my knowledge of the men. Intuitively I felt a revelation was coming. He continued: "These men covet a coal mine that is now being worked. The mine shows prospects of making its owner a millionaire in the very near future. To-day a number of posts were placed in the first excavation. These can be shifted to such positions that when the boss and miners begin work to-morrow morning all the props will suddenly collapse. That diabolical act has been accomplished. The two men who did this are desperadoes and will stop at nothing if they find out we have had a hand in preventing the slaughter. The premeditated deaths not taking place will be ignored by them, but not getting possession of the coal mine would make them furious. What do you suggest?"

Realizing the deep significance of what he disclosed, I needed to reflect seriously. The two desperadoes—especially one of them, and this one controlled the mind of the other—were well known to me. The coal mine is located at some distance from Trinidad. Should I absent myself from school, it would be noticed. To go out to the mine would cause a sensation. So I revolved the matter over in my mind, while my informant waited for some suggestion. There was no time to lose.

Among my former pupils is a level-headed Indian. Mentally I had already sent for him. Continuing the conversation, I said: "Leave this affair to me; rumor is often unjust. Only assure yourself of this: if there is truth in what you were told, the supports in that mine will not collapse to-morrow."

To keep everything under cover, a small Mexican boy carried this message to the Indian: "I have some work for you, come." The Indian arrived some time before the return of the boy who took the message. When the messenger came back, the Indian was cleaning the windows in my schoolroom.

After the boy left, the Indian and myself got to work. His first question was, *"Qué, hay, Hermana?"* (What is it, Sister?) I answered: "A big one this time. Working men are wanted at the mine—go to the boss and hire yourself this evening. Be the first at the mine in the morning. Bring your miner's light with you. Inspect the supports and call the attention of the boss to anything that looks dangerous to you. You understand?"

"Sí, Hermana." (Yes, Sister.)

"Remain working at the mine, and instruct the natives how to detect danger in wrongly put-up supports and tell them to inspect the posts every time they resume work. Watch for powder and fuses. Instruct those most capable to carry out what you say."

"Sí, Hermana, yo voy." (Yes, Sister, I go.)

This Indian has the instinct of silence: to this, add that of loyalty to goodness, and you have the character of the one intrusted to frustrate the murderous design of the desperadoes. No long explanation was needed. I give you the conversation as we had it.

The mine remained in possession of its rightful owner, and no one was injured by the infernal plot to kill boss and miners. In my estimation, a good Indian is the best ally in an emergency. . . .

Nov. 14. . . .

One of my oldest pupils came to ask to have his sister excused from school. He looked so deathly pale that I inquired, "What has happened?" He answered, "Haven't you heard?"

"Nothing that should make you look as you do."

"Sister, dad shot a man! He's in jail. A mob has gathered and placed men about forty feet apart from the jail to Mr. McCaferty's room. The instant he breathes his last, the signal of his death will be given, and the mob will go to the jail and drag dad out and hang him."

"Have you thought of anything that might save him?" I asked.

"Nothing, Sister; nothing can be done."

"Is there no hope that the wounded man may recover?"

"No hope whatever; the gun was loaded with tin shot."

"John, go to the jail and ask your father if he will take a chance at not being hanged by a mob."

"What do you propose doing, Sister?"

"First to visit the wounded man and ask if he will receive your father and forgive him, with the understanding that the full force of the law be carried out."

"Sister, the mob would tear him to pieces before he was ten feet from the jail."

"I believe he will not be touched if I accompany him," I said.

"I'm afraid he will not have the courage to do as you propose."

"That is the only thing I can see that will save him from the mob law. Ask your father to decide. This is Friday. I'll visit the sick man after school this afternoon. Let me know if he will consent to go with me to the sick man's room."

Immediately after school, with a companion, I went to see the wounded man. Sister Fidelis had preceded me. She was writing a letter to his mother bidding her good-bye until they would meet where the Judge was just, and their tears would be dried forever.

I looked at the young man, a fine specimen of honesty and manliness. My heart ached for the mother who expected frequent word from her son, then to receive such news! To be shot unjustly, to die in a strange land, among strangers, so young!

As soon as Sister Fidelis and companion took leave of the sick man, the subject of the present visit was broached. The young man was consistent. He said, "I forgive him, as I hope to be forgiven, but I want the law to take its course."

Fully agreeing with him, he was asked: "Will you tell Mr.——— this if he comes to beg your pardon?"

"Yes, Sister," he answered.

Friday evening the prisoner's son came to say his father was very much afraid to attempt to walk to Mr. McCaferty's room, but if Sister would walk with him, he would take the chance of having the court pronounce sentence on him.

Early Saturday morning we presented ourselves to the Sheriff in his office.

"Good morning, Sister!" was the Sheriff's pleasant greeting.

"Good morning, Mr. Sheriff. Needless to ask if you know what is taking place on our two principal streets."

"You mean the men ready to lynch the prisoner who so unjustly shot the young Irishman?"

"Yes. What are you going to do to prevent the lynching?"

"Do! What has any sheriff here ever been able to do to prevent a mob from carrying out its intent?"

"Be the first sheriff to make the attempt!"

"How, Sister?" Standing to his full height—he must be six feet four—he reminded me of a person with plenty of reserve strength, and on the *qui vive* to use a portion of it.

"The prisoner was asked if he would be willing to walk between the sheriff and Sister to the victim's sick bed and ask his pardon." The sheriff interrupted:—"Sister, have you ever seen the working of a mob?"

"A few, Mr. Sheriff."

"And would you take the chance of having the prisoner snatched from between us and hanged to the nearest cottonwood?"

"In my opinion, there is nothing to fear." He straightened himself and looked at me, shrugged his shoulders and said, "If you are not afraid, neither am I."

We—the sheriff, my companion and myself—started to walk to the jail. All along the main street and leading to the jail were men at about a distance of a rod apart. These were the men who were to signal Mr. McCaferty's death by three taps of our school bell, in order that the mob might proceed to the jail, take the prisoner and hang him. Our group arrived at the jail, where we encountered the greatest discouragement. The prisoner saw us coming. When we got near enough to speak to him, he was trembling like an aspen. We saw his courage had failed him. We paused while we assured him he was safe in going with us.

He hesitated, then said: "I'll go with you." All along the road we kept silence, and no one spoke to us. When we got within a block of the sick man's room, we saw a crowd of men outside his door. It was at this juncture that my fears for the prisoner began. Intent upon saving our protégé from mob law, we hastened to the sick man's door. The crowd made way. Intense fear took possession of me. "Will the prisoner be jerked away when he attempts to enter his victim's room?"

The Sheriff and I remained at the foot of the few steps which led into the room. Meanwhile, I quietly said to the prisoner: "Go in," which he did, myself and companion following. The sheriff remained outside. The door was left wide open that those standing outside might hear the conversation taking place within.

The culprit stood before his victim with bowed head. Fearing a prolonged silence, I addressed the prisoner: "Have you nothing to say?"

He looked at the man in bed and said: "My boy, I did not know what I was doing. Forgive me."

The sick man removed the blanket which covered his tin-shot leg, revealing a sight to unnerve the stoutest heart. The whole leg was mortified and swollen out of proportion, showing where the poisonous tin had lodged and the mortification creeping toward the heart.

"See what you have done!" said the wounded man.

"I'm sorry, my boy, forgive me."

"I forgive you, as I hope to be forgiven, but the law must take its course."

I added, "Yes, the law must take its course—not mob law." Those outside the door with craned necks distinctly heard the conversation.

We returned to the jail where the prisoner was to remain until the Circuit Court convened.

From the time Judge Hallet became judge of the Circuit Court, he and his court members have regularly made a visit to the Convent.

June, 1876.

Dear Sister Justina:

To-day I asked Sister Eulalia if, in her opinion, we did not need a new school building, which would contain a hall and stage for all school purposes. She said: "Just what we need, Sister. Do you want to build it?" I answered, "Yes, I do." She added, "We have not enough cash to pay interest on our indebtedness. Have you a plan by which you can build without money? If so, I say build."

"Here is my plan, Sister. Borrow a crowbar, get on the roof of the schoolhouse and begin to detach the adobes. The first good Mexican who sees me will ask, "What are you doing, Sister?" I will answer, "Tumbling down this structure to rebuild it before the opening of the fall term of school."

You should have seen Sister Eulalia laugh! It did me good. After three days' pondering how to get rid of low ceilings, poor ventilation, acrobats from log-rafters introducing themselves without notice, and now here is an opportunity to carry out a test on the good in human nature, so I took it. I borrowed a crowbar and went on the roof, detached some adobes and began throwing them down. The school building is only one story high.

The first person who came towards the schoolhouse was Doña Juanita

Simpson, wife of the noted hero of Simpson's Rest. When she saw me at work, she exclaimed, "*Por amor de Dios, Hermana, qué está Vd. haciendo?*" (For the love of God, Sister, what are you doing?)

I answered, "We need a schoolhouse that will a little resemble those we have in the United States, so I am demolishing this one in order to rebuild."

"How many men do you need, Sister?"

"We need not only men, but also straw, moulds, hods, shovels—everything it takes to build a house with a shingle roof. Our assets are good-will and energy."

Earnestly Mrs. Simpson said: "I go to get what you need."

The crowbar was kept at its work. In less than an hour, Mrs. Simpson returned with six men. One carried a mould, another straw, etc. The mould carrier informed me at once that women only know how to *encalcar* (whitewash), the men had the trades and they would continue what I began. In a few days the old building was thrown down, the adobes made and sun-burnt. In two weeks all the rubbish was hauled away. The trouble began when we were ready for the foundation. Keep in mind it was only by condescension I was permitted to look on. At this juncture I remarked to the moulder:

"Of course, we will have a stone foundation."

"Oh, no!" he answered, "we use adobes laid in mud."

"Do you think if we laid a foundation with stone laid in mortar, the combination would resist the rainy season better than adobes laid in mud?"

"No, no, Sister, we never use stone for any of our houses," he replied.

I was at the mercy of those good natives and my best move was to let them have their way. Moreover, I recalled the fact that in the Far East there are mud structures centuries old in a good state of preservation. No mistake would be made by not changing their mode of building in that one point. We got the necessary lumber, sashes and shingles from Chené's mill, sixty miles from Trinidad. Wagons hauled the material. As the Chené family has a daughter at our boarding school, there will be no difficulty in meeting our bill. Mr. Hermann's daughter is a resident student, and Mr. Hermann is a carpenter and will pay his bill by work.

When the schoolhouse was ready for roofing, a number of the town carpenters offered to help. The merchants gave nails, paints, brushes, lime, hair, etc.

But now came the big obstacle. There is but one man who calls himself a plasterer, and his method is to plaster with mud. It is impossible to get a smooth surface with mud. I remarked to the plasterer: "You will use lime, sand and hair to plaster the schoolrooms."

His look plainly said: "What do women know of men's work?" Yet he condescended to explain: "I am the plasterer of this part of the country; if I should use any material but mud, my reputation would be lost."

I said to him, "But if lime, sand and hair made a better job, your reputation would gain."

He made answer, "Sister, I'll make a bargain with you. I will do as you suggest, but I will tell my people I carried out your American idea of plastering."

We both agreed to this. Meanwhile, the other men had shouldered their implements and were on their way home. The plasterer had to mix the sand, lime and hair following my directions. All that was done satisfactorily to me, at least. But there was not a man to carry the mortar to the plasterer, so I got a bucket and supplied a man's place. The comedy follows:

Rev. Charles Pinto, S.J., pastor, took pleasure in telling his co-religionists that the study of human nature, combined with good will and tactfulness, were building a schoolhouse.

On this day of my hod-carrying, the Rt. Rev. Bishop Machebeuf of Denver, Colorado, arrived on his visitation. The first place to which he was taken was the schoolhouse being built without money. Bishop and Pastor had just turned the kitchen corner when the three of us came face to face. Both gentlemen stood amazed. I rested my hod-bucket. Father Pinto looked puzzled. The Bishop remarked:

"I see how you manage to build without money." I laughed and explained the situation.

They took the bucket, and the three of us went to where the plasterer was working. After the welcome to the Bishop, the plasterer said:

"Your Reverence, look at me, the only Mexican plasterer, and I am putting aside my knowledge to follow American ways of doing my trade; but I told Sister the failure will not be pointed at me." The Rt. Rev. Bishop analyzed the material at a glance, then said: "Juan, if this method of plastering is better than yours, come again to help Sister when she needs you. If it fails, report to me and between us we shall give her the biggest penance she ever received."

The schoolroom walls turned out smooth, the plaster adhesive, and the plasterer will now make a lucrative living at his American method of plastering. . . .

We have not had any mob to hang delinquents since the Sheriff and some members of the Vigilant Committee asserted the rights of courts instead of unauthorized groups to carry out the interest of the laws.

The Circuit Court came to Trinidad. At its sitting it sentenced the prisoner to ten years in the penitentiary. Mr. McCaferty had lived three days after being shot, hence the deed is called manslaughter, minimum, one year, maximum, ten years.

Shall I prophesy? The prisoner will be at large in less than two years. Yet this small unmapped town is making strides in the right direction.

To-day we went to visit our cripple—spinal invalid—who was once the best horseman of the Southwest. His eyes are hungry for someone to speak to, and his appetite craves a change of diet. Among the edibles we brought him was a baked custard, which he literally devoured. During the time he was eating, his look was frequently directed to one particular part of the room.

When we turned to leave, my attention was arrested by a crouching figure. The object looked like a huddled dressed-up skeleton, head bald, eyes as if they had been placed in the sockets. The only indication of life was a terrified expression from the orbs that looked from the hollow sockets. I walked toward the bundle and said:

"Poor child, what can we do for you?"

"You do not recognize me, Sister? I am Crazy Ann! They told me you come to see this cripple, and I came to see you. I have no place where I can go to die."

"We shall find a place for you, Ann. You are one of God's children, but forgot you once loved Him, yet He still loves you."

Her sobs were sincere. We found a room and bed for her yesterday, to-day we went to see her. Her first request was for the scapulars. Oh! the feeling of repugnance that came over me to put the image of the purest of creatures on this all but God-forsaken, shriveled creature! But she was a "Prodigal Son." She told us she had cast off the scapulars when she began her downward career. She had but a few days to live. Her repentance is sincere, not because she now cannot sin, but because the faith instilled in early years has revived and prevented self-destruction.

Three days later, "Crazy Ann"—we knew her by no other name—was buried. The corpse was carried on a sort of stretcher covered with a sheet. she was lowered into a hole 3x6 ft. May her soul rest in peace, for surely peace left her from the moment her downward course began, and only returned when she came back to God.

Sept., 1876.

The pupils and myself will have to be introduced daily to our schoolroom. It will take some time to wear off the novelty of entering a well-lighted, well-ventilated room, flowers in blossom on window sills, blackboard built into the walls, modern desks, and a stage for Friday exercises. I think one of my ambitions has been reached, viz.: to walk into my schoolroom and feel that it is "up-to-date" and I, "Mistress of all I survey," particularly of the minds to be taught.

My scattered notes on "Billy the Kid's Gang" are condensed, and some day you will be thrilled by their perusal.

The Trinidad Enterprise—the only paper published here—in its last issue gave an exciting description of how a member of "Bill's Gang" painted red the town of Cimarron by mounting his stallion and holding two six-shooters aloft while shouting his commands, which everyone obeyed, not knowing when the trigger on either weapon would be lowered. This event has been the town talk, excluding every other subject, for the past week.

Yesterday one of the Vigilant Committee came to where I was on our grounds—acting as umpire for a future ball game—and said: "Sister, please come to the front yard. I want you to see one of 'Billy's gang,' the one who caused such fright in Cimarron week before last." My informant passed the news to the Nine and their admirers, so that it became my duty to go with the pupils, not knowing what might take place.

When we reached the front yard, the object of our curiosity was still many rods from us. The air here is very rarefied, and we all are eagle-eyed in this atmosphere. We stood in our front yard, everyone trying to look indifferent, while Billy's accomplice headed toward us.

He was mounted on a spirited stallion of unusually large proportions, and was dressed as the *Toreadores* (Bull-Fighters) dress in old Mexico. Cowboy's sombrero, fantastically trimmed, red velvet knee breeches, green velvet short coat, long sharp spurs, gold and green saddle cover. A figure of six feet three, on a beautiful animal, made restless by a tight bit—you need not wonder, the rider drew attention. His intention was to impress you with the idea "I belong to the gang." The impression made on me was one of intense loathing, and I will candidly acknowledge, of fear also.

The figure passed from our sight. I tried to forget it, but it was not to be. Our Vigilant Club, at all times, is on the alert to be of service. William Adamson, a member of the Club, came excitedly, to say—"We have work on hand!"

"What kind of work?" I asked.

"You remember the man who frightened the people in Cimarron, and who passed our schoolhouse some weeks ago?"

"Yes, William."

"Well, he and Happy Jack, his partner, got into a quarrel, and each got the drop on the other. They kept eyeing and following each other for three days, eating at the same table, weapon in right hand, conveying food to their mouth with left hand.

"The tragedy took place when they were eating dinner. Each thought the other off guard, both fired simultaneously. Happy Jack was shot through the breast. He was put in a dug-out 3 x 6 ft. Schneider received a bullet in his thigh, and has been brought into Trinidad, thrown into an unused adobe hut, and left there to die. He has a very poor chance of living."

"Well, William, we shall do all we can for him. Where did this all take place?"

"At Dick Wootton's tollgate—the dividing line between Colorado and New Mexico."

At the noon hour we carried nourishing food, water, castile soap and linens to the sick and neglected man. After placing on a table what we had brought, my two companions, William Adamson and Laura Menger, withdrew. I walked towards the bed and, looking at the sick man, I exclaimed, "I see that nothing but a bullet through your brain will finish you!"

I saw a quivering smile pass over his face, and his tiger eyes gleamed. My words seemed heartless. I had gone to make up for the inhuman treatment given by others, and instead, I had added to the inhumanity by my words.

After a few days of retrospection, I concluded it was not I who had spoken, but Fear, so psychologists say.

At our first visit I offered to dress the wound, but to my great relief the desperado said, "I am glad to get the nourishment and the wherewith to dress my wound, but I shall attend to it myself." Then he asked: "What shall I call you?"

"Sister," I answered.

"Well, Sister, I am very glad you came to see me. Will you come again?"

"Yes, two and three times a day. Good-bye."

We continued these visits for about two months, then one day the sick man asked: "Sister, why is it you never speak to me about your religion or anything else?"

I looked and smiled.

He continued: "I want to tell you something. I allude to the first day you came. Had you spoken to me of repentance, honesty, morals, or anything pertaining to religion, I would have ordered you out. 'I see that nothing but a bullet through your brain will finish you.' Sister, you have no idea what strength and courage those words put into me. I said to myself, 'no shamming here, but the right stuff.'" . . .

Sept., 1876. . . .

Another month passed by and the patient was visibly losing strength. I managed to get his mother's address. She lives in California.

After a week we resumed our visits. At the noon call our patient was quite hilarious. I surmised something unusual had taken place. He lost no time in telling me that Billy and the "gang" are to be here, Saturday at 2 P.M., and I am going to tell you why they are coming.

"Do you know the four physicians who live here in Trinidad?"

"I know three of them," I answered.

"Well, the 'gang' is going to scalp the four of them" (and his tiger eyes gleamed with satisfaction) "because not one of them would extract the bullet from my thigh."

Can you imagine, Sister Justina, the feeling that came over me? One of the gentlemen is our Convent physician!

I looked at the sick man for a few seconds, then said: "Do you believe that with this knowledge I'm going to keep still?"

"What are you going to do about it?"

"Meet your gang at 2 P.M. next Saturday."

He laughed as heartily as a sick man could laugh and said, "Why, Sister,

Billy and the gang will be pleased to meet you. I've told them about you and the others, too, who call themselves my church people," but seeing the conversation did not please, he said no more.

In the interval between this visit and the Saturday 2 P.M., which was to be such a memorable day for me, I wrote to his mother not in an alarming strain, but enough to give her to understand he might not recover. Fourteen days later, she arrived. That was quick time, for she depended on mules and horses for conveyance. I cannot give you any idea of the anxiety of the days previous to the coming ordeal of meeting the gang.

Saturday, 2 P.M., came, and I went to meet Billy and his gang. When I got to the patient's room, the men were around his bed. The introduction was given. I can only remember, "Billy, our Captain, and Chism."

I was not prepared to see the men that met me, which must account for my not being able to recall their names.

The leader, Billy, has steel-blue eyes, peach complexion, is young, one would take him to be seventeen—innocent-looking, save for the corners of his eyes, which tell a set purpose, good or bad. Mr. Chism, of course this is not his real name—has a most bashful appearance. I judge he has sisters. The others, all fine looking young men. My glance took this description in while "Billy" was saying: "We are all glad to see you, Sister, and I want to say, it would give me pleasure to be able to do you any favor."

I answered, "Yes, there is a favor you can grant me." He reached his hand toward me with the words: "The favor is granted."

I took the hand, saying: "I understand you have come to scalp our Trinidad physicians, which act I ask you to cancel." Billy looked down at the sick man who remarked: "She is game."

What he meant by that I am yet at a loss to understand. Billy then said: "I granted the favor before I knew what it was, and it stands. Not only that, Sister, but at any time my pals and I can serve you, you will find us ready." . . .

July 31, 1877. . . .

Here is a scene of weekly occurrence. Saturday morning come into Santa Fe the superannuated, the blind, and the lame, who are incapacitated for work. They make their rounds of visits usually in groups of two or three. Each carries a bag or basket into which charitable persons may put whatever they wish. At noon time they all have found their way to our *placita.* They arrange themselves as comfortably as they can in a sitting position where the sun shines, and await the coming of Sister Catherine, who moves among them with an air of benevolence truly charming.

Whatever the convent has been able to put aside for them during the week Sister distributes. Then takes place what in my estimation is the essence of unselfishness. Each recipient looks into his basket or bag. Those who can see do this act for the blind. Then they equalize the edibles. They who have more than can be consumed for the week give to those who have less, the quality is also changed, giving to those who prefer one thing more than another.

Is not this a beautiful miniature picture of the first Christians?

Our closing exercises will take place August 29. The invitations are limited on account of the smallness of the hall. During the intermission—ten minutes—a cool drink will be served the audience by white aproned gentlemen.

Sept. 1.

The "Charity Girls" had their inning. The closing exercises were a revelation to all present. The first number "Art Gallery" represented a series of masterpieces in painting, the most prominent being Dolce's *Madonna.* The audience was busy studying the paintings in order to name the artists. Meanwhile Bengal Lights were flashed over the gallery to enhance the beauty of the scene. In the audience were several connoisseurs. The study was interrupted by a widow exclaiming in an ecstatic voice, *"Es mi hija! Es mi hija!"* (That is my daughter! That is my daughter!) pointing to the most attractive painting on the stage. Then the talk and laughter began, while the actors remained statuesque. When the curtain dropped the assembly as one became magpies. Every number on the program was greeted with genuine enthusiasm. My theory is fully vindicated. The children of toil given the same opportunity as children of luxury, will excel.

What do you think is strongly agitated? The building of an Industrial School.

Jan. 16, 1878.

One year ago I arrived in Santa Fe with the feelings of a shrunken resurrection plant, and a sincere desire to be immersed or remain dry. But lo! I've been plunged into a whirlpool of work.

The Legislature meets in Santa Fe biennially. Members of the present session are arriving from all parts of the Territory. Major Sena made a speech at our closing exercises which gave me thought for a territorial hospital appropriation. The inhabitants here do not seem to have the same diseases as we have in the States. The majority take a daily sun bath— though I do not vouch they take a water bath as frequently. The hospital would be a vacated building, did we depend on native patients. Those who are admitted are men who come from the States seeking health or prospecting for gold; some are under the impulse of wanderlust, and others simply to get away from everybody. These are the ones who are likely to succumb to the climate.

A bill introduced to protect the interests of our native population passed over the Governor's veto. He has the unsavory reputation of being a Mormon, though I believe the odium comes from the fact that he was Governor of Utah before his appointment to the gubernatorial chair here.

A bill has been drafted, the gist of which is to allow the St. Vincent Hospital $100.00 monthly. This will help support the penniless who come for admission.

Jan. 18.

The Territorial Appropriation Bill for the relief of the Hospital passed. *Deo Gratias!*

Our orphans gave a special entertainment for the House and Senate. All members attended. Mr. Jaramillo, a prominent Senator, found out that the piano used was a borrowed one. After the "Little Show" he, in the name of a number of friends, placed money enough in my hands to order a new piano. The order goes in the next mail.

April, 1878.

The question of building is assuming large proportions. I smile, knowing the financial condition of the convent treasury. . . .

Sister Augustine called me to her office and very suavely broached the subject of building. In part she said, "Most Rev. Archbishop Lamy thinks one great need in the Territory is a Trade School for girls. Now, Sister, will you undertake to build it?"

"How much money have we with which to begin building?"

"Nothing, Sister. Do as you did in Trinidad. I was told you had not a cent when you started to build your adobe schoolhouse, and you finished it without debts."

"Ah! Sister, that was only an insignificant matter compared to what a Trade School should be."

"Well, Sister, keep the size of the building within the boundary of your judgment."

"And the money within the same boundary?"

She smiled and continued, "Use your originality as you did elsewhere, and with God's blessing you will get through."

I immediately thought of the young artist, Mr. Projectus Mouly, son of Antoine, whose feelings made him shrink from meeting his friends.

Mr. Mouly has come to the Convent. I saw at once he was strangely touched that I should send for him. I told him my plans for building an Industrial School. The plans are out of all proportions to any building here, and far away from the imagination of the present population of Santa Fe. Keep in mind the fact that the inhabitants of the territory are still on terms of enmity with the Apaches and Navajos, and any railroad is yet three hundred and some miles from here.

Was it the extreme pressure of mental distress being experienced by this young genius, or his determination to get away from what he believes would be his ultimate downfall, or my enthusiasm in plunging into a great undertaking requiring large sums of money and not a cent on hand, that made him say: "I'm with you, Sister, when do you wish to begin?"

"As soon as I consult with His Grace and the Rector of the Cathedral."

I must confess, I have a strong repugnance to building; not on account of the hardships the work will entail, but because some things are not clear to me. At an interview with His Grace, he said: "One great need of the territory is a Trade School. Go at it with my full blessing." Here is the interview with the Rector of the Cathedral, Rev. Augustine Truchard. He thinks the object of the training school is most laudable and greatly needed.

"How much money have you to begin with, Sister?"

"Not a cent, Father."

"And you want to build a three-story house in a country where there is not a planingmill, not a brickyard, not a quarry of your own, nor limekilns, and, worst of all, not a cent on hand! Yet you want to begin to dig the foundation Monday morning. Do you know what some of us will say of you?"

"I can surmise, but if you will do what I ask of you I'm not afraid to begin work Monday morning."

"Let me hear, Sister, what you wish me to do."

"Simply to announce at the next Sunday Masses that the Sisters of Charity wish to build a house where girls in need can be trained in industries by which they can make a livelihood. Please say that our present wish is that a number of peons be paid by those disposed to do so, and sent to our front grounds to work on Monday and continue daily until the foundations are laid, each man to bring pick and shovel."

"Well, Sister, I will make the announcement, but I do not believe the men will come."

Monday, June 3, 1878.

Seven o'clock. Twelve men with picks and shovels came to work. I registered the names and became timekeeper.

June 17, 1878.

Two weeks ago we started work on the foundations for an Industrial School. Part of the land excavated makes a natural foundation, so we are ready for masonry work.

I had another interview with the Rector of the Cathedral. When he saw me he said: "Now, Sister, what do you want?" The answer was, "Wagons, mules, drivers."

"And how do you propose getting them?"

"If you please, in the same way we got men, picks, and shovels."

"Well, Sister, I shall announce your second plea at all the Masses tomorrow."

Meanwhile, a quarry had been opened and the men who were not needed to work on foundations were quarrying stone. After the second announcement in the church so many men and wagons were sent to us that they were in one another's way. A Mr. Antonio Ortiz y Salazar, who has taken an active interest in our plan of building without money, said to me:

"Sister, when you dismiss these men and wagons, I shall send you a regular team on one condition that when the mules need shoeing and the wagon needs repairs you send them to Mr. Paul's blacksmith shop and charge to me."

"Thank you, Sir!" I said gratefully. You will note, Sister Justina, that by this arrangement we will have a steady team to depend on.

Dr. Longwell said to me this morning, "Sister, there is an American who has a splendid pair of horses which he will let you have on ninety days' time."

"And the price?"

"One hundred and fifty dollars."

"Please tell the American that I shall take the span on his own terms."

Some time before this I had seen a jolt ranch wagon warping in the sun and ascertained that the owners had no further use for it. As the family who owned the wagon was poor, I asked them to let me have it for some time, which they cheerfully did. You know, Sister Justina, that there are here no planingmills, no brickyards, nor regular limekilns.

We have given a contract to a native who will employ his own men to cut the trees and handsaw the lumber to the dimensions required. The nearest place trees are available for lumber is twenty-three miles from Santa Fe.

We have started our own brickyard. 250,000 bricks will be burnt at the first firing. We have eight gentlemen pledged to send workingmen to wait on the bricklayers.

The intersecting interior walls are to be of adobe laid in mortar. This will make the school cool in summer, and warm in winter. The work is to settle for months before the bricks and adobe walls are interlocked.

We have neither gas nor water-works here, but we are going to install pipes for both commodities in case we ever "wake up." This place is not a "Sleepy Hollow" only "Sunshine Asleep."

July 26, 1878.

The bricks are all piled ready to use.

I sold the span of horses and the wagon for $200, paid the owner of the horses $150, and gave $40 to the poor family who had no use for the wagon, and thereby gained $10. This will help pay for lime.

We have made no financial appeal to the people of Santa Fe, yet they have shown themselves most liberal. Seldom do I go to the plaza to order supplies, but I return with much more money than I started out with. God provides when one does his best. . . .

August 14. . . .

"Very well, Mr. Mouly, when do you want to start for Denver?"

"I have a mule, but no credit there."

"The credit will arrive in Denver sooner than you will on mule back. A check will be sent you by mail, so go when you are ready."

"May I suggest that I remain until after the open air exercises, for which you are preparing the orphan girls, are over?"

"I am more than pleased at your suggestion, because I know I could not carry out the drafted programme without your help."

About two months ago I was measuring lumber which had been hauled in when I heard someone say, "Ma, I wager that is the Sister we want to see."

I turned to face a tall woman, who introduced herself.

"I am Mrs. Dana, the General Quartermaster's wife. This is my daughter, Mary."

"You are speaking to Sister Blandina," I said.

"Mary thought so. My daughter would like to read *Promessi Sposi* with you and review some of her music."

"My work is such that I cannot assure you a lesson without interruption. If you are willing to come with that understanding I accept you as a pupil."

Mary came. Miss Dana is much interested in our orphan girls. She has every lady at the military post anxious to assist us in any way she can. For quite a while I was annoyed at her calling our girls "brats," so I asked her what meaning she attached to the word "brat." She laughed. "By 'brat,' I mean every girl in your school is a love of mine."

Miss Dana is a unique character. She comes frequently to assist us. When she leaves she goes straight to the Cathedral—the side chapel opens into our placita (yard) and there remains half an hour in His presence. The Danas are not Catholics.

A messenger from the General Quartermaster says that he will send an orderly and a squad of soldiers to put up awnings for the open air exercises. The rainy season begins about the middle of August.

If the programme we have on paper can be carried out in reality, no one in the audience will regret the dollar entrance fee. I was coerced in charging for entrance.

The stage is topped by two large acacia trees. The stage proper is divided into three stages, each with its curtain. Carolina's voice has been placed. One year's training has accomplished much. Her voice is a rich mezzo-soprano, and can easily support twenty-five voices without effort.

Carolina's mother had been a traveling opera singer and harpist. Years ago she left this child with the Sisters and forgot to call for her.

Sept., 1878

The Open Air Exercises surpassed all I had hoped. I am going to explain two scenes.

First stage. The curtain rose on a tableau of our Blessed Mother, angels clustered about her, ascending into heaven. Slowly she disappeared, the angels accompanying her. The illusion was perfect. No one suspected a second stage.

The second curtain rose. Carolina, a captive knight, dressed in the full armor of knighthood, sang, "The Captive Knight." Above the dungeon scattered in two acacia trees were many brilliantly dressed fairies, with bows and arrows, awaiting to defend the Knight, in case of treachery. A third curtain rose, showing a garden. The fairies had carried the Captive Knight to the fountain, which was throwing intermittent sprays of sparkling water, and the Knight was made to drink. This turned him into the leading fairy just as the court officers came to recapture him. During all this scene, dreamy music was heard from the distance. The would-be captors fell asleep. The fairies disappeared. The perspective from the first stage to the end of the garden was enchanting. The play was part of an original one, written to meet the capacity of the orphans.

As nothing of this kind had ever been produced here, the circulating gossip had it that the trainer of the orphan children must have been an actress!

·   ·   ·   ·

Sept., 1879.

Dear Sister Justina:

Looking over the scribble I wrote on scraps since January, I notice they were not entered in this journal, which I trust some day you will enjoy. I have condensed the scraps and here is the result:

The legislature was in session the early part of the year.

Many tramps came from the East and Northeast.

Need I say that, as usual, everywhere attempts were made to get rid of them?

Yet these same poor tramps are human beings with immortal souls. Repeatedly we were told that many of these trail-pilgrims were succumbing to fatigue, climate, and want of nourishment. Those who reached Santa Fe found their way to our hospital and often gave us the information that quite a number of fortune-hunters were perishing on the Santa Fe Trail. At the time I scribbled this on waste paper every bed in the hospital was occupied. Like King Richard who offered his Kingdom for a horse, I would offer mine for a mattress. But there were no mattresses to be had. I took the mattress from my bed and had it placed on the porch for a patient. Then came two more patients. By the time their brief history was recorded, another mattress was placed by the side of the other. Without a word, every Sister deprived herself of her mattress for the poor patients.

Then came the question of nourishment. Sisters denied themselves milk and sugar to give their portion to the convalescents. . . .

Some weeks after we had permission to take in patients who had no money, the head of the culinary department said to me: "Sister, we have not a handful of vegetables to prepare for dinner, and seventy-two patients, thirty-five orphans, and sixteen Sisters to feed. Please figure it out, you, who, I have been told, are never daunted!"

Smiling, I replied, "That problem will be solved in ten minutes."

I went to the rear of our empty vegetable garden and looked over the adobe wall into the Archbishop's garden. There I saw an abundance of cabbage, turnips, carrots, and what not. Most of the vegetables were buried heads down in the ground, roots showing above ground. I made one athletic spring (old habits die slowly) and landed near the cabbage patch. Throwing over into our vacant garden at least two dozen cabbage heads, I did the same with each of the other vegetables, only in greater number, as the sizes were smaller. Then I went to His Grace's door and rapped.

"Come in."

I opened the door and stood, saying: "I have come to make a confession out of the confessional." He looked at me with that benevolent expression which once seen can never be forgotten. In that look he also saw that I was covered with dust, and he said, "My little Sister, what have you been doing?"

"Stealing, Your Grace. With never a thought of restitution, I dug up enough vegetables from your garden to last us three days."

"And then?"

"Whatever you say."

"Tell Louis to give you all there are."

"Thank you very much," is all I could say.

Shortly after this, Mr. Frank Manzanares, of the firm of Browne and Manzanares, sent sacks of coffee and sugar. I think His Grace is guilty. . . .

Nov., 1882. . . .

(Sister Segale made a trip to Santa Fe from Albuquerque.) When I boarded the Lamy branch to the ancient city, I noticed a number of Pino Indians. Scarcely was I seated when a blanketed chief came to ask me in incorrect Spanish:

"Tu vas Carlisle, Santa Catalina escuola?" (Are you going to Carlisle, to Saint Catherine's School?)

"There is no Santa Catalina School in Carlisle."

"No Santa Catalina School, no papooses!"

With this the Indian agent, Thomas by name, came to ask me if the atmosphere was too oppressive, meaning the nearness of the Indian to me. I retorted: "The oppression just now comes from another quarter." Thus by all sorts of deception the Red Man is deprived of the little he desires. . . .

That English phrase, "The survival of the fittest," is being applied to the rightful owners of this country. Let us stretch our imagination and see ten million Chinese suddenly descend on us! Would we not, if given a new chance, be more considerate with the Indians? The money supplied by our government and misapplied by the agents helps the extermination.

What does the whole amount to anyway? A few more years and we lay our burdens down, close our eyes and carry in our hands the good or otherwise we did during the test of our pilgrimage. There will be no deceptions at the bar of the Supreme Judge.

December, 1883.

Sister Pauline and myself have returned without reaching where we intended to go, namely, the San Bernardino Mountains. We started from Albuquerque and reached McCarthy's Camp by railroad. From this camp, we were to travel by an uncovered jolt wagon.

When we arrived at McCarthy's Camp, the whole place was in confusion. Several workmen came to inform us that a man by the name of

D—— had been selling liquor to the Indians, and he, himself, drank heavily—during which time he killed his father-in-law and another member of the family, and then ran away with a young girl—dressed in man's attire—leaving his wife and children in destitution.

"Will you go see the murdered two?" said a kind Irishman to me. "No, but I will give you a message to his abandoned wife and children. Give this note to show the conductor on any train she may take to Albuquerque. Give her this second note and have her present it to our Sisters in Old Albuquerque—they will supply all her wants—rooms included."

"But, Sister," said the Irishman, "none of them is of our faith."

"A bigger reason why we should come to their aid."

"God bless you, Sister, that is not the way England would treat Ireland."

"We are living in a country where every Christian should be neighborly."

We left McCarthy's Camp in an uncovered freight wagon and had traveled until 3 P.M. before we saw any sign of habitation. This was represented to us by a large commissary tent. Looking at the sun, I remarked to the driver, "We can still travel three hours before camping." While I was saying this, a gentleman left the tent and came toward us. I soon recognized our friend, Mr. Louis Grant, the youngest of the Grant Bros., Bridge Contractors. Mr. Grant looked the picture of a corpse. He cautiously approached and said, "You can go no farther, and neither can you return, the Apaches are on the war path."

Turning to the driver, he ordered him to unhitch and come into the tent. We followed. Mr. Grant, the driver, and Sister Pauline went into the tent. I stood at the opening flap facing twenty-two men with set teeth, each holding a gun, and showing a determination to protect his own life. Soap boxes, nail kegs, etc., were used for chairs. I asked Mr. Grant, "What does this all mean?"

He replied: "The camp ahead of us is a grading camp. At noon to-day a number of Apache Indians galloped in to gather up food that had been discarded by the workingmen. One of the graders said to a group of men near him, 'I'm going to let you see how an Indian kicks the bucket.' He went to his tent, brought out a gun, took aim and shot an Indian through the heart! The Indians looked at their fallen companion, raised him—he was dead, strapped him on his pony and made for their reservation. In less than an hour they returned demanding the man who shot the Indian. They were told he had gone to the Bridge Builders. The Indians came here demanding the murderer. We told them the man had not come to our works, nor had we seen him. The Indians told us, 'We are not an American ball, if he is not here we must go there to get him, he not there, we come back, we not get him we whoop, whoop, whoop,' making gestures with his mouth. This conversation was carried on with one of the Indians who spoke a little Spanish and a little English. We managed to understand what he wanted to tell us."

While Mr. Louis Grant was saying this to me, the men in front of me who could see through the open lapel of the tent, became more tense, if possible. I looked at Mr. Grant, who also could see over my head, and watched his eyes focused on a point.

I asked, "What now?"

He replied: "Scout Indians on the knoll opposite us."

Instantly I determined to go meet them and so stated. Looking at Sister Pauline, I said, "Pray, pray." Then raising my crucifix from my rosary, I turned. The scouts were fully two rods from us. The first sight I got of the Indians my teeth began to chatter and my knees to knock against each other, but my brain worked fast. Twenty-two men and Sister in the tent. If I can make these scouts realize I am the Sister who received the message from their chief to teach their papooses, we are safe. This reasoning had the effect of partially controlling the fright I was thrown into at the first sight of the scouts. Well, I realized the two Indians could not conquer the men in the tent who were prepared to protect all our lives, but the two scouts only needed to give the war signal and our doom was sealed. So bracing myself with prayer, and utilizing my natural courage, I slowly walked to meet them. As I approached, my eyes caught sight of their armor. Each had a gun on his right shoulder, bow and arrows on left shoulder, a belt alternating with bow knives and pistols, as many as could be placed in belt, war paint, red and yellow. Again fear tried to gain ascendancy, but will power won. Holding the crucifix in both hands, and steadily looking at the elder of the two Indians, I said, "*Buenas tardes*" (Good evening). Showing no expression whatever, he answered, in lower chest tones, "*Buenas tardes.*"

I added: "*Me conoce?*" (Do you know me?)

He replied, "*No eres tú tata?*" (No, are you a priest?)

I made answer, "*No, yo nana*" and continued, "I am to your squaws and papooses what the priest is to your chief and braves."

He added, "What are you doing here?"

I told him another Nana and myself were journeying to the San Bernardino Mountains, but the chief of the workmen, who is my friend, told me someone has done a wrong to the Apaches, but the one who did the wrong is not here.

"Do you believe him?"

"Yes, because my friend has never told me a lie. Let us go to the tent and I will tell my friend what you say and tell you what he says."

"Do you believe him?"

"Yes, because he has never told me a lie."

We walked to the tent. I asked Sister Pauline for some medals which we always carried. Stringing them, I placed a number around the neck of each scout, then resumed the conversation, saying to the elder Indian:

"What do you wish to say to my friend?"

He responded: "Do you believe him?"

I answered, "I do, because he has never told me a lie."

"Ask him if the American who killed our Indian is here."

Mr. Grant said, "No, he is not here." The Indian looked at me.

"Do you believe him?"

"I do, because he has never told me a lie."

"Ask your friend if he or any of his men know where he is."

I put this question to Mr. Grant, who said, "Neither I nor any of my workers saw the man the Indians are looking for."

The elder Indian asked again, "Do you believe him?"

"I do, because he has never told me a lie."

Then fixing his eyes on me, he said, "Tell your friend, the chief, to put his men to work; we will not touch them. We will go to the other camp for the American who killed our Apache. If they do not give the man we whoop, and then we (passing his hand around his head) scalp." Our intensified feeling relaxed. The scouts started on the trail to the next camp. I said to Mr. Grant, "I suggest you send a messenger on horseback to the grading camp and advise giving the wanton murderer over to the Apaches to prevent many complications with the Government, Apaches, and railroad officials. It is plain that, unless the Apaches are pacified, they will break from their reservation and then who can hold Geronimo and his band?" I added, "When you come to Albuquerque, please do not mention this incident to me, or what became of the man. The advice to turn the murderer over to the Apaches is given, as my conscience dictates. I'm not certain that theology bears me out." Mr. Grant is a Catholic. Sister and myself retraced our journey to Albuquerque.

Sister Blandina Segale, *At the End of the Santa Fe Trail* (Milwaukee: Bruce, 1948), pp. 27–33, 55–62, 67–69, 74–75, 104–10, 141–45, 216–20.

"This is desolation itself"

Angie Mitchell (1854–1909) was born just two years before her parents joined other antislavery settlers moving from Massachusetts to the strife-torn Kansas frontier. In 1876 they moved on to Prescott, Arizona, where her father was a government surveyor and justice of the peace. Angie herself, "one of Prescott's most accomplished young ladies" (according to the local newspaper), taught school in various districts. She married George Brown, a sheriff and territorial legislator, in April 1881, just after the teaching assignment described in this diary excerpt.

Brown's lively narrative contains vivid details about herself and about the household of women and children with whom she lived in the frontier Tonto district, west of Prescott. As on many frontier ranches in Arizona, the household functioned most of the time without men, who were generally miles away herding cattle. But it included several women of different generations, a variety of children, and frequent visitors. Schoolmarm Mitchell boarded there while teaching twenty-five children in what newspapers called the "new and thriving community."

One remarkable episode, related here, was an encounter with terrorizing Indians, who later complimented the women on their bravery. Brown also explored ancient Native American pueblo ruins with students and friends, and survived almost daily crises and adventures. As she returned home for Christmas, her stagecoach was almost swept over a waterfall, and later a team of runaway horses nearly pulled the coach off a mountain cliff. Perhaps it was her coolheaded good humor that endeared her to the Spanish-American senora who insisted on entertaining her without her fellow passengers.

Sept. 5th Sunday

I wrote Hancock [to accept the Tonto School] and Geo. [her fiance] went down about 10 & found out from Dan O'Leary and St. James concerning the Tonto road—then came back at 12 and "said things" about my *craziness* in wanting to go to such an out of the way place & I merely reminded him that I promised him I'd go to the most "barbarous" country I could if he ran for anything on the ticket & he promised not to and I abandoned my intention of going to St Johns-Apache Co.—that he broke his share of the agreement and I thought *Tonto* would answer my purpose *nearly* as well as *St Johns* (which latter school was now engaged) and therefore I should go to Tonto. That I hoped he'd be willing to take me there but if he wasn't I'd go to Phoenix by Stage & get some way of going to Tonto Basin from there. He looked disgusted—but the whole thing is a little amusing & we both laughed & he said he'd assuredly take me if I was going anyhow, & that settled it. . . .

Sept. 6th

Washed my duds, then sorted trunks & boxes for Tonto. Can only take a little trunk & it is hard to decide what I can do without. Geo. went home at 1. Josie & Mrs K. came out & they said more "things". Mother will go with us, & she is merely *resigned* not *jubilant*. Really one would think I was going to the Feejee Isles.

Sept. 7th

Ben Weaver wanted me to see about getting a select school instead of going away & Ma, Josie & Mrs K all agreed so that I agreed to try & if I could get 15 good paying pupils I'd stay. I got 12 without any trouble & was actually scared, lest I'd get 3 more but Fortune favored me & I couldn't get any more positively promised tho' I honestly did my best, and so that settled it & today since I got home at 3, I've been packing & getting ready. . . .

Sept. 16

Rained all night but our camp is "high & dry" among the cedars & our improvised tent kept us dry & comfortable (Ma & I) while Geo. fared equally well in the wagon: Got up early & found the sun shining over the Mts., eat a hearty breakfast & started on. Went to Mud Tanks about 4 miles over a *fearful* road. There Geo. fed & watered the horses & we started again—only went about a mile when a big black cloud came overhead & promised to "hail" us out of existence. In a jiffey Geo. unhitched the team & in two jiffeys fixed a shelter under the wagon for us. The storm passed by us & we only got a very little of it & were very thankful. . . .

Sept. 17

Ma sick with crampcolic part of the night. All right today, also had a bad pain in her lungs so I did her up in mustard, rubbed her in liniment & dosed her with hot wiskey & she got better. Started at 7 without breakfast as water was non est. Went to a grove of fine pines & there got breakfast. Drove to Strawberry & then to Pine Cr. & camped at the Mormon's ranch. This man has 2 or else 3 wives & we saw 16 children sitting on some logs, that seemed to be nerly the same age & size & looked exactly alike, about as wild as quail. There are also an assorted variety of dogs. . . . Tonight after the cows were milked the 16 *twins &* about as many older ones each with a bowl of bread & milk, scattred around the yard and eat their suppers. Geo. says he counted them & there were 73—but he exaggerates a trifle tho'. There really are 22 or 23 of the kids but I don't suppose they belong to one family.

. . . [After a horrendous journey down a precipitous canyon, caused by deliberately wrong directions from another Mormon, whose wife called it "the meanest trick I've ever known him to do," they arrived on September 20 at Judge John Blake's, with time to "rest-up" for a week before the start of school.]

Sept. 23

Geo. & Ma started for Green Valley & today for the first time in my life I know what it is to feel utterly cast away & homesick. This is desolation itself here, high frowning hills, long stretch of dusty road, no fields, no trees except a few near what is, part of the year a creek, no shade near the house, no porch around it, no furniture in it, except a broken cook stove, two shaky tables, a rough board bedstead, 3 or 4 home made camp stools, an almanac & 3 or 4 papers a month old, and a law book & book of forms—½ a dozen plates, 3 saucers, 2 cups, & 3 or 4 tin cups & 3 or 4 tin plates, steel knives & forks—a tin can lid for salt & lard buckets to cook in & a wooden box or two—a gourd dipper, an old tin water pail & ditto milk pail & a nice new style churn, 2 battered tubs, a broom, & a rough bench & 1 dozen good milk pans, a piece of tin with holes punched for a skimmer & a lot of iron & tin spoons, ass't sizes & all ages constitute the house hold goods of this family. I'm not sherring them, I'm simply filled with amazement that people sensible, nice people can live in such a way! Oh yes—there's a block with 3 nails in it for one candle stick & a bottle for another! The beds are ticks filled with hay the pillows about the same hard anyway & there's only *one:* Heavens! will my boarding place be a duplicate?

Sept. 24

I climbed to the ruin above the road on a hill & explored it.

Sept. 25

Mrs. Blake washed & I helped her & washed my trip clothes. Judge B. went to Reno. . . . I had another surprise about noon just after I had changed my clothes, "banged" my hair afresh and was wondering what upon earth I was going to do with myself the balance of the long hot day—a stranger rode up—a rough kindly looking miner. He viewed me with a surprised air & asked for Judge B. the folks had all gone across the creek after some stock or something & I said so. He accepted my invitation to come in and wait & suddenly turning said, "My little lady, where on earth did a dainty bit of humanity like you drop from to light in this dirty valley?" Who'd look for *flattery* of such broad description from such a source! I told him I had come to teach the Lowes Tonto school & would go there tomorrow: he started & exclaimed, "You, teach down there? Its like putting a humming bird into a mud lark's nest!" Now *thats* what I call encouraging. I had on to be sure, my pet dress for hot afternoons, a white lawn with delicate pink flowers made with a ruffle, edges with lace & headed with same & broad sash of lawn tied at back (of the lawn) tucked waist trimmed with insertion & lace & a little pink bow, cut pointed in neck & filled in with lace & rather short ruffled sleeves trimmed with more of the lace all of ordinary quality & common style & not new, but clean & crisp all my own make. My stockings were flesh color ballriggan with pink

Indo on the instep & my slippers (I *never* wear shoes except when I *must*) one strap black opera sandals with bows & have been worn lots. My skirts of course were all white & all trimmed & he may have seen the edges of them as I sat on the step, but I haven't got a perfectly plain garment in my wardrobe & I wonder now seriously if I had not better have made some. While thinking about it the Blakes came & Janie & I retired to the kitchen & I heard the stranger say, "Thats a dainty bit of girlhood, but I'm sorry for her if she's to teach down yonder" & Judge Blake said, "She looks more like a living rosebud in that dress than anyone I ever saw, but she's got grit enough to teach any school around this country & she'll run it to please herself." Janie looked at me and laughed & said, "You'll need your grit in lots of ways." The miner's name is Louis Horediu. *Next* time I go into "barbarism" I'll wear nothing but dark calico & unbleached sheeting for underclothes & hob nail shoes!

Sept. 26

Andy & Jane B. & I went to Vinyards at Adams. . . . We reached John Vinyard's about 5. Mrs V—— is a sister of Mrs. Blake's. Mr. Harrer father of the girls was there also, & their younger sister Alice. The V's have 5 children, Will, John, Green, Ezra, & baby Agnes. The house consists of 1 room 16 x 16, dirt floor, pole house, thatched flat roof, no windows but open spaces (small) in the sides: It has a rough fireplace & in this house live V & his wife & 5 children and Alice & I are to stay temporarily: Great Stars! It is located in a lovely place: trees & fine views on all sides & nothing bleak or dreary about it. As to the furniture, 2 rough double bunks for bedsteads & hay filled ticks (but 4 pillows & thats *luck*) clean, abundant, home made quilts, a long home made dining table, uncertain on one leg, two or three boxes, used as trunks pushed under the "bunks", 6 or 7 home made stools; a rough kitchen table; a fair cook stove, & a fair collection of heavy white crockery & quite a lot of tins. Calico curtains round one "bunk", & a cracker box cradle, a small lamp & some more block or bottle candle sticks, a bible, almanac & one or two stock books & a few old papers &——, that's about all! Everything is clean & tidy tho' and the family are very kind & pleasant spoken. V. is over six ft. & built in proportion while Mrs V—— is not much over 4 & weighs, I guess almost 90 lbs!

Sept. 27

Mrs Blake went home (25) miles, Mr Blake staid to help work on the school house. He & Mr V & Mr Harrer & one or two more finished it tonight. It is about 1¼ miles from here, on the bank of Tonto Creek. . . .

Oct. 2 Sat.

Taught to make up for Monday. One week is over & it has been very pleasant. The school house resembles V's abode, only it has no door & is not as high or as large.

Oct. 3rd Sunday

Board consists of coffee, milk, bread, bacon & dried apples, all well cooked however, & twice we had beans & some "jerky." Today it is bread & boiled chicken. Alice, Willie & I took a long, long walk. Got home at 7 A.M. Persons has come to work for V. This house is like a New York Omnibus!

Oct 4th Mon.

Sarah & Melinda Armer aged 14 & 13 came to school this morning. They live a little over 7 miles from here on Salt River.

Oct. 5th Tuesday

26 years old today: Tom and Frank Armer came to school today.

Oct. 6 Wednesday

Last night I was wakened from sleep sometime after midnight by a tremendous purring noise and while wondering what it could be I partly raised in bed and looked through a chink some 3 inches wide—at the side of the bed where a pole was taken out from the wall for ventilation & was teribly frightened by having the mouth & nose of some animal thrust just opposite my face—in an attempt to reach me—&, as I darted back with a scream, to see a big, furry paw stick through the crack evidently trying to catch hold of me. I nearly fell out of bed over Alice in my anxiety to get out of the vicinity of that paw & roused the family with my shrieks which were echoed from outside by a long, peculiar wail like a woman or child crying. Then I knew what it was for I've heard that wail many a time before—it was a "cougar"—or "mountain lion" or "California lion". Vinyard had hung a small piece of beef up in the house close to the roof & on this same side—near a "chink or two"—not as wide as the "window" over the bed. The lion had scented it & was trying to reach it when my moving about attracted his attention & I presume angered him. The sound that awakened me was his purring, which I had never before happened to hear one of them do. Peering cautiously out of a smaller crack we, Alice and I—could see in the clear moonlight three of them prowling around—1 a cub—& probably the others were its parents. After watching awhile & being certain that no amount of clawing, even if he tried it again—would admit—of the lion reaching me while I lay down—I fell asleep again & the last sound I heard was one of the big "cats" climbing up the side of the house to the roof—probably thinking to reach that much desired beef from there. . . .

[She soon moved to the Harers' newly built house closer to her school.]

Oct. 16

Washed & ironed my belongings & it is quite a new way. We go to the Creek bank, set a few rocks & build a fire, put a big zinc pail over it on the rocks & fill it with water—Then we take the one tub & put some water in it & soak the clothes, and as we have at present no wash board we hunt up a big (as nerly flat as possible) rock "tote" it to the edge of the water in the creek & get another smooth round or oval one not very large, take the clothes a piece at a time from the tub put them on the big rock over which the creek flows and soap them then pound them well with the smaller rock, keeping them under the surface of the creek as much as we can—after we've hammered them as long as we care to, we drop them into the zinc pail of hot water & cook them. Then we get another bucket, smaller, & a tin milk pan or two & rinse them and hang them out to dry on the sage brush and arrow weeds & various bushes—to my surprise my clothes look white & nice as if I'd had all the modern conveniences & I washed over 80 pieces. There are 2 irons which we heat on the stove & I laid a long rather wide board on the dirt floor and put an old bedspread over it & my ironing sheet over that & we knelt down on the spread & ironed on the board & it worked fine. We will have a table before next Sat. & ironing will be easier. Made Clara's doll a dress this eve. John Vineyard went to Reno this Morn. I finished the edging (crochetted) for the Blake baby's shirt.

. . . [Janie Blake had a three-pound baby born two months early on October 4. They came for a few days' visit on October 17.]

Oct 18th Monday

This morning we rose about our usual time. Alice, Clara, Abbie, Mrs. H. and I. Clara went to Vinyards for milk and the other four of us and oh yes, I forgot Janie & the baby—well, the other 5 of us (baby don't count) were eating breakfast when a great hullabaloo arose at the creek crossing just below our house, shouting and splashing of water. Alice remarked, "That's Bal, crossing his band of cattle, I guess," when up to the house with a horrible whoop rode a band of Indians. The chief rode his horse into the house but when he found he could not sit erect on the animal after he got inside & could barely turn around on him he dismounted, turned (walking him all over Mr. H's bed which was still on the floor) and led him out. Then returned followed by Indians till they quite filled the small room. We counted 14 & 1 half grown boy. The bucks were in war paint & each had on a cartridge belt well filled pistol in holster, a fine Gov't rifle in his hands and all but one or two had big wicked looking knives. The boy had a knife & bow & arrows. We sat as if petrified thinking our time had come when Mrs Harer (who is as brave a frontier woman as ever lived & is quite accustomed to the Indians as she has long lived near the San Carlos Reservation) arose put on a brave face and stepping to the Chief held out her hand with the customary, "How." The Chief only gave a savage grunt and put his hand behind him. Janies baby on our bed in the corner cried & she trying to profit by her mothers example rose & during the second while every Indian watched her movements Alice close to the middle door, slid thro it like a flash, seized Abbie (who on the chief's first appearance had hid in the corner of the back room & whom the Indians had not seen) and squeezing thro' a narrow space near the kitchen chimney fled, as I was certain, to Jon. V to warn them & get help if she could. Baffled in her first overtures to the chief Mrs H. demanded their passes but the chief said they had none as they were not from San Carlos. Mrs. H asked where they were from (the conversation was principally in Mexican which all the Indians of this country speak) & he said they were "Papagoes",—that was an awful lie for there's very little similarity between the Apache & Papago tribes. Janie was trying to hush her baby & the chief glanced her way as if anxious to see the child, now usually the greatest mark of friendship one can show these savages is to exhibit their tiny white & pink babies to them & usually the Indians consider it an honor, so Janie plucking up courage moved a little nearer & unrolled the shawl & showed the chief what a tiny morsel he was but he only frowned the fiercer & made a motion as if to seize the child & fling him down but Janie clasped him closer & carried him to the farthest corner & deposited him & then resumed her seat at the table near me, close by her baby & between the Indians & it. The Chief and his band surveyed us in ominous silence, three lone defenceless women, one old, small & gray, one a slender girl, & the third, weak from recent confinement & now pale as death; then after a few guttural sentences to each other, they seemed to decide on a plan. Grasping Mrs H firmly the chief held her hands behind her while one of the others tied them tightly with a buckskin thong. Then she was led to the opposite corner from us placed in a chair & tied to the chair while a handkerchief lying handy was bound over her mouth. She struggled desperately but uselessly. During this performance Jane & I sat motionless—I could not have moved an eyelash—if by doing so I could have escaped what I believed to be the awful & certain death that awaited, for I was actually paralyzed by fright—& I believe Janie was in a similar condition. I sat with my head a trifle drooping & my hands folded—pushed just a little back from the end of the table—one of the ugliest & most hideously painted of the Indians came & stood as nearly in front of me as my position permitted. Of course I did not look up at him, I *couldn't,* but putting his hand under my chin he jerked my head back with a force that nearly broke my neck. I looked at him then straight, & unflinchingly in his cruel gleaming eyes & I know I wondered if Satan in all his kingdom had a more fiendish looking devil—something in my expression seemed to please him—the fear I could not hide probably, & with a wild whoop that made our nerves tingle (tho' neither Janie nor I jumped as one would suppose we would) he grabbed that great knife of his & grabbing me by my hair threw my head back & drew his knife, I thought, over my throat but he did not touch it—that's sure or I wouldn't be writing this tonight. I think he must have touched my flesh with the back of the knife for I am sure I felt the cold of the steel. I think I must have looked surprised when he dropped my head & I discovered it still rested securely on my shoulders, at any rate another pleased look came into his eyes— then he tore my sleeves open & pinched my arms & shoulders till I am blue-green & black most all over them, he slapped my cheeks pulled my ears & pinched them—& then grabbed me by my bangs & pretended to scalp me & not a sound did I utter all that time—I really believe if he had tied me to a stake & set fire to me I could not have even groaned, & I'm sure I could not have resisted. At last as if tired he paused a minute & I glanced at Jane. Poor girl—she had been submitted to the same torments only she wore earrings & the brute had torn one entirely down thro' her ear & the other nearly & the blood was running freely from them. She like myself had not made a sound & for a similar reason. At last my tormentor returned to his charge but he wheeled the chair around & caused me to face the others & I suddenly saw that one Indian had my trunk open and had turned over some ribbons & things & I knew in a minute he'd reach my bundle of photos & a lot of little keepsakes & that would be the last I'd see of them—queer notion, to think of a trifling thing like that when I was *positive* that in an hour or whenever that fellow got done amusing him- self—I'd be killed—but I'm not accountable for the vagary—but the thought put life into me and I sprang from my chair so suddenly that the buck did not have time to stop me if he had wanted to, rushed to the In- dian at my trunk who had just got a photo in his hand, grabbed it from him & delt him a blow in the face so unexpected that he fairly staggered, flung the picture into the trunk—& the lid down—turned the key, & snapped the catches & put the key down my neck. The Indian whom I struck made a move as if to spring upon me but the chief said a word or two & he slunk back scowling. The buck to whom apparently the others had given me, stepped forward—gave me a jerk & fling & sat me down so solidly that it took my breath, in the chair I had left. He stood & looked at me a while & I felt again as if paralyzed & not able to stir. Then he, still regarding me closely, spoke to Jane's persecutor & they talked (in Apache) a little. Then my demon spoke to the chief, he in turn, to the other Indians & to my horror they all filed out got on their horses & rode off leaving those two with us. Then the one I seemed to belong to said something to the other and walked out. I sat still for there did not seem to be anything else to do. Suddenly Jane's possessor grasped me by the arm, jerked me out of the chair & led me to the third & unoccupied corner of our brush house—stopped me about two ft. from it & dropped my arm. I stood as he had left me—head a bit forward arms by my sides, motionless; a rustle made me raise my head a bit and there within a foot of me & aimed squarely at my head was a Winchester rifle & as I gazed squarely at it I wondered that it had never before occurred to me what a *big barrel* those guns had. I heard the click of the trigger *very* clearly—then—instead of finding myself dead—I was again grasped by Jane's Indian & dropped into my chair while *my* Indian—who had had the rifle at my head came in & up to me and said, "Heap brave squaw, mucho brave—mucho. Una pocita (thats not spelled right but it sounds like it) muchacha esta much brave"—! Such a funny mixture of Spanish & English! Then they turned to Jane and called her, "mucho brave", "una bravisto mujer" & lots of such phrases, all meaning that they thought we were "brave". At first I thought they were making game of us but soon realized they were serious & really thought that it was courage that had prevented us from screaming or fainting or crying when they tormented us and that while we had been so paralyzed with fear & terror as to be utterly powerless to scream or even speak or to move hardly of our own volition. They ascribed it to pride & bravery. Well! thats good! Mrs Harer says she thinks the manner in which I sprang on that Indian at my trunk & made him leave it went far toward causing them to think that if I wished to I could cry or scream or struggle but then Jane & I were both acting on the principle that we would not give them the satisfaction of acting as though they hurt us. She also says that it was an inspiration that seized me to do that as the Apaches are great admirers of courage in anyone particularly white women & that she believes we would have suffered much worse indignities if they had not been forced to respect our stoical courage! It looks to me like a silly piece of extreme idiocy on my part to think of trifles like that—with death by torture staring me in the face, for not till they led me to the chair away from the gun—did one gleam of hope dawn on me. Well to return to my story. After praising us awhile they said to us—(each of them addressing one of us)—several rapid sentences in Spanish which I only half understood but the little I did "sabe" turned me cold! Seeing, I suppose, that we did not comprehend all they said, they made a few rapid & unmistakable gestures and exhibited a certain portion of themselves to us that *decency* usually keeps covered & while we grew fairly frozen with an awful terror—they adjusted their garments again and led us to the doorway where my tormentor pointed to the

Outdoor school. A dramatic illustration of adaptation to the new environment. Courtesy of the Western History Collections, University of Oklahoma Library.

sun. Then towards the west with this remark, "Bimeby four o'clock come— we come" and waited a minute and said again more emphatically—"Four o'clock come we come" & I found my tongue & exclaimed, "The dickens you will! Well you won't find *me* here"—but they did not understand & leading us back sat us down in our chairs & left the house & in a minute were riding rapidly northward to the mountains near by. It dawned on us slowly that we were alone and we both sprang to our feet, but poor Janie's slight strength was gone & with a moan she fell to the floor; I went to Mrs Harer & cut the cord that tied her hands and the strings—(buckskin thongs) that bound her to her chair and was trying to untie the handkerchief that was used as a sort of gag, when everything got black & the rest is a blank as far as my personal knowledge goes for about half an hour when I found myself lying on Mrs Harers mattress with an odor of camphor- ammonia & H.H.H. all about me & considerable dampness of hair & clothes. Mrs Harer says that I remarked while at work on the knot of the handkerchief: "Poor Janie I'll", and then with some incoherent exclama- tion fell to the floor like a dead person. She grabbed a butcher knife from the table, cut the handkerchief loose—dashed a pitcher of water over Jane—then grabbed the bucket from the kitchen & treated me to its con- tents after which she got the camphor etc & treated us to alternate applica- tions to our noses & rubbed camphor on our faces & slapped us vigorously

& did everything else she could think of but without much success—about that time Alice (who with Mary V & all the children had hid in the brush) who had seen the Indians (the last two) ride away & could endure the agony of suspense as to our fate no longer—had arrived on the scene by creeping thro' the brush and along the creek cautiously till sure no more Apaches were there. She thought we were dead but her mother reassured her as regards that and set her to work over us and Alice—whose hands were not numbed (as her mothers were by the cruel thongs) soon brought Janie to and a little while after, me, but when Jane & I tried to move—oh what torture! Our shoulders, arms, necks, heads, ears, & faces were so sore, & there were black & blue & discolored spots all around. Our hair had been pulled so hard as to pull our heads nearly loose & we did feel as if it was impossible to move—but move we had to for it was eleven o'clock then (the Apaches came at 7 and left about quarter past ten) & unless we desired a worse fate to befall us that afternoon, we had much to do. . . . [The women got on horses and rode in different directions to look for miners and cattlemen to help them. When the Apaches returned at four o'clock, they explained that they were only hunting and had scared the women as a joke, not to hurt them. Angie closed her school that day and the next.]

Oct. 25

My goodness—but this is a lively place to live—only its a bit wearing on one's nerves. Last night at Mrs H's request [after a skunk came in the night before] I "exhumed" my 42 caliber pistol from the bottom of my trunk & laid it handy when we retired about 9. Baby cried steadily till 12, then grew quiet & everyone went to sleep. About 1 a skunk got in & Mrs Harer sprang up & called me and run outside after the skunk & tumbled him over but in a second he jumped & ran into a catclaw bush. Mrs Harer seized a pole from the wood pile and beat round till she dislodged him & he broke for another bush, she following striking violent blows at him without however damaging anything but the ground. Meanwhile Jane & Alice had put a board about two ft high across the door & stuck two stools against it to prevent his coming back into the house—& I, out in the sand-rocks & brush had concluded that bare feet were not best calculated to run around on & went back to the house on the run to get my slippers & go back to help Mrs H, knowing nothing of the girls' barricade I struck it with a good deal of force fell over it & onto it and through it—& recochetted wildly around with those stools till I finally landed in a heap under the table at the other side of the room with several abrasions on my limbs & the more *prominent* portions of my anatomy uncertain whether it was myself or some other person & not quite clear as to what had happened to me for the room was dark—neither of the girls having lit a candle. While I was slowly collecting my scattered senses and the girls were trying to explain & baby was yelling at the top of his lungs we heard Mrs H—calling Alice & I—so she ran out and I gathered myself up & followed, and arrived just in time to see Mrs Harer aim a blow at the skunk who by this time had got some ways from the house, miss it again but hit Alice—luckily with the extreme end of the pole—on top the head. I decided that in this case discretion was the better part of valor & fell into the rear of the procession. His skunkship crawled into a sage brush and then Mrs H Alice & I among us demolished him with poles & met with no more accidents except that we got a liberal dose of perfume. Then we retreated to the house, got Jane who held her nose—to get us some clean clothes & bring them to the creek bank & also soap & towels, while we plunged into the creek, which is cold enough to nearly freeze one, got rid of the smell as well as we could, got on clean night gowns—(all any of us had on to begin with) & carried the old ones on sticks a little way down the creek & buried them in the sand. Then we went back to bed. . . .

Oct. 26

Worse and more of it:—Baby grew easier about 1 & we went to sleep—Mrs Hook slept with me & she snored & snorted so & then tossed around like a restless child that my sleep was of short duration. While I was meditating about sliding out on the floor with a quilt, there arose a great barking of coyotes & bellowing of cattle some ways up the mountain side above us. It awakened us all and in a minute we heard the hoof beats of the panic stricken cattle & their bellowing grew nearer. We sprang out of bed & rushed in a body for the door sure that the stampeding herd would rush straight thro' our frail house & probably crush us as well. Everyone grabbed the first thing they could that would aid in frightening them. Alice & I were first out & each had a sheet so we ran round to the side the cattle were coming from & faced them & indeed it was a sight. Not more than a hundred yards away, tearing along in that manner peculiar to a badly

Domestic interior. Everywhere in the West, women worked to establish and maintain the routines of daily life. Mrs. Clough and Norah, in this picture, are mentioned in portions of Angie Brown's diary not reproduced here. Courtesy of the Sharlot Hall Historical Society, Prescott, Arizona.

frightened herd of stampeding cattle & making straight for our house in their mad rush for the creek & safety—were about 100 head of stock. We took a firm hold of our sheets flapped them up & down & ran forward yelling as loud as we could while directly behind came Mrs Harer & Mrs Hook each beating a tin pan with a stick & yelling & behind them Clara & Belle with an old tin can & a spoon for Belle and a big white apron & an old tin horn of Abbie's (who is at Vinyard's) for Clara, each swelling the noise as well as they could & Clara wildly waving her apron in one hand. Such an awful pow-wow was too much for the cattle & they swerved passed each side of us & our house, so close they nearly grazed us and went on tearing thro the bushes & rushed across the creek—then we returned out of breath & badly scared to find poor Janie lying just outside the door in a faint with her baby wrapped in a blanket close to her. Her strength was not sufficient for the shock. We brought her to & took care of baby & built up a little fire & got hot water to make tea for Jane & at last subsided into our "peaceful beds." This morning we find that the cattle demolished our brush shade that we fixed to wash under—trampled our one tub & the wash bucket & bench & a stool we had there into a shapeless mass of sticks and battered tin. Also that a skirt of mine & some things of Alice & Clara's have been either trampled under the wreck of a clump of bushes we used as a "clothes line" or carried in fragments away on their horns. Thank Heaven the damage is no more serious—five minutes of inaction on our part & awful would have been the results. . . .

Oct. 27

Baby cried all night last night & we gave up trying to get a night's rest & took turns tending him. He is better this eve. Our light—nights now is bacon grease in a tin plate with a rag rolled up & put in.

Oct. 28

Once more we had to rush out & save ourselves from a band of stampeded cattle. This time it was lions probably for we heard their screaming upon the Mt awhile before the cattle started. This trip the band was not quite as large as before & we met them farther from the house. Then we barricaded the door & took turns tending baby and watching that open space over the old chimney in the back room lest some stray lion might pay us a visit. A few more nights of this sort of business & we'll all be crazy. Andy B came this eve & a little later Mr Jas Harer—David's oldest brother arrived unexpectedly from Oregon and says a lot more of their relatives will be here in a few days. . . .

Nov. 4

More excitement last night. We retired—Alice, Mrs H & I—about 10. Mattie, Belle & Clara & Abbie were asleep much earlier in the back room. About 12 I who was sleeping uncommonly sound—was awakened by something warm and moist licking the little finger & one next it of my hand which hung down over the side of the bed. I drew it up with a jerk and raised & looked down on the floor and beheld a pretty little, spotted skunk—nothing more nor less than one of the dreaded "hydrophobia cats" of Arizona. My but I did scream. Mrs H sprang up barefooted on the floor in the other part of the room but I told her to look out for we had a little skunk in the house & she scrambled on to a chair till she got her shoes on—then, striking a light before she crossed the room—she saw [it] sitting close to the head of my bed with our chicken, which was "roosting" in a box under the bed (an uncovered box) for the night, beside it, dead. She threw me my shoes, into which I scrambled quickly and got out at the foot of the bed, we both got a long stick & standing at a respectful distance we urged his departure—he took the hint and moved to the door—stopping every second or two, to face us & "pat" (as the way they move their fore feet on the ground when angry—is aply described out here) finally we got him outside and we had the good luck to kill him—but our chicken was useless to us now—so we flung it away too. The younger ones had watched this performance from the safe shelter of their beds. No Arizonian attacks a "hydrophobia cat" unless it is necessary, for their bite is almost certain death. It is not long since two men living up the creek aways, died in the terrible agonies of hydrophobia induced by the bite of one of these pretty looking little animals under circumstances similar to ours. We examined my finger & found it was not bitten, he had only lapped it—kitten fashion & wasn't I grateful! . . . This evening at 8½ our family received quite an accession. Mrs "Obedience ("Beady") Hazelton"— 2 sons—3 daughters—grown—and "Newton Green Nathaniel Harrer" and the relatives from Oregon who were expected next week. . . . [She names them all.] Such another time as we've had getting settled for tonight. Mr Green H. & the 3 older boys slept in the wagon. Mrs Hazelton with Mrs Harer & Regie & May; Sarah—Alice & I together, Laura & Ida on one pallet and Belle & Clara on another & we made a bed for little Abbie on the table & tucked Frances crosswise in Ida's bed. . . .

Nov. 8th

Quite a school. . . . 23 pupils in a house 10 x 12, dirt floor, brush sides like *our* house & no door! And only seats for 12. On looking back I see that I have never described the style of architecture adopted for "our" mansion—so I'll do it now.—A space is cleared on the ground from brush—& levelled—then poles mesquit in this case—no they are lighter than that, well—poles about as large as a medium size fence post and 8½ ft long are set into the ground for a depth of 2 ft—& another pole of the length of the house (or perhaps 2 poles are required to make the desired length) smaller around than those set in the ground is fastened on top of the row of posts—this is repeated till the four sides are made. Then two big posts are set at equal distances from those forming the ends—midway between those for the side. [. . .] Our house is 14 ft wide by 18 ft long & the poles on two sides & one end are 2 ft apart but on the end . . . a space of nearly 4 ft is left & the rest of that end had poles 2 ft apart again—then a row of poles about a foot apart is set for a partition between the rooms & covered with strips of canvass—leaving near the middle of the partition a door 2½ feet wide: the two rooms thus formed are respectively 14 x 12 & 14 x 6. Now across the top are laid first some poles stout ones extending from the end of the house to the middle posts (which are 10 inches thro' & they are cut so as to leave a crotch at the top. . . . Next smaller poles 3 or 4 inches thro' are nailed from ridge pole to side poles—2 ft apart. Then brush & yucca plant leaves & tules—either or all are woven thro & secured—in our case they are only lain on top of the poles & fastened—then mud—the regular adobe clay kind—is plastered several inches thick over the outside of the (hut) etc. on the roof & that is finished. A chimney is built with a fireplace in our parlor of rough rocks laid up in mud. . . .

Nov. 12

. . . I furnished a good deal of amusement for my school today quite unexpectedly. I was hearing a Geography class & feeling something tugging at my dress as if there was a weight on it—shook it and went on with my class; presently feeling it again I looked down & there lying on my dress skirt in a ray of sunlight was as hideous a reptile as I've ever seen. He was black & yellow & tawny & had a body like a monstrous lizard & a "spiky" looking tail & a head like a snake & was over a foot long—Lord! I gathered up dress & with a yell one could hear a mile jumped on the stool [where] I had been sitting: The commotion that ensued beggars description. Ida & Laura nearest me—glanced down saw the reptile & promptly followed my example—the littler ones cried from fright at our strange antics and everything was confusion, but when the Arizonans saw the hideous thing—they laughed and said, "Why, teacher thats nothing but a Gila Monster"—Well I've heard lots of stories about those uncanny dwellers in Arizona but I've never seen one before—at least on his native heath. I was sufficiently reassured to collect my wits but I took pains to jump off my stool on the side the "monster" was not—then I gave a sudden recess & asked for information. The scholars said that, by some, the Gila's were believed to be poisonous—(that I had heard) but that they personally knew that some people actually petted them, & that they did not bite unless very angry & it was not an easy matter usually to make one angry enough for that but they could "blow themselves up" as Willie phrased it and "puff their breath in your face & make you awful sick." In the meantime one Gila had leisurely taken himself home & disappeared down a hole in the corner near my desk. Soon after we resumed the interrupted lessons & things went more smoothly than I hoped after that unseemly performance of mine. . . .

Dec. 2nd

I've forgotten to say that the Gila monster who gave me such a scare comes out every morning & sun's himself & I've taken to picking him gingerly by the tail & putting him back of my desk where he lies out at full length in the sun & sometimes snaps up an unwary fly & seems to enjoy himself greatly. I've ceased to fear him tho' it will be long before I shall consider him handsome. I stroke his scaly back with a pencil & he likes it apparently. Someday I'll try to make him mad, I want to know if it is true about their "blowing." . . .

Wed. Dec. 15

School closed today. It rained awfully but the whole Armer family, Geo Moore & Hook, Mr & Mrs Harer, Mrs Hazelton, the Vinyard's, Fannie, Laura & Adeline Gordon came at 9½ & staid till the close & I've an idea now about how much room Noah had left in his Ark. 19 pupils & myself and 18 more counting babies (2 of them) and all—is a good many on a rainy day in a room 10 x 12! I don't quite know how we did it! After school Sarah & I cleaned everything up inside as well as we could, barricaded the doorway with boards, & went home & packed up for the Phoenix trip. . . .

Dec. 22nd

It rained most of the night but this morning is pleasant tho' the mud is absolutely without bottom. Started fairly early but only got to the neighborhod of Tempe & camped tonight near a Mexican's house—as it is the only place one can get good drinking water—every ditch etc. is so muddy. The Mexican came out to camp and talked to Mr Harer and after he went back she, the senora, sent a message inviting the "senoras" to come up to the porch which was dry. We went & it was clean & we were muddy—but she insisted so shedding our rubbers we went up & soon she brought us a brush to brush the mud from our shoes if we wished as we most certainly did wish to. . . . She speaks a little English, I a little Spanish (Sarah doesn't know any yet) and we *pretended* to understand & got along fine. She *watched* me so closely it was uncomfortable & paid some attention to Sarah & was kind to us both. When we came out to go to camp where the men had supper ready she stepped up & kissed me Spanish style to my great surprise. Sarah & I discussed it & concluded I must resemble some dear friend—& I'm tanned enough to resemble *any* Mexican! Mrs Hazelton was in a bad humor evidently at the woman's preference for me tho! I can't see how I was to blame. We were just eating supper when a fine looking lad appeared & addressed me in Spanish—I shook my head for I did not understand him & he spoke to Mrs Harer who is "up" in the lingo. She told me Senora—(we disagree as to the name. *I* think it was Garcia—) has invited you to supper. "Only me?" I asked & she said "Thats all he said," "Then tell him it is impossible." She did so after telling me I had best go as it would be a novelty but I wouldn't. . . . [The Senora sent another invitation] Then he and Mrs Harer held a conversation and Mrs H, with fun in her eyes, translated, "She wants the young lady & when I asked which he said she wanted the one with the red lips, the eyes & the hands." . . . "he says the *tall* young lady—and she wants her to come up for a while as she will have some friends arrive soon & she thinks the young lady may enjoy it." . . . I thought a minute and Sarah urged me to go—& I decided I'd see what a Mexican evening party might be like. I *did* want Sarah to go for I'd enjoy it lots more but how could she when she was not asked! I said, "Tell him I'll be there in ten minutes." . . . The young fellow had put some boards down from the camp to the walk inside the gate (about 50 ft I guess) and I got there without getting at all muddy. He led me to his mother who kissed me twice then introduced the boys as Ramon & Manuel. She insisted on my eating some "dulcies" (delicious cookies) and drinking some coffee in spite of my assurance that I was not hungry. Then Ramon took a guitar & played and she showed me a number of curiosities from Old Mexico & from Arizona ruins & seemed delighted to find that "specimens" were something I delighted in. After that a dozen young "senors" and "senoritas" arrived and I found they were celebrating some kind of a fete day—of the Senora's, birth, wedding, or something. They seemed surprised to see me & well they might be—but she introduced me to them as kindly as if I were a long lost relative just arrived. . . . We had music, singing also & dancing & games till we were all tired & then refreshments of all sorts of "dulcies" (sweets of any kind) preserves, bread, "chicken

Tomales" & goodness knows what and some sort of Mexican liquor, coffee and chocolate. At last I said I must go and they came over & bade me "good night" or "buenos noches" one by one & wished me a pleasant journey and a speedy return to Tonto—(as I had promised to stay a day on my way to the Basin, if I could) and the girls kissed me Spanish style—and the young men shook hands—then the Senora went on the porch with me & kissed me again & Ramon took me home. I certainly had a jolly time—I crawled in, after getting into my flannel gown, beside Sarah & was soon sound asleep.

Dec. 23rd

This morning we were up early & just after breakfast the Senora appeared and after talking to all of us she said she had some "panoche" at the house for me to take home if I wished—I *did* "wish" and I took Sarah with me and went up with Senora to the house. She talked to us and once in a while we understood!—and took us out to her cellar & it was a nice one too, full of preserves & jams & jars of butter & of panochi and all sort of things mostly in pottery, ollas & large bowls. She gave me a gallon crock of panoche, & said I'd find the crock or olla handy about the house. She also gave us some preserves made of the wild date for dinner & then gave me some specimens for my cabinet. I was aghast at the size of the crock of panoche & wanted to pay but she said, "No, no," and seemed so hurt that I thanked her the best I could. She went back to our camp & carried the panoche for me & we found a box & got some hay & packed it well. Then she told me (Mrs Harer) that if I wanted a good tamale receipt she'd give me one. I wanted it for hers last night were the finest I ever eat so she told it to Mrs H & she translated & I wrote it. Then she brought out a cheese of goat's milk & added that to our bill of fare for dinner. Soon after we left and reached Phoenix about 11. Hancock had letters for me from home & Geo. and I sent the folks a telegram. . . .

Angeline Mitchell Brown, "Diary of a School teacher on the Arizona Frontier," September 5, 1880, to February 10, 1881, Angie M. Brown Collection, Sharlot Hall Museum, Prescott, Arizona.

This detailed memoir by a well-educated woman describes Arizona ranching from 1888 to the early 1900s. Though her husband, an irrigation engineer, was dubious about the wisdom of her coming from Iowa to that "'God forsaken country,'" Martin insisted upon joining him as a young bride and makes it clear that she never regretted doing so. The Martins, like many other settlers in arid areas of the West, believed that canals and reservoirs would soon make "life in Arizona . . . little short of Paradise for us."

Referring often to the "hypnotic" spell of the desert and its beauty, Martin describes her "comfortable, rambling house (if only a log one) with a dirt roof," as well as various times when they had to live in outdoor camps. She loved the land, despite the hazards and trials of heat, flood, isolation, three pregnancies, and even near death from infection after childbirth. When the "boys" went duck hunting by the river, she "always went with them as any form of recreation was acceptable in those days." Among other details, she describes folk remedies for various illnesses; and her favorable comments about Indians and Mexicans contrast notably with the prejudices of other pioneers. Because of her husband's poor health and the difficulties they encountered as farmers, the Martins regretfully sold the ranch in 1897, still in debt, because they "could never have been successful there." Nevertheless, Sadie Martin's memories of Arizona remained generous and heartwarming.

*I*t was early on the morning of the 22nd of August, 1888, when my train rolled into the most desolate little town I had ever seen or ever expected to see. Nevertheless my heart was beating high as I was to meet my husband, who had preceded me to Arizona five months before.

As I stepped from the train I could hardly realize that the young man coming toward me was my John. He was as dark as an Indian and only his height, eagerness and familiar smile made me recognize him.

It was a happy reunion. We had been married less than a year, when he left me behind in Iowa and the five months had been long and lonely ones for us both. Early as it was, it was hot; but I could say nothing, as he had tried to warn me and had advised me to wait one or two months longer, but I would not listen. I was so tired visiting around and was homesick for him, so I had no one to blame but myself and was not going to complain.

As we walked toward the little home of the Southern Pacific agent to get breakfast, John was telling me how the agent had talked to him far into the night, trying to persuade him not to take me into that (as he called it) "God forsaken country". And I am afraid he had dampened my husband's ardour, as his ideas had changed somewhat since his letters, which had been so full of the future and promise of the land when water should be developed.

And while we were eating our simple meal, the agent commenced again. He said we were so pitifully young and inexperienced for pioneer life on the desert. But what was there to do? My father-in-law had come to Arizona a year before to take a contract to build a large canal—"The Toltec"—in the vicinity of what was called the Gila Valley. His wife and youngest son had come with him—my husband following later. Shortly before John came, the company Father was working for had failed with their pay checks and Father had to file a lien on the property. This meant a long delay, so while waiting for the case to be tried, he and the boys went ten miles below Agua Caliente and each had filed on a quarter section of land where they had established a home. Sentinel was the railroad station, and was twelve miles from Agua Caliente and such a long twelve miles in the hot sun. Our conveyance was a lumber wagon without any cover. Fortunately I had an umbrella, which proved to be a life saver. I had been told before leaving Iowa to take as thin a garment as I had to put on when I reached Arizona. So I made up my mind that my new "Peek-a-boo" blouse, which had three rows of coarse lace running the length of the sleeves, was the very thing. Shall I ever forget that ride? It took us all day long, the sun growing hotter and hotter (and I mean hot, not warm). There was nothing to look at but sand—and not a house nor a tree until we were near the Gila River. I had taken a wash cloth out of my grip and

John wet it with water from his canteen. I held it up in front of my face. It was cool for the time being, but was the very worst thing I could have done, I found, when I looked in the mirror that night. A boiled lobster could not have been any redder.

We reached Aqua Caliente, about noon and stopped to rest and eat our lunch. It was a picturesque place with many mesquite trees and little streams of water. We found a nice tree and sat down under it to eat our lunch and look at the scenery. There was a store building and little shacks and tents here and there. The tents were mostly occupied by people taking baths for their health, as the water was warm and of medicinal value, much liked for rheumatic ills. The man who owned the springs had a good sized house and nice surroundings, but the bath houses were made of ocatillos standing upright close together without roofs. In later years, after we left the country, this place became quite a health resort and more substantial bath houses were built. There were better facilities for taking care of the sick after they built a hotel and installed nurses. I was loath to leave the pretty spot, but if we were to reach home by sundown, we must go, as it was so hot the horses were obliged to walk every step of the way. From there on, there was little more to see. The first home was about a mile below the Springs and we stopped and bought some honey and melons. I met some of our future neighbors. This family had five or six children, who wore very little clothing. Their little tummies podded out full of melon. I never tasted such honey. It was light in color and made from the mesquite trees. That was chiefly the business of this family—honey.

Houses were a mile or so apart now. One held a Mexican family, with little naked children playing around the door. Another, an old man, who had the reputation, John said, for killing snakes. All the Arizona settlers killed snakes, but this man was particularly skillful in tracking a snake to its hole, where he would dig it out and do battle to the death.

The ranchers up and down the valley, for twenty or twenty-five miles, had formed what was called the "Farmers' Canal Group." Once in a while, we would pass a camp of men working on one of the smaller connecting canals, as the principal canal ran at the foot of the mesa, not far from the road we were traveling.

Little did either of us realize then the long years of struggle, hardships and disappointments that lay ahead of us. But we were young and together again: and now the future began to look as bright and prosperous as it had before. We were already beginning to come under the hypnotic influence of the desert and we said to each other that with the completion of this canal, life in Arizona would be little short of Paradise for us.

We reached the ranch about sundown, tired, warm and hungry and were met by the members of the family who had preceded us. My! What a sight I was—my face burned to a deep and unbecoming red and down my left arm were three rows of blisters in the design of the lace in my sleeve. It was so good to have that sun go down and to take a long cool drink of delicious water from the great Mexican olla—a porous clay vessel, which was kept cool by a covering of wet gunny sacks. There was no ice on the desert, but I was soon to find that we could keep our milk and butter cool and sweet, by wrapping damp cloths around the receptacles that held them and setting them in the air. And as we were everlastingly thirsty it was a relief to find there would be no dearth of cooling drinks.

The family consisted of John's father, mother and brother and four or five Indian helpers. These were the first Indians I had ever seen and I must say I was greatly disappointed. Of course, I was not exactly expecting to see war paint and feathers, but I was hardly prepared for such harmless looking creatures in overalls. One of them had a light blue handkerchief draped around his neck in picturesque fashion and was grinning in an embarrassed way. They told me afterwards that he had been to school at the Yuma reservation, that his experience there had rather dissatisfied him with life among his own people and he was the laziest one of the lazy bunch.

I found that the family was living in the tents Father had used at the Toltec camp and were quite comfortable while the cabin of cottonwood logs (cut from the river bottom) was being built for a permanent home—how permanent you are soon to hear. And I was soon to ask myself, "Is there anything permanent made by the hand of man on this great beautiful desert?"

Our great interest was the building of this log house. The Indians of the Yuma Apache tribe were there for the purpose of "chinking" and "mud-ding," as they called it, and for making adobes for the fire-places. The one in charge was named Steve and he had been a scout in one of the Indian wars and was mentioned in some of Captain King's novels. His father was one of the old timers—no overalls for him—nothing but a "gee string." His skin was like wrinkled leather. I was quite pleased to find him, as he more nearly typified what I was expecting to see in the way of an Indian. I was greatly impressed by the Indian story John had told me on our way to the ranch that day. It was called the Oatman Massacre and had occurred in the year 1851. The father, mother and one child were murdered. Two daughters were taken captive and a boy who had been clubbed and left for dead, had been rescued later. The girls were sold to a visiting band of Indians on the Colorado river, where the younger one soon died. Oatman flat was only about thirty miles above Aqua Caliente—which to me seemed altogether too near.

Father had taken plenty of time to consider the site for the new home. He did not want to build too close to the river, the mischievous Gila, that had a reputation for changing its banks in heavy rains, he did not want to build too close to the road, so he chose a beautiful spot about a half mile from the river and the same distance from the main road. John's piece lay west and his brother Rube's north.

And now, after I had been there only three days, I was to experience my first sand storm. When the desert does things, it seems to do them in a great big way. It may only have been doing what it conceived to be its duty, but sometimes I have felt that back of it all there was a sort of resentment toward human beings who dared to come in there and meddle around in a puny way, to make things more comfortable for themselves. The longer I lived there, the more I felt this Spirit of the desert, sometimes benign, but often the opposite, as though it must make up for those heavenly days of smiling sunshine by a tremendous blast which would show those humans their absurd insignificance.

A neighbor had killed a beef and sent word to father, as was the desert custom. I went with him for the meat and we were all anticipating the great treat, as fresh meat was scarce on the desert. We cooked some delicious, tender steak for our evening meal and set the table outside, as was our custom. Just as we were ready to sit down someone shouted, "Sand Storm!" That was all that was necessary to start things moving. We covered the food with dish towels and aprons. The boys picked up the table to carry it inside—mother and I running along by the side to hold the covers. We couldn't see three feet in front of us. I stumbled and fell and the covers took wings. The food was coated with sand in a second and we could not eat a bite of it. When the worst was over, Father called the Indians and we had the rueful enjoyment of watching them dispose of it—sand and all.

We were indeed glad when the house was finished and I think we were in it by October. It was such a comfortable, rambling house (if only a log one) with a dirt roof. It was built in two parts with a twelve-foot alley way between. In one part was the long living room and two bedrooms, in the other part a dining room, long kitchen and another bedroom. A ten-foot porch ran all the way around the house, but with a dirt floor like the alley way. The folks had cots, tables, chairs, etc., which they had used at camp, and the boys made other things that we needed until we could have our furniture shipped out from Iowa.

In order to prove up on our quarter section John and I had to sleep on our own land. I did not like the idea of sleeping outdoors on account of snakes, so John made a high bedstead of lumber and we sewed gunny sacks together for a mattress, which, when filled with straw, made a bed so high that I had to get on a chair to climb up to it. What fun John had watching me make the ascent! I told him I could almost hear the snakes "gnashing their teeth" at my having eluded them!

There were few settlers in the valley at that time and it would be two or three months at a time that Mother and I would not see another white woman. Men would stop in often and sometimes Indians would come around—the squaws appearing without a sound and put their faces against the window pane to peek in at us. It took me some time to get used to this, but they were quite friendly and meant no harm and really were just as curious about us and our methods of living as we were about them. After a few years, they moved their tepees nearer us, as the men worked on the ranches and the women washed for us. What a boon that was for the boys, who up to this time, had insisted on doing the rubbing for us, which John said was the hardest work a woman could do. He was always considerate and helpful, so that life was well worth living even under such conditions. I was extremely lonely at times, but through it all felt that I had much to be thankful for.

The boys often had to go up on the canal to do their share of the work, and once in a while, they allowed me to go along. But during the time that Father was going back and forth to Phoenix to attend to his law suit, I had to stay with Mother. At such times, the boys always came home at night, as it was not considered safe to leave us alone. But the law suit was finally decided in Father's favor and great was our rejoicing to have things settled. He succeeded in getting a lien on the property and the next thing was to form a new company, which he was fortunate enough to do in Phoenix, through a banker whom he had known in Iowa.

It took so much time and many trips to and from Phoenix for the men of the company to thoroughly examine the property. The head waters of the Toltec were about twenty-five miles above Aqua Caliente, I think, not far from Gila Bend.

The boys, when not working on the farmers' canal, were getting part of our land fenced and ready for water. One of the first things they did was to plant some potatoes in the river bottom, where the soil was moist and needed no irrigating. And one of our recreations was to walk down every Sunday morning to see how they were doing and if they needed hoeing. One day was quite exciting. We were walking single file, John first, I next and Mother bringing up the rear. We had gone a little way, when Mother called John. I had stepped right over a snake that was crawling across our path. It was not a rattle snake, however, tho' quite as exciting. As we were returning we were startled by the real thing. On the opposite side of a bush—his head at least two feet in the air—was a rattler—coiled ready to strike. Mother and I stood guard until John secured a shovel to kill it. When the cool October days came, the boys went to the river duck hunting. I always went with them as any form of recreation was acceptable in those days.

Mother and I took pleasure and pride in our chickens. We had a number of hens and had them all named. Some of them developed almost human qualities and we made great pets of them. One of them—a black one, we named "Molly", was unusual. She would sneak into the living room (before the screens were hung) and we used to watch her tip-toe across the room and go way back under the bed in the bedroom to lay her egg, then tiptoe out again, before she commenced to cackle. Another thing that happened before the screen doors were put on was not so pleasant. A sidewinder had coiled behind the outside dining room door and when I was sweeping, he did not seem to like it, nor did I. These snakes were new to me though I had been told to look out for them, so I ran for Indian Steve. This snake was small and so vicious that I shudder to think of the consequences if it had crawled just a little farther to our bedroom, which only had a curtain for a door. By the way, that curtain was a pretty piece of satine which I had brought from Iowa for a dress, and it was only a short time until I had to take it down and put it to such use.

Clothes were a problem on the desert. Mother Hubbards happened to be in style at that time and a veritable God's blessing they were. Made of a material called cheese cloth, they were very cool and comfortable. It seems absurd now, but they even seemed to be stylish in those days. There was a store in the little nearby settlement called Palomas, where we had a limited choice of dress material and we made the most of it, just as the Indian squaws did, who appeared in wonderful creations made of turkey red calico. When Arizona winter came and the days began to get cooler, we decided we must have warmer dresses. I can't remember how we got the idea, or the goods, but I remember the dresses very well. They were made of tan bed ticking with fancy stripes. I think Mother's had navy blue stripes. Both were made with tight waists and full skirts. Such splendid dresses for winter and how we did enjoy them! No thorns or brush could tear them and I am not sure but that Mother and I set the style for the Valley that winter. It was a pleasant occupation for us too, as we were by ourselves so much. When Father was on the ranch, I could go occasionally with the boys, but when I had to stay at home day after day, the days were so long. We spent the time knitting yards of lace and all the sewing we did was done by hand.

Mother was invited to go to Phoenix with Father on one of his trips and the dress question loomed prominently. Bedticking was definitely out. We looked through her wardrobe and found a black and white satine, which I thought I could make over for her. I had been sewing ever since my stepmother came into the family, when I was thirteen years old, but what was I to do without a machine? There was a woman in Palomas who had a machine and we thought that she might loan it to us to make the dress, but she was not willing to do so. I asked if she would let me stitch the long seams at her house. But no—she may have thought I was too young to know how to sew, or something may have been wrong with the machine—anyway I had to do every stitch by hand and it was such hard work and Mother and I were both so proud when it was finished. Mother was a pretty woman and liked pretty clothes and I still remember how she looked when she drove away with Father that day. She was worrying up to the last moment for fear we would starve while she was gone or that something dreadful would happen to us. But we were glad to have her to go, for the ranch life was taking its toll and she was very frail and needed a change badly.

She returned with Father, in September, much improved. Father was very much encouraged and enthusiastic about making improvements. He made a driveway around the house and excavated for a pond, which fate decreed was never to be finished or enjoyed.

Now that Father and Mother were home, I went with the boys to camp and we were gone two or three weeks. They were all so anxious to get the water turned on in the canal so we could get things started to growing on the ranch. Everything depended on the success of the canal. One afternoon, Rube was away and I offered to drive the mules for John who was plowing. It was great fun. The mules were lively and I had to go so fast that John could hardly hold the plow straight for laughing. At this time, we had to go back on the mesa to get hay for the horses. Gulleta was a wild hay and did not grow everywhere and we were at some trouble to find it, but amply repaid by watching the horses and mules enjoy it. Other hay was expensive and had to be hauled even farther.

Quail were so thick that first year that we had all we could eat. Trappers were up and down the river and shipping them out. Father loved to hunt and he was called on to do most of it. He would stand almost in the back door and kill enough birds for a meal. After that year, they were never so plentiful and we missed them very much, as they helped out wonderfully with our menus.

Snakes were our greatest worry (especially mine) that first summer. I did not venture far from the house alone. We had one building that had never been finished. One morning, Mother had gone inside and I was standing by the door talking to her when she screamed "Snake". I turned and saw a big rattler coming right toward me. Instead of jumping to one side, I stepped in beside Mother, never dreaming the snake would follow, but it came as far as the door sill. We both got up on boxes. I grabbed a broom and struck at it several times. When it finally turned, Mother ran out and saw it disappear around the corner. She followed and found it was trying to push through between the logs, but it was too large. When I reached the scene the snake had coiled, but was able to keep out of its way, until Mother brought help. Father would come any distance to kill a snake, as he said it was his greatest pleasure. This was the closest call I ever had. Finally, I became quite expert at killing them and tried never to let one get away.

For some time, all of our trips had to be made in the lumber wagon.

John and I drove in it to Phoenix, and were two and a half days on the road. We slept in the wagon going, but on the return trip, it was loaded with provisions and supplies for the ranch, so we had to sleep on the ground, which was always a trial to me. On the way up, when we came to the Buckeye country and saw that little stream, the green fields of alfalfa and big trees, I just begged to get out and put my feet in the water and feast my eyes on the trees. John was glad to humor me as it had been so long since we had seen any thing so lovely. It looked like heaven to us. We stopped quite a while and nothing ever seemed so restful and cool.

On our trip back, we noticed new tents and strangers, at Aqua Caliente. We could hardly wait to return and make their acquaintance. The etiquette of the desert was at that time on a basis of complete informality. There was little class consciousness. Settlers of education and refinement made no distinction among their acquaintances, so long as they were decent and law-abiding. If the loneliness was at times so intense that even dogs, horses and chickens seemed to take on a personality, to encounter a human being of any description assumed the proportions of an adventure.

We found the newcomers at the Springs very interesting and made many trips to visit them. There were the father and mother (elderly people from Phoenix) with a daughter and grand daughter. The daughter was crippled with rheumatism and in a wheel chair. The grand daughter was a charming young girl who was especially attractive to John's brother Rube. They remained three months at the Springs and we all made the most of our time during wonderful moonlight nights, with Rube playing his banjo and all of us making heroic attempts to vocalize on such current hits as "After The Ball" and "The Band Played On". Of course, we couldn't remember all the words, but we carried on any way and felt well repaid for the long trips back and forth. No, Rube didn't marry the pretty girl. The pretty girl went back to Joliet, Illinois, with her invalid mother, and neither the girl nor her mother lived very long. Rube continued to be a perfectly contented bachelor until past middle-age. This family thought it was too bad for us to spend our young lives in this desert country and constantly urged us to go back to a more settled condition of life, but we never even considered it.

Soon after this, on Father's next trip to Phoenix, he brought back a light spring wagon, with two seats and canvas top. This was quite an innovation for that desert country and a blessed relief after the lumber wagon.

Naturally, there had been from the very first, at the back of John's head and mine, the thought of a home of our very own on our own land. We did not say much about it, only when we were by ourselves, but it helped us over the roughest trials and made our heavy tasks seem lighter. And now in November of 1889, there was a very real reason for having our own little home, for we were getting ready to welcome a permanent guest, who would make the journey via Stork, and we wanted as fine a landing place as possible for the gallant bird and his precious cargo. But the dream of having our own cozy place was not realized so soon nor so easily.

John used to work in the cool of the afternoon, clearing a piece of land for the house and I would go with him. One night he was burning brush and I was helping him, when my dress caught fire, which frightened us both so much that I could help no more.

Our furniture came and we had great fun unpacking and arranging it. A bed was put up for me in the living room and there our baby boy was born the 18th of November, 1889. I think we were all more or less nervous on account of a dream I had about six weeks before this time. I thought I was walking with a stranger up a beautiful wide street and seemed to be hunting for some one. My own dear father was at the top of a hill (he had passed away the winter before) when there appeared in the sky a hand holding a wreath of flowers, which turned to evergreen as I watched. Three times as I went along, the wreath appeared. It seemed an omen some way, and afterward, John told me that he and Mother had been afraid for me. Later, I was to think of that dream.

However, everything went well with me. Brother Rube went for a neighbor and John had to cross the river and ride ten miles below, for the doctor, a stranger who had come into the valley with a colony from St. Louis. Both the doctor and nurse gave me good care and from this time, little Brayton was the center of our universe, and the family his devoted and admiring subjects. There was nothing to use for a bassinet, so we took a wooden canned goods box, cutting it low in front and at the foot, but leaving it high at the head and back. I lined it and used a pillow for a mattress, putting it on a chair by the bed and it answered the purpose very well for a few months. By summer, the baby was big enough for a larger bed, so John made one as high as ours and we moved out in the alley way to sleep, as it was cooler. One night I was in the house getting ready for bed, when Brayton cried. John took him up, and as he did so I opened the screen door to go out, when the light from the lamp fell on a big rattler crawling toward him. I screamed "Snake" and John jumped just as it coiled. I brought the light and the snake was killed—another narrow escape.

A little later, one of the men interested in the canal, offered us his house, in Phoenix, for a couple of months. We were glad to have the vacation. John clerked in a grocery store while there and we did enjoy the change. The owner wanted John to stay on in the store, but he knew he was needed on the ranch, so we went back. Sometimes, I have wondered what our life would have been if John had accepted this offer. While in Phoenix I secured a second-hand baby buggy, not a very good one, nor safe, as we were soon to find out. When Brayton was eleven months old, I had him in it and had pushed him up to the back door to get something inside. I was gone only a minute—as it seemed to me—when I heard him scream. I rushed out and found that he had evidently turned around and when he stood up the buggy had tipped backward with him. Right under it on the ground was a twenty-pound lard pail, and the baby had cut his lip clear through on that. The edge of the pail was as sharp as a knife. Father took four stitches in the wound, but Brayton sucked his thumb and try as I would to keep it out of his mouth, some of the stitches pulled out and a lump formed on his lip.

Our own little house was being completed and that winter we moved into it. It was not far from Father's which was handy. In February, John's eldest brother, Ancil Martin (a doctor), came out from Iowa to visit us, and also to look around Phoenix with the intention of settling there to establish a practice. While with us, he and John took Brayton over to our house, gave him chloroform and Ancil operated on his lip. After a year, we could hardly see the line. That Spring, the doctor settled in Phoenix. He was the first oculist in the state of Arizona and became nationally known for his skill as a surgeon.

Along in the Spring, Brayton became ill with a fever. My sister-in-law was with us at the time and she said we must "make him sweat". So we filled bottles with hot water and put around him, using such simple remedies as we knew. When the doctor came, he said she had saved his life. It took some time for him to recover and as the sister was there to help Mother, John thought it would be wise for me to take Brayton and go back home for a visit. Father had a friend who was warden of the penitentiary at Yuma, so John applied for a position as guard, and secured it. The first day of June John went to Yuma and Brayton and I were on our way to Iowa. We were gone six months and on our return, stopped off at Yuma, but we found it was too expensive to try to live there, so the baby and I went back to the ranch. It was quite different living on the ranch without John. It had been fine so long as he was with us. I was not of a despondent disposition, but the days were so long and unbearable, I could not stand it. So John came home in the Fall and again we lived in our little house across the way and we were all happy and contented.

Brayton was two years old now, full of life, and into everything. We had a team of large mules and they were so mean that even the men were afraid of them. One day when Brayton was missing, we looked every place for him and found him right up in the manger of one of the mules, feeding it. After that we enclosed the porch with a fence to insure his safety.

So far there had been no picnics or parties of any kind, so when an invitation came from a family several miles down the valley to attend a dance, I was thrilled. I was so fond of dancing and of course wanted to go. My brother and sister-in-law were going, but I could not persuade John to go. He said I could go and he would stay home and take care of Brayton. The last thing I saw as we drove out of the gate and down the road was John with Brayton in his arms, watching us. Some way it took all the pleasure out of the trip. I kept trying to think it was right for me to go, but in my heart I was sorry I had ever considered it, and it was the first and last party for years that I ever attended without John.

Our outside pleasures were few. We were too far from Yuma to have church services. As I remember, only three or four times a year, a wandering preacher would stop in Palomas for one meeting. But what a sermon it would be! It was good for us to be reminded of our short comings, but some times we came away with the feeling that the preacher thought we were more wicked than we actually were. We had a Sunday School for a little while but so few came or showed any interest, that we had to give it up.

More settlers were coming in to the valley now that we had some water, but were the wandering "covered wagon" kind from Texas and the South— nothing against them, but they were the shiftless type who took no pride in improving their places, thinking perhaps they might move on, which many of them did. So the better families began to stand out in the community, and we came to the point where we could pick and choose our acquaintances.

Little Brayton was now two and old enough to enjoy Christmas. We were determined to have a Christmas tree for him. We had to use a branch of a mesquite tree, but when it was decorated with silver balls made of cotton, covered with tin foil (which came with tobacco or cigars) and strings of popcorn, and other home made decorations, it all looked very lovely to us. Of course there were toys for Brayton. My Christmas gifts that went home that year were made from pieces of lace and silk from wedding gifts and from my trousseau, but it gave me pleasure to make them and our friends understood.

Father's place was lovely now. Little trees were leaving out and one was in blossom. We had all worked so hard to accomplish our hearts' desire—a real home on the desert. Little by little we had developed improvements and conveniences that made the work easier for all of us. But we were so soon to have nothing left of that precious spot but memories.

In February of that year the treacherous river ran true to form. In fact, it out did itself. We had been notified that the river was on a rampage, but we had no idea that the flood waters would reach us so quickly or run so high. The boys were piling up the furniture as fast as they could, but before they knew it the water was around the house. The adobe fireplaces melted and things began floating away. So many articles were ruined, not being put up high enough. However, the water began to recede a little, when in a couple of days, a "Paul Revere" rode through the valley shouting that Walnut Creek dam had gone out. Then there was scampering in every direction. We had a pretty good idea by that time what this would mean to us. When everything in Father's home was piled as high as possible the bedding and articles the family most needed were brought over to our house, as it was on higher ground. It was in the evening, so we made beds on the floor, but were careful to have things ready to move out in case of an emergency. Then we all went to bed, leaving John and his brother Rube sitting in front of the fireplace to keep watch.

Along in the night John's sister woke up and looked out of the window to find water completely surrounding the house and the boys sound asleep. It did not take long to load the wagons that stood ready—the horses being near at hand—and I, being the last to leave, Father had to jump me over the water. We went up on higher land and camped under a mesquite tree for three weeks. We had two tents with a large piece of canvas stretched between, so we got along pretty well, but it was very cold. The river was three miles wide I was told, and it certainly looked it. We saw all sorts of things floating down the stream. There were great hay stacks, little shacks, wood piles and one log appeared to have a man clinging to it.

As the water receded, the ground began to cave—sometimes six feet at a time. Father and I walked down one day to look at it and he reached over and picked an almond blossom off the little tree he had planted, and the next minute the tree was gone. Father's ground was going so fast they knew there was no hope for the house, so the neighbors assembled and tore it down, afterward re-building it on Rube's land which was much higher. Every foot of Father's land caved off into the river and about a quarter of John's. When Father rebuilt, there was just one large room with a smaller one at the side, to cook and eat in. We all lived there together again, as our house though still standing, was right near the edge of the bank now six feet above the river bed.

Here was another period of adjustment not easy for any of us, but far less trying on the younger ones than on Father and Mother, who had already passed through so much. However, they were courageous. We were all of the "tender foot" variety, but were beginning to feel like seasoned pioneers. We never complained even to each other, but it was all pretty discouraging.

If it hadn't been for Brayton in those trying days, I do not know what we would have done. He was growing dearer each day.

We had beds in three corners of the big room and a trundle bed for Brayton. He seemed to heed everything we tried to teach him, never forgetting anything. As it grew warmer, we had a little fence made around the porch so he could be outside most of the time. He loved to ride, but I began to notice along in May that he wanted to be held so much, and if riding, would put his head in my lap and his feet on John and ask me to sing about Jesus. About that time a friend spent Sunday with us, and he and Brayton had such a nice time. When he went home he said to his mother, "That little boy of John's is too sweet to live." That does not seem an exaggeration now. The next Sunday we buried him. He must have been ailing for some time, as I have described, but he was only dangerously ill a day and a night. We sent to Yuma for a doctor, as it took so long for John's brother to reach us. When he did come it was too late. Brayton was gone and the Yuma doctor could only attend to sending a little grey casket. We buried him on Sunday morning at Aqua Caliente. We had a few wild flowers and father read the burial service. It seemed that our one bright star had set. When I look back on that time, and think what that loss was to John and me, I can hardly see how we could have gone on, had we not meant so much to each other. We were so young and there was so little in that country for us, living as we were, with no home of our own. Our house had been given to a man (with a family) who was putting in a vegetable garden for all of us. I went every where with John, and I would sit by the hour on a bank and watch him plow or irrigate and every Sunday we went to the little grave.

In 1893 Father and Mother took a vacation and went to the World's Fair in Chicago. They needed a change badly. Of course, after the flood, there was nothing left of the head gate as it had not been finished and what work was done had been washed out, so it was decided not to go on with it. This was a great disappointment to Father and he was very much discouraged, as there was nothing to do now but farm, and not a real farmer in the family. It was a problem to know what was best to do. Many advised we should leave while the boys were yet young.

John and I were looking forward with pleasure to an "event" in the Fall and he was unwilling to have me to remain on the ranch. Some time before, we had become acquainted with a woman who came out to Arizona with the St. Louis colony. She had been a nurse and had gone to Phoenix with the idea of continuing her profession. She and her husband had bought a small ranch about four miles out from Phoenix and John thought this would be the very place for me at this time, so we left the home in July and I was placed in her care. An old family physician of my father's from Iowa was now in the office of John's brother, so John made all arrangements with him to look after me and we were both so satisfied and happy, when he left me to return to the ranch.

The house was small, but it was really a lovely little place and I was quite contented until the nurse rented the two front rooms and put me in a back bedroom which had only one window without any glass in it. A curtain hung over the opening. The furnishings were very meagre but I told John nothing of this for I knew how angry and worried he would be. Our baby girl came the 14th of October. All went so well that the nurse thought we didn't need a doctor, so she did not send for him. John's brother was down in Mexico on a vacation or he would have inquired for me. Time went on and I was neglected in some way and for three weeks I had chills and fever.

At last I became frightened and insisted upon seeing the doctor. Several times the nurse sent her husband for him, each time he returned, saying the doctor was not in. Knowing him to be a drinking man—I doubted his word. Finally I insisted upon the woman writing a note to the doctor and sending it in by some friends who were visiting with her. That brought the doctor out to see me early the next morning—and such an indignant doctor. John's brother had gotten back by this time, so he came out with Dr. Ward and John came that night. When they saw my condition and realized how I had been neglected, they were all very angry. John stayed right beside me and would not permit the woman even to make my bed. The doctors agreed I would not have lived three days longer. To make a bad matter worse, I had gotten "milk leg" and was obliged to remain there ten weeks more. Such a serious time! And it had all looked so right and bright in the beginning.

At last the terrible nightmare was a thing of the past and I was leaving that place with my precious baby in my arms. We named her Gladys. My days were never to be so lonely again and the anguish of Brayton's passing was to grow less keen as this little one developed and my time and strength were taken up in ministering to her needs.

That summer while I was gone, the boys had added three rooms to the south side of the house and it made the greatest difference in our comfort. The rooms were small, but it gave *us* a bedroom and later, we used the others for dining room and kitchen. You cannot imagine how childishly delighted we all were over every added improvement. And the fact that it was the work of the boys themselves made us prouder still. Father and Mother came back that Fall and John's sister was also with us.

About this time John began to have trouble with dysentery. He grew so weak and white with the heat of summer, that we became frightened and wrote his brother for advice. As our Phoenix Doctor had moved to Los Angeles, he suggested that John go there without delay and put himself under the care of Dr. Ward, which he did. He was there six weeks and began to feel much better. He became quite interested in the oil business, going to the fields every day. One day he ran on to a little place for lease—with one well producing, and room for drilling others. There was also a small furnished house on the property. It looked good to John and he immediately wrote the folks about it. Father went in to Los Angeles to look things over. I think John had hoped to lease the property for himself, but

Ladies with cactus. Sightseeing excursions to the giant saguaro were common among leisured Arizonans; even as they reveled in the western landscape, women dressed with care and style. Courtesy of the Sharlot Hall Historical Society, Prescott, Arizona.

when he saw how eager Father was to have it he didn't say a word. That was John—he always gave up to others. He came back on the ranch and soon began to run down in health again. My story might have been very different, if a cousin had not written Mother of a simple remedy which cured him. Just two cubes of sugar crushed and mixed with the yolk of an egg, taken every night. I have passed it on to so many and it has proved a wonderful cure.

There had been great excitement over the finding of gold in the Harqua Hala mountains about seventy-five miles north of us. I can't remember what year it was—but some time in 1892 to 1893, and Oh how the boys longed to go up there! But help was not easy to find at that time so they could not leave the ranch. However, they always kept the "mining bug", as you will see later. There was much activity in the valley, with people coming and going all the time. We were two miles from Palomas where the road to the mine lay; many came to us to buy hay for their horses, and freight teams often camped on the ranch, so we felt the excitement too.

Father and Mother were getting ready to move to Los Angeles now and as we were expecting another "arrival", I was to go with them so I could be near our doctor. I had been suffering with rheumatism in my hands and arms all Fall and didn't know how I was going to manage. The neighbor who had cared for me when our little boy was born, told John of a remedy if I would use it—I consented, and he was so faithful with it. I am going to tell you what it was. He took dry cow manure and powdered it, then heated it thoroughly, put my hand and arm down in it and wrapped something around all to keep in the heat. It was a heroic remedy but it brought results and we could not be too particular about methods in the desert. John would get up about three or four times in the night to re-heat the mixture. Mother made more of a fuss about it than I did, as the odor was most unpleasant. I could only use it on my left arm, as I had to take care of Gladys with the other. I wondered what I was going to do when I went to Los Angeles, but from the first night on leaving home I was free of pain in both arms and it never returned.

Father, Mother and I were very comfortable in the little house in Los Angeles—but how I missed John! Dear little Marcella, our second daughter, was born on New Years day, 1895. I stayed about a month longer then started home with two babies. Fortunately there were no complications this time. Gladys could not walk, but there is always some one to help on the train and John met me in the middle of the night at Aztec. So we got along very well.

Soon after the folks left, Rube went with a surveying party into Mexico, so we were alone on the ranch. John had a good Mexican boy and persuaded an Indian to move near, so he could irrigate for him. His tepee was across the canal on the mesa and his squaw washed for me. Mollie had washed for us before, but had been living down in the valley until now.

We had a very nice school teacher at this time. Her school was at Palomas, but she lived with her family about two miles east of us and was much company for me. She stopped often when going by, and when John had to be away over night, she would come and stay with me. On one of these nights we had a very unpleasant experience. I was awakened by the barking of the dogs and knew in a moment what was the trouble. We had a wonderful watch dog, a hound, but once in a while he would wander too far from home and encounter our neighbor's dog and then there was mischief to pay, as the two would chase the hogs. I knew that was what they were doing. I tried to call the Mexican boy but could not make him hear. I knew I could do nothing myself, yet I could not go back to bed, knowing a nice fat hog was being killed. The teacher begged me to go to bed and told me I was sure to take cold, which I did—and a fearful one. What a time I had with those babies! They were both as good as could be and I could dispose of Marcella by putting her in her basket on a table. But it was so cold on the floor for Gladys and I was afraid to hold her. I sat by the kitchen stove, my feet in the oven, suffering agony with a sore throat, but nature finally came to my relief.

Our Indian had not been well for some time—"tuberculosis," they said. So many of them died of it during those years. They would work on the ranches in shirt and overalls, then go home at night and take them off and lie on the cold ground. The morning before John got home I was awakened by much weeping and wailing at the Indian's camp. I had heard the "medicine man" at times all night, so I knew that Indian Jim had passed on. When the Mexican boy came that morning he showed me the smoke away back on the mesa where Jim and his pony (he told me) and everything belonging to Jim, had been burned. Even Mollie's clothes were burned, for about nine o'clock when she came to tell me she was going away, she had on the dirtiest rags I ever saw. Such a sudden weird incident it was and it left me very down-hearted all day and so very sorry John had to be away. He was fond of Jim and might have been able to do something for him. There was nothing to be done now, because when there was a death in an Indian family, those that were left were supposed to move away. We missed them both very much.

Now that Rube was gone we had been thinking of moving into his little place. The house wasn't much, but it had two rooms and John added two more. It was under one of the largest mesquite trees I ever saw, and around it and enclosing the dining room door, a fence was made to protect the children. There was a nice little orchard that extended from the house to the main road and a line of tall poplar trees west, along a fence, which was a protection for the house and orchard. We were more content and cosier here than we had been since coming to Arizona—no doubt because we were by ourselves.

The following winter my niece from Iowa came to be with us and we were so thankful we were in this place, yet we wondered what we could do to entertain so lovely a young girl. She was as happy as a lark all the time she was there, and we need not have worried about that.

One day a young man from the St. Louis Colony came along and seeing John busy digging a well, stopped to talk with him. John liked his appearance very much and finally asked if he would like to work for him. Frank Snowden was with us for over a year. He was one of the family, more like a younger brother, and such a comfort to us. One day when John was in the saddle his horse reared and fell, crushing John's knee. I do not know what we would have done without Frank. He picked John up as if he were a child, took him to Aztec and put him on the train for Phoenix, where he would be under the care of his brother.

The year that Frank was with us on the ranch we decided to celebrate Christmas in a big way. My niece was there to help and we asked our friends to send us scraps of silk and lace and any ideas for making little gifts, also fancy pictures, tissue paper and patterns for cloth dolls. I was so surprised and delighted at the outcome. Everyone was keen about helping me, even sending me dolls already made and so many ideas.

It was a grand success and there were sixty-five at that Christmas celebration. John and Frank dug a barbecue pit and roasted in it an immense piece of beef and a whole pig. I asked the neighbors if they would help with the dinner by bringing cakes, pies, and bread, and we did the rest. One woman brought a cake and when John tried to cut it he could not make a dent in it with the knife. Something was wrong, but we could not bother to investigate, so when no one was looking John slipped the cake under the cupboard on the floor. He was pretty embarrassed when the woman asked him for the plate as she was leaving. John happened to think where he had put it and told Frank to engage her in conversation until he could get it out.

We put the big tree over in Father's house and it really looked lovely and the children loved Santa Claus. At night the guests danced in the big room—a few playing cards at our house. A number of the neighbors wanted another Christmas party the next year, but John and I remembering the hard work and responsibility were not so keen about it though we were very glad we had given it the year before.

After Frank left us he went to the "Fortuna" mine near Yuma, then moved to California and married, settling in Orange. We did not see him again until February 1937, when we were living in Arcadia, California. I was returning from a trip to Los Angeles and Gladys met me at the train. She had a strange man with her, who greeted me with, "Well, how are you, Aunt Sadie?" I should have known it was Frank, but forty years makes quite a difference in one's appearance. He had been out on the Arizona desert and heard someone talking about the Martins, so he was able to secure our address. We had a little visit and I have seen him once since, but would give a good deal to see him again and talk over those old days.

But to resume my story—

The "prospects" in the Harqua Hala country had developed into a real gold mine and a lively little camp had been opened. The property had been taken over by an English company who had engaged an American mining engineer to run it, and by this time there were a number of men employed, many of whom had brought their families. We had become quite well acquainted with a few of these people and they had entertained my niece quite royally. She was such a sweet girl, whom everyone loved and missed when she went back home. Many times we had entertained the people from the mine when they would be passing through Palomas. Occasionally some of the ladies would come down from the mine and wait with us to meet their husbands who might be returning from a business trip. It was such a pleasure to us as we saw so few people. We had often been invited to go up to the mine and at last we accepted the invitation. It was a long day's drive over desert roads. We arrived about dark and as we came up out of a wash, a beautiful sight met our eyes. The camp was electrically lighted and the cyanide plant was a mass of brilliant lights. We were so splendidly entertained while there, and it was hard to return to the ranch after so much excitement.

However we were not quite so lonely as we had been a few years before. My father had an old-fashioned organ that had been stored from the time he remarried. When he died the relatives sent it to me, knowing I had no instrument and would appreciate it. I loved it and John and I sang often in the evening. Especially was it a joy, when a young lady who was visiting her brother (the agent at Aztec) came to see us. She was a brilliant girl, full of fun and with such a sweet voice. She could play and sing anything and I am afraid we over taxed her as she was always willing and we enjoyed the music so much. She also was invited to visit at Harqua Hala mine and later became engaged to the manager of the mine, whom she married. In all the years that have passed, we have kept in touch with each other and I esteem her friendship very highly. The summer following her visit we were away and we let our nearest neighbor use the organ. While we were gone their house burned and with it the dear old organ. I was very sorry but as things turned out, there was no telling what fate would have befallen it anyway. As I have said before, "nothing seemed permanent on the desert."

Our land had been advertised for sale or trade and in the spring of 1897, John had a letter from a man who asked him to meet him at Aztec, as he wanted to look over the ranches, and if satisfactory, trade a place in Los Angeles for them.

The ranches looked lovely when he arrived, all in alfalfa and all so green. We had three jersey cows, a number of fat cattle, hogs and horses. I fed the gentleman everything he could eat with cream; also cottage cheese, and gave him all the milk he could drink. John said that was what made the trade. The house in Los Angeles was furnished, so the hogs were traded for the furniture. We left the ranch $200 in debt. We were rather sad about leaving, for after all, it had been our first home. However we could never have been successful there. When the crops were good there was apt to be some trouble with the canal—or rain to spoil great stacks of wheat ready to be thrashed. When we had fat steers, prices were low—same with hogs, and when later John made the remark that those nine years were the only part of his life that he regretted, I could hardly blame him. Nine years out of a young man's life when he could have been getting a valuable start in some business. By that time we were sure he was a business man, not a farmer. Often we were to remember the advice of those friends from Joliet, who begged us to leave and not bury ourselves in that desert life, when we were so young. We were not in any way fitted for such a life, nor was John strong enough. Hard work and disappointment took its terrible toll and he looked much older than his years.

It seemed now we were to start out all over again. John's health was a handicap. He had been on the desert so long he felt he was incapable of starting a business life. This was probably the reason he decided to send the children and me into California. Father and Mother were now moved and settled in their beautiful new home in Los Angeles, in one of the best residential districts. Now John felt at liberty to go out to some gold mining claims that his doctor brother had gotten hold of. His younger brother, Rube and my brother went with him.

The new home in Los Angeles was very lovely and we were comfortable and well taken care of, yet it was the longest year and a half of all the years I have experienced. The children had colds all winter long, besides Marcella had membraneous croup and typhoid fever during that time. As the boys were living in tents again, and had to have water hauled in barrels for all uses, for a distance of six miles, and had to go six miles in another direction for mail and food, with one burro for transportation, there was no immediate hope of our going to John. However after two summers and a winter in Los Angeles, I wrote and begged John to let us come to him even if we had to live in a dugout. I knew we would be happier together and no one blame me. Of course he told me to come. He never refused me anything.

We were all so happy to be back with him. The camp was arranged very well. There were three tents, one to cook and eat in, one for the boys and one for us. In the boys' tent and in ours, they had ripped up the corner and built a stone fire-place in each. You can't imagine how wonderful these seemed to us. When I looked at the boys I felt that they needed me. They showed plainly that they were happy to transfer the cooking and dishwashing to someone else, after they had been down in the mine all day. The children and I did not get away from camp very often but we were satisfied. We did go a few times when it was John's turn to go for the mail. We would go as far as the Reid ranch (about five miles)—John and I walking and the girls riding on the burro.

Our camp was in a lovely spot on the side of a mountain and we could see many miles in three directions. If anyone was coming on the main road we could see the dust at least twenty miles away, the air being so clear and dry. The August sand storms would come rolling down the valley in great clouds and faster than a team could travel, but we would just get the edge of it and were so grateful to escape. We were never really lonely. Someone came by nearly every day and our friends, Mr. and Mrs. Quinn, drove out from Harrisburg to see us from time to time. The water wagon came now twice a week, so there was almost always something to look forward to.

About this time we experienced a snow storm—most unusual in this part of Arizona. One morning we were awakened by the boys scraping snow off the tent and as this was their first snow, the children were delighted. John helped them make a snow man which was of good size, but it was about gone by noon. Later in the winter we had a terrific rain. We tried to protect the beds as much as possible and then we only had a dry space as big as a card table—to eat our supper on. We could cook nothing. I can't describe "the wetness" of it. The next morning I had everything out on the lines and on chairs drying, when in came Rube bringing the teacher from Harrisburg to spend the week end. Needless to say we found a way to take care of her.

In the early fall when the weather was settled and beautiful a friend came out from Phoenix for a visit. I was rather expecting her yet had not heard definitely when she was to arrive. Rube brought her in one night when he came home with the mail, and her letter was in the mail bag. The poor girl had been through quite a distressing experience and showed it. She had arrived at Congress during the night and soon after started out in a light rig with a Mexican driver. On that long drive of about sixty miles, it seems the driver would fall asleep and then my friend, quite unused to the easy going ways of our Mexicans, would poke him, for fear the horses would leave the road. When they finally reached "Pete's Well," (where our water came from) and no one was there to meet her, the Mexicans persuaded her to go on to Harrisburg. When nobody met her there, she was told to sit in the boarding house and if no one came for the mail they would find a way to get her out to our camp. Imagine her relief when Rube arrived. We had a wonderful time while she was with us. The boys liked her so much. She was clever and full of fun, there was something doing every minute, and we missed her so when she left.

Our next excitement came a few days later when a man rode into camp, asking if a Mexican riding a horse, had passed that way. The store keeper at Harrisburg had been murdered the night before and there was a search warrant out for the murderer. It seems this merchant, Mr. Moffett, had his cot on the porch in front of the store, so it was easy for the man to approach from the rear and hit him over the head with a drill, then steal the gold dust from under the pillow. It looked as if Mr. Moffett had tried to get his gun which was also under the pillow. The Mexican had removed his shoes but he was easily traced to the place where he had tied his horse some distance away. He had not planned very well. They first found where he had changed horses, then soon caught him. It was a bold and brutal murder and created great excitement for some time. Harrisburg had been quite a mining town and there was still an old mill there, but at this time it was quiet. A nephew of the murdered man came out from the East and stayed until things could be settled and the store sold. Two old men took it over for a time, but finally John bought them out and we moved to Harrisburg.

And now another adjustment had to be made. We had left the camp life behind us and were to live in a house again. There were two buildings alike made of adobe, one housed a saloon and the other a store with the Post Office in one corner. Then there was a boarding house, a school house and a few tents and houses scattered about. The house we were to occupy was adobe and at least a quarter of a mile from the store.

That first summer I was called upon several times to cook for strangers passing through, but it was too hard for me; so in the Fall John hired a Chinaman and started the boarding house which was just across the street from the store and quite handy. We took our meals there also as there was no need of running two houses. We had friends who lived at the other end of town and about two miles away—was the ranch I have mentioned, where we enjoyed going and where we could get fresh meat and vegetables—a rare treat on the desert.

It was really the first little *town* we had lived in since coming to Arizona and we found it quite entertaining. Our house being rather isolated, we thought we should have a dog, so the doctor sent a large black one out from Phoenix. He proved to be just what we needed. A stranger could not get inside the fence and at night, when we went home before John, he would find our dog lying right in front of the door, on guard. He hated the Mexican dogs and there were many fights in consequence. Even my

Mexican washerwoman could not get in until I rescued her. We had a living room, two bedrooms and a large kitchen, so when it was necessary for the teacher to live with us, John took some space off one end of the kitchen and made a bedroom for the girls.

At this time there was much excitement about the new railroad going through from Wickenburg to California. The surveyors were busy and according to their stakes, the railroad would run about six miles from Harrisburg, quite different from the way it now was—sixty miles by stage to the place where we took the train.

I think they started work on the road west from Wickenburg about 1904. This was when we met Dick Wick Hall. He and others expected to build a town on the new railroad and made their headquarters in Harrisburg. That town is now Salome. The survey had been made a half mile west of where it is now, so that later (before the road was finished that far) the buildings were moved to the present site of Salome. I understand the town acquired its name a short time before Dick Wick had opened his Laughing Gas station. A covered wagon rolled in to town and a comely barefoot girl jumped out. Finding the sand too hot she started dancing. Dick Wick was amused and asked her name. She replied, "Salome." He gazed at her bare feet for a while. "I know what I'm going to name my town. It will be Salome." (where she danced.)

A short time before Dick moved to Salome we gave a Hallowe'en Party and he was the life of it. As it was seldom he attended any social gatherings, we felt quite honored to have him. He was so witty that night and so full of stories he seemed to enjoy our party as much as we did. Dick was well known as a wild and tall story teller. That evening there was a young man—a tenderfoot from the East—(visiting his sister) who sat entranced, drinking in every word of Dick's and believing it all. But we who understood, enjoyed watching the boy quite as much as the boy enjoyed watching Dick.

There was another interesting young man in Harrisburg who was on the desert for his health. He was clever and full of fun and we were all fond of him. He was around the store so much and was good company for John. He came from a Chicago family (one of six children). They visited him at different times, as did his father and mother. We came to know and like them all and the friendships started then have lasted through all these years, though I regret to say there are only three of that family left.

During the last year of our stay in Harrisburg (we lived there about four years) John, through a man from New York who was prospecting in our vicinity, became interested in the mines at Harqua Hala. By this time the English company had gone. The property had reverted to the owner and had been idle for some time. John made several trips to see him and finally an agreement was reached to buy the property. We planned to move to the camp in 1906. That summer the mine was bonded to the Ironwood Michigan Co. and we went to Los Angeles and then as far east as Chicago, before returning to Harqua Hala. John had been given the privilege of running the store and boarding house there. He had sold the store in Harrisburg before we left on our trip. When we returned, we found John had been nominated for a position in the Arizona legislature. He refused to run as he knew he was due in Harqua Hala to get the store and boarding house started, also he had to build a home for us. But men came to him from Yuma and plead with him until he finally consented to run and was elected.

Until the house was finished at Harqua Hala, we had to live in a room adjoining the store (which later became John's office). We took our meals at the boarding house.

The father of the young man from Chicago, (whom we first met in Harrisburg, Mr. Scales,) now became interested in some mining claims in the vicinity of Harqua Hala, and built a home at the camp called "Hercules". He wanted his family to be comfortable when they came out on their frequent visits, and he was particularly concerned for the welfare of his invalid son, who, I am sorry to say, passed away that summer in Prescott. One of the daughters, Elizabeth Scales, applied for the school and we were delighted to have her, but by Christmas time she found it too hard and thought best to resign. We were fortunate in locating another teacher immediately through the State Normal School and John felt relieved as he was soon to leave for the legislature. John's brother had found a capable young man to run the store and boarding house for him. Also a good Chinese cook was employed. A niece from Iowa came to visit me and the teacher had a room with us.

We moved into our house the day before New Years, and the next day found that we had nearly burned out during the night. Mexicans had made our fire-place of rocks and there were cracks which had not been filled with cement. The wall boards had been charred half way through, so they had to cut out the boards and put a cement wall back of the fireplace.

The mining company brought their own officials. Two of them had families and there were some unmarried men. There were also several Mexican families, so we had a good sized school that year.

When a mine is running it does not take long for men to wander in, seeking work. A number came up from old Mexico, unmarried and not desirable. I believe it was along in February when our deputy sheriff was murdered. He had come to camp in the late afternoon and laid down to rest just inside the bunk house. He was there when the miners went to their evening meal. According to the testimony there was one Mexican who reached the bunk house quite late and he met two other Mexicans as he was coming over. There had been a dance a short time before and these two had attended in a drunken condition, causing some trouble, so the deputy took their guns from them. They vowed they would "get him" and he had been warned, but did not take it seriously. It was proven that they stopped at the bunk house and while one of them held the deputy, the other shot him with his own gun. Then they left him. He tried to reach the store, but fell on the way and when a boy who saw him fall reached him, he was just able to say, "Well, they got me."

The Mexicans were arrested, tied to posts on the office porch and guarded until the sheriff and coroner arrived the next day. The deputy died toward morning. In his delirium during the night he kept repeating the name of one of the men.

How I did long for John who was so calm in an emergency and always knew just what to do. The mine superintendent did not understand nor know how to manage Mexicans. He drove them all over in their part of camp, called them "dogs" and much worse names, not realizing that there were many decent ones among them. Naturally the Mexicans hated him and I was afraid there would be a riot. A day or so after this the superintendent came to our house wanting any firearms we might have and said he expected trouble that night, that they had planned to put all the women and children in the store, so the men could protect them better. I was not afraid; I told him our Mexicans would protect us instead of harming us. John came in on the stage that afternoon and he certainly told the superintendent what he thought of him for creating such a commotion, and there was no trouble then or later.

We were in for all kinds of frights that Spring, while John was away. One night we were sitting in front of the fire-place after dinner, when we saw a light flash on the corner of the porch and a man climbing up. The porch was quite high at that point and the steps were not far away, so we wondered at such a performance. As he passed the window I could see his face plainly and it was not only a strange face to me, but it was so white and wild looking. My niece ran into the other room and the teacher rushed for the stairs, but the children sat perfectly still. I was at the door by the time the man was and put my knee against it, so he would not hear me turn the key. As the upper part of the door was glass, I could see him and I asked him what he wanted. He mumbled a name and it was hard to per-saude him to go to the store, where I said this person might be found. We heard afterward that he was inquiring for himself. He had delirium tre-mens. Someone took him home, which was to a saloon, the allotted dis-tance from camp. His father was the owner of the saloon and had left his son with a trusted Mexican in charge, but he had made his escape and later that night got away again. Nearly every man in camp was out looking for him, but finally, an Indian discovered him after searching two days and a half. He was hanging dead over a limb of a tree.

As I have said, the camp was full of strange men that winter, mostly Mexicans, and many tents were scattered around. At the foot of the hill, where our house was located, we were not so far from some of these tents, and we could hear the people quarreling and fighting over cards, which seemed to be one of their principal pastimes, but they never came near us, nor did any harm on the outside, that we could see.

When John came home from the Legislature, he brought the Speaker of the House with his wife and sister. John hired a three-seated rig with four horses and driver and we had several nice days with them.

The mining company operated for about two years, when the president got into some kind of trouble in Michigan and had to give up the prop-erty. He was a banker—but a gambler by nature—and had misused bank money or something to that effect. We had liked him and felt sorry for his wife and children. After a time another company of Prescott men was formed, but it was never a great success. The president of the company went East to raise money and sent it back to the mine, but he found on his return that his money had been spent on road building, instead of in the mine; and under the contract, a certain amount of work was to be done underground within a specified time, so the president was displeased and discharged everybody. John was placed in charge, as watchman, and acted as such for several years.

Engineers came to examine the mine and at times the mill would run. The greatest disappointment was when an engineer was with us for a week and gave John every encouragement as to the report he was handing in. Then we read in the Los Angeles Times that some members of the company which he represented, had been in Los Angeles and had gone to an Arizona mine. They never came, however, and after some time, John found that they had been ready to make a deal, but the president of our company was not willing to give them control and the deal was off. We always felt a little hard toward hm. He never accomplished anything for the property.

We lived on at the camp for several years, having many disappointments, but much happiness as we went along together. Our new home was comfortable and we had many good friends.

The railroad was finished about 1912. In 1909 Gladys was ready for High School, so we sent both children to a Girls' School in Los Angeles. This was the year the railroad was finished past Salome. So they came home for vacation by way of Wickenburg, and on a caboose as far as Salome. John had remarked to me when they left for school, in the Fall, "Well Sadie, this is the beginning of the end." We both believed they would never again be happy and satisfied on the desert. But we were wrong. Imagine our joy when they were so eager to get home that they never stayed for any final exercise, until Gladys graduated in 1913. She went to Flagstaff Teachers College the next year, and while there, met a young man to whom she was married in 1917, just before he went into a training camp during the World War. Marcella had gone into a bank in Phoenix, so we were alone again that winter. Gladys' husband, Fred, was over seas for eighteen months and on his way home she met him in New York and they went to Iowa to visit his people. Fred lost his father in January of that year; then they came to Arizona and settled in Phoenix.

In August, John and I went to Phoenix for a month to be with Marcella, and while there, he had the flu, and was never strong again. It was thought best to go to Los Angeles, out of the heat. I felt now that my pioneer days were over. John passed away in July, 1920.

In conclusion, I want to say I realize, that my life was an ordinary one, but it was a different kind of a life from that which most people experience and so very trying at time, that if I had not had the love and devotion of one of the finest men that ever lived—tender, sympathetic and understanding—it would have been unbearable. If I have gone into detail about the happenings from day to day in our desert life, it is because I want my children to know and appreciate (and their children after them) what John was to me and to them. He never failed one of us in any relation of life and no sacrifice was too great for him to make, where the welfare and happiness of his family was concerned. He did not accumulate much of this world's riches, but he left us a heritage far more precious than silver or gold—and he died as he had lived—smiling.

Years later I had an opportunity to return to Arizona and visit some of the old familiar places. I was reminded of my early prophesy—"Is there anything permanent on the beautiful desert"? In Harrisburg I found only ruined walls of the adobe buildings and not a trace of anything resembling a house. At Agua Caliente I visited the little knoll where we buried our baby boy. I was not quite sure that I found the little grave—as many others had been placed around it.

When we neared the location of our ranches—imagine my astonishment and bitter disappointment at not being able to find one of them. Not a tree, a fence post or even the ruins of either house could be seen anywhere—search as I did I could see nothing but desert.

What was the cause? I could not say—perchance the river was in sympathy with the sand-storms and seemed (as I had said) to have a resentment for human beings who dared to come and change things for their own comfort and pleasure.

Sadie Martin, "My Desert Memories," typed manuscript, Arizona Historical Society Library, Tucson, Arizona, 1939.

Selected Bibliography

GENERAL SURVEYS

Armitage, Susan, and Elizabeth Jameson, eds. *The Women's West*. Norman: University of Oklahoma Press, 1987.

Bataille, Gretchen M., and Kathleen Mullen Sands. *American Indian Women: Telling Their Lives*. Lincoln: University of Nebraska Press, 1984.

Jameson, Elizabeth, and Susan Armitage, eds. *Writing the Range: Race, Class and Culture in the Women's West*. Norman: University of Oklahoma Press, 1997.

Jeffrey, Julie Roy. *Frontier Women: The Trans-Mississippi West 1840–1880*. New York: Hill and Wang, 1979.

Jensen, Joan. *One Foot on the Rockies: Women and Creativity in the Modern American West*. Albuquerque: University of New Mexico Press, 1995.

Luchetti, Cathy, and Carol Olwell. *Women of the West*. St. George, Utah: Antelope Island Press, 1982.

Myres, Sandra L. *Westering Women and the Frontier Experience 1800–1915*. Albuquerque: University of New Mexico Press, 1982.

Peavy, Linda, and Ursula Smith. *Pioneer Women: The Lives of Women on the Frontier*. New York: Smithmark, 1996.

Reiter, Joan Swallow, ed. *The Women*. The Old West Series. Alexandria, Va.: Time-Life Books, 1978.

Schlissel, Lillian, Vicki L. Ruiz, and Janice Monk, eds. *Western Women: Their Land, Their Lives*. Albuquerque: University of New Mexico Press, 1988.

LOCAL AND SPECIALIZED STUDIES

Beeton, Beverly. *Women Vote in the West: The Woman Suffrage Movement, 1869–1896*. New York: Garland Publishing, 1986.

Benson, Bjorn, Elizabeth Hampsten, and Kathryn Sweeney. *Day In, Day Out: Women's Lives in North Dakota*. Grand Forks: University of North Dakota Press, 1988.

Blair, Karen, ed. *Women in Pacific Northwest History: An Anthology.* Seattle: University of Washington Press, 1988.

Bopp, Georgia Kinney. *Summers Family of California.* Kailua, Hawaii: self-published, 1994. This includes a reprint of *Early Days in California* by Lee Ann Summers Whipple-Haslem.

Bushman, Claudia, ed. *Mormon Sisters: Women in Early Utah.* Salt Lake City: Olympus Publishing, 1980.

Butler, Anne M. *Daughters of Joy, Sisters of Misery: Prostitutes in the American West, 1865–90.* Urbana: University of Illinois Press, 1985.

Cross, Mary Bywater. *Treasures in the Trunk: Quilts of the Oregon Trail.* Nashville: Rutledge Hill Press, 1993.

De la Torre, Adela, and Beatriz Pesquera, eds. *Building With Our Hands: New Directions in Chicana Studies.* Berkeley: University of California Press, 1993.

Deutsch, Sarah. *No Separate Refuge: Culture, Class and Gender on an Anglo-Hispanic Frontier in the American Southwest, 1880–1940.* New York: Oxford University Press, 1987.

Etulain, Richard, and Glenda Riley. *By Grit and Grace: Eleven Women Who Made the American West.* Golden, Colo.: Fulcrum Press, 1997.

Faragher, John Mack. *Women and Men on the Overland Trail.* New Haven: Yale University Press, 1979.

Fischer, Christiane. "A Profile of Women in Arizona in Frontier Days." *Journal of the West* 16, no. 3 (July 1977): 42–53.

———. "Women in California in the Early 1850s." *Southern California Quarterly* 60, no. 3 (Fall 1978): 231–53.

Garceau, Dee. *The Important Things of Life: Women, Work, and Family in Sweetwater County, Wyoming, 1880–1929.* Lincoln: University of Nebraska Press, 1997.

Georgi-Findlay, Brigitte. *The Frontiers of Women's Writing: Women's Narratives and the Rhetoric of Westward Expansion.* Tucson: University of Arizona Press, 1996.

Goldman, Marion S. *Gold Diggers and Silver Miners: Prostitution and Social Life on the Comstock Load.* Ann Arbor: University of Michigan Press, 1981.

Gray, Dorothy. *Women of the West.* Millbrae, Calif.: Les Femmes, 1976. Reprint. Lincoln: University of Nebraska Press, 1998.

Griswold, Robert L. *Family and Divorce in California, 1850–1890: Victorian Illusions and Everyday Realities.* Albany: State University of New York Press, 1983.

Hampsten, Elizabeth. *Read This Only to Yourself: The Private Writings of Midwestern Women, 1880–1910.* Bloomington: Indiana University Press, 1982.

————. *Settlers' Children: Growing Up on the Great Plains*. Norman: University of Oklahoma Press, 1991.

Hermann, Ruth. "'More than Gold,' An Authentic Story Never Before Told," *Grass Valley Union*, Nov.–Dec. 1963.

Jensen, Joan, and Gloria Lothrop. *California Women: A History*. Boston: Boyd and Fraser, 1987.

Jensen, Joan, and Darlis A. Miller, eds. *New Mexico Women: Intercultural Perspectives*. Albuquerque: University of New Mexico Press, 1986.

Kaufman, Polly Welts. *Women Teachers on the Frontier*. New Haven: Yale University Press, 1984.

Kolodny, Annette. *The Land before Her: Fantasy and Experience of the American Frontiers, 1630–1860*. Chapel Hill: University of North Carolina Press, 1984.

Levy, Joann. *They Saw the Elephant: Women in the California Gold Rush*. Norman: University of Oklahoma Press, 1992.

Matsumoto, Valerie. *Farming the Homeplace: A Japanese American Community in California, 1919–1982*. Ithaca: Cornell University Press, 1993.

Norwood, Vera, and Janice Monk, eds. *The Desert Is No Lady: Southwestern Landscapes in Women's Writing and Art*. New Haven: Yale University Press, 1987.

Pascoe, Peggy. *Relations of Rescue: The Search for Female Moral Authority in the American West, 1874–1939*. New York: Oxford University Press, 1990.

Peavy, Linda, and Ursula Smith. *The Gold Rush Widows of Little Falls*. St. Paul: Minnesota Historical Society Press, 1990.

————. *Women in Waiting in the Westward Movement: Life on the Home Frontier*. Norman: University of Oklahoma Press, 1994.

Petrick, Paula. *No Step Backward: Women and Family on the Rocky Mountain Mining Frontier, Helena, Montana 1865–1900*. Helena: Montana Historical Society, 1987.

Riley, Glenda. *The Female Frontier: A Comparative View of Women on the Prairie and the Plains*. Lawrence: University Press of Kansas, 1988.

————. *Women and Indians on the Frontier, 1825–1915*. Albuquerque: University of New Mexico Press, 1984.

Schloff, Linda Mack. *"And Prairie Dogs Weren't Kosher": Jewish Women in the Upper Midwest since 1855*. St. Paul: Minnesota Historical Society Press, 1996.

Yung, Judy. *Chinese Women of America: A Pictorial History*. Seattle: University of Washington Press, 1986.

————. *Unbound Feet: A Social History of Chinese Women in San Francisco*. Berkeley: University of California Press, 1995.

Zanjani, Sally. *A Mine of Her Own: Women Prospectors in the American West, 1850–1950.* Lincoln: University of Nebraska Press, 1997.

BIOGRAPHIES AND AUTOBIOGRAPHICAL NARRATIVES

Alderson, Nannie T., and Helena Huntington Smith. *A Bride Goes West.* New York: Farrar & Rinehart, 1942. Reprint. Lincoln: University of Nebraska Press, 1969.

Arnold, Mary Ellicott, and Mabel Reed. *In the Land of the Grasshopper Song: Two Women in the Klamath River Indian Country in 1908–09.* New York: Vantage Press, 1957. Reprint. Lincoln: University of Nebraska Press, 1980.

Benson, Maxine. *Martha Maxwell: Rocky Mountain Naturalist.* Lincoln: University of Nebraska Press, 1986.

Berry, Alice Edna. *The Bushes and the Berrys.* Los Angeles: 1941.

Bird, Isabella L. *A Lady's Life in the Rocky Mountains.* Norman: University of Oklahoma Press, 1960.

Brown, Mrs. Hugh. *Lady in Boomtown: Miners and Manners of the Nevada Frontier.* New York: Ballantine Books, 1968.

Bruyn, Kathleen. *"Aunt" Clara Brown: Story of a Black Pioneer.* Boulder, Colo.: Pruett Press, 1970.

Cabeza de Baca, Fabiola. *We Feed Them Cactus.* Albuquerque: University of New Mexico Press, 1954.

Calof, Rachel. *Rachel Calof's Story: A Jewish Homesteader on the Northern Plains.* Bloomington: Indiana University Press, 1995.

Canfield, Gae Whitney. *Sarah Winnemucca of the Northern Paiutes.* Norman: University of Oklahoma Press, 1983.

Churchill, Caroline M. *Over the Purple Hills, or Sketches of Travel in California.* Denver: Mrs. C. M. Churchill, 1884.

Clappe, Louise A. K. S. *The Shirley Letters: From the California Mines, 1851–1852.* New York: Alfred A. Knopf, 1949.

Cleaveland, Agnes Morley. *No Life for a Lady.* Boston: Houghton Mifflin, 1941. Reprint. Lincoln: University of Nebraska Press, 1977.

Farnham, Eliza Woodson. *California, In-Doors and Out.* New York: Dix, Edwards & Co., 1856.

Fischer, Christiane, ed. *Let Them Speak for Themselves: Women in the American West, 1849–1900.* Hamden, Conn.: Shoe String Press, 1977.

Foote, Mary Hallock. *A Victorian Gentlewoman in the Far West: Reminiscences of*

Mary Hallock Foote. Edited by Rodman Paul. San Marino, Calif.: The Huntington Library, 1972.

Frazier, Mrs. *Reminiscences of Travel from 1855 to 1867, By A Lady.* San Francisco: 1868.

French, Emily. *Emily: The Diary of a Hard-Worked Woman.* Lincoln: University of Nebraska Press, 1987.

Greenwood, Annie Pike. *We Sagebrush Folks.* Moscow: University of Idaho Press, 1988.

Guerin, Elsa Jane. *Mountain Charley, or the Adventures of Mrs. E. J. Guerin, Who Was Thirteen Years in Male Attire.* Norman: University of Oklahoma Press, 1968.

Hazzlett, Fanny. "Historical Sketches and Reminiscences of Dayton, Nevada." *Nevada Historical Society Papers* (1921–22): 3–93.

Holdrege, Helen. *Mammy Pleasant.* New York: Ballantine Books, 1972.

Holmes, Kenneth L., ed. and comp. *Covered Wagon Women: Diaries and Letters from the Western Trails, 1840–1890,* Vols. I–II. Glendale, Calif.: Arthur H. Clark, 1983–1988. Bison Books reprints of Vols. 1–7, Lincoln: University of Nebraska Press, 1995–98. (More volumes forthcoming.)

Jeffrey, Julie Roy. *Converting the West: A Biography of Narcissa Whitman.* Norman: University of Oklahoma Press, 1991.

Jenkins, Malinda. *Gambler's Wife: The Life of Malinda Jenkins.* Boston and New York: Houghton Mifflin, 1933. Reprint. Lincoln: University of Nebraska Press, 1998.

Judson, Phoebe Goodell. *A Pioneer's Search for an Ideal Home.* Bellingham, Wash.: Printed by Union Printing, Binding and Stationary, 1925. Reprint. Lincoln: University of Nebraska Press, 1984.

Kohl, Edith Eudora. *Land of the Burnt Thigh: Women Homesteaders on the South Dakota Frontier.* St. Paul: Minnesota Historical Society Press, 1986.

Linderman, Frank B. *Pretty-shield: Medicine Woman of the Crows.* (Originally published under the title *Red Mother*). New York: John Day, 1932. Reprint. Lincoln: University of Nebraska Press, 1974.

Love, Barbara, and Frances Love Froidevaux, eds. *Lady's Choice: Ethel Waxham's Journals and Letters, 1905–1910.* Albuquerque: University of New Mexico Press, 1993.

Magoffin, Susan Shelby. *Down the Santa Fe Trail and into Mexico: The Diary of Susan Shelby Magoffin 1846–1847.* Edited by Stella M. Drumm. New Haven: Yale University Press, 1962. Reprint. Lincoln: University of Nebraska Press, 1982.

Mathews, Mary McNair. *Ten Years in Nevada; or, Life on the Pacific Coast.* Buffalo: Baker, Jones, 1880. Reprint. Lincoln: University of Nebraka Press, 1985.

McCunn, Ruthanne Lum. *Thousand Pieces of Gold*. San Francisco: Design Enterprises, 1981.

Megquier, Mary Jane. *Apron Full of Gold: The Letters of Mary Jane Megquier from San Francisco, 1849–1856*. Edited by Robert Glass Cleland. San Marino, Calif.: The Huntington Library, 1949.

Moynihan, Betty. *Augusta Tabor: A Pioneering Woman*. Boulder, Colo.: Johnson Books, 1988.

Moynihan, Ruth B. "Children and Young People on the Overland Trail." *Western Historical Quarterly* 6, no. 3 (July 1975): 279–94.

Moynihan, Ruth B. *Rebel for Rights: The Life of Abigail Scott Duniway*. New Haven: Yale University Press, 1983.

Mumey, Nolie. *Poker Alice: History of a Woman Gambler in the West*. Denver: Artcraft Press, 1951.

Niederman, Sharon. *A Quilt of Words: Women's Diaries, Letters, and Original Accounts of Life in the Southwest, 1860–1960*. Boulder, Colo.: Johnson Books, 1988.

Pender, Rose. *A Lady's Experiences in the Wild West in 1883*. London: G. Tucker, 1888. Reprint. Lincoln: University of Nebraska Press, 1985.

Reid, Agnes Just. *Letters of Long Ago*. Boise: Caxton Printers, Ltd., 1923; 2d ed., 1936.

Royce, Sarah. *A Frontier Lady: Recollections of the Gold Rush and Early California*. New Haven: Yale University Press, 1932. Reprint. Lincoln: University of Nebraska Press, 1977.

Sanford, Mollie. *Mollie: The Journal of Mollie Dorsey Sanford in Nebraska and Colorado Territories 1857–1866*. Lincoln: University of Nebraska Press, 1959.

Schlissel, Lillian, Byrd Gibbens, and Elizabeth Hampsten. *Far From Home: Families on the Western Frontier*. New York: Schocken Books, 1989.

Schlissel, Lillian. *Women's Diaries of the Westward Journey*. New York: Schocken, 1982.

Stewart, Elinore Pruitt. *Letters of a Woman Homesteader*. Boston: Houghton Mifflin, 1914. Reprint. Lincoln: University of Nebraska Press, 1990.

Summerhayes, Martha. *Vanished Arizona: Recollections of the Army Life of a New England Woman*. Salem, Mass.: Salem Press, 1911. Reprint. Lincoln: University of Nebraska Press, 1979.

Tanner, Annie Clark. *A Mormon Mother: An Autobiography*. Salt Lake City: University of Utah Press, 1969.

Thompson, Era Bell. *American Daughter*. St. Paul: Minnesota Historical Society Press, 1986.

Trupin, Sophie. *Dakota Diaspora: Memories of a Jewish Homesteader*. Lincoln: University of Nebraska Press, 1984.

Vielé, Teresa Griffin. *Following the Drum: A Glimpse of Frontier Life*. New York: Rudd & Carleton, 1858. Reprint. Lincoln: University of Nebraska Press, 1984.

Ward, Jean M. and Elaine A. Maveety. *Jottings and Journeys: The Writings of Abigail Scott Duniway in the* New Northwest. Corvallis: Oregon State University Press, forthcoming.

———. *Pacific Northwest Women: 1815–1925*. Corvallis: Oregon State University Press, 1995.

Wilbur-Cruce, Eva Antonia. *A Beautiful, Cruel Country*. Tucson: University of Arizona Press, 1987.

Wynn, Marcia Rittenhouse. *Pioneer Family of Whiskey Flat*. Los Angeles: Hayes Corporation, 1945.

Young, Carrie. *Nothing to Do but Stay: My Pioneer Mother*. Iowa City: University of Iowa Press, 1991.